McCarthy and His Enemies

The Record and its Meaning

WM. F. BUCKLEY JR. *&* L. BRENT BOZELL

McCARTHY

AND

HIS ENEMIES

The Record and its Meaning

PROLOGUE BY WILLIAM SCHLAMM

Chicago · HENRY REGNERY COMPANY · *1954*

First Printing, 10,000—March, 1954
Second Printing, 10,000—March, 1954
Third Printing, 10,000—April, 1954
Fourth Printing, 5,000—April, 1954

For

P.B.B. *and* **P.T.B.**

PROLOGUE

THE TWO AUTHORS of this book have chosen to study and take sides in the most scandalous fracas of the century. For the intellectual brawl that has evolved around McCarthy is, in fact, just about the most offensive kind of scandal the human intellect can be dragged into: a scandal of the mind gone manifestly irresponsible. And the authors contend that this ultimate felony of reason has been committed, not by McCarthy, but by McCarthy's opponents.

It is the bold assumption of this book that the incredible Senator Joe McCarthy, who has replaced the weather and even existentialism as the main topic of civilized dinner conversation, actually exists. The two authors, that is to say, chose not to accept the judgment of the day (which, in politics, tends towards fiction); rather, they decided to investigate the mythical Grand Investigator's three-dimensional record.

Right here, of course, we have a violation of current intellectual etiquette. For nobody is deemed so uncouth by certified gentlemen as a writer who dares take their favored figures of speech literally. The sweeping and unsupported generalization is nowadays absolutely *de rigueur*—so long as it aims at the allegedly supreme dispenser of the sweeping and unsupported generalization, that man from Wisconsin. The gentlest President this Republic has ever known gets up and delivers a downright inflammatory speech against the burning of books; yet, when asked by mortified reporters a few days later which books have in fact been burned by his government, he reassures them that he had been speaking metaphorically of purely metaphoric perils in an altogether metaphoric world. The stage, in short, is set for a Jonathan Swift (who, however, would have to be awfully careful with such ironical stunts as those about abolishing Christianity and eating babies: for, in this somewhat psychopathic era, the highest political authority would greet Swiftian satire with solemn appeals to the citizenry *not* to abolish Christianity and *not* to eat babies).

Consequently, the authors would seem to be in for some unusual and cruel punishment from the American Academe which will stand for no such nonsense as a material probe of metaphoric political contentions. As it happens, I know the two authors well, and I have no doubt that they can take it. Still, I gratefully avail myself of the publisher's invitation to explain my considered solidarity with them and their book. I do so, not because of any delusion that my endorsement could add one whit of luster or validity to their argument, but because I appreciate every opportunity to clarify an unorthodox position; and what could be more unorthodox in this era than intellectuals engaged in hot pursuit of *Anti*-McCarthyism?

When McCarthy proceeded to uncover the immense Communist infiltration of democratic government and free society, his conduct was sometimes objectionable (as this book demonstrates), but his activating premise was not: At the heart of what is derisively called McCarthyism lives, in paradoxical fact, the very principle of Western civilization—the axiomatic tenet that man is entirely responsible for the intellectual choices he has made in an exercise of his free will. The essence of what we have learned in five thousand years about the nature of man is that the inviolable sovereignty of the person presupposes his inseparable responsibility for the positions he takes, including wrong ones. A man can stumble into grave error for the noblest of reasons, God knows; and only Satanism denies man's inalienable capacity to recover from error. But man can neither grow, nor err, nor reform, nor even exist, unless he is taken seriously, and so takes himself. The true difference between McCarthy and his allegedly sophisticated opponents is not that they propose a charitable and civilized course, while McCarthy is Caliban; the difference is, in truth, that he, often crudely instructed, takes man seriously, while they insist that man is morally a vegetable and intellectually an eternal child. The intellectual scandal around McCarthy is primarily the frightening frivolousness of his opposition which holds that man's choices signify nothing; that on his walks through the valley of decisions man picks and discards commitments with the abandon of Peter Pan picking daisies.

And the scandal becomes wholly insufferable when the private commitments for which pardon is asked—on the peculiar grounds of moral idiocy—involve no less than the fate of man. Conceivably, an artist can justly demand that no importance be attached to his early endorsement of, say, stark atonality: for this, surely, may have been the commitment of a playful hour of nihilism involving, after all, nothing but his own creative self; and so it must not be held against whatever preference he later chooses. But what is one to say of an intellectual who, having advocated in the past a tragic interference with innumerable lives, now thinks himself entitled to claim for his immense act the irrelevancy of a meaningless infatuation? To a man who leaves an indefensible position, society owes understanding and confidence, provided his motives in taking the indefensible position had been in themselves defensible, and provided he himself tries to understand the impact of his error and to atone for it. But to a college professor who, on leaving organizations which are demonstrably engaged in a total upheaval of human existence, says "Ooops, so sorry, and let's not ever mention it again!"—to such a man society owes nothing but contempt.

Yet this is precisely the measure of the scandal: that the most audible intellectuals of our era invoke for themselves a special dispensation from intellectual responsibility, a kind of license to philander through the moral order, a fool's franchise never to be taken at their word. This, I submit, is the ironical essence of what America's and Europe's intelligentsia consider their battle royal with McCarthy: that he ascribes to the intellectual a serious impact on society.

I do not know Mr. McCarthy's innermost thoughts on the subject. But judging by what he has done and said in public, I am compelled to conclude that he is one of the few contemporary politicians who earnestly believe in the efficacy of ideas. He respects reason so much, in fact, that he clearly overemphasizes its part in the shaping of national policies. For his rationale is invariably the same: certain people have certain ideas—*ergo,* whatever they do in positions they have obtained must have been determined by, and serve, these ideas. The shameful joke of the era is that this compliment to the supremacy of the mind is being taken by the Liberal intelligentsia as the supreme affront against the intellect, as a sordid assault of Know-Nothingism on reason.

Honesty and worldly experience compel me to warn Mr. Mc-Carthy that he may overrate the mind's supremacy over character. In sad truth, a great many intellectuals put income above convictions and, consequently, have no scruples in acting contrary to their beliefs. There must be, for example, quite a few Marxians in government and in the professions who, in exchange for a regular salary, do their utmost to promote capitalism. The Senator from Wisconsin, in short, underestimates the frequency and the compe-

tence of prostitution. But unless we renounce rationality altogether, we are forced to assume that, once an intellectual disagrees
with his society, only two consequences are logically permissible:
either he infuses his considered bias into every phase of his professional work—in which case society is surely entitled to retaliate;
or he suppresses his innermost beliefs for a fee—in which case he
proves himself so depraved that his services ought to be discon-
tinued on grounds of moral hygiene. For on two points have revolutionaries and conservatives agreed, from the dawn of time up to
the appearance of Anti-McCarthyism: both always acknowledged
man's privileged duty to live by his convictions, and both always
despised the purchasable libertine. Of all changes that have occurred in my lifetime, none is more catastrophic than this: that the
Liberals, in their brawl with McCarthy, no longer defend man's
glorious burden of living his beliefs, but now stipulate a brand-new
inalienable right of man—the right to sell his soul.

No, the disclaimer that the concentric and unprecedentedly
savage Liberal attack on McCarthy is motivated by nothing but
the celebrated crudity of his rhetoric and his investigative methods
will just not wash. Crudeness is of course deplorable, even in a
politician, and must be censured by the sensitive; consequently,
this book censures McCarthy whenever its authors found him
guilty of recklessness or just plain exaggeration. But no honest
book has ever been written about any American politician, alive or
dead, that has not censured him on these very grounds. Mass
democracy apparently invites shouting, and this country, at any
rate, is used to a pretty high pitch. In fact, I for one can still remember the learned American Liberal's sheepish pleasure with the
demagogic cleverness of F.D.R. and the murderous invectives of
Ickes; mind you, not that the learned American Liberal "philo-
sophically" approved of demagoguery and venom—he just wanted
you to know that he was "realist" enough to "understand" how
indispensable such gimmicks were in mobilizing the lazy "masses"
for the righteous cause. Now, unlike that American Liberal, the
authors of this book apply one standard to both camps: objectionable techniques they find objectionable even when employed on
their side of the issue, and they say so quite unequivocally. But—
and for such astuteness I want to congratulate them particularly—
not for a second did they believe that the hectic growth of Anti-
McCarthyism has been really provoked by "McCarthy's methods."

Some day, when there has developed a new science of political ethnology, a patient scholar will undoubtedly produce the *Golden Bough* of Anti-McCarthyism—a definitive critical catalogue of its mythology, its lore and its obsessions. And though the area of that fascinating inquiry has as yet hardly been mapped, I would hazard the guess that its future Sir James Frazer will define the great affliction of the 20th-Century intelligentsia as a collective mental inversion. Not for the first time in history, but more fiercely and more uninhibitedly than ever before, a closed group was exorcising the devils of its collective mind by projecting all its own vices onto a personalized demon: what McCarthy's opposition calls "McCarthyism" will no doubt be found the observable sum total of their own techniques, aggressions and attitudes.

McCarthyism, indicts the opposition, is a technique of the fantastic and reckless exaggeration. Yet, typically, when a lady in a small Indiana town ventures to warn that the Communists are exploiting the delightful tale of Robin Hood (which, to be sure, they indubitably are), the ubiquitous anti-McCarthy press blankets the several continents with editorial chants that this worrisome lady from Indiana represents America gone mad over suppressive censorship.

McCarthyism, accuses the opposition, is the technique of establishing a lie simply by referring to it as a well known fact. Yet Mr. Walter Lippmann, a senior saint of certified liberalism, did not hesitate to misinform the world in his globally syndicated column that "an American who dared to suggest the relinquishment of American sovereignty to a supernational, to a super-American federation would be hauled up before the McCarthy committee." (Whereupon Mr. Clarence Streit, President of the manifestly supernational "Federal Union," reminded Lippmann that, on the contrary, the Senator from Wisconsin had co-sponsored the Kefauver Resolution "calling for a Federal convention of delegates to explore the possibility of the U.S. and Canada forming an Atlantic Union with Britain, France and other European members of NATO.")

McCarthyism, claims the opposition, is the technique of the gratuitous smear. Yet, for one of innumerable examples, the liberal *Saturday Review*, reviewing an innocuous book on Formosa, suggests without the slightest provocation that "it may be denounced by the China Lobby's *kept* journalists and legislators."

McCarthyism, protests the opposition, subverts the very essence of free society by charging a person's private associations against his fitness for positions of public trust. Yet no American Liberal has ever objected to this finding of the U.S. Supreme Court: "One's associates, past and present, as well as one's conduct, may properly be considered in determining fitness and loyalty."

McCarthyism, thunders the opposition, slaughters civic rights by dragging private citizens through the mud of congressional investigations. Yet when the U.S. Senate was investigating some wretched capitalists, and foolhardy conservatives objected to possible congressional violations of privacy, Professor (later Justice) Felix Frankfurter, another senior saint of certified liberalism, thus found in *The New Republic* (of May 21, 1924): "The question is not whether people's feelings here and there may be hurt, or names 'dragged through the mud,' as it is called. . . . Critics, who have nothing to say for the astonishing corruption and corrupting soil which have been brought to light, seek to divert attention and shackle the future by suggesting restrictions in the procedure of future congressional investigations."

Anti-McCarthyism, one can see, throws the liberal mind into distressing inconsistency: contortions of such severity have not been observed since the St. Vitus Dance epidemics of the Middle Ages. That the McCarthy-obsessed intelligentsia enjoy their sprained logic is inconceivable; to make them endure that self-imposed pain, their fixation must be profound. What is it?

Is it a dread that McCarthy may be America's Hitler? To my knowledge, not even McCarthy's worst-balanced opponents have ever publicized such a dread. True, some conscientious objectors to "guilt by association" have, somewhat inconsistently again, tried to hold against the Senator that several denizens of America's lunatic fringe have accosted him. But McCarthy's rebuke of such advances was each time so unequivocal and spiteful that the whisper died on the rotten vine.

Indeed, nothing perhaps embitters McCarthy's opposition so much as the, to them, confusing fact that he has never indicated the slightest sympathy for Fascism. For, surely, one is allowed to presume a general consensus that these are the two irreducible tenets of any Fascist ideology: the transfer of undivided social and political power into the hands of an executive which reigns supreme; and the abolition of all political parties, save a "people's" militarized rally around a deified leader and his appointed "elite." Different color schemes of Fascism (black, brown, or red) may, as it suits, drape this skeleton of the Fascist doctrine with different sets of racial or social or philosophical canons; but, so long as we propose to make semantic sense, we confine the term Fascist to revolutionary movements only when they embrace the two generic creeds of totalitarian social organizations—an all-powerful executive and a one-party system.

By no stretch of the imagination, or logic, could anything McCarthy has ever done, or said, or written, be interpreted as a malcontent revolutionary's critique of America's traditional system. He is, come to think of it, the exceptional politician who advocates no social reform, recommends no surgery, and sells no medicine. Here indeed, if anywhere, McCarthy would appear seriously vulnerable: authentic American liberals could reasonably admonish him that a politician of his stature and eloquence owed to himself, and to the nation, a far more sharply profiled approach to the authentic dilemmas of our social, economic, financial and foreign policies. To this McCarthy might reply that the hectic circumstances of his crusade against the Communist infiltration of government force upon him a singlemindedness which precludes expert concern for much else.

And this would be a persuasive reply because McCarthy believes (backed up by excellent evidence and excellent compatriots—the authors of this book among them) that his country is at war with Communism, war pure and simple; and that therefore, as there is in war "no substitute for victory," all other policy concerns must recede for the time of fighting. "This war will not end except by either victory or death for this civilization," McCarthy asserted in a recent speech; and it is this hot sense of urgency which distinguishes him from the more conventional practitioners of the political trade—and also explains, altogether satisfactorily, his nonconformance with pastoral etiquette.

Still, an authentic American liberalism could, perhaps convincingly, insist that a Senator of McCarthy's fame ought to work harder on his political rationale. But it is a measure of the stupefaction which has befallen American liberalism that, instead of demanding that McCarthy talk more, and about more things, its only intent is to shut him up about everything. For, inasmuch as a modicum of coherence can be interpolated into their frantic utterances, the program of American Liberals seems to have atrophied to just this one plank: Shut him up—in the name of free speech!

What *is it* they want? That it be made illegal for the citizens of Wisconsin to vote for McCarthy? That he be forbidden to speak his mind when, nonetheless, elected? That at a time when some liberals proclaim the *de luxe* "right to be wrong," one man *(that man)* be forbidden to be right? In bizarre fact, Anti-McCarthyism seems to be campaigning for a veritable Rube Goldberg of a Constitutional Bill of Attainder—a repeal of the Constitution for just one Joseph R. McCarthy, Jr.

For the same Constitution that evidently grants a Communist the privilege not to *answer* a Senator's questions, surely grants a Senator the concomitant privilege to *ask* them. And that privilege of a Senator happens to coincide with his sworn duty to ask any question he deems relevant to pending or contemplated legislation. Yes, here stands the American Liberal, stuck with a Constitution which guarantees freedom of speech even to Senators; with a political system whose effectiveness depends on unfettered congressional hearings; and with the Senate's indisputable right to elect its own inquiring officers. But the American Liberal is also stuck with that Senator whom, one gathers, he dislikes. And so the American Liberal, cutting his nose rather than the Gordian knot, suggests that Constitution, political system, and Senatorial statute—just this once, please!—be damned. Such are the fevers of McCarthophobia.

Now the origin of this novel disease is still unknown. It can not, as we have seen, have been caused by a sincere apprehension of incipient Fascism; for to suspect McCarthy of Fascist intent would be just another symptom of McCarthophobia—not its causation. Nor can the affliction stem from an irritated concern for civil liberties; for we have seen that the afflicted have always considered what they now call "McCarthy's methods" to constitute a most legitimate exercise of those very same civil liberties. Nor could it be a case of plain allergy; for while anybody is of course entitled to dislike an incumbent Senator, nobody can be such an ass as to make his private hate-affair the very center of his *Weltanschauung* —nobody, that is, who is not stricken by a serious malady. So we will have to be patient for a while; it may take years before the elusive virus of McCarthophobia is finally separated.

Until then, I venture to predict, this book will remain a unique source of illumination for anybody who wants to move through our darkened political neighborhood. I venture to predict that the reader of this heavily documented volume will discover how exciting documentation can be—incomparably more exciting, in pleasurable fact, than the banal irrationalism which nowadays simulates political debate.

This book refutes the insolent contention that those millions of Americans who share McCarthy's sense of urgency, though not necessarily all his judgments, are sons of Neanderthal. And it reduces the peddlers of this falsehood to their size: if the entrenched and the conformists, the Babbitts and the snobs, have ever agreed on a common enemy, and made utter fools of themselves, they have done so in the case of McCarthy.

There came from the heartland of America a tenacious and quite traditional politician who had much to learn about the nature of evidence and the manners of public debate. He occasionally misjudged the motives of men, but not worse than two generations of American liberals have misjudged men and motives. Yes, he called Mr. Owen Lattimore the top Soviet agent in this country, and he has not produced conclusive evidence. But two generations of American liberalism have called honorable men "merchants of death" and Stalin a protagonist of human liberation; and for either misjudgment they had far less evidence than McCarthy had for his.

And consider what happened! On the one side, there were the pundits and opinion-makers, the professional thinkers, the teachers and artists and critics—and they have been proved fatally wrong in a stubborn misjudgment that may involve the end of everything they were educated to uphold. On the other side, there was a young, not at all subtle, entirely self-made Midwestern politician— and he was wrong in several judgments that involve some members of the club. Whereupon the Liberal supreme court of columnists, editors, commentators and critics, of thinkers and comedians, of statesmen and account executives, of publishers and piccolo players, convened in permanent mob session and found: the atrocious misjudgment of the certified gentlemen, who have dropped ("Oops, sorry!") half of the world into irrevocable perdition, are not merely forgivable but downright honorable; while the erring young man from Wisconsin is the hound of hell.

With this book, William F. Buckley, Jr. and L. Brent Bozell have liberated a territory which for four years was terrorized by the nervous shriek; liberated and restored it to orderly argument. Now anybody who wants to remain an Anti-McCarthyite in good standing, and at the same time intellectually respectable, will first have to read and disprove this book.

WILLIAM S. SCHLAMM

CONTENTS

PART THREE

PART ONE

CHAPTER I

The Problem

ON THE 31st of March, in 1949, Mr. Winston Churchill (he was then ungartered) was to address the Mid-Century Convocation of the Massachusetts Institute of Technology, and he had advertised his forthcoming remarks as "not unimportant."

After it was delivered, the press services had a hard time deciding what aspect of Churchill's address was most newsworthy. They settled, finally, on this: "It is certain that Europe would have been communized like Czechoslovakia, and London under bombardment some time ago, but for the deterrent of the atomic bomb in the hands of the U. S."

Sir Winston, of course, normally speaks with a robust certitude about everything. It is perhaps not "certain" that our monopoly on the atom bomb served during those years as the controlling deterrent to Soviet expansion. But whatever Churchill's extravagances, he cannot be taken lightly. This time, no doubt, he put his finger on the dominant feature of mid-twentieth century international relations: conceivably a single individual could shift the balance of power by delivering to the Soviet Union technological secrets through the use of which they could overcome their strategic disadvantage and proceed to communize Europe.

This is something new in the world. Traitors have played critical parts in the past. But many factors—primarily the indecisiveness of any single weapon—have mitigated the consequences of treason. The great traitors of the past have swung battles, but not wars. The situation is different today. An Alger Hiss, critically situated, can, conceivably, determine the destiny of the West. A Klaus Fuchs can deliver to "the thirteen scheming men" what may well be the key to world conquest.

It is largely because of this new face of treason that we in the free world are writing, preaching and discussing ways to adapt our traditional concepts into serviceable weapons with which to protect ourselves from hazards the architects of our society never contemplated. The job will be hard. The new consequences of treason will not allow us to settle for a security program based on the idea —in itself venerable—that ten suspected traitors working in the State Department should not be molested lest one of them should prove to be loyal. It is one thing for Lizzie Borden to benefit from the charity of the doubt; it is something else again to protect Klaus Fuchs until after he has committed the "overt" act.

By 1950, we were more or less agreed that the overt act a Fuchs might commit was something we dared not risk. The majority of us now knew that, for all the twists and turns of the Party Line, the Communists have never swerved and, barring a philosophical or political revolution, never would swerve from their ambition to occupy the world. And we knew, moreover, that they had hit upon an uncommonly successful formula for achieving their goal. The era was past when Americans needed to be educated about the *threat* of Communism.

But a new era arrived, the dominant characteristic of which was—and remains—indecision. Undecided how to cope with the new menace, we lacked even the will to find a solution. Our confusion and our purposelessness were crippling. A symbol of it, perhaps, was our society's relentless persecution of what John Chamberlain has shrewdly labelled "premature anti-Communists." The evolution from pro-Communism in the direction of anti-Communism seemed to have ground to a halt in an intermediary stage, aptly described as *anti*-anti-Communism.

This, then, was the overriding problem when Senator McCarthy made his entrance on the national stage: having acknowledged the nature and the immediacy of our peril, how might we get by our disintegrated ruling elite, which had no stomach for battle, and get down to the business of fighting the enemy in our midst?

CHAPTER II

The Background

CERTAINLY one of the most effective arms of Soviet imperialism has been the strategically placed native of the free world who, for whatever perverse reason, has determined to serve the Communist cause.

As far back as the twenties, many Americans were aware that Communism was more than a proposal for political change which would take its chances "in the marketplace of ideas." Communism, it was recognized, was a relentless political-military conspiracy. A Committee of the House of Representatives was soon instructed to investigate the Communist conspiracy in the United States. The Committee operated in the increasingly difficult climate of the Popular Front, when great numbers of Western intellectuals had entered into an enthusiastic concordat with Stalin. Slowly and haphazardly our lawmakers sought to adjust our statute books to the realities of the Communist menace.

In 1938, the McCormack Act ordered all agents of foreign governments to register with the Department of Justice. The Hatch Act of 1939 excluded from Federal employment members of any organization that advocates the forcible overthrow of our constitutional form of government. The Smith Act of 1940 forbade Americans to conspire to teach or advocate the overthrow of the U. S. government by force or violence.

In 1942, surprisingly, an alert Civil Service Commission enunciated loyalty criteria which were to govern federal agencies in determining whom to hire. It was stipulated that, in case of "reasonable doubt" as to his loyalty, an applicant must be regarded as unemployable.

These, of course, were primitive and inadequate tools for dealing with the kind of penetration against which our best students of Communism were warning us. It is best to think of them as the first efforts of the American people, acting through their representa-

tives, to master by fiat a problem that, in the long run, would require much more, perhaps even a Constitutional Amendment.*

Moreover, the laws were not enforced; or, insofar as they were
enforced, they were enforced tardily and halfheartedly. The Hatch
Act bothered nobody. Even after it was passed, no less than 537
members of the American League for Peace and Democracy alone
(as palpable a Communist front as ever existed) remained in federal service.

However, the Civil Service Commission's "reasonable doubt" criterion for applicants moved toward the heart of the matter. The
Commission made a start toward committing us to the principle
that the federal government has the right to draw up its own requirements for government service—that employment by the Government is a privilege, not a right.

The Commission's effort did not, however, prevent further Communist penetration of the government, much less undo that which
had already occurred. For the Commission did not rule on personnel already hired. Moreover, the Commission, under existing statutes and budget limitations, could not use the FBI in its investigations. Consequently, most of the Commission's information was obtained from the files of the House Committee on Un-American
Activities. The rest came from a handful of its own investigators.

Meanwhile, the Attorney General had entered the field. In 1941,
he directed the FBI to probe complaints of alleged disloyalty
among Federal personnel. The FBI reported its findings to the appropriate agencies, and these agencies made their own decisions. It
soon became clear that standards varied widely from agency to
agency. In 1942, therefore, the Attorney General created an Interdepartmental Committee on Investigation to assist in standardiz-
ing procedures and evaluative criteria. This Committee, like the
Civil Service Commission, confined itself to regulating applications
for employment; and even then it recommended a manifestly inadequate standard: rejection on loyalty grounds was to be based on
proof that the applicant *personally* advocates the overthrow of the
government; or else that he is a *conscious* and *willing* member of
an organization advocating such overthrow.

* The Smith Act, in our opinion, in effect did amend the Constitution,
the circumlocutions of the slim majority of the Supreme Court that upheld
it notwithstanding. The First Amendment states that "Congress shall make
no law . . . abridging the freedom of speech." It does not go on to say that
certain social exigencies, as for example war, or a foreign conspiracy, invalidate this explicit limitation of congressional competence.

But the Civil Service Commission was making enough headway to inconvenience some Communists on the government payroll. Consequently, a sustained cry went up from the Communist-influenced Federal Workers Union which demanded, among other things, that the Commission cease to affront the dignity of the individual by interesting itself in his allegiance. The Bureau of the Budget heeded the Union's protests and cut the funds required to implement the loyalty program. And Communist after Communist worked his way into the assorted wartime agencies.

Thus, during the war, there was no effective program to keep Communist agents out of sensitive government areas. In some cases, the most incriminating evidence against an applicant or, worse still, against a highly situated incumbent, failed not only to produce action but even to get attention. The case of Alger Hiss, the *Amerasia* case, and the Doxey Wilkerson case, are monuments to America's early incapacity to defend herself against her enemies.

Responsible officials, both in the State Department and in the White House, were twice informed about Alger Hiss. Mr. Adolph A. Berle relayed Mr. Whittaker Chambers' report on Hiss to his superiors in 1939. In 1943, Chambers spoke with the FBI, who presumably submitted the information to the State Department. There was either a conspiracy of silence among those officers who knew the information about Hiss, or else they were so persuaded by pro-Communist propaganda, much of it of their own making, that they simply did not think it made much difference whether or not Hiss *was* a Communist. The last is less astounding if one recalls the celebrated statement of the influential Mr. Paul Appleby, of the Bureau of the Budget: "A man in the employ of the government has just as much right to be a member of the Communist Party as he has to be a member of the Democratic or Republican Party."[1]

Chambers also revealed to the FBI his personal knowledge of the fact that Lee Pressman, Nathan Witt, John Abt, Charles Kramer and others—all of them government employees at one time—were members of the Communist Party. Yet no action was taken even on those who were still employed in the government.

The *Amerasia* case is the second-most publicized dereliction of the State and Justice Departments in loyalty matters. Six persons were apprehended and charged with delivering at least 1700 classified government documents to the magazine *Amerasia*, a dimly veiled Communist publication run by a named Communist, Philip

Jaffe. Many of the documents were top secret, and some of them contained information still affecting American security. But so reluctant was the Justice Department to press the case that charges against four of the individuals involved were dropped altogether, Jaffe was let off with a fine of $2,500, and Emmanuel Larsen, an employee of the State Department, with one of $500.

Throughout the war, to the extent that limited funds and overworked personnel made it possible, the FBI kept up a steady flow of reports to government agencies on the results of its inquiry into the affiliations of various employees. But no matter how conclusive its evidence, the FBI could never count on prompt action. One example: Before the Committee on Un-American Activities, Mr. J. Edgar Hoover testified on March 26, 1947, that on March 7, 1942, the Bureau had transmitted to the Federal Security Agency a 57-page report indicating that one of its employees, Doxey Wilkerson, had been, and in all probability still was, a Communist. The FSA nevertheless retained Wilkerson (who later left it for another government agency, the Office of Price Administration). On the 19th of June, 1943, Mr. Hoover continued, Wilkerson left the government altogether—to become a "Communist Party Organizer" and a member of the National Committee of the Communist Party. Mr. Hoover was able to cite a regulation of the Communist Party which stipulates that, to be eligible for its National Committee, an individual must have been a Party member in good standing for at least four years.

The government's wartime record on security was so bad that inadequate laws and sloppy administrative procedures cannot fully account for it. There must have been a total absence of the will to do the job. Understandably, after all. For this was the era when our government was using its propaganda machine to trumpet the virtues of our noble and democratic Soviet ally. Into this propaganda effort our leaders put their hearts. It could hardly be expected that, at the same time, they should consider as unfit for government service Americans who had merely shown themselves to be deeply attached to that ally.

CHAPTER III

The State Department, 1945–1947: An Earnest Effort

M R. J. ANTHONY PANUCH, Deputy Assistant Secretary of State for Administration between September, 1945, and January, 1947, asserted recently that, the scandal of Alger Hiss notwithstanding, "the hard core of the State Department remained [under Cordell Hull] impenetrable—a stockade of conservatism and traditionalism." It is, of course, now a matter of record that Hiss was not the sole representative of proletarian democracy in Hull's State Department. Still, Mr. Panuch may be almost right; for it was not until the fall of 1945 that the State Department became the haven for every jobless ideologue in Washington. Then, at the behest of the all-powerful Bureau of the Budget, roughly 13,000 employees of wartime agencies were transferred to the State Department, *en masse*, in the interest of "economy." As we shall see, the "Merger of 1945" presented almost insuperable problems for the Department's security officers.

Yet before examining this critical turn of affairs, we must take note of concurrent events at the policy-making level of the Department. By the summer of 1945, the State Department had a New Look, even though James Byrnes was its head. Assistant Secretary Adolph Berle had been eased out by those who, as he put it, were opposed to "a pretty clean-cut showdown" with Soviet Russia— "Mr. Acheson's group, of course, with Mr. Hiss as principal assistant in the matter."[1] Next to go was anti-Communist Under Secretary Joseph Grew, who, in August of 1945, was replaced by Dean Acheson. Similar shifts followed on lower levels.

The now powerful left-wing faction within the Department set itself a whole series of administrative and policy objectives, most particularly:

1) transfer of the policy-making function from Foreign Service career officers to new State Department personnel;

2) centralized control of sources of foreign intelligence;

3) adoption of a global (as opposed to a nationalist, alliance-type) approach to foreign policy, centered on the United Nations.

Already, Alger Hiss, as Director of the State Department's Office of Special Political Affairs, exercised broad powers. The charter of Hiss' office—drafted by himself—delegated to it "charge of international organization [UN] and security affairs, for the formulation and coordination of policy and action relating to such affairs, with special emphasis on the maintenance of international peace and security through organized action."

After organizing the United Nations Secretariat in London, in March, 1946, Hiss proposed a reorganization of the State Department. Had this plan been approved, and had Hiss attained the personal power which, under the plan, he staked out for himself, the State Department would have taken a long step forward in the direction of becoming an adjunct to the Soviet Foreign Office.

The Deputy Assistant Secretary for Administration, Mr. J. Anthony Panuch, transmitted an analysis* of Hiss' plan to his superiors which said in part:

I have read with mingled feelings of admiration and horror the outline of the above as revealed in . . . memorandum to the Secretary of State, March 5, 1946. The plan's simplicity of design is admirable; its conception is grandiose. . . .

In examining the plan and assessing its implications in terms of control, it should be remembered that Dr. Hiss exercises Svengali-like influence over the mental process of (Blank). Through (Blank), his designee for the post of Secretary General of the U.S. Delegation to the UNO, Dr. Hiss will enjoy "working control" over the flow of papers in and out of the Secretariat of the U.S. group. The proposed plan would establish a similar control set-up within the State Department, where Dr. Hiss already wields considerable influence with (Blank). . . . Under the plan, the Director of this new office (Dr. Hiss) would be the under Secretary's Deputy for United Nations Affairs.

If this ambitious project should be approved, it is obvious that the operations of the new Office, as the "initiating and coordinating center with the Department" for UNO affairs will, for all practical purposes, supplant and supersede the functions of the geographic and economic offices of the Department. . . . If Dr. Hiss should succeed in causing

* This memorandum was treated as confidential until it was read on the floor of the Senate, on July 24, 1950, by Senator Homer Ferguson. Senator Ferguson, even then, suppressed many of the names mentioned, substituting, in each case, "Blank." The names were revealed by Panuch before a subcommittee of the Senate Judiciary on June 25, 1953; for various reasons, however, they are excluded here.

(Blank) to be designated as the UNO Assistant Secretary General for Administration, *the Hiss group will have achieved infiltration in, or control of, four critically strategic points, i.e.,* a) *UNO itself (Blank),* b) *The U. S. Delegation (Blank),* c) *State Department (Blank) and* d) *Bureau of the Budget (Blank).* . . . [Italics added.]

God was surely in His heaven on that particular day: Secretary Byrnes rejected the proposed reorganization plan. Had Byrnes accepted it, and had Whittaker Chambers remained silent, Alger Hiss would have emerged as our virtual Secretary of State. As it happened, Hiss was defeated—on this point, at any rate. A few months later, he resigned, to labor in the vineyards of International Peace as President of the Carnegie Foundation.

Though he cannot be credited with being a pioneer in the fight against Soviet infiltration of government, Secretary Byrnes frustrated the aspirations of the Hiss group and maintained a determined, if sometimes shortsighted, team in the security division. He brought with him, as Assistant Secretary, his long-time friend and former law partner, Mr. Donald Russell. And at the suggestion of General Clay and others, Russell persuaded J. Anthony Panuch, a successful New York attorney with ten years' experience in various government jobs, to take the post of Deputy Assistant Secretary for Administration.

Panuch was assigned the task of integrating the new "merger" personnel into the State Department. He insisted that this responsibility called for complete authority over the Department's security program. Byrnes agreed and named Panuch "Coordinator" in October, 1945. Panuch retained from Cordell Hull's regime Mr. Tom Fitch, head of the Bureau of Special Investigation, and Mr. Fred Lyon, Chief of Counter Intelligence, both of whom had made conscientious and sometimes telling security efforts during the war. Mr. Robert L. Bannerman came in as Special Assistant and Security Officer.

Panuch's responsibilities were legion. He had, on the one hand, to concern himself with internecine struggles raging between various agencies in the Department. Many of these were over competing proposals for reorganization of the Department; and some, as we have noticed, were but thinly disguised attempts to center power in the hands of ideologues congenial to the schemer. Notwithstanding, Panuch and his associates waded into the security quagmire. They faced a number of grave problems.

There was, first, the sheer volume of work involved in screening

the personnel entering the Department under the "merger" program. Another problem was the reorganization of security procedures with an eye to separating the investigative and evaluative
functions. A third was the adoption of a loyalty standard exacting
enough to protect the Department in case of doubt about an employee's reliability. And a fourth concerned the legal problems
involved in firing "status" employees.

Top priority was given to the "merger" program. The task was
difficult. There had been a total of 12,797 "transferees," as the State
Department called them. Although most of them left the Department almost immediately, as a result of the post-war retrenchment,
approximately 4,000 stayed on. The personnel records for many of
these, however, were far from complete. The State Department
listed some of its difficulties in a memorandum to the Tydings Committee,[2] emphasizing both the administrative confusion of the day
and the sloppiness of the wartime security program:

Thus, as to one of these agencies [the OWI], it was determined that of
the entire staff of 7,482 transferred to the Department, only 2,687 had
been cleared by the Civil Service Commission. Investigations were dis-
continued before completion in 1,113 cases and were pending in 262
cases when the transfers were made. Thus, there were thousands of
cases of employees in this and other agencies transferred to the Department who had apparently never been fully investigated. . . .

During the first hectic months of the new security program, investigators were often called upon to evaluate their own findings,
and even to make final disposition of the cases, though a strict
separation of fact-finding and evaluation has for centuries been
basic to justice. This deficiency was, however, spotted before much
damage had been done, and Mr. Panuch eliminated it. Thenceforth
individuals were investigated at one level, the findings evaluated at
another. Moreover, employees could appeal to the Secretary of
State, who was empowered to reject the recommendations of the
final screening board.

But what loyalty and security standards were to be established?
Here Panuch aligned himself with the realists. He ordered his
security personnel to observe the standards set up by the Civil Service Commission in 1942: if there was "reasonable doubt" as to an
individual's loyalty to the U.S. government or if there was "reasonable doubt" about his reliability, the panel should recommend his

dismissal. On this point—that the government, not the individual jobholder, should benefit from any doubt—Panuch and his assistants remained emphatic. On July 29, 1946, the State Department security office was able to advise Mr. Bartel Jonkman of the Foreign Affairs Committee of the House of Representatives that the "reasonable doubt" standard had been in effect for months. "The Department," it stated,

is thoroughly cognizant of the security problem and its implications, and any reasonable doubt of an employee's loyalty to this Government or its institutions will be resolved in favor of the Government. However, the doubt must be based on substantial evidence.

This view of the State Department coincided with that of the Civil Service Committee of the House, which, after a long investigation into the problem of subversives in government, had recently declared:

Adequate protective measures must be adopted to see that persons of questioned loyalty are not permitted to enter into federal service. These protective measures should of course be absolutely fair and impartial, but doubts must, in the nature of things, be resolved in favor of the government.

Note that the State Department did not restrict the application of the standard to individuals *seeking* employment; but in dealing with persons already employed, the Department clashed with Civil Service regulations protecting certain classes of government personnel from "arbitrary dismissal." In short, rules fashioned for one purpose—to protect non-policy-making public servants from the ravages of incoming, patronage-starved administrations—had become a major obstacle to the realization of another legitimate objective—a strong internal security program.

At its inception in 1884, the Civil Service Code prohibited inquiry into the political beliefs of civil servants: "No question in any form or application or in any examination shall be so framed as to elicit information concerning the political or religious opinions or affiliations of any applicant, nor shall any inquiry be made concerning such opinions, or affiliations, and all disclosures thereof shall be discountenanced."

The Hatch Act of 1939, however, and subsequent legislative and administrative orders, set aside parts of this prohibition. They authorized inquiries meant to determine whether or not an individual's employment jeopardized the nation's security. But when exercising the "reasonable doubt" standard, security officers—in the State Department—were treading on loose ground, especially when there was no conclusive evidence that the investigated individual was still a member of a party advocating the violent overthrow of the government. The Hatch Act merely forbade employment to *members* of the Communist Party or of subversive organizations; and an employee, even if detected as having been a member of such a group, had only to resign from it to avoid the sanctions of the Hatch Act. If his job had tenure rights, he was thereafter virtually immune against dismissal on loyalty grounds.

The old Lloyd-LaFollette Act in effect permitted the dismissal of any federal employee in the interest of efficiency. It stipulated, however, that proposed dismissals be submitted for approval to a board of the Civil Service Commission. Here the procedural requirements were so angled in favor of the employee, and the sheer time and manpower needed to press the government's case were so exorbitant, that it was entirely impractical to rely on this authority to dismiss overt Communists, let alone suspected Communists.

In short, no one really knew how to get rid of persons whose continued presence in the State Department jeopardized national security without violating their rights as civil servants. While Federal agencies now had the authority to question employees about their political opinions and their affiliations, "status" employees could not be discharged on a "reasonable doubt" judgment. Nothing less than provable present membership in the Communist Party, or in an organization cited as subversive by the Attorney General, would do.*

Secretary Byrnes, Assistant Secretary Russell, and Deputy Assistant Secretary Panuch discussed this conundrum with Senators Bridges and McCarran. McCarran suggested a way out, and the conference led to the attachment of the so-called McCarran Rider to the State Department Appropriations Bill, passed on the 6th of July, 1946, and renewed yearly until 1953. The Rider authorizes the Secretary of State "in his absolute discretion" to discharge any em-

---

* And even this was made risky when the Supreme Court declared in 1943 on the Schneiderman case that mere membership in the Communist Party is insufficient proof that a given individual advocates the violent overthrow of the government.

ployee "whenever he shall deem such termination necessary or advisable in the interests of the United States."*

But during the six months following the passage of the McCarran Rider, it was used only once.** A few weeks after the enactment of the Rider, Secretary Byrnes wrote a much-discussed letter to Congressman Adolph Sabath reporting that of 284† "adverse recommendations" thus far made against Department personnel, 79 had been acted upon. Of the 79, 40 were loyalty and security cases, Byrnes added. Yet these 40 were *not* fired under the authority of the McCarran Rider.‡

How account for this apparent dereliction? In Mr. Panuch's opinion, the McCarran Rider did not definitely settle the question whether or not a discharged employee could successfully appeal to the courts on the grounds that, when all was said and done, he had been discriminated against because of his political opinions—in violation of the First Amendment. In the absence of a firm legal precedent to sustain him, Panuch believed the issue of thought control would inevitably arise. Might not the point be made that a govern-

* Similar powers had been conferred upon the Secretaries of War and Navy during the war. Subsequently, the Director of the Atomic Energy Commission was also empowered to discharge summarily. On August 26, 1950, this privilege was incorporated into an independent bill which also extended the privilege to the Departments of Justice and Commerce, the Coast Guard, the National Security Resources Board, and the National Advisory Commission for Aeronautics. The Bill passed the House of Representatives by a vote of 327–14.

** Perhaps twice, for there is conflicting evidence as to whether Mary Jane Keeney was got out under the Rider. It is established, however, that the Rider was used for the first time in dismissing Carl Marzani on December 20, 1946. (See below.)

† This letter has been widely misrepresented. Various commentators have suggested that the figure 284 represented *all* the final adverse determinations. But the security board's work had then only begun, and at least a thousand "transferees" were yet to be processed. And the twenty-odd thousand standing personnel of the Department had not yet been re-examined.

‡ The authority under which the 40 individuals were fired as security risks remains a mystery. The McCarran Rider was not used, and the President's loyalty order had not been issued. It was by no means proved that all the individuals in question were members of the Communist Party, and hence violators of the Hatch Act. Mr. Panuch does not "remember how they were gotten rid of." The man most directly concerned, Mr. Robert Bannerman, is now working with the Central Intelligence Agency, and refuses to comment. Only two explanations spring to mind: (1) the individuals in question were not dismissed, but were persuaded to resign, or were transferred to a unit destined for liquidation at the war's end; or (2) Byrnes' letter was inaccurate.

ment which extends job protection privileges only to employees holding a particular set of beliefs is abridging freedom of speech? In Panuch's opinion, in other words, the legal issue had by no means been definitely settled, notwithstanding congressional authorization of the McCarran Rider. What was more, relative apathy to the menace of Communism, the action of the Supreme Court in the Schneiderman case, and an academic groundswell (to which the Supreme Court would be predictably sensitive) against "witch-hunting," were all storm signals which Panuch decided to take seriously. The stakes were too high. The danger of the moment, as he saw it, did not lie in postponing the day of reckoning for pro-Communists in the Department. It lay, rather, in judicial torpedo-ing of the entire federal loyalty program.

He decided, therefore, to take a calculated risk. He retained in office all security and loyalty cases who had committed no overt illegal act. And carefully preparing his case, he trained his guns on one individual.* On the 20th of December, 1946, Carl Aldo Marzani was fired by the Secretary of State, under the authority of the McCarran Rider.

Marzani had lied to Panuch when he denied having been actively associated with the Communist Party in the late 30's and early 40's. He was convicted on May 22, 1947, on eleven counts, the crucial one being his misrepresentation of his political affiliations to security officers of the State Department. Exactly two years after he was fired by the State Department, Marzani's conviction was upheld by the Supreme Court. The Court's decision affirmed the right of security officers to ask political questions relevant to a security investigation, and the duty of employees to answer them truthfully.

Two months before Marzani's conviction, the Supreme Court had refused to review the complaint of Morton Friedman, who had been fired from his post with the War Manpower Commission in 1944 on the grounds that he was pro-Communist. On March 22,

---

* Panuch's wisdom in postponing a purge of pro-Communists in the Department is, unlike his good faith in doing so, open to question. There are convincing grounds for believing that, had he eliminated them as soon as he had amassed evidence supporting "reasonable doubt," the Court would have sustained him—especially since it was faced with an aroused Congress which had already recorded its solidarity on this issue by its overwhelming approval of the McCarran Rider. Panuch's timidity in this respect reflects the legal fastidiousness of his boss, Secretary Byrnes, who on this and other occasions (see, for example, the section on the United Nations) hesitated to risk judicial rebuke, even in matters affecting the national security.

1947, President Truman had issued Executive Order 9835, establishing a federal loyalty program that forbade the employment of loyalty risks. The "trusteeship" view of federal employment—the doctrine that public service is a privilege rather than a right—had thus won legislative, executive, and judicial recognition.

But neither Panuch nor his principal assistants were to be given the opportunity to carry out their long-range, earnest program to rid the State Department of security risks. On the 22nd of January, 1947, James Byrnes resigned, and George Marshall assumed office. The following day, after a protracted interview with Dean Acheson, Under Secretary of State and long-time foe of Panuch, Marshall consented to the firing of Panuch. Acheson ordered Panuch out of the Department, at the close of business the same day.

Within a few weeks, every vital member of Panuch's security staff was retired, demoted, transferred to another branch of the Department, or fired. John Peurifoy succeeded Panuch. President Truman's loyalty directive established the inadequate "reasonable grounds" standard in loyalty cases. The State Department security program was now dead in its tracks.

CHAPTER IV

The State Department, 1947–1950: Three Years of Inertia

THE premise of virtually all non-Communist attacks on McCarthy is that for three years before Senator McCarthy made his sensational charges in February, 1950, the State Department had maintained an effective security division. The sun never sets without some editorial writer, some professor, or some radio commentator having asserted that the pre-McCarthy State Department was doing a magnificent job of weeding out security risks, and that therefore McCarthy's charges were sheer demagoguery.

Here are a few examples, taken at random:

From the *New York Times*, breathless with indignation after McCarthy was renominated in Wisconsin on September 9, 1952:

The plain fact of the matter is that the Government's own loyalty program was initiated almost three years before McCarthy made his first national impact with [a] ... discredited allegation. ...

From *Life* Magazine, October 1, 1951:

If Houdini were a suspected Communist,* he couldn't get near a sensitive government payroll today. In short, Communist infiltration of Government is no longer a legitimate worry.

From *McCarthy: The Man, The Senator, The "Ism"*:[1]

... of all the government departments probably the most security-conscious has been [i.e., before McCarthy] the State Department.

State Department officials have energetically attempted, with remarkable skill, to foster national confidence on this score. General

* Which of course begs the question of what Houdini has to do to get himself "suspected."

Conrad Snow, Chairman of the State Department Loyalty Security Board, for example, met any doubts about his efficiency and judgment head-on in a nationally circularized speech delivered on the 21st of October, 1951:

What, then, is all the shouting about? The best and shortest answer I can give you is to ask you to read the article "Demagog McCarthy" . . . in *Time* magazine, October 22, 1951. . . . What about the loyalty program, designed to prevent infiltration of Government by Communism, and, in fact, ante-dating McCarthyism for two full years? . . . it is effectively protecting not only the Government of the United States, but also the loyal employees of that Government.

General Snow might, of course, be suspected of speaking *ex parte;* for an indictment of State Department security is in large measure an indictment of General Snow. The defenders of the Department's program, therefore, have relied heavily on other documents to sustain their point of view. One source to which they turn is the report of the Tydings Committee. Tydings did more than brand McCarthy a liar, and the persons McCarthy had denounced, patriots. He handed down a studied endorsement of the entire State Department security program:

Our investigation reveals . . . B) *That the State Department's Security Division is efficiently operated by highly qualified personnel.* C) That the loyalty and security Board of the State Department is made up of high-type individuals of unquestioned loyalty and integrity, and sound judgment. [Italics added.]

Some of the pleaders for the Department reach back to the 2nd of August, 1948, and quote a self-effacing Republican Congressman from Michigan, Mr. Bartel Jonkman, who announced on the floor of the House that after conducting a one-man investigation in behalf of the House Committee on Foreign Affairs, he had something he wanted to say:

. . . before the 80th Congress adjourns, I want the members to know that there is one department in which the known or reasonably suspected subversives, Communists, fellow-travelers, sympathizers, and persons whose services are not for the best interests of the United States, have been swept out. That is the Department of State. For this job the people of the United States can thank to a great extent in the order in which the work was done: First, Congressman Bartel J. Jonkman of the Fifth District of Michigan, who on July 10, 1946, was appointed a Committee of one—from the Committee on Foreign Affairs—to investigate Communism in the State Department; second, the people themselves . . . and third, Mr. John E. Peurifoy . . . Assistant Secretary of State for Administration. . . .

Defenders of State Department security action during this period neglect, almost conspiratorially, to point out that, after March of 1948, *the data necessary to the making of an informed evaluation of the security program were inaccessible.* For on March 13, 1948, President Truman issued an order instructing all federal officials to withhold personnel loyalty and security information from members of Congress; and from everybody else, of course. This order was of critical importance, for several reasons.

For one thing, it served notice on Congress that it had better not concern itself with loyalty and security; the Executive would shoulder the job itself without any outside help. But further, since the concern of Congress over security in sensitive government agencies cannot be foreclosed by presidential fiat, the Executive Order was to invite uneasiness on Capitol Hill—and consummate arrogance on the part of federal security personnel. The Order created the combustible frustration which McCarthy detonated two years later.

President Truman's directive read, in part, as follows:

. . . all reports, records, and files relative to the loyalty of employees or prospective employees . . . shall be maintained in confidence, and shall not be transmitted or disclosed except as required in the efficient conduct of business.

Any subpoena or demand or request for information, reports or files of the nature described, received from sources other than those persons in the executive branch of the Government who are entitled thereto by reason of their official duties, shall be respectfully declined. . . . There shall be no relaxation of the provisions of this directive except with my express authority.

Members of Congress were thenceforth left without information on which to base a vote either of confidence or of no confidence in the Administration's handling of security matters. For it obviously does not follow that, because the proclaimed security standards are acceptable, the personnel of, say, the State Department Loyalty Security Board will *apply* the standards in such a way as to merit Congressional confidence.

The important fact is that vital security data were withheld from

Congress. This alone would invalidate such claims as that "the Senate Committee on Appropriations gave the State Department a clean bill of health in 1948." Yet much has been made of such alleged clean bills of health. The Tydings Report stated, for example, that the Appropriations Committee had cleared the State Department—for it had not even published a report on concluding its investigation into Department security.

Senator Homer Ferguson, a member of the Appropriations Committee, coped with this claim on July 24, 1950. He stated that, despite concerted pressure from some sources, the Committee had been making gradual progress *up to the moment* of the President's directive of 1948.

As I have stated [Senator Ferguson told the Senate] our Committee did not consider the situation [security in the State Department] as one which did not merit a report because we did report to the Secretary of State and we cited names [of security risks]. *We gave no clearances,* as the subcommittee [Tydings] report and the Senator from Maryland inferred we did. As I have said before, *we were confronted in March 1948 with the closing of all the files,* and therefore it was impossible for us to look into the files any further, or continue the examination of them. [Italics added.]

Thus, not only was it impossible for a responsible Senate Committee to *clear* the State Department after the promulgation of Truman's censorship order; there also is evidence that a specific committee of Congress was preparing to do just the *opposite* when the Order made it impossible to pursue the matter.

The preliminary report to the Secretary of State, cited by Senator Ferguson, was a confidential memorandum which the Committee transmitted to General Marshall on the 10th of June, 1947:

It becomes necessary, due to the gravity of the situation, to call your attention to a condition that developed and still flourishes in the State Department under the administration of [Under Secretary] Dean Acheson.

It is evident that there is a deliberate, calculated program being carried out not only to protect Communist personnel in high places, but to reduce security and intelligence protection to a nullity.

Regarding the much-publicized MARZANI case, the evidence brought out at his trial was well known to State Department officers, who ignored it and refused to act for a full year.

MARZANI and several other Department officials, with full knowledge of the State Department, and with Government time and money, promoted a scheme called PRESENTATIONS, INC., which contracted with a Communist dominated organization to disseminate propaganda.

Security objections to these and other even more dangerous developments were rebuffed by high administrative officials; and there followed the substitution of unqualified men for these competent, highly respected personnel who theretofore held the intelligence and security assignments in the Department. The new chief of controls is a man utterly devoid of background and experience for the job, who is and at the time of his appointment was known to those who appointed him to be, a cousin and close associate of a suspected Soviet agent. The next development was the refusal of the FBI, ONI and other federal investigative agencies to continue the whole hearted cooperation they had for years extended to the State Department.

On file in the Department is a copy of a preliminary report of the FBI on Soviet espionage activities in the United States, which involves a large number of State Department employees, some in high official positions. This report has been challenged and ignored by those charged with the responsibility of administering the Department with the apparent tacit approval of Mr. Acheson. Should this case break before the State Department acts, it will be a national disgrace.

Voluminous files are on hand in the Department proving the connection of the State Department employees and officials with this Soviet espionage ring. Despite this, only two persons, one of whom is MARZANI, were released under the McCarran rider because of their subversive activity.

1.	[names omitted]	6.
2.		7.
3.		8.
4.		9.
5.		

are only a few of the hundreds now employed in varying capacities who are protected and allowed to remain despite the fact that their presence is an obvious hazard to national security. There is also the extensive employment in highly classified positions of admitted homosexuals, who are historically known to be security risks.

The War and Navy Departments have been thwarted for a year in their efforts to carry out the German Scientist program. They are blocked by one man in the State Department, a protégé of Acheson, named [name omitted], who is also the chief instrument in the subverting of the over-all security program.

This deplorable condition runs all the way up and down the line. Assistant Secretary Braden also surrounded himself with men like [name omitted] and with [name omitted] who has a notorious international reputation. The network also extends into the office of Assistant Secretary Benton.* [Italics added.]

The nature and intent of Truman's Executive Order are disclosed by the following colloquy between Senator Ferguson and a State Department official, in which Ferguson virtually threw up his hands in despair:

SENATOR FERGUSON. The way I find myself here in this committee as a representative of the people is that we can review the procedure but we cannot review any substantive evidence.

MR. HUMELSINE. That is right, and that is not my regulation but the directive of the President.

SENATOR FERGUSON. I understand. But he tells the people, "You are not entitled to know anything except the machinery." That is true, is it not?

MR. HUMELSINE. Yes, sir; that is true.[2]

The fact that legislative committees could not possibly go on record as approving State Department security practices sheds light on the performance of the press and other special pleaders for the Department. For it follows from Congressional inability that laymen—and we dare include here the editors of the *New York Times*—were alike unqualified to talk authoritatively on the subject, though in their efforts to discredit McCarthy they have not hesitated to do so.

Every Executive effort has been made to maintain a full blackout of security information. But an occasional failure of these efforts has brought to light sufficient data to justify a preliminary answer to the one question at issue: whether the State Department's loyalty-security program had adequately protected a most sensitive government agency from Communist penetration.

Before going into that, however, it is necessary to define the authorities under which the Department's program operated after 1947, the different standards under which its personnel were

* In his book, *McCarthyism, the Fight for America* (New York; Devin-Adair, 1952), Senator McCarthy states, "This warning was disregarded by Marshall" (p. 23). This is only partly true. On the 24th of June, 1947, Assistant Secretary John Peurifoy notified Senator Ball, chairman of the subcommittee of the Committee on Appropriations handling State Department matters, that ten persons had been dismissed. Five of them were listed in the above memorandum. Their separation was, let us assume, urged by General Marshall.

tried, and, of course, the difference between the loyalty and the security risk.

Until the 17th of December, 1947, the State Department operated under the "reasonable doubt" standard with respect to both loyalty and security cases; and it had the power, under the McCarran Rider, to discharge at will. From December, 1947, on, federal agencies were under a directive (the President's Executive Order No. 9835) which required the dismissal of *"loyalty* risks," but set up the "reasonable grounds" rather than the "reasonable doubt" standard for determining whether a person *was* a loyalty risk. In doing so, the President went contrary to the recommendations of the House Civil Service Commission, and moved away from the standards the State Department itself had adopted—on paper at least.

The President's Order also directed the Civil Service Commission to establish a Loyalty Review Board which was empowered to review, at its discretion, the findings of agency loyalty boards; to reverse them if it saw fit; and to adjudicate appeals from adverse findings of subordinate boards. The Loyalty Review Board could not, however, entertain an appeal by the government against the clearance of an employee by an agency board.* Moreover, it had no jurisdiction at all over *security* cases.

The language of the President's Order ("on all the evidence reasonable grounds exist for belief that the person involved is disloyal to the Government of the United States") set up a standard that is far more lenient than that included in the words, "on all the evidence there is reasonable *doubt* as to the loyalty, etc. . . ."

The difference in standards can be shown with the following illustration: An employee is identified, let us say, as a former member of the Communist Party. If he specifically pleads change of heart, it is difficult to find *"reasonable grounds"* for concluding that the alleged change has *not* in fact taken place. Under the *"reasonable doubt"* standard, by contrast, only clear-cut, substantial *evidence* of reform would prevent dismissal. In fact, State Department regulations based on *"reasonable doubt"* stipulate that *"A former course of conduct or holding of beliefs will be presumed to continue in the absence of positive evidence indicating a change, both in course of action and conviction, by clear, overt, and unequivocal acts."*[3]

---

* The Government has never formally recognized the "prosecutor" (i.e., those members of a security division who recommend dismissal of an employee) as its representative. Appeals in the loyalty field, consequently, should always be understood to mean appeals from *adverse* findings.

In all justice, then, the fact that the State Department suddenly found itself saddled with what appeared to be a stringent *pro-employee* standard made dismissals *on loyalty grounds* more difficult than they had been formerly.*

Actually, however, the change in standards was meaningless. *For what the apologists for the State Department studiously neglect to mention is that the President's Loyalty Order did not rescind the McCarran Rider; that the State Department's security standard continued to be based on "reasonable doubt"; that every loyalty risk is ipso facto a security risk; and that therefore the promulgation of the Loyalty Order in no way affected the Department's authority to discharge suspect personnel in the security category under the "reasonable doubt" standard.*

The State Department, in short, was not actually handicapped— provided it was willing to proceed against employees in the *security* rather than the *loyalty* category. And responsible State Department officials were demonstrably aware of the decisive difference between the two standards. The indispensability of the "reasonable doubt" standard to an effective security program was stressed by Mr. John Peurifoy on June 13, 1947—*after* the promulgation of the President's Loyalty Order (but before it began to operate). Mr. Peurifoy, who as Deputy Under Secretary of State for Administration was directly in charge of the State Department's security division, appeared before the Appropriations Subcommittee of the Senate. Former Senator Joseph Ball asked him:

Would you say that in our present situation, internationally, particularly in a Department like the State Department, dealing with foreign questions, it is essential that there be absolutely no question as to the loyalty of its employees?

Mr. Peurifoy. Absolutely, sir.

Senator Ball. . . . *any doubt as to an individual's loyalty should be resolved in favor of the Government?*

Mr. Peurifoy. *Any reasonable doubt should be resolved in favor of the Government.* I believe it is a privilege to work for this Government, and not a right.[4] [Italics added.]

Now: How to distinguish between the two classes of "risks?" Here is one explanation:

* Though having said this, we must hasten to add that the Department never exercised even the power the Loyalty Order left to it. Other agencies subject to the Order managed to dismiss their more flagrant loyalty risks. But the State Department did not.

Suppose the District Attorney in your county called together police officials to plan a series of raids against gambling spots.

If an official at that meeting carelessly told a newspaper reporter about the plans, then he would be a *security risk*.

If this official, however, immediately telephoned a gambler and warned him of the coming raid, then the official would be *disloyal* to his government—the county in this case.

Thus, a "security risk" might be an employee who talks too much, or who drinks, or who is careless in the kind of people with whom he associates.[5]

Another explanation:

SENATOR FERGUSON. How can there be security when there is disloyalty? Will you please tell me.

MR. HUMELSINE (Assistant Secretary of State—Administration). *Well, a person that is a loyalty risk is also a security risk.*

SENATOR MCCARRAN. Certainly.

MR. HUMELSINE. But a person can be a security risk without necessarily being a loyalty risk. The reverse of that would not be true.

SENATOR HILL. You mean by that that a person might be a drunkard, say, a habitual drunkard.

MR. HUMELSINE. Yes, he might be a habitual drunkard who went into a bar and talked too much and allowed some of our very vital information to fall into the hands of our enemies. . . .

SENATOR MCCARRAN. He would be termed a security risk, would he not?

MR. HUMELSINE. Yes, sir. Now a person who takes a confidential document from the Department of State and sees to it that it gets into the hands of an alien power—if that sort of thing were to take place—that person would be a loyalty risk.

SENATOR MCCARRAN. He would be both, would he not?

MR. HUMELSINE. And also a security risk; yes sir. *When I use the term loyalty risk, that includes security.*

SENATOR MCCARRAN. That is what I wanted to know. How can there be a loyalty risk and not a security risk?

MR. HUMELSINE. *There cannot be,* Senator.[6] [Italics added.]

However, neither of these explanations is adequate. While it is true that an individual may be a security risk and yet a patriot—he may be alcoholic, homosexual, forgetful, or artless—the term, as used by the State Department when referring to *political* suspects, very simply denotes disloyalty. For the loyalty and security criteria of the State Department are virtually identical, except for one thing: guilt by association is more heavily stressed in the security category, which, for example, cites as pertinent evidence against an employee, "voluntary association with persons known or *believed* to be" Communist sympathizers.

The fact that a "security risk" may also be a *conscious* threat to the United States is clearly indicated in Paragraph 3 (Section VA) of the State Department's security regulations. A security risk is, among other things,

A person who has knowingly divulged classified information without authority and with the knowledge or belief or with reasonable grounds for the knowledge or belief that it will be transmitted to agencies of a foreign government, *or* who is so consistently irresponsible in the handling of classified information as to compel the conclusion of extreme lack of care or judgment.[7] [Italics added.]

Clearly, there was nothing to prevent Department officials from putting every "loyalty" suspect into *security* channels, and thence examining him under the "reasonable doubt" standard. What is more, the Department had no choice in the matter; as security officials themselves never tire of repeating, "Whoever is a loyalty risk is also a security risk." As it happens, the preponderant majority of employees discharged under the *security* category during the years 1948 through 1952 had been previously cleared in the *loyalty* category. What is more, Under Secretary of State for Administration, Carlisle Humelsine, unambiguously admitted that there is no such thing as examining a man on loyalty and neglecting to look at him on security:

SENATOR MCCARTHY. Am I correct in saying that you have had over 800 cases that went through the loyalty-security channels [since 1947]?
MR. HUMELSINE. That is right.
SENATOR MCCARTHY. And all 800, you say, were considered as security risks as well as loyalty risks?
MR. HUMELSINE. Yes.[8]

In short, the President's 1947 Loyalty Order notwithstanding, the State Department's mandate after 1946 was to apply the reasonable doubt standard on all its suspect employees. *

How did the State Department use, after 1947, the broad powers it had to purge the Department of dubious personnel?

---

* The same does not hold true for all other government agencies, some of which were not granted the authority of the McCarran Rider to discharge at will, and were hence without the effective power to set up their own standards.

Security information on specific persons is still inaccessible—even to Congressmen. But general figures are available and may be assembled from testimony squeezed out of Department officials by Congressional Committees. While the Executive Order forbids disclosures which involve names and which reveal the current security status of a given employee, it does permit Department officials to reveal the *number* of cases that are being handled or that have been disposed of in some way or other.

During the period here in question, the State Department had roughly 20,000 employees, all of whom it was required to process on loyalty (under the Presidential directive) and on security (under its own regulations).

On June 10, 1947, Assistant Secretary John Peurifoy testified before the Senate Committee on Appropriations that, until that time, the authority of the (then eleven months old) McCarran Rider had been used to discharge exactly two persons from the State Department.* One of these, as we have seen, was Carl Marzani, discharged under the Rider in December, 1946.

In March of 1950, Peurifoy appeared again before the Appropriations Committee, and in the presence of Mr. Acheson testified again about the use of the Rider:

SENATOR BRIDGES. How many employees, Mr. Secretary, have been dismissed under the McCarran rider in the years since its inception?
SECRETARY ACHESON. I will have to get the statistics.
MR. PEURIFOY. May I answer that?
SENATOR BRIDGES. Yes.
MR. PEURIFOY. Since January 1, 1947, there has been one.[9]

This testimony, in conjunction with the Marzani facts, establishes that the Rider was exercised for the second time between January 1, 1947, and June 10, 1947. *It establishes also that the Rider*

---

* [*Hearings, Committee on Appropriations, U. S. Senate, for 1948,* p. 646.] In June of 1947, ten persons were discharged under the McCarran Rider. One of them appealed to Washington lawyers Thurman Arnold and Abe Fortas, old hands at defending loyalty suspects. Mr. Bert Andrews of the *New York Herald Tribune* took up the cause of this same man, Mr. X (his name was not publicly discussed), and wrote a series of articles which won him a Pulitzer Prize, and which later appeared in book form with the title *Washington Witchhunt,* no less. Secretary of State Marshall succumbed to mounting pressure and rescinded the dismissals, allowing the ten to "resign without prejudice." Thus, the McCarran Rider is not theoretically on record as having been used on the ten.

was not used from June of 1947 until McCarthy made his charges in the spring of 1950.

But this does not mean that no security risk was removed during this period, not by any means. The Loyalty Security Board of the Department made *one* adverse security finding in 1948 and *one* more in 1949.* Both employees were allowed to resign.

As regards loyalty, not only did the Department fail to discharge anyone on these grounds, the *Department's Board made not a single adverse determination—not, in fact, until early 1952!*

In short, throughout a period of two and one half years preceding McCarthy's entry into the picture (during which time 16,000 investigations had been conducted), the State Department's record was as follows: fired as loyalty risks—none; fired as security risks—none; adverse loyalty determinations—none; adverse security determinations—two.**

"But this is surely not a fair picture," Department defenders will say. "What about those persons who resigned before their cases were finally adjudicated? Did not the Department get most of its risks out by *scaring* them out?"

The Department put at 182 the number of persons who had resigned and about whom "security or loyalty questions have been raised and not cleared up."[10] We have Mr. Peurifoy's own word for it that this statistic does not shed much light on the problem at hand: it should *not* be inferred, he told the press in February, 1940, "that these employees were security risks. . . ." There may, of course, have been some Communists among them; but if so, there is little reason to suppose they left the Department because they feared exposure. The record of the Loyalty Security Board, which was spotting security risks at the rate of one a year and had never found a loyalty risk, was not such as to have caused widespread panic among them. A Mother Bloor, hawking membership in the Party during the lunch hour, might have chosen the discreet occasion to make for the door; but certainly not an Alger Hiss.

But most State Department defenders take the position that, if no adverse loyalty determinations were made, the presumption is

---

* These statistics were given to the authors by the office of the Chief Counsel of the Loyalty Security Board. They are confirmed by the testimony of Mr. Sam Boykin of the Department before the Senate Appropriations Committee for 1951, pp. 603, 610, 611.

** During the same period, from 1947 to 1951, a total of well over 300 persons were discharged *for loyalty alone* in other branches of government.

not that the State Department's program was inadequate, but that, very simply, there were no loyalty risks around.

Now of course an evaluation of a security program must not be based on the number of scalps offered up to the public every fiscal year. If the State Department harbored only two security risks from 1947 to 1950, then obviously only two should have been discharged. If the Department employed no loyalty risks until 1952, then we must commend the courage of its officers in refusing to sacrifice innocent people to the appetites of lustful witch-hunters. The important question is, *Were* there any security or loyalty risks in the State Department during this vital period?

This question we will attempt to answer in analyzing the Tydings investigation. But let us first look at the security record of the State Department as regards the protection of American interests in the United Nations.

The State Department and the United Nations

On December 29, 1952, foreman Joseph P. Kelly of a New York Grand Jury appeared before a House Investigating Committee and reiterated, under oath, an astonishing charge he and fellow jurors had made earlier in the month. The State and Justice Departments, Mr. Kelly declared, had put pressure upon him and his colleagues to "postpone" or "tone down" a finding to the effect that an "overwhelmingly large group of disloyal" Americans had successfully penetrated the United Nations. He, and fellow jurymen, further stated that the refusal of Secretary Acheson to divulge the names of State Department officers responsible for passing judgment on the loyalty of American personnel in the UN Secretariat had made it impossible for them to conduct a definitive inquiry into the employment of American Communists by the UN.

The State Department promptly denied virtually everything: at no time had it obstructed the work of the grand jury; and, in any case, the UN Charter does not permit the Department to "interfere" with the Secretary General in the hiring of personnel for positions in the UN Secretariat.

An explosive issue was touched off. Its repercussions would have received more notice had they not occurred in the headline-filling weeks of the Republican return to power. However, a subcommittee of the House Committee on the Judiciary summoned Secretary Acheson on the last day of December, 1952. Mr. Acheson persisted in refusing to divulge the names of responsible State Department officials. And anyway, Acheson maintained, while subversive Americans in the United Nations might damage American "interests," certainly they could not damage American "security"—a distinction not entirely clear to some members of the Committee.

The new Administration promised to press the investigation, and subsequent hearings before the House Committee led to significant revelations.

The architects of the United Nations had stipulated in Article 101 of the Charter that

Each member of the United Nations undertakes to respect the exclusively international character of the responsibilities of the Secretary General, and the staff, and not to seek to influence them in the discharge of their responsibilities. . . . The staff shall be appointed by the Secretary General under regulations established by the General Assembly.

The Soviet Union (through Yugoslavia) had objected to the principle that the personnel of the Secretariat should not be responsible to their own governments. The Western world, the United States in particular, had expressly sought the internationalization of the Secretariat, and had won the day. The Russians finally approved Article 101, in return for Western support of an administrative provision which bars from UN employment any person who has a background of sympathy for Fascism or Nazism.

Thus, on the basis of Article 101, Secretary of State Byrnes took the position in 1946 that the State Department ought not to intrude in any way in the affairs of the UN Secretariat. "It was my opinion," Byrnes wrote to the chairman of the Judiciary Subcommittee in January, 1953, "that the Department of State should not assume responsibility when it had neither the power to hire nor the power to dismiss employees. . . . Under these circumstances, I did not wish to offer any recommendations of persons seeking employment at the United Nations nor did I want subordinate officials to offer recommendations without my knowledge or authority. I made known my views to the Assistant Secretary for Administration, Mr. Donald Russell, in March, 1946."

But in the early days of the UN, its Secretary General was short-handed. To help him out, the State Department's office of Special Political Affairs (in charge of relations with the UN) submitted in the early spring of 1946 about 300 names of "qualified individuals." One set of names was sent to Mr. Lie on March 25. On March 29, Byrnes laid down his directive. On April 4, a second list was sent to Mr. Lie completing the roster. (Secretary Byrnes was not aware that such lists had been drawn up, or submitted, until six years later.) But Lie wanted more. The State Department—again, mostly through SPA—obliged by detailing 193 government employees to work, on a contractual basis, for the UN.* Of this group 43 became permanent UN employees.

The head of the office of Special Political Affairs was Alger Hiss.

A few years and many disillusions later, the prevailing American philosophy about the United Nations moved a little way towards

---

* President Truman authorized this procedure on May 10, 1946, in Executive Order 9721.

realism. The change was reflected in an incident described to the Judiciary Committee on March 23, 1953, by Mr. William Franklin, a State Department security officer:

At a luncheon in 1949, [Mr. Franklin testified]—in the summer of 1949—it developed here that Mr. John D. Hickerson, Assistant Secretary of State, of the Bureau of United Nations Affairs, met with one of the principal assistants of the Secretary General's staff, who asked Mr. Hickerson if there was not some help that *we* could give to help *him* get rid of undesirable Americans on his staff. [Italics added.]

The initiative, then, in formulating a program to protect American security interests was taken, not by the U.S. government, but by the UN! Mr. Franklin continued:

Then following that meeting, there was scheduled within the areas of the Department other meetings to determine what could be done, and out of that developed this secret arrangement.

The secret arrangement was designed this way, on this basis: the Secretary General would send to the Department of State lists of names of United States nationals employed on his staff. It was agreed that the Department of State, through the Division of Security, would conduct what we call a namecheck operation. . . . When this information was assembled it was reviewed by an official in the Office of Security, the Chief of a branch, who looked at and kept it secret; and if it were derogatory, the Bureau of United Nations Affairs was informed of that and that they were to review the information, and if it was of such nature, to put them on notice that the person was a Communist or under Communist discipline.[11]

In other words, the security division of the State Department was to act as a security office for the Secretary General of the UN; and it was to do so unbeknownst to the Secretary of State:

MR. FRANKLIN: The record as far as we can determine is clear on that point, that Mr. Acheson did not know about this arrangement until October 8, 1952, at which time Mr. McGranery, the Attorney General, told him that the Grand Jury for the Southern District of New York was about to hand up an interim presentment critical of [Communist infiltration in] the United Nations.[12]

The rationale of concealing the Secret Agreement from Mr. Acheson appears to have been as follows: Had he known of the Agreement his subordinates entered into, and had he subsequently faced a charge from a representative of a member nation that the United

States was violating Article 101 of the United Nations Charter, he would have been placed in an intolerable position; i.e., he would have had to choose between confessing all and lying—with the possibility of future exposure.

To protect the confidential nature of the Agreement, investigation of Americans in the United Nations was to be confined to a "namecheck operation." (That is, no field investigations aimed at corroborating or dispelling charges were to be conducted, since this might alert others to what was going on.) The resulting appraisals would accordingly be based, exclusively, on information *already on file* in some government agency. Upon arriving at an adverse decision about the loyalty of an individual, a State Department official would confidentially inform the UN of its finding. And, Mr. Franklin told the Committee, the UN had pledged itself to act upon adverse Department recommendations.[13]

The Committee set out to assess the administration of the Secret Agreement by studying the negotiations between the State Department and the UN over each of the 47 UN employees whom the New York Grand Jury had examined.* Secretary Dulles directed Mr. John W. Ford, the Director of Security of the State Department to assist it in every way. Mr. Ford, among other things, prepared charts illustrating the operation of the program as far as the 47 individuals were concerned.

And they were unquestionably a rum lot. Department evaluators, after studying information, had transmitted to the UN "adverse judgments" on no less than 35 of the 47. And Committee members were soon expressing surprise that the UN had not been warned against five of the remaining twelve.

The high percentage of adverse judgments was by no means the most arresting information the Committee turned up. Mr. Hickerson, Assistant Secretary of State for UN Affairs, testified to the Committee that the average interval between the Department's receipt of an individual's name from the UN and a reply, based on nothing more than an examination of the individual's file kept in the various Washington departments, was "three to four months." Later, correcting himself, he put it at six months. The real state of affairs turned out to be even worse than that. "We find, however,"

* Five of the 47 witnesses were individuals included in the Hiss list referred to above: Cases 12, 26, 36, 43, and 46. It is an interesting and relevant sidelight on State Department security attitudes that, as late as 1951, Alger Hiss was referred to in State Department security reports as a "suspected Communist"![14]

said Robert A. Collier, Chief Counsel of the Committee, "that in analyzing these 47 cases, in the adverse comment cases, *there was a total of 15.6 months average . . . to process those cases. . . .*"* (Italics added.)

In short, the State Department took an average of 12–15 months to check *existing data* in personnel files, evaluate these data, and report back to the UN.

"In case after case," the Committee reported, "it was revealed that the FBI had transmitted highly derogatory information from sources of known reliability, and that the State Department had either refrained from making any adverse comment to Lie or had delayed for periods up to more than 3 years."[15]

The delays of the State Department in passing judgments to the UN were matched by the delays of the Secretary General in acting on the Department's recommendations. Some notorious U.S. Communists remained with the UN more than two years after the State Department reports had been submitted.**

Of the 35 UN employees on whom the State Department reported adversely, only 15 had left the UN when the McCarran Committee and the New York Grand Jury investigating Communism in the United Nations blew the lid off the Secret Agreement in October, 1952. Lie forthwith suspended, and subsequently dismissed, 19 more employees who had refused to answer questions before the McCarran Committee.

The inertia, the apparent lack of interest, and the total absence of effective statecraft exhibited by the State Department in dealing with loyalty in the UN, can only be understood when one recalls the whole security picture in the Department during the Acheson period. The fact that neither Secretary Byrnes nor Secretary Marshall took a stand on the matter of disloyal Americans in the UN does them, of course, no credit. But they must not be judged too severely; anyone tempted to do so must bear in mind the intellectual climate of the day. Any effort the Department might have

---

* The discrepancy between this and Hickerson's average figure is presumably accounted for by the fact that Hickerson was referring to *all* cases, and Collier to the 47 mostly adverse judgments.

** Trygvie Lie has stated that he proceeded cautiously because he was never sure the General Assembly would sustain him if he fired individuals against their protests. He therefore adopted the practice of putting pressure on suspect employees to resign, assigning them to less important posts, and otherwise harrassing them; but he did not feel he could terminate their employment until their contracts ran out.

made at that time to prescribe standards of employment for Americans at the UN would have been generally denounced as a sacrilegious maneuver to destroy the integrity of the international body; though this is not to say, of course, that the effort should not have been made anyway. But by 1949, America's back had stiffened. The Communist technique of policy sabotage had been exposed so completely that the legitimacy of the United States government's interest in its nationals working in the UN became widely accepted. (The public debates of the time seldom centered on the question whether the United States had the *right* to screen American employees in the UN for Communist sympathies but on whether there were in *fact* American Communists in the UN.)

There are, then, two counts on which to base a severe judgment. One, of course, is that State Department underlings failed to attend with even minimum dispatch to a highly important matter dealing with American security. The other is that Dean Acheson failed to seek an agreement with the UN on what to do about American Communists in the UN Secretariat.

The rather desperate "explanation"—that Mr. Acheson did not attempt to take such steps because as a lawyer he knew that, in view of Article 101 of the Charter, they would be fruitless—will not hold up. On November 30, 1953, a UN Special Commission of Jurists, to whom Trygvie Lie had submitted the question of the legality of firing American Communists from the UN staff, ruled unanimously that nothing in the Charter could be construed to protect American Communists in their jobs. On the contrary, the Commission recommended immediate dismissal of (a) American Communists, (b) members of organizations officially listed as subversive, (c) employees with respect to whom the Attorney General might find "reasonable grounds" for regarding them as "likely to be engaged in any activities regarded as disloyal by the host country." Belatedly, the President issued an Executive Order (10244) directing that Americans in the UN be screened for loyalty.

The presumption is that the UN's ruling would have been identical had it been sought three years before. And it is difficult to avoid the conclusion that the interests of the United States would have been better served had Mr. Acheson requested a ruling on the matter.

On August 21, 1953, in adjudicating a number of individual complaints from dismissed UN personnel, the Administrative Tribunal of the United Nations handed down a series of judgments, the moment of which reversed the advisory finding of the Special Commission of Jurists: that the Secretary General is entitled to dismiss persons whose employment constitutes a risk to the security of the United States. The new ruling was greeted in this country by a bipartisan uproar. Dag Hammarskjold immediately refused to reemploy the persons involved and thus, for the moment at least, mollified the American people.

The ruling of the UN Tribunal* indicates not only the dogged ignorance of its members about the realities of the Communist conspiracy, but also, we suspect, a profound miscalculation of the temper of the American people. The United States has been temporarily assuaged by Hammerskjold's decision not to reemploy the ousted persons; but it will probably insist in due time on an unambiguous legalization of the Secretary General's right, and duty, to dismiss security risks.

Be that as it may, the effect of the State Department's inertia, and of its incorrigible insensitivity to the demands of national security, was the retention in positions of varying importance in the UN of dozens of American Communists and pro-Communists. To this price we must also add the embarrassment to the United States involved in the revelation that State Department officials were carrying on secret business with the United Nations, behind the back of the Secretary of State and in possible violation of the UN Charter; and that these officials were prepared not only to lie about the existence of the Secret Agreement, but also to allow Secretary Acheson to deceive the United Nations and his own countrymen by blandly asserting that no such agreement existed. And finally, one must add to the price the humiliation in learning that the only measures taken to guard against disloyalty in the UN were suggested not by our own representatives but by officials of the UN who had apparently pre-empted American concern for American security.

---

* It is difficult, incidentally, to pinpoint the ruling because it uses different terms in the various judgments handed down. It appears most baldly, perhaps, in Judgment No. 18, upholding the complaint of Ruth E. Crawford: ". . . membership of [sic] any particular party would not, of itself, be a justification, in the absence of other cause, for dismissal." (*Administrative Tribunal,* Judgment No. 18, 21 August 1953, p. 6)

PART TWO

CHAPTER V

The First Charges

O N THE 9th of February, 1950, Senator Joe McCarthy struck his first important blow at the criminal nonchalance of State Department security practices. He knew, he told the Ohio County Women's Republican Club of Wheeling, West Virginia, the names of a number of Communists working in the State Department. Just how *many* Communists McCarthy claimed to have knowledge of is still being hotly argued. In fact, his enemies have made so much of the alleged disparity between what McCarthy actually said in Wheeling and what he subsequently claimed he had said, that one of them—Senator William Benton—seriously proposed he be expelled from the Senate as a perjurer.

For this reason we will examine in some detail the two versions of McCarthy's Wheeling speech. We will do this by canvassing the evidence dug up by the Senate Committee that explored Benton's allegations. (The authors have had access to the confidential report of the Committee's staff.)[1]

Senator McCarthy, Benton told the Senate subcommittee on Privileges and Elections (the Gillette-Monroney Committee) on September 28, 1951, "shows himself a calculating dispenser of false and perverted information." For, said Benton, McCarthy lied to the Senate on February 20, 1950, and to the Tydings Committee on April 24, 1950, when he denied that he had said at Wheeling on February 9, 1950, "*I have here in my hand a list of 205—a list of names that were made known to the Secretary of State as being members of the Communist Party and who nevertheless are still working and shaping policy in the State Department.*" Rather, McCarthy claimed to have said at Wheeling, "*I have in my hand 57 cases of individuals who would appear to be either card-carrying* *members or certainly loyal to the Communist Party, but who never-theless are still helping to shape our foreign policy.*"*

The speech was recorded, and broadcast the same day over radio station WWVA in Wheeling, but the recording was erased on the following day (a routine practice of that radio station). And persons who had heard McCarthy deliver his speech were vague as to just exactly what figures he had used and in what context he had used them.

On July 20, Senator Millard Tydings presented the report of his committee to the Senate, and startled the press and the Senate by telling them that, at last, he had the goods on McCarthy: he had the recording of the Wheeling speech and proposed to play it on the Senate floor. But as we shall see in a later chapter, Tydings did *not* in fact have the recording and only an adroit bit of maneuvering on the floor kept the Senate from baring his hoax. Thus, the Gillette-Monroney Committee had to proceed with its inquiry without direct evidence.

Benton insisted, however, that the circumstantial evidence was conclusive, and that even in the absence of a recording of McCarthy's own voice, he must be found guilty of lying. Benton set forth his evidence. He gave the committee:

A. An affidavit signed by Mr. James E. Whitaker, News Editor of Radio Station WWVA. The affidavit was attached to a copy of the speech Benton insisted McCarthy gave, i.e. the version which contained the statement that McCarthy knew the names of 205 members of the Communist Party known to the Secretary of State and nevertheless still working in the State Department. The affidavit read:

As News Editor of Radio Station WWVA I was in charge of the tape recording of Senator Joseph McCarthy's speech at the Hotel McLure, Wheeling, West Virginia, on February 9, 1950. At the hotel I followed the prepared script as I listened to the speech. I certify that the delivered speech, as recorded by me, and on that evening broadcast by the Station WWVA, was in the same form as the attached photostat of the prepared script—with the exception of the usual added connective

---

* The most striking difference between the two versions, it would certainly seem, is that in the one McCarthy in just about as many words accused Acheson of treason—for not having got rid of 205 "members of the Communist Party" although their identity had been "made known" to him. But curiously, this was not the difference which elicited most comment. Rather it was the sheer discrepancy in the number of Communists McCarthy claimed to have personal knowledge of.

phrases and the addition or deletion of such words as "a's"; "and's", and "the's" which to my thinking did not materially change the meaning of the text. I have initialed each page of the attached photostatic copy of Senator McCarthy's speech.

B. An affidavit identical in all material respects with that of Whitaker, attached to the same version of McCarthy's speech, signed by Paul A. Myers, program director of WWVA.

C. A reproduction of a news story that appeared in the Wheeling *Intelligencer* the day after the speech, written by Mr. Frank Desmond of the *Intelligencer* staff. A part of that story reads:

Referring directly to the State Department, he [McCarthy] declared: "While I cannot take the time to name all of the men in the State Department who have been named as members of the Communist Party and members of a spy ring, I have here in my hand a list of 205 that were known to the Secretary of State as being members of the Communist Party and who, nevertheless, are still working and shaping the policy in the State Department."

Benton also told the Committee that Mr. Austin V. Wood, vice-president and general manager of the *Intelligencer*, had written to Senator Tydings on March 25, 1950, as follows:

I have today talked with Mr. Frank Desmond, the reporter who wrote the story in question. He tells me there can be no doubt that Senator McCarthy did use the figure "205" in referring to his list of men in the State Department who have been named as members of the Communist Party, and members of a spy ring.

D. A copy of Senator McCarthy's speech to the Senate on February 20. In this speech, McCarthy in effect denied having used the "205" version at Wheeling. He told his colleagues that he would read to them a copy of the speech he had *actually* delivered in Wheeling. The figure mentioned in this version was "57." McCarthy furthermore stated that the speech he was then reading to the Senate "was taken from a recording of the speech. I did not use a written speech that night."

Since McCarthy at no time had access to a recording of the *Wheeling* speech, Benton claimed that his Senate denial of the "205" version was without foundation.*

* It will be seen below, that McCarthy must have been referring to a recording of a speech delivered *in Reno* on February 11. The two speeches, McCarthy claimed, were identical.

E. A copy of *U.S. News and World Report,* September 7, 1951, including an interview with McCarthy, who had been asked,

Senator, there was, we've heard, a great deal of talk about your changing your numbers. What is your explanation for that—205 charges in one speech up in West Virginia, and then 81—

[McCarthy.] Up in West Virginia we read to the audience a letter written by Jimmy Byrnes, the then Secretary of State, to Congressman Sabath, in which he said that out of the 3000 employees screened— employees who were being transferred from other departments into the State Department—they found 284 unfit for government service. He said of the 284 we discharged 79, leaving a total of 205. That night I called upon Acheson and the President to tell us where those 205 were, why they kept them in if the President's own board says they were unfit for service. . . .

This statement, Benton told the committee, directly contradicts even McCarthy's own claims; for in the speech he read to the Senate which he represented as the speech he gave at Wheeling, *no mention whatever* was made of the figure 205.

"To me," Benton concluded his statement on the first charge, "Senator McCarthy shows himself a calculating dispenser of false and perverted information. If your Committee, upon investigation, decides that Senator McCarthy has committed perjury, I assume it will bring the facts to the attention of the proper authorities for prosecution in the courts. I concede cheerfully that if this is done my resolution asking for his expulsion from this body becomes somewhat academic. After all, a Senator in jail, for all practical purposes, has been expelled."

Here is what the Committee's staff, after a thorough investigation, were able to report:

McCarthy flew from Washington to Wheeling and arrived "somewhere between three and five o'clock" on the day he was scheduled to speak. He was met at the airplane by Mr. Tom Sweeney, his host at Wheeling, Mr. Francis J. Love, a Republican member of the 80th Congress, and Mr. Frank Desmond, the reporter from the *Intelligencer.* McCarthy was told that WWVA was planning to broadcast his speech later in the evening and so required an advance copy of the script.

McCarthy told Sweeney, Love, and Desmond that he had with him only a *rough draft* of the speech he intended to deliver; that it would take him several hours to put it in shape. He consented to turn over the draft, as it stood, to the radio station, but only on the understanding that the WWVA executives should consider it a rough draft.

Sweeney took the script to the radio station. Desmond was given another copy. McCarthy took a third copy to his rooms to work over it.

This rough draft contained the "205" version. And it was this rough draft that WWVA employees Whitaker and Myers were subsequently to swear was delivered by McCarthy, "word-for-word," at the night's meeting.

The Committee's investigators questioned Whitaker.* Who had asked him to sign the affidavit? *A representative of the State Department*—he did not know his name. How was Whitaker able to certify that McCarthy had followed the rough script word for word? Because he was checking the script (the rough draft that had been given to WWVA) while McCarthy spoke: his role had been to watch for "libel, profanity, or slander," and to see to it that the recording being made by a WWVA engineer was broken off at a logical point, not more than 29½ minutes after McCarthy had begun to speak.

Could he positively remember that McCarthy had used the figure 205? He could not remember any longer, but he *had* remembered at the time he signed the affidavit.

Did Whitaker realize that, if McCarthy *had* read word-for-word from the rough draft, he would have been saying some rather extraordinary things? For example, did Whitaker remember McCarthy's saying, *"Today less than 100 years have come under Communist domination?"* Whitaker did not remember. Did he remember McCarthy's saying, *"Today, only 6 years later, there are 80 billion people under the absolute domination of Soviet Russia—an increase of over 400 percent. On our side the figure has shrunk to around 500 thousand. In other words in less than six years, the odds have changed from 9 to 1 in our favor to 8 to 1 against us"?* Did Whitaker remember McCarthy saying *that?* Whitaker could not be sure.

"It should . . . be mentioned," the Committee's staff reported after reviewing the evidence, "as a factor to be considered in evalu-

---

* The reader should recall that the Gillette-Monroney Committee revealed itself from the outset of its investigation as predisposed to find *against* Senator McCarthy. So much so that one of its assistant counsels, Mr. Dan Buckley, resigned in protest against the partisanship of the inquiry in December, 1951. Later, two senators on the Committee, and another member of the staff resigned, giving similar reasons.

ating the credibility and scrupulosity of Whitaker, that he was very evasive—i.e., was unwilling to give a definite affirmative or negative answer—when he was asked whether or not Senator McCarthy in fact orally uttered the grossly erroneous population statistics contained in the script attached to his, Whitaker's, affidavit, *notwithstanding that the only possible answer was 'yes' if the affidavit was accurate and truthful.*" (Italics added.)

Mr. Bill Callahan, chairman of the meeting at which McCarthy spoke, was asked to comment on Whitaker's competence to make such an affidavit; he said:

> If Whitaker says that, he is right. I did not have that impression. . . . I was to give a signal to McCarthy when he got to 3-2-1 or 5-3-1 minutes and I was to stand up and show him by fingers how long he had to go. When Whitaker was "following" the script, he was watching his watch because he was looking up to me and I was looking down to him. [Whitaker claims to have looked at his watch only two or three times.] I would be amazed if he could follow the written speech, give me signals and make sure I gave them to McCarthy and nodded back to him. If he could do that, he was a miracle man. . . . I would say Whitaker would be absolutely honest in his opinion, but, again, I do not think that Whitaker, in watching his watch, tape, engineer and me . . . would be able to follow accurately a written prepared speech . . . with all that on his mind and know it was going word-for-word. I would say—having seen McCarthy with a big sheaf jumping from page to page and turning many pages and skipping—that Whitaker could not possibly have followed a script.

This last sentence of Callahan's statement introduced a highly relevant factor. Every person interviewed—Desmond, Callahan, Sweeney, Love, Mr. Herman Gieske (editor of the *Intelligencer*) and a Mrs. Eberhard (President of the Wheeling Women's Republican Club)—testified that McCarthy had spoken in part extemporaneously, in part from "a sheaf of notes." Samples:

> SWEENEY. McCarthy was not reading the speech. It was a combination of both [reading and extemporizing]. He was walking around the platform. He left the center part two or three times. But he did have some type of manuscript. . . . He referred to the manuscript from time to time. He did not read the speech.

> LOVE. It seems to me that McCarthy talked extemporaneously but that he had papers in front of him and might have read a paragraph now and then. My impression was that McCarthy did not read the speech but now and then looked at papers before him.

CALLAHAN. I have a distinct impression that McCarthy cut, eliminated, passed over, jumped through parts of his speech. He did have a
thick sheaf of papers on the desk. . . . Sometimes he appeared to be
looking at the papers and just glanced over the script and read some
part . . . and then did not read for a minute and then read for a minute
again.

It is not easy to understand, in short, how McCarthy could have
clung literally to the text of the rough draft—even assuming he was
using this draft—if he had danced all over the platform, and spoken
largely extempore.

Unlike his colleague in WWVA, Myers, under examination, in
effect repudiated his affidavit. "Admissions made to our investigators by Myers," the Committee's staff reported, "proved that his
certification of virtual identity between the tape-recording of Senator McCarthy's speech and the text of the script attached to his
affidavit was not based on personal knowledge."

Myers had not attended McCarthy's speech. His affidavit was
based on a technical check of the recording prior to its broadcast
over the radio. The Committee's staff reported:

Myers later admitted (1) that his first "review" of the tape-recording—
the one which occurred between delivery of the speech and the broadcast—consisted merely of a "spot-checking" of the recording to make
sure that it was "of broadcast character," i.e., free of mechanical defects,
and involved no textual comparison whatever of the recording against
the script; and (2) that in his second review of the tape-recording,
"against the script," on the following day, only "certain portions" of the
recording were textually compared with the script.

Myers did insist, however, that Senator McCarthy had used the
figure "205" somewhere in his speech. But note the exact extent of
Myers' recollection:

Q. [by a Committee investigator] Did you play back the portion
concerning 205? Can you religiously state that the figure 205 was used?
A. Yes, that was what I have been concerned about. He used the
term 205. . . . I can recall the figure 205. . . .
Q. To make the matter entirely clear, Mr. Myers, will you now read
page 7, paragraph 3, of the script which you had in your hands that day
when you checked, as you say, portions of the script against the recording, and tell us whether you can now recall not merely that the figure
205, which appears in that paragraph, was in the recording, but also
that the *entire* paragraph was in the recording, word-for-word?

A. *I cannot state that the entire paragraph was in the recording word-for-word. I did not compare that closely.*

Q. Can you say what the *substance* of the paragraph was in the re-cording, including the idea expressed by the words [205 Communists] made known to the Secretary of State?

A. No, sir. I did not check that closely. [Italics added.]

In short, Myers could only remember that McCarthy had used the figure "205" in *some* connection. McCarthy himself has repeat-edly acknowledged having used that figure: he had drawn atten-tion to the fact that in 1946 Secretary of State Byrnes had written that 205 persons recommended for dismissal by a security screening committee had not yet left the Department.

The third of Benton's exhibits was the news story of Frank Des-mond citing the "205" figure exactly as it appeared in the rough draft. Desmond had attended McCarthy's speech. Had he written his story on the basis of the speech itself, or on the basis of the rough draft that McCarthy had given him (with due warning as to its crudity) during the automobile trip from the airport? Austin Wood, general manager of the *Intelligencer* told the Tydings Committee that Desmond had said to him that there could "be no doubt" that his news story had correctly quoted McCarthy. Asked to amplify on his meeting with Desmond, Wood told Committee investigators that on Tydings' request he had asked Desmond whether "the fig-ure he quoted McCarthy as using was accurate"; that Desmond had "stated that it was"; and that he had therefore so reported to Tydings in his letter of March 25. However, Wood told the investi-gators he would nevertheless "bet 10 to 1 [that] Desmond got the story from the script."

Herman Gieske, the paper's editor and a member of the audience that heard McCarthy, also told investigators that he had ques-tioned Desmond's figure "205" when he saw it in the paper the next day; and that Desmond, although he at first defended it, later "qual-ified" his answer. The end of the road came when Desmond himself was questioned. He frankly admitted to the investigators that he had "got the figure from the script."

At this point, little was left of the case on the basis of which Sena-tor Benton proposed McCarthy be sent to jail. But the Committee's investigation was to yield more than a point-by-point discreation of Benton's charges: it yielded positive evidence supporting Mc-Carthy's Senate version of what he had said at Wheeling. On the other hand, none of the witnesses interviewed by the investigators, aside from Whitaker, said anything that tended to confirm the Benton-Tydings version of the Wheeling speech.

(1) Two persons, Love and Callahan, distinctly remembered that McCarthy had used two numbers. Love: "There was certainly another figure mentioned other than 205 and I think it was stressed more than 205. I am not sure if 205 was mentioned. It seems to me that he talked about another number. . . ." Callahan: "McCarthy definitely talked about two different figures. . . ." which represented (a) State Department employees identified as Communists about whom McCarthy "had gotten information which he considered authentic" and (b) Department employees who were "fellow travelers or suspected [as such] who ought to be investigated." (Presumably Callahan was referring to the 57 and 205 figures, respectively.)

(2) Herman Gieske, the editor of the *Intelligencer*, wrote an editorial the day after the speech presumably based on his own recollection of what McCarthy had said. "Senator McCarthy shocked his audience," the editorial said, "when he charged there are *over fifty* persons of known Communistic affiliation still sheltered in the U.S. Department of State." (Italics added.)

(3) On June 28, McCarthy wrote to Herman Gieske of the *Intelligencer*:

The thought occurs to me that there is a sizeable number of people who make a hobby of recording almost any and every program on the air. There must be someone someplace who has a recording of my speech in Wheeling.

It would be tremendously valuable to me to obtain a recording. Normally it would be of very little importance but the State Department and the Tydings group have spent so much time building up the importance of the [charge] . . . that I said 205, a recording would effectively discredit. . . . the false claim.

McCarthy asked Gieske to use the facilities of his paper to locate a recording. "If you could do this, Herman, I would not want it to appear to have been initiated by me because if it were I would have the press service on my neck looking for a statement."

Though nothing came of Gieske's attempt to unearth a recording, the Committee's staff interpreted McCarthy's spontaneous effort to get hold of an authentic transcript as evidence of his own confidence that such a transcript would vindicate him. If McCarthy's effort had been sheer bravado, it is unlikely that his approach to Gieske would have been confidential.

(4) A final and highly relevant consideration. Within a period of 48 hours after he spoke in Wheeling, McCarthy made the charge, on three separate occasions, that there were 57 Communists in the State Department; and during this period all mentions of the figure 205 were confined to remarks on the old Byrnes list.

On the night of February 10, in Salt Lake City, McCarthy said over the air:

Last night I discussed the "Communists in the State Department." I stated I had the names of 57 card-carrying members of the Communist party.... [Italics added.]

On February 11, McCarthy wired President Truman:

In the Lincoln Day speech at Wheeling Thursday night I . . . further stated that I have in my possession the names of 57 Communists who are in the State Department at present. . . .
While the records are not available to me, I know absolutely of one group of approximately 300 certified to the Secretary for discharge, because of communism. He actually only discharged approximately 80. [Herein, obviously, the reference to the 205.]

On February 11, McCarthy spoke in Reno and said:

I have in my hand 57 cases of individuals who would appear to be either card-carrying members or certainly loyal to the Communist Party, but who nevertheless are still helping to shape our foreign policy.

If McCarthy had told a large audience on Thursday night that he had in hand a list of 205 State Department Communists, known to the Secretary of State as such, why did he say something so very different on Friday, and again on Saturday? An explanation has on occasion been advanced: McCarthy was so alarmed Friday morning by the reaction to his explosive Thursday-night statement in Wheeling that he immediately took counsel with himself and, after looking over his meager data, decided that discretion was the better part of valor. Whereupon he took the square root of his original figure, and for good measure multiplied it by four, and started talking about 57 Communists.

This might be a cogent argument except for the fact that there *was* no uproar Friday morning! McCarthy was too little known, and Wheeling was too remote. Only the Wheeling paper, and the *Chicago Tribune,* as far as we have been able to discover, reported

McCarthy's speech of Thursday night on the following day. It was another two or three days before his Wheeling statements reached a national audience. That audience was aroused by the charge that there were 57, not 205, Communists in the State Department.

To sum up: there is no conclusive evidence (i.e., evidence provided by a tape recording or by numerous and unambiguous affidavits from a cross-section of McCarthy's audience) that McCarthy said "57" or that he said "205". The available evidence, however, clearly indicates that McCarthy used "57"; and that therefore Senator Benton and others are unjustified in accusing McCarthy of having lied to the Senate. There is, on the other hand, no accounting for McCarthy's having represented to the Senate, as a verbatim transcript of his Wheeling speech, a version in which the figure 205 never appeared—since, on repeated occasions, he has acknowledged having used both figures in the speech. Benton was correct in pointing out this contradiction; though it is not one that buttresses Benton's main argument.

Let us turn now to the impact of the Wheeling speech and the two or three public appearances McCarthy made in the ensuing few days. McCarthy accomplished two things. He served notice that nothing short of an exhaustive investigation into State Department security practices would satisfy him. And he committed an egregious blunder which continues to furnish grist for the mills of those many whose first goal in national affairs remains the political assassination of McCarthy.

In Wheeling, as we have seen, McCarthy said, "I have in my hand 57 cases of individuals who would appear to be either card-carrying members or certainly loyal to the Communist Party, but who nevertheless are still helping to shape our foreign policy." The following evening, in Salt Lake City, he went even further. He was on the air with Senator Malone. The interrogator, Mr. Dan Valentine, asked him to elaborate on his speech the night before:

McCARTHY. Last night I discussed the Communists in the State Department. I stated that I had the names of 57 card-carrying members of the Communist Party.

VALENTINE. . . . In other words, Senator, if Secretary of State Dean Acheson would call you at the Hotel Utah tonight in Salt Lake City, you would tell him 57 names of actual card-carrying Communists in the State Department, actual card-carrying Communists?

McCARTHY. Not only can I, Dan, but I will, as I say, on condition. . . .

"Not 'members of the Communist Party,' not 'people who were alleged to be Communists,' but 'the names of 57 card-carrying members of the Communist Party,' " Senator Tydings was to taunt McCarthy on the Senate floor upon submitting the Tydings Report on July 20, 1953; and the refrain has never died down: "57 *card-carrying* Communists?" it goes; "where are their cards?"*

The following day, McCarthy wired President Truman the flat statement: "I have in my possession the names of 57 Communists who are in the State Department at present." Six paragraphs further on, in the same telegram, McCarthy repeated his unambiguous charge: "Despite this State Department blackout, we have been able to compile a list of 57 Communists in the State Department."

McCarthy, of course, could never hope to prove that specific charge, and hence should not have phrased it in the way he did. This does not mean that there were not at the time, or that there are not today, 57 Communists in the Department of State; nor does it mean that McCarthy did not actually name 57 Communists to the Tydings Committee. It means simply that McCarthy never offered proof that he had in hand the names of 57 State Department employees loyal to the Communist Party, much less "card-carrying" members.**

These are difficult things to prove at best; and, as experience shows, all but impossible to prove to the satisfaction of the Liberals. At this writing, a book has appeared contending that even Alger Hiss was not a Communist—that he was framed. Reputable folk continue to insist that Harry Dexter White, that Lauchlin Currie, that Nathan Gregory Silvermaster were not Communists. "Insufficient proof," we are told; and indeed, at least one court has ruled that anyone who calls somebody a Communist had better be pre-

---

* We asked Senator McCarthy why he described the 57 as "card-carrying" Communists, and he answered that he had in mind the discipline under which the persons in question worked, and the regularity with which they served Communism: he had meant it as a figure of speech to emphasize the seriousness of the evidence against them. "Card-carrying" *could*, in certain circumstances, mean simply that; but it should be so used only in pretty sophisticated company, and even then subject to proper inflection and emphasis. And even a poet would not press a figure of speech if he were challenged as Mr. Valentine challenged McCarthy in asking ". . . actual card-carrying Communists?" McCarthy should have answered, of course, "Probably not actually 'card-carrying'; but what difference does carrying a card make anyhow?"

** As a matter of fact, in 1950 there were no card-carrying Communists in the State Department—or anywhere else. The Party had recalled all membership cards several years before.

pared to furnish either a certified photostat of that person's Communist Party card or sworn affidavits from at least two people to the effect that they have with their own eyes seen him at meetings of the Party open to members only.

Probatory evidence of Party membership is *ipso facto* hard to come by. If we have learned anything about the scope and the techniques of the Communist conspiracy it is that only a small percentage of the Communist faithful take out membership cards; and that, what is more, many Communists are not identifiable on the basis of their overt political activities. Whittaker Chambers has a great deal to say on the subject, as do a dozen equally authentic witnesses to the conspiracy. Moreover, the Party's increased emphasis on underground activity and its current discouragement of overt support of Russian policies are well known, thanks in part to the published findings of FBI undercover agents. It can be imagined, indeed, that disciplined Communists in strategic posts in the federal government are now enjoined to frequent in far greater force meetings of the National Association of Manufacturers than the functions of the National Council for American-Soviet Friendship.

Perhaps McCarthy deliberately sensationalized the evidence he possessed in order to draw attention to the gravity of the situation. Perhaps, again, the complexities of the Communist problem were lost on Joe McCarthy in the early days of his venture. After all, he had seen alarming reports of various investigating agencies on certain employees of the State Department. And who, McCarthy may have asked himself, who but Communists would do and say such things? That only Communists would so act is perhaps a logical answer to the question; but logic in our age, must be strained through the woof of irrationality and the warp of ignorance. Many non-Communists behave in a baffling manner, and McCarthy should have taken this into account—all the more since he was prepared to challenge the President of the United States, the political party in control of Congress, and the vigilantes of Liberalism in the press and the classroom.

McCarthy could have said: "I hold in my hand investigative reports on 57 members of the State Department. The evidence of pro-Communism on the part of these 57 is so substantial that, in my opinion, no loyalty-security board composed of conscientious men who know the score about Communism would, after weighing it, clear them for sensitive positions. The Communists don't often give us a break and expose themselves. But here we have 57 people whose activities and associations are ominous. Perhaps some of them, perhaps many of them, are not Communists. But none of them should be working in the State Department."

But McCarthy did not put it that way; and it quickly became evident that it would be difficult, if not impossible, for him to pull himself out of the hole he had dug himself into. And to those who were above all concerned with getting the dupes and the fellow travellers out of the State Department, McCarthy's blunder would prove costly. His specific charges, just to the extent that they were incautious, would make a cleanup more difficult because attention would be drawn away from loyalty *risks* (the real problem) to Communist Party card-carriers (a marginal aspect of the real problem).

If, however, McCarthy at first disappointed his potential allies, he was soon to surprise them by the speed with which he got educated to the kind of warfare in which he found himself engaged. By the 20th of February, when McCarthy faced a hostile Senate, and a press aroused to a fever pitch of excitement, he had changed his tack notably.

When he got up to speak in the late afternoon, the Senate embarked upon a rowdy six-hour session. The Democrats had been clamoring for McCarthy to state his case against the State Department. When he tried to do so, they made it all but impossible. Senator Lucas interrupted no less than 61 times, Senator McMahon no less than 27 times, while the more restrained Senators Withers and Lehman satisfied themselves with 22 and 13 insertions respectively.

McCarthy presented material, most of it developed several years earlier by the State Department Security office, on "81"* cases. He has since stated, "This list included the 57, plus additional cases of less importance against whom the evidence was less conclusive."**

---

* Actually, he omitted a few. See below.
** [Joe McCarthy, *McCarthyism*, (New York; Devin-Adair, 1952), p. 10.] McCarthy did not segregate the 57 from the others. And since in the course of his harried six-hour presentation, he spoke several times of numbers 1, 2, and 81 as the most dangerous on his list, he left his listeners no grounds for concluding that numbers 1–57 were the ones he had in mind at Wheeling and Salt Lake City, and in his wire to President Truman. (No. 1 was finally suspended by the Department, pending the adjudication of loyalty-security charges against him. No. 2 was ultimately found to be a loyalty risk by the Loyalty-Review Board. No. 81 had been "separated" from government service four months before McCarthy spoke.)

In his Senate speech, *McCarthy did not contend that his material conclusively proved membership in the Communist Party*. He spoke of *loyalty risks*. These we propose to classify, roughly, in five groups. One category includes persons suspected of being disciplined Communists and/or espionage agents; that is, persons who may fairly be described as "first-degree security risks." A second group includes persons with provably suspicious associations and activities, whom we may call "second-degree security risks." A third category includes persons who have associated with *suspected* Communists and shown themselves to be in sympathy with assorted Communist objectives, or "third-degree risks." A fourth includes sexual deviates, persons with mental or character weaknesses—let us say, "moral risks." A fifth group includes persons who are both "third-degree" and "moral risks," or "combination risks."

McCarthy went into 76 of his 81 cases.* They break down as follows: 25 first-degree risks, 13 second-degree risks, 30 third-degree risks, 2 morals risks, and 5 combination risks.**

There was here a perceptible change in the nature of McCarthy's charges—a change to which his critics have paid scant attention. They have preferred to call him to an accounting on the basis of his early scattered references to "57 members of the Communist Party presently in the State Department" rather than on the basis of his detailed Senate speech. They keep insisting that he stand or fall on a political peroration rather than on his more or less formal indictment.

Several misapprehensions are, consequently, current about what McCarthy set out to do in his Senate speech. We are told, for example, that he was attempting to prove, case by case, that 81 members of the Communist Party were employed in the State Department—although quite early in the speech, and again and again later, he discouraged such expectations. "I shall not attempt to present a detailed case on each one, a case which would convince a jury. All I am doing is to develop sufficient evidence so that anyone who reads the record will have a good idea of the number of Com-

* One of the 76 persons (No. 72) McCarthy highly approved—his quarrel with the State Department was that it had refused to *hire* him! He read one duplication (he confused No. 77 with No. 9) and omitted, without explanation, four cases—Nos. 15, 27, 35, and 59.

** First-degree risks: 1, 2, 4, 5, 7, 12, 16, 17, 19, 28, 29, 30, 31, 32, 33, 36, 38, 39, 47, 53, 58, 68, 74, 75, 81. Second-degree risks: 3, 8, 9, 13, 34, 37, 46, 54, 55, 57, 64, 67, 73. Third-degree risks: 6, 10, 11, 21, 22, 23, 24, 25, 26, 40, 41, 42, 43, 45, 48, 49, 50, 51, 52, 56, 60, 61, 63, 65, 69, 70, 71, 78, 79, 80. Morals risks: 62, 76. Combination risks: 14, 18, 20, 44, 66.

munists in the State Department." (*Congressional Record,* Feb. 20, 1950, p. 1959.) "It is possible that some of these persons will get a clean bill of health. I know that some of them will not." (P. 1967.) "I have said to the Senator that I am not indicting the 81. *I have said there is sufficient in the files to show that there is something radically wrong.*" (P. 1968. Italics, here and throughout the balance of this chapter, are added.)

McCarthy is frequently accused of having said that all his targets worked in the State Department whereas it later developed that many of them did not. Yet McCarthy was quite clear about this also:

I may say that I know that some of these individuals whose cases I am giving the Senate are no longer in the State Department. A sizeable number of them are not. Some of them have transferred to other Government work, work allied with the State Department. Others have been transferred to the United Nations. (P. 1961.)

About several of the persons on his list McCarthy stated frankly that he did not know their whereabouts.

I . . . told the Senate earlier that I have no way of knowing definitely which of these persons are still in the employ of the State Department. I know they have all been there at some time.* A sizeable number is still there. (P. 1964.)**

McCarthy made it clear why his interest in a case did not lapse the moment the person involved left the State Department. And the Senate went along: its Resolution 231 authorized the Tydings Committee to investigate present and *former* employees of the State Department whose loyalty was in question.

I do not claim that all the cases I am reporting to the Senate refer to persons working in the State Department, but in view of the fact that most of them were in the State Department and had top secret clearance, I think the Senate could call them before a committee and find out in what Government work they are now engaged, or, if they are not engaged in Government work, what they have been doing in private employment, and whether they are members of espionage rings. (P. 1971.)

* All but six were or had been. Five of the six had applied for work in the State Department, but had never been hired.

** McCarthy commented similarly in discussing Cases 29, 33, 34, 39, 42, 45, 57, 78, 81.

In the light of these facts, which are available in the *Congressional Record,* it is surprising that McCarthy is so universally judged by an irrelevant yardstick. McCarthy's excesses in Wheeling, Salt Lake and Reno were not repeated in the Senate and are unrelated to his later performances—for example, before the Tydings Committee. In the Senate speech which occasioned the creation of that Committee, McCarthy did not commit himself to reveal the names of 57 card-carrying Communists presently working in the State Department, but, rather, to present evidence against individuals whose survival of the State Department's security program was a *prima facie* indictment of that program.

The further charge is made that McCarthy "introduced no new evidence"—that, insofar as he said anything that was correct, it was old stuff. This is a curious accusation, if only because McCarthy's claims about what he was doing before the Senate were extremely modest. "This information is nothing new," he said. "It has been there a long time. If the Senator or anyone else who is interested had expended sufficient effort, he could have brought this to the attention of the Senate." (P. 1968.) Indeed, this was the crux of McCarthy's argument. It is, McCarthy was saying, precisely because the cases are "old" ones that the situation is so serious. For if the employees he had in mind had been under fire several years before (as they *had* been), and if the State Department had kept them on anyway (as it *had* with respect to the majority), then the Department security picture was all the more alarming.

At this juncture, however, McCarthy should have given his colleagues some information highly relevant to what he was doing. Yet he chose not to; and so he gave the Tydings Committee an opening for the sweeping charge in its Report, that "in securing [an investigation] . . . a fraud was perpetrated upon the Senate."[2]

Having told his colleagues that his information was "nothing new," and having, in fact, gone so far as to chide them for not having "expended sufficient effort" to bring this information "to the attention of the Senate" at an earlier date, McCarthy should have told them just exactly *where* they could have got hold of the information. Virtually all the data McCarthy was giving them were to be found in the files of the House Committee on Appropriations which two years before, prior to the imposition of the ban on the release of security data, had conducted its own investigation of State Department security. McCarthy kept this highly relevant fact from the Senate. And at the same time he was telling the Senate that the information "has been there a long time," he was also telling it that "all the records are completely secret except what I could get from loyal State Department employees"! And again, "I know the State Department is very eager to know how I have secured all this information. I know that the jobs of the men who helped me secure this material would be worth nothing if the names were given.* If it were not for some good, loyal Americans in the State Department—and there are many of them—I should not have been able to present this picture to the Senate tonight. . . ."

Now this amounts to misleading the Senate as to the *source* of his information—but only, be it noted, because McCarthy intimated that the data he was presenting to the Senate *that night* had been gotten together for him by Department informants. As we shall see in subsequent chapters, a great deal of the information McCarthy gave to the Tydings Committee was indeed fresh information; and some must have come through leaks from the Department. Moreover, it is likely that confidential information from the Department had already begun to reach him before he delivered his Senate speech. But the point is, of course, that McCarthy was not using that material *on the night of February 20th;* or, if he was, it constituted only a very small portion of his presentation.** McCarthy had put himself in an embarrassing position because the assorted factors could be so arranged, by adept partisans, as to add up as follows: (1) By referring to Department informants McCarthy gave the Senate the impression that he was presenting it with *fresh* information; (2) the Senate, taking McCarthy's word for it that his charges had not previously been reviewed and discredited, voted an investigation; (3) the investigation would not have been voted had McCarthy advised the Senate that his data had previously been gone over by a committee of Congress. *Therefore*, McCarthy got his investigation by perpetrating "a fraud upon the Senate."

Actually, no such offense could be proved against Senator McCarthy by the Tydings Committee—nor was the Tydings Committee entitled to reprimand McCarthy in the language it did. As we have said, McCarthy may have misled the Senate as to the source

---

* This was no exaggeration. See Humelsine's warning to State Department employees, in Chapter XI, "Confrontation."

** The exceptions: McCarthy referred sketchily to seven employees with bad security backgrounds who were working in the State Department's Office of Information and Education in New York (Cases 21-27). There are no identifiable counterparts for these persons on the old House list. Hence it is likely that their names were indeed given to McCarthy by what he termed "good loyal people in the [OIE]."

of his information; but steps 2 and 3 in the Committee's reasoning involve a couple of false premises. For one, the House committee that had gone over the data that McCarthy presented on the Senate floor had *not* cleared the suspect employees*—in fact, it had done everything in its power to urge the State Department to dismiss them. That was in the early months of 1948. In the early months of 1950, McCarthy found that a number of these people were *still* working in the Department. Such a situation clearly called for an investigation. But most important, Tydings' premises are that, if McCarthy had enlightened the Senate about the history of his 81 cases, an investigation would not have been voted; and that Senator McCarthy, therefore, defrauded the Senate. This is nonsense.

Since 1948, no Congressional probe into State Department security had taken place, for the simple reason that security data on federal employees had been withheld from the legislature. In the meantime, President Truman had called the Hiss investigation a "red herring"; Hiss had been convicted; the ideological coloration of the Institute of Pacific Relations was becoming increasingly evident; Judith Coplon and Klaus Fuchs had been caught; and we had lost China. The public's reaction to McCarthy's charges in Wheeling and elsewhere was unmistakable: the country wanted an investigation. *The Senate would in no circumstances have denied it one.* It would have made no difference whatever if McCarthy *had* told the Senate that his material had been developed by the 80th Congress.

To get on: McCarthy not only told the Senate that his information was not new, he went further and said that even the evaluation of the information was not, by and large, his own:

I am not giving my evaluation of the evidence. I want it understood. If the Senators will listen, they will note that what I am doing is to recite the facts, which the State Department's own security agency dug up, and which information acted as the basis for *their* recommendation that the individuals in question, because of being security risks, be discharged and not retained in the service.

And finally, McCarthy admitted that the information he was presenting was not necessarily complete; though he assumed that, in arriving at the conclusion that the individuals in question were security risks, the original evaluators had taken stock of mitigating evidence:

* See Chapter VIII.

I think the Senator [McMahon] flatters me when he says it is my duty to present the *entire* file to the Senate and to give *all* the information. The President has said we shall not get that file, and, as of the present moment, since we are not on a "Dear Joe, Dear Harry" basis, I cannot go to the White House and say "Harry, give me this file because Senator McMahon insists that you give me the information." All I can do is to give Senators what I can dig up. I have given Senators the fullest, most complete, fairest resume of the files that I possibly could. (P. 1969.)

On this point, McCarthy deserves to be censured. For his resume of the information that had been developed by State Department security investigators, and synthesized by Congressional investigators two years before,* was neither full nor fair. A comparison of the dossier from which McCarthy got his material with McCarthy's own version of this material reveals that in 38 cases he was guilty of exaggeration. On some occasions "fellow-traveller" had turned into "Communist"; on others, "alleged pro-Communist" had developed into "pro-Communist." In most cases, however, McCarthy's exaggerations were neither detailed nor emphatic enough to shove a given case into a higher security category. However, after McCarthy got through improvising on them, fifteen cases seemed indeed to move up a notch in the security ladder.**

In the course of the debate, McCarthy was asked several times why he had not presented his evidence in an "orderly fashion" to the President, or to the Secretary of State, or to the Senate Committee on Foreign Relations. McCarthy's answer, precise and on occasion eloquent, was as follows:

Mr. President, I have before me information from the State Department files, information which the President says the Senate did not have. Having this information, it is a serious question as to what should be done with it. I originally thought possibly we could hope for some cooperation from the State Department and the President. However, in going over the material and finding that all of it, of course, has been available to the State Department, for it is all from their files, it seemed that nothing would be gained by calling it to their attention again. The President, I felt, had demonstrated his lack of interest quite thoroughly, during the Hiss investigation. Then, when I sent him a telegram and said, "Mr. President, I have the 57 names; they are yours if you want them"; and when he answered by calling me a liar, I felt I could get no cooperation from the President. (P. 1958.)

* See Chapter VIII.
** They are Cases 1, 4, 14, 17, 18, 20, 28, 30, 31, 32, 33, 34, 37, 58, and 68.

To those who say, "Why do you not tell the State Department; why do you not give the names to the State Department?" I say that everything I have here is from the State Department's own files. (P. 1959.)

[Re McMahon's suggestion that he should have reported his findings to the Senate Foreign Relations Committee:] the Senator suggested a course of action which he thinks I should have followed. As I explained earlier this evening, I thought of that. I thought there was some possibility of accomplishing the desired results in that fashion. However, keeping in mind that the members of the Foreign Relations Committee and all the Senators have had substantially the same knowledge and opportunity that I have had, I questioned whether anything would be gained unless the President changed his mind and said "I will give you the information." . . . I thought the only thing to do was what I have done, namely, to let the people of the country know what is going on, and then hope that the pressure of public opinion would be great enough to force the President to clean house. Frankly, I think he will not clean house until he determines it is politically inexpedient for him to do otherwise. I think the President is one of the cleverest politicians this Nation has ever had. I think when he discovers that the people of the country do not want a continuation of what is going on, there will be a housecleaning. (P. 1970.)

Here is a précis of McCarthy's position in his speech to the Senate:

1. In 1946 and 1947, security investigators in the State Department developed convincing evidence that a substantial number of Department employees are disloyal to the United States or that they are, at least, security risks.

2. Three years have gone by, and yet, I have reason to believe that a number of the individuals in question remain on duty in the State Department.

3. If there are mitigating circumstances in these cases, if there exists new evidence that exonerates them, I do not know what it is, and the Presidential ban on releasing material in the files precludes my finding out what it is.

I am not prepared to take the word of the Secretary of State that his security program is serving the national interests. I find it difficult to believe that the retention in office of a number of these individuals is justified. I want an independent judgment—the judgment of a Senate investigating committee.

This may not fit in very well with the press picture of McCarthy the loud-of-mouth, McCarthy the irresponsible. But it is the position McCarthy actually took and said he was taking.

CHAPTER VI

The Tydings Saga: Introduction

THE Tydings Committee investigation "made" McCarthy. This is true in two senses. The investigation established McCarthy in the eyes of a few articulate, and millions of inarticulate, anti-Communists as the standard-bearer in the fight to expose Communist infiltration of the Federal Government. In the eyes of many other Americans, especially of almost all members of our intelligentsia, it established McCarthy as the arch-villain of mid-twentieth-century American politics.

It was in the course of the Tydings investigation that McCarthy earned his stripes as a "wholesale character assassin." There he got his reputation for "publicly smearing innocent people." There "McCarthy" became (or soon was to become) synonymous with the irresponsible, reckless accusation. There he became known as the unconscionable and insatiable publicity-seeker, the crude and ambitious political adventurer. There the "Big Lie," "misrepresentation" and "innuendo" became known as McCarthy's "methods." There he was "ismized": "McCarthyism," the derisive epithet coined by Owen Lattimore, became, with a boost from the Tydings Committee, a household word. And there, most important of all, McCarthy's fundamental charge that the State Department had been guilty of lax security practices was consigned to history as a "fraud and a hoax."

All this is not to say, of course, that McCarthy stopped offending people when the Tydings hearings closed. But it was in the course of that investigation that he got branded—indelibly, so it seems—as someone nice people are, as a matter of course, against.

The Tydings investigation occupied less than four months of McCarthy's tumultuous career—something less, surely, than the span of time normally allotted to a man for defining himself, his life work, and his methods. It might, therefore, seem sensible for us to treat the Tydings episode as an isolated item in McCarthy's record and speedily move on from there to consider the present-day McCarthy whom even his critics acknowledge to be wiser, more cautious, and more sophisticated. But such treatment of the episode would keep us from coming to grips with the over-arching issue of the whole McCarthy controversy: Is the view of Mc-Carthy cultivated by the Liberal intelligentsia something for which McCarthy himself is responsible, or something for which persons other than McCarthy are responsible? Is it traceable to things McCarthy has *really* done and *really* said, or to things he is merely *alleged* to have done and said? If the responsibility does lie with persons other than McCarthy (or even if only part of it does), intelligent discussion of McCarthy requires that we know who has so misled large numbers of Americans, and what, in so misleading them, they have been up to.

The answer emerges, in full, from the Report of the Tydings Committee, a subcommittee of the Senate Committee on Foreign Relations, which in the spring of 1950 investigated charges that disloyal persons were employed or had been employed by the De-partment of State. This Committee returned the verdict that the man who had made most of the charges had perpetrated a "fraud and a hoax" upon the American people. Since the Liberals seem to want it that way, we shall let it be that way: we shall take the Tyd-ings episode as the testing ground for judging both McCarthy and McCarthy's enemies.

For such purposes, however, a hasty précis of the hearings will not do. We shall, rather, survey in some detail the data McCarthy presented to the Committee; note the precise charges McCarthy levelled—both those that do him credit in retrospect and those that do not; examine the defense offered by each of the persons accused; and give close attention to what the Tydings Investigating Com-mittee did, and failed to do, with the evidence put at its disposal by McCarthy and other witnesses. This will involve our devoting a sizeable portion of our book to the Tydings proceedings.

In three particulars, however, we shall move faster than in all others. The *Amerasia* case will be dealt with only to the extent that it sheds light on the Committee's performance and attitude, and thus, briefly: the *Amerasia* story is well known, and McCarthy's role in it was a minor one. Similarly, we shall take a short-cut in dealing with the cases of Owen Lattimore and John Stewart Serv-ice. The Lattimore and Service cases were highly publicized at the time of the investigation, and most Americans are now more or less conversant with their details. And these two cases are beyond any question McCarthy's *strongest* cases; so that in abbreviating them rather than, for example, the Hanson and Kenyon cases, we do not open ourselves to the charge of stacking the cards. (McCarthy has been dramatically vindicated in the Service case, by the finding of the Loyalty Review Board that "reasonable doubt" existed as to his loyalty; and in the Lattimore case by the findings of the McCarran Committee and by Lattimore's subsequent indictment for perjury.)

The following review by no means purports to be an exhaustive account of the Tydings proceedings. (There are 1498 pages of testimony in the Committee's record, plus 1024 pages of documentary evidence.) But it does purport to be a fair one. We propose to present the reader with sufficient data on both sides to enable him to make informed judgments about McCarthy and the forces which were arrayed against him. These data are the raw materials out of which the political pundits, the press, and most of our intellectuals, have constructed the most publicized if not necessarily the popular notion of what McCarthyism is. Upon them was based the judgment, handed down many months ago, that the State Department's security record has been as pure as the driven snow, and that Senator McCarthy is Lucifer looking for headlines. We are urging that they be freshly considered. Is the picture of McCarthy painted four years ago a good likeness? Was the indictment, then handed down, in accord with the facts and was it brought against the right people?

Finally: the requirements of impartiality, which we have strived to observe in the ensuing pages, apply only to the *presentation of the facts*—they do not commit us to reticence in stating our own conclusions. We do not, in other words, intend to repress the contempt that familiarity with the Tydings record breeds.

Two days after McCarthy first aired his charges on the floor of the Senate, Democratic Majority Leader Scott Lucas—McCarthy's principal heckler—introduced Senate Resolution 231, which authorized an investigation of the State Department.

The wording of the resolution needs careful attention since there is a striking discrepancy between what the Senate unanimously instructed its Committee to do and what the Committee later did. "Resolved," the Resolution reads,[1]

That the Senate Committee on Foreign Relations, or any duly authorized subcommittee thereof, is authorized and directed to conduct a full and complete study and investigation as to whether persons who are disloyal to the United States are, or have been, employed by the Department of State. The committee shall report to the Senate at the earliest practicable date the result of its investigation, together with such recommendations as it may deem desirable, and if said recommendations are to include formal charges of disloyalty against any individual, then the committee, before making such recommendation, shall give said individual open hearing for the purpose of taking evidence or testimony on said charges.

In the conduct of this study and investigation, the committee is directed to procure by subpoena and examine the complete loyalty and employment files and records of all the Government employees in the Department of State, and such other agencies against whom charges have been heard.*

The reader will note at once that some of the language here is ambiguous; that, for example, the Resolution leaves in question the exact scope of the Committee's inquiry. Thus, a dispute over technicalities plagued the Committee from the beginning, particularly the question whether it should investigate only *State Department* employees (past and present) or, additionally, employees of "other agencies against whom charges have been heard." For example: was William Remington (a Commerce Department employee, yet one of Senator McCarthy's cases) a proper subject of the investigation?

McCarthy has attacked Tydings for not having investigated Remington, maintaining that the "other agencies" phrase in the Resolution's second paragraph brought within the Committee's purview *all* government employees "against whom charges have been heard."[2] Yet the Committee's refusal to take up the Remington case was, from a strictly technical point of view, justified. (The first paragraph of the Resolution fixes the limits of the inquiry,

---

* There is no evidence that McCarthy objected to the phrasing of the Resolution—which he should have done. For it is virtually impossible to prove that persons "are disloyal" to the United States. In February, 1950, the question was whether the President's Loyalty Program was being *adequately administered*. The committee should have been asked to ascertain whether "reasonable grounds" existed for questioning the loyalty of persons who are or have been employed by the Department of State; or, foreshadowing the momentous change in loyalty standards of a year later, better still, "whether persons about whose loyalty or reliability there is reasonable *doubt* are or have been employed by the Department of State."

and includes only past and present employees of the State Department. The second paragraph is clearly procedural, authorizing the Committee to procure the files of suspect State Department personnel from other agencies where such individuals may also have been employed.) But it is another question entirely whether the Committee *ought* to have stuck to a strict interpretation of its mandate when it was confronted with a man like Remington who, while never on the State Department payroll, nevertheless engaged in interdepartmental work that included the State Department.

Traditionally, the Senate gives its investigating committees a measure of discretion. Thus it is unlikely that the Senate intended this Committee to call back the hounds whenever a disloyalty trail led to individuals who did not present themselves fortnightly to a State Department cashier. Moreover, the Committee *did* adopt the "broader" view in the case of Owen Lattimore.* "We find," the Committee said in its final report to the Senate, "that Owen Lattimore is not now and never has been in any proper sense an employee of our State Department."[3] Yet this did not deter it from hearing 191 pages of testimony from Lattimore, or from devoting 26 pages of its final Report to his exculpation. The Committee's comments on the charges against Lattimore were advanced "as a matter of elementary fairness to Mr. Lattimore . . . [and] to scholars and writers throughout the country and to the American public generally."[4] But no such tender concern was shown for an inquiring public, or a harassed Senator, when the Committee refused to look into the record of William Remington who has since been convicted of perjury for having testified under oath that he had never been a member of the Communist Party. But we are getting ahead of the story.

Whatever lingering doubts there may have been in the minds of Committee members as to the propriety of investigating personnel on the State Department periphery, Senate Resolution 231 spelled out one unequivocal directive: it ordered the Committee to find out whether disloyal persons were being, or had been, employed by the State Department. Yet a majority of the Committee either misunderstood the assignment or deliberately perverted its meaning. For the majority's operating assumption was, from the very first, that the Senate had ordered an inquiry concerning McCar-

---

* Nor is this the only instance in which the Committee displayed its willingness to stretch and contract its mandate as it saw fit.

thy's reliability—or, concretely, the validity of his contention that such and such a number of loyalty risks were working in the Department of State. And this untenable notion of the Committee's task was so promoted by the press that the public remains ill-informed even today as to what the Tydings Committee was supposed to do.

The difference between investigating "McCarthy's charges" and investigating the loyalty of State Department personnel is obvious and important. A committee conducting a "full and complete study . . . as to whether persons who are disloyal to the United States are, or have been, employed by the Department of State" will itself assume the burden of investigation. It will seek out information from every available source; it will follow up leads; it will pore over personnel files; it will subpoena key figures to testify; and it will draw the conclusions to which its evidence points. A committee investigating "McCarthy's charges" will—as the Tydings Committee did—turn to McCarthy and demand conclusive proof from him. It will content itself with evaluating McCarthy's cases on the basis of such evidence as *McCarthy* is able to produce.

McCarthy's approach to the Committee was consistent with the Senate Resolution. "I intend," he told the Committee when he first appeared before it, "to submit to the Committee information bearing upon the disloyalty, the bad security risks in the State Department. Then it is up to the Committee to investigate those particular cases. The Committee has been allowed, I believe, $25,000 or $50,000 to do that. I do not have the investigative staff, I do not have access to the files, to make any complete investigation and make any formal charges. All I intend to do, Mr. Chairman, is to submit the evidence I have gathered."[5] What is more, in his major Senate speech, McCarthy specifically *disowned* exhaustive knowledge of all his cases. And, of course, he repeatedly called for the establishment of an *investigating* committee; which would hardly have been necessary if, in his view, there had been nothing left to investigate.

Senator Tydings lost no time in setting the course we have attributed to him. Pointing his finger at McCarthy on the opening day of the hearings, he said:[6] "You are in the position of being the man who occasioned this hearing, and so far as I am concerned in this Committee you are going to get one of the most complete investigations ever given in the history of the Republic, so far as my abilities permit."* The Tydings group faithfully steered this course through the succeeding four months. Yet the notion is abroad in the land that a Senate Committee, four years ago, conscientiously and impartially canvassed McCarthy's charges, found them baseless, went on to explore security in the State Department, and gave the Department a clean bill of health.

Our contentions are that the Tydings Committee did *not* go into the Department security at all; that it did not adequately canvass *even the charges themselves;* and that in failing to do the one, and in only half-doing the other, it violated the express mandate of its parent body.

* Perhaps Tydings misspoke; perhaps he meant McCarthy's *charges* were going to get a complete investigation, rather than McCarthy personally. But then it becomes hard to explain why the Committee sent investigators to Wheeling, West Virginia, to seek proof that McCarthy, in insisting he had used the figure "57" rather than "205," had lied (which certainly had nothing to do with investigating the State Department). Or why the Committee made a compilation of the State Department publicity releases dissecting McCarthy's public speeches, and included it in the Appendix to its Report.

Public Hearings: Whose Responsibility?

On March 8, 1950, the Tydings investigation opened, with Senator McCarthy on the dock. It was time for the showdown, and McCarthy started in. But no sooner was the name *Dorothy Kenyon,* the first case McCarthy presented to the Committee, out of his mouth than the Tydings claque went into action with a charge that has figured incessantly in the subsequent history of anti-McCarthyism. Namely, that McCarthy "accuses in public persons who have no opportunity to answer." The second part of this charge, that the persons he accuses have no opportunity to answer the accusation, is, as we shall see, without basis in fact.

But let us at the start place where it belongs the responsibility for the public identification of McCarthy's cases. And the question here is not *Ought* the names to have been divulged? (That question we shall consider in the chapter "Senator McCarthy's Method.") But: What parties are responsible for these names having been divulged?

That McCarthy would give the Tydings Committee the names of the persons whose loyalty or reliability he had questioned on the Senate floor (plus those of other persons who might subsequently have come to his attention) was a foregone conclusion when the Committee was set up. Indeed, McCarthy had been under great pressure to reveal the names in a *public* Senate session; and the pressure had come precisely from Democratic senators—among them, Senator Lucas, the Majority Leader, who rose four times to demand that McCarthy name, right there and then, the individuals described in the 81 cases.[7]

Even before McCarthy began his formal Senate presentation, Lucas had asked for the names. "I want to remain here," he said, "until he names them. That is what I am interested in."[8] McCarthy refused. But he had only half completed what he referred to as "Case Number One" when Senator Lucas interrupted him again to ask, "Will the Senator tell us the name of the man for the record? We are entitled to know who he is. I say this in all seriousness."[9] Senator Withers (D. Ky.) was even more insistent: "I should like to ask the Senator what reason he has for not calling names. Does not the Senator think it would be a fine thing to let the public know who the guilty are? Is not the Senator privileged?"[10] McCarthy did not acquiesce in these demands. He took the position, from the very beginning of the debate, *that the names should be submitted only to a Senate committee authorized to investigate the cases; and that they should be withheld from the public till the committee itself saw fit to disclose them.* Later in the session he stated this position as follows:

The Senator from Illinois [Lucas] demanded, loudly, that I furnish all the names. *I told him at that time that so far as I was concerned, I thought that would be improper; that I did not have all the information about these individuals. . . .* I have enough to convince me that either they are members of the Communist Party or they have given great aid to the Communists: *I may be wrong. That is why I said that unless the Senate demanded that I do so, I would not submit this publicly, but I would submit it to any committee—and would let the committee go over these in executive session. It is possible that some of these persons will get a clean bill of health. . . .*[11] [Italics added.]

Senator Lucas finally shifted his emphasis and said, "The Senator should name the names before the [proposed] committee."[12]

Thus the only question left open was whether the committee hearings should or should not be held in executive session.* And on this point, too, the record disproves what most Americans have been led to believe. For McCarthy expressed his desire to name the names in executive session, in order to protect individuals who, in his words, might "get a clean bill of health." It was left to the Democratic Majority Leader to urge maximum publicity. "*So far as I am concerned,*" said Senator Lucas, "*it will be in the open, where every individual in America, every newspaperman can attend, so that they will know definitely, as soon as possible, just who is being charged, and who is not being charged with being Communists. This is only fair. . . . every individual in the State Department tonight is under a cloud. . . .*"[13]

But McCarthy stuck to his guns. A few days later, after Senator Tydings' appointment as chairman of the inquiry, McCarthy made a personal request that the forthcoming hearings be held in secret. Here is the story—plus its sequel—as McCarthy told it to the Senate some five weeks later, after the dispute had exploded into a major Party issue.

---

* Senate Resolution 231 was silent on this issue. Indeed, its sole procedural directive was to the effect that persons against whom the committee determined to bring formal charges of disloyalty must be allowed to testify in open hearings.

At the time [February 22?] I urged that the hearings be in executive session, and reminded him [Tydings] of the statements which I had made on the Senate floor. He informed me that the first hearings would be in public, and that later we would go into executive session. Later I was informed by the press that the Senator from Maryland had made the statement that I could present my cases as I saw fit. I again contacted him and told him that if that were the case I thought the names should be given in executive session, but was again informed that the hearings would be in public.[14]

But the actual power of decision rested, of course, not with McCarthy, nor even with Tydings, but with the Committee itself; and the matter was decided at the first executive session to consider procedure. Senator Hickenlooper later told the Senate what transpired at that meeting:

It is a matter of fact . . . that the junior Senator from Massachusetts and I, . . . at the first executive meeting of the subcommittee, suggested and proposed the procedure, that the subcommittee meet in executive session, call the Senator from Wisconsin before it, and ask him to disclose names in private, together with whatever information he had in connection with the names; but the majority of the subcommittee said no, this must be brought out in public. . . . the Senator from Wisconsin was required, or requested, to come before the committee in public hearing, with klieg lights, television, and all the rest of the fanfare of such an emotional occasion, there to bring out his cases, name names, and produce facts.[15]

Any attempt to make McCarthy, in the teeth of such evidence, responsible for "the public naming of names" would have to rest on his role in the jockeying for position *after* the *public* hearings were under way. The sparring began when Senator McMahon interrupted McCarthy's introductory remarks with a question: "Senator, is it your intention to name individuals against whom you are making charges?"[16] McMahon, in other words, now deliberately dumped in McCarthy's lap the issue that he, as a member of the Committee majority, had already resolved *against* McCarthy in executive session. If names were named, McMahon continued, and the charge turned out to be incorrect, would it not result in "great injustice to decent American citizens?"[17] McCarthy reminded McMahon that he had expressed misgivings precisely on that point on the Senate floor; and for that very reason had requested that his charges be heard in executive session.[18]

The ensuing brush between Tydings and McCarthy is of great interest:

SENATOR McCARTHY. Let me make my position clear. I personally do not favor presenting names, no matter how conclusive the evidence is. The committee has called me this morning and in order to intelligently present this information I must give names. I think this should be in executive session. I think it would be better. However, I am here. The committee has voted to hold open sessions, so I shall proceed. Let me take the case of Dor—

SENATOR TYDINGS. I told you when I invited you to testify that you could testify in any manner you saw fit. If it is your preference to give these names in executive session we will be very glad to have your wishes acceded to. If it is your desire to give them in open session, that is your responsibility. Now, if you will indicate how you want to proceed, the committee will take it under advisement and give you an answer in 2 minutes.

SENATOR McCARTHY. Let me say this first case has been handed to the press already. I think we will have to proceed with this one in open session. When we get to the next case, let us consider it. Let us take the case of Dorothy Kenyon.[19]

Wrapped up in this passage is the "proof" offered by McCarthy's enemies for the contention that the responsibility for naming names in public was his. For, they ask, did not Tydings call McCarthy's palpable bluff by giving him the opportunity to go into executive session, thus forcing him to admit that he had already handed to the press his proposed testimony? Here the disturbing fact is not so much Tydings' attempt to make McCarthy appear responsible for the holding of public hearings. The shameful fact is that Tydings was allowed by subsequent commentators to get away with his incredible ruse.

Let us put the above colloquy in its proper setting. When McCarthy entered the conference room, it was his understanding (a) that names were to be given out, and (b) that the hearings were to be open to the public. It was therefore perfectly natural that he should have handed the press advance copies of what he was going to say: as every congressman and Washington reporter knows, advance press releases of public statements are unchallenged routine. Thus, that Tydings' last-minute maneuver should have succeeded in impressing the public that McCarthy was responsible for naming the names in public incriminates others besides the Committee members. For it is quite clear that this misinformation could not have been palmed off to the American people solely through the artful play-acting of the Tydings Company; cooperation was required from members of the press who, although they could see plainly what was going on in the Committee room, popularized and perpetuated a malicious myth.

And why did not McCarthy move to have the subsequent cases heard in executive session? In view of the reception accorded the Kenyon case by press and radio, a later request by McCarthy to ring down the curtain on publicity at that point would have been interpreted as his effort to run for cover. Moreover, McCarthy, as a mere witness, had every right (having raised the issue, and made his own position clear) to deem the procedure, from the Kenyon case on, a proper matter for determination *by the Committee—and no one else*. As a polemicist, he had everything to gain by doing so. Thus, he acquiesced in the decision the Committee had taken *before the hearings began*—the decision to hold, over McCarthy's protest, open sessions at which the public would learn the names of suspected State Department personnel.

CHAPTER VII

The Nine Public Cases:
An Invitation to Investigate

LORD ACTON advised us never to rest content with a point of view "until we have made out for our opponents a stronger and more impressive case than they present themselves." Objectivity and charity demand that we search out a propositional justification for the Tydings Committee's amazing refusal to investigate—the more so since its friends and admirers have never attempted one themselves.

The "stronger and more impressive case" for the Committee's performance would run something like this: Granted, the Senate ordered an investigation. But it was implicit in the mandate that the Committee should not expend time and money on an exhaustive probe that might jeopardize Department morale and, perhaps, even our foreign relations, unless the chief accuser presented a *prima facie* case against the Department's loyalty and security program. And this—so the case would run—McCarthy did not do.

Let us, in other words, give the Tydings Committee the benefit of the doubt here and agree that, unless McCarthy produced a persuasive *prima facie* case against the State Department's loyalty program, the Tydings Committee was entitled not to investigate, not to subpoena witnesses, not to follow up leads, not to take more than a furtive peek at the loyalty files of suspect personnel. Let us even concede that the Committee should have adjourned its inquiry into the problem, should have silenced McCarthy at crucial points in the proceedings, and should have used State Department press releases to disprove charges against the State Department— *if* McCarthy failed to bring a persuasive *prima facie* case in support of his contentions. Thus, we shall fix our attention on one simple question: *Did McCarthy present enough evidence to raise reasonable doubt as to whether all loyalty and security risks had been removed from the State Department?*

To answer this question we propose close scrutiny of the Nine Public Cases. The nine individuals whose cases McCarthy discussed in public are not necessarily the most important in terms either of their influence on the State Department or of incriminating evidence McCarthy brought to light. But they were the first group of cases about which an amount of useful information was made available to Congress and to the nation, both thirsty for facts on which to base an opinion on State Department security. None of these nine cases, let us agree at once, was backed up by definitive or even particularly impressive research. They were the product of more or less sustained homework by a single Senator to uncover hard-to-come-by loyalty and security data on employees, or consultants, or associates, of the United States Government. The evidence was obtained from multifarious sources—from the files of private researchers, from informants working in the government, from old newspaper clippings, from forgotten speeches of a few congressmen who had sensed the danger long before McCarthy, but had for the most part failed to find a listening audience.

Such evidence is unlikely to provide unassailable and unambiguous proof that a government employee is disloyal. The question is whether McCarthy's evidence added up to a *prima facie* case against State Department security practices.

The story of the Nine Public Cases was not adequately told at the time. It was adumbrated here and there, in lurid news stories, and between the lines and words of excited columnists and commentators. But most of the factual data never did get out; and those that did were quickly forgotten in the backwash of angry partisanship. We have, therefore, attempted to run the story down. We will tell it here, hoping to slight neither McCarthy's evidence, the counter-testimony of the accused, nor the Committee's investigative efforts.

The Case of Dorothy Kenyon

SENATOR McCARTHY's choice of the Kenyon case to lead off his presentation came as a surprise. The name of Dorothy Kenyon was little known to the public—much less in association with Communist activities. Judge Kenyon was a reputable New York City lawyer, had once served as a municipal court judge, and had attracted some attention as a political activist, especially in the advancement of women's causes. She had been hired by the State Department in 1947 to serve as American delegate to the United Nations Commission on the Status of Women.

"This lady," Senator McCarthy explained, "has been affiliated with at least 28 Communist front organizations, all of which have been declared subversive by an official government agency."[1]

McCarthy thereupon handed the Committee a series of documents, mostly photostats, allegedly establishing Judge Kenyon's connection with various front organizations. He cited the government groups (including state legislative committees) that had designated these organizations as "subversive" or as "Communist fronts." Nine of them, McCarthy said, had been cited as subversive by the Attorney General of the United States.[2] The documents themselves were of several types. Most were official organization letterheads that listed Miss Kenyon either as a sponsor or as a member. Some were official programs of organization-sponsored dinners. A few were newspaper reports of open letters that Miss Kenyon had allegedly signed in such fashion as to connect her with this or that organization.* All in all, it looked as though McCarthy had a pretty good *prima facie* case.

McCarthy, to be sure, was not permitted to lay out his evidence in neat, orderly fashion. The presentation summarized in the preceding paragraph took the better part of two days, during which McCarthy was plagued by constant interruptions—a kind of sustained heckling that finally prompted Senator Lodge to intercede on McCarthy's behalf: "I think to interrupt the witness [McCarthy] every time and break up his continuity and destroy the flow of his argument, the way we are doing, is not the right procedure.

---

* A summary of McCarthy's evidence on Miss Kenyon's front affiliations, along with official citations, is set forth in the Appendix.

... For some reason that has not been made clear to me, whether it is to rattle or whether it is to confuse, I don't know, we have an entirely different procedure today. . . . I am objecting to the constant interruption of the witness so that he never gets a fair shake."[3]

McCarthy's opposition was rallying—and not only within the Committee. That night, the State Department issued the first of its almost daily communiques on the investigation: Dorothy Kenyon, the Department said, was *not* one of its employees, since her appointment to the UN had terminated some two months earlier. McCarthy shot back that the implications of the case were not in the slightest affected by the fact that Miss Kenyon's term of employment happened to have lapsed: "Even though this individual may no longer be with the Department, the case in my opinion, is still extremely important in that it will shed considerable light on the workings of our loyalty program."[4]

This, then, was the issue as McCarthy drew it: Is it not a persuasive indictment of the State Department loyalty program, he asked, that an important Department employee had successfully weathered loyalty and security screening processes in spite of her sometime affiliation with "at least 28" Communist fronts?

Now let us get before us the salient points of Judge Kenyon's defense. But first we must put to rest one of the most vicious of the anti-McCarthy canards. Long-standing evidence to the contrary, one hears again and again that the people McCarthy accuses in public are not given a chance to answer. The fact of the matter is that *every person McCarthy publicly accused before the Tydings Committee was invited to appear before the Committee to reply to the charges.* Six of the nine persons accused availed themselves of the opportunity. The others submitted statements to the Committee. All were permitted counsel. Affidavits on behalf of the accused, and all other exhibits offered, were entered in the Committee's records. The accused could bring in witnesses to testify for him, and the Committee offered to subpoena any reluctant witness the accused wished to call.

Judge Kenyon's reply to McCarthy's charges was flat and unequivocal. "I am not," she declared, "and never have been disloyal. I am not, and never have been a Communist. I am not, and never have been a fellow-traveler. I am not, and never have been, a supporter of, a member of, or a sympathizer with any organization known to me to be, or suspected by me of being, controlled or dominated by Communists. As emphatically and unreservedly as possible, I deny any connection of any kind or character with communism or its adherents."[5]

On the specific question of her affiliation with Communist fronts, which Senator McCarthy professed to have documented a week earlier, this was Miss Kenyon's testimony: She had been affiliated in the past with 12 of the front organizations mentioned. She had withdrawn from 4 of the 12 upon discovering their communist "complexion." She denied affiliation with two of the fronts mentioned (the Consumers Union and the Veterans of the Abraham Lincoln Brigade). She had "no recollection" of having been affiliated with the remainder. In no instance, she emphasized, had she continued her affiliation with an organization that she knew to be Communist. Finally, she was not at present connected with any of the groups Senator McCarthy mentioned.[*]

Judge Kenyon went further and offered evidence that she was, on the record, an active and determined opponent of Communism. In the fall of 1939, the American Labor Party, for many years a prime target for and later the captive of Communist infiltrators, had split wide open on the subject of the Hitler-Stalin pact. Miss Kenyon, an ALP candidate for re-election as municipal court judge, had been asked by ALP state secretary, Alex Rose, to state her views on the pact; and she did so, she told the Committee, as follows: "I regard with horror and loathing the Hitler-Stalin pact. . . . I agree with you that any fusing of the brown and red dictatorships is a treacherous blow to world civilization."[6] Moreover, the following spring she had been vice-chairman of the "Liberal and Labor Committee to Safeguard the American Labor Party," a group formed to "fight the Communist attempt to capture the Labor Party."[7] And by way of clinching the argument as to her views during the German-Russian honeymoon, she showed the Committee her signature on an open letter, dated May, 1941, of the interventionist (William Allen White) Committee to Defend America by Aiding the Allies.[8]

Miss Kenyon also called attention to her clashes with the Russians during her stint on the UN's Commission on the Status of Women. She had told a woman's club audience back in 1948, "Women in Russia undoubtedly have more equality in a greater variety of jobs than do American women, but it is the equality of slavery."[9] Several weeks later, the Soviet short wave radio had ac-

---

[*] Judge Kenyon's description of her connection with each of the fronts is summarized in Appendix A.

cused her of "slandering the Soviet people" with her "irresponsible drivel."[10]

Her summary was plaintive but eloquent:

With all the mistakes and errors of judgment which the best of us can and do commit only too frequently, I submit that the record proves without a question that I am a lover of democracy, of individual freedom, and of human rights for everybody, a battler, perhaps a little too much of a battler sometimes, for the rights of the little fellow who gets forgotten or frightened or shunned because of unpopular views. . . . The converse of these things: dictatorship, cruelty, oppression and slavery, are to me intolerable. I cannot live in their air, I must fight back. This is not perhaps a very wise or prudent way to live, but it is my way. . . . There is not a Communist bone in my body.[11]

One further point in Miss Kenyon's testimony deserves special notice. When Senator Hickenlooper asked her whether any State Department official had ever questioned her about her affiliations with subversive organizations, her answer was: "Never."[12]

Let us return now to the evidence presented by Senator Mc-Carthy and evaluate it in the light of both Judge Kenyon's reply and other data the Committee could easily have laid its hands on, and let us attempt to answer three questions: (1) To what extent did McCarthy show himself to be an accurate and reliable witness? (2) How well did the Committee perform its job? (3) What did the evidence disclose about the adequacy of the State Department's loyalty and security precautions?

The first of these questions must be answered, in part at least, adversely to McCarthy. He had said things about Judge Kenyon that he clearly had no business saying—especially since he had insisted early in his testimony that characterizing the accused was not his task. "I am not making charges," McCarthy had said, "I am giving the Committee information on individuals who appear to all the rules of common sense as being very bad security risks."[13] On his own showing, that is to say, McCarthy should have confined himself to the evidence and should have made observations concerning only Miss Kenyon's fitness for government employment. But he said: ". . . the Communist activities of Miss Kenyon are not only deep-rooted but extend back through the years. Her sponsorship of the doctrines and philosophy of this ruthless and godless organization is not new."[14] And again: "Here again we have this prominent State Department official, Judge Kenyon, crying aloud in anguish for a fellow red."[15]

These, however, are the only instances in which he referred to Miss Kenyon otherwise than as a security risk. But the words *are* McCarthy's, and their use was, in our opinion, unjustified, for the case against Miss Kenyon was not strong enough to warrant such language.

The main thrust of McCarthy's argument, however, was that Judge Kenyon had belonged to a flock of Communist fronts and, by that token, was a poor security risk. Here he was on firm ground.

Insistence on the relevance of Communist front affiliations in determining the security status of a government employee is not a McCarthy innovation (as his enemies often imply). Ten days before the Tydings Committee convened, Secretary Acheson had told the Senate Appropriations Committee about the criteria *he* used to determine who was a security risk. Quoting from the Department's security regulations, Acheson said: "Participation . . . in organizations which are fronts for, or controlled by, [the Communist] party . . . whether by membership therein, taking part in its executive direction or control, contribution of funds thereto, attendance at meetings . . . or by written evidences or oral expressions by speeches or otherwise, of political, economic or social views will be taken into account, together with such mitigating circumstances as may exist."[16] McCarthy, then, was simply asking, Does the State Department adhere to its own standards in evaluating security risks? His answer: it had clearly not been doing so, as witness the fact that the Department had cleared someone with a record of 28 front affiliations. And the Department could not very well plead "mitigating circumstances" in this instance *since it had not even bothered to question Miss Kenyon about her affiliations.*

Close examination of the Committee's published record reveals that McCarthy showed evidence of only 24 Communist front affiliations for Miss Kenyon (rather than 28) and that two of her affiliations (that with the Consumers Union and that with the Veterans of the Abraham Lincoln Brigade) were backed up only by a news story and an advertisement, respectively, in the *Daily Worker.* Curiously, however, the Tydings Committee did not itself take notice of the discrepancy between the 28 alleged affiliations and the 24 actually suggested by the documentation. The likely explanation, in the light of the Committee's yen for pointing out each and every McCarthy misstatement, is that someone on the Committee had consulted Appendix IX of the House Committee on Un-American Activities which lists 28 Communist fronts after Dorothy Kenyon's name.

Only four of the 24 groups had been cited as subversive by the Attorney General; not, as McCarthy had stated, nine.* Except, however, for purposes of nailing down a McCarthy inaccuracy, this fact is of little significance. For absurd emphasis is normally put on the Attorney General's list—as though it were the only authentic compilation of Communist fronts. The Justice Department usually does not get around to citing an organization as subversive until many months (and sometimes many years) after it is so recognized by most other people conversant with the subject. Sometimes the Attorney General waits until an organization has disbanded, and then passes a post-mortem. The House Committee on Un-American Activities lists almost five times as many organizations as the Attorney General, and has yet to be embarrassed by having to retract one of its listings.

It is interesting that the Tydings Committee exploited none of these inaccuracies. It did not, indeed, so much as mention them in its report. Thus, for all its eagerness to nail McCarthy whenever the opportunity arose, the Committee neglected to comb McCarthy's data with sufficient thoroughness to discover his mistakes! Instead, as far as the Kenyon case was concerned, it contented itself with urging two themes: (a) some "pretty prominent people" had joined with Miss Kenyon in several of the fronts mentioned, and (b) the dates of Miss Kenyon's affiliations (in every instance but one) preceded the dates on which the groups were officially cited as "Communist-fronts."

Time and again during McCarthy's testimony it was remarked that Miss Kenyon had "distinguished company" in her connection with this or that front organization. A United States Senator was noted here, a prominent diplomat there.[17] Now such observations might be expected from a high school senior but, coming from

* The four: American-Russian Institute of New York, National Council of Soviet-American Friendship, Conference on Pan American Democracy, and the Veterans of the Abraham Lincoln Brigade. A fifth, the Political Prisoners Bail Fund Committee, might be included since the House Committee on Un-American Activities had indicated that during the period of Miss Kenyon's affiliation, the "Bail Fund" was an adjunct of the notorious International Labor Defense, which Attorney General Biddle, in 1942, had labelled the "legal arm of the Communist Party."

United States Senators presumed qualified to investigate subversion, they are rather baffling. For a Communist front is, *by definition,* an organization that uses innocent people (the more prominent the better) to conceal its real nature. The California Committee on Un-American Activities, for example, cautioned the readers of its report "to hold in mind that a Communist front organization is characterized by the fact that a majority of its members are non-Communists. *If this were not true, it should be quite obvious that the organization would be actually a Communist organization, and not a front in any sense.*"[18] (Italics added.)

Whether or not an individual has been "duped," McCarthy suggested to the Committee, can be quite reliably established by looking at the number of fronts he has joined. For experience with Communist groups presumably educates even "innocents" to recognize a front. "I think that it is possible that you yourself may be duped into joining, or having your name used on some Communist-front organization," McCarthy told Senator Tydings. "The reason I submit the vast number [of Miss Kenyon's affiliations] is that it is impossible for any normal individual, of normal intelligence, to be so deceived that they can act as sponsors for 28 different Communist front organizations."[19]

The Committee made the further point that only in one case (re the National Council of American-Soviet Friendship) did Mc-Carthy's evidence show that Miss Kenyon's affiliation post-dated the official citation of the group as subversive. McCarthy's answer: This is not significant "where we are dealing with a person who belongs to 25 or 30 of them."[20] A seasoned joiner, he reasoned, should not depend on the invariably belated judgment of the Attorney General for information as to the nature of an organization he has joined. And McCarthy might well have gone on to point out—though he did not—that there was no reason to assume Miss Kenyon's affiliation had lapsed on the date mentioned by the single document McCarthy gave the Committee. His documents merely showed Miss Kenyon's connection with each organization *as of a given day;* only by further investigation could the Committee have learned the dates on which she had *severed* the connection. The Committee could easily have learned, for example, that Miss Kenyon was still signing petitions of the Veterans of the Abraham Lincoln Brigade in March, 1945—a year *after* the organization had been officially cited as Communist by the House Un-American Activities Committee and five years after the date mentioned in

McCarthy's document. The Committee's bald statement in its final report, that Miss Kenyon "was found to be connected on but one occasion with an organization after it was cited as subversive,"[21] reveals both the Committee's indolence and its intellectual dishonesty.

In "investigating" Miss Kenyon's alleged addiction to front-joining, the only documents the Committee examined were McCarthy's photostats and clippings. How could meaningful conclusions be reached on the nature and extent of an individual's connection with an organization on the basis of one solitary document countered by the individual's self-serving explanations and denials? The unavoidable result of the Committee's decision not to press the investigation was that *the validity of McCarthy's documentation was not disproved*. Thus it had no grounds on which to challenge the presumption that Miss Kenyon was affiliated, as charged, with 24 (or 28) Communist fronts. That presumption—arising from the fact that greater credence is normally given to written documentation than to simple denials—accordingly stands.

As for Judge Kenyon's own evidence relating to her attitude during the Hitler-Stalin pact, the situation is more complicated. Her documents indicate that she was opposed to the pact—that she was, in fact, an "interventionist" at the time. They therefore weigh strongly in her favor; for seasoned students of party-lining are unanimous in attaching great significance to an individual's attitude during that period. So it is understandable that the Tydings Committee should have been "especially impressed" with Miss Kenyon's record on this point. "Of great significance," the Committee reported, is "the undisputed evidence of her pro-Allied feelings in 1940 and 1941. . . ."[22]

The complications arise because the evidence was *not* "undisputed." For the Committee also had before it evidence that Miss Kenyon had signed a party-lining Open Letter on February 21, 1940, which supported the Veterans of the Abraham Lincoln Brigade* and deplored the "mounting war fever," the "hysteria," and the "terror" encouraged by the Roosevelt Administration.[23] To be sure, the validity of this evidence is questionable: it appeared as a paid advertisement in the *Daily Worker,* and Miss Kenyon denied having authorized the use of her name on the letter. But

---

* What is more, there was the evidence, mentioned earlier, which lends credibility to the 1940 "Brigade" allegation; namely, the Brigade's own press release which *in 1945* listed Judge Kenyon as one of its sponsors.

there it stood: a photostat of an advertisement in the *Daily Worker* bearing Miss Kenyon's name—versus Miss Kenyon's insistence that her name had been used without her authority. And there is not the slightest indication, on the record, that the Committee ever attempted to secure the original of the letter or even a reliable copy of it. The "investigators" preferred to treat this disruptive bit of evidence as though it had never existed. But if it were true that Miss Kenyon did, in fact, join with the Abraham Lincoln Brigade to protest against American "war hysteria" in 1940, then her real sentiments during the Hitler-Stalin Pact are in doubt. We then would have to conclude that she was working both sides of the street—as the strenuous demands of a political career in New York's American Labor Party have obliged many a man and woman to do.

On balance, we believe that Dorothy Kenyon is and has been a loyal American. By that we mean that a person is innocent until proven guilty—a presumption Americans traditionally indulge in when deciding whether a fellow citizen is guilty of a crime. But Miss Kenyon indiscriminately joined numerous Communist fronts and this clearly disqualified her from government service. It makes her, as McCarthy claimed, *a security risk*. For where government employment is involved, the benefit of the doubt must (and does, by recent tradition) go to the government.

The Tydings Committee made no such observations about Miss Kenyon. Rather, in handing down its categorical clearance of her, the Committee indulged in several remarks which throw light on the attitudes—and incapacities—of its members. Their job was to assess the Kenyon case in the context of prevailing security standards in the Department of State; instead of doing that job, the Committee launched into a rollicking cliché about jurisprudence, sportsmanship, and other matters. "While the number of admitted affiliations by Miss Kenyon," the report stated,[24] "are sufficient to suggest a high degree of naivete and perhaps gullibility" (we disagree: with McCarthy, we believe that, in general, naivete and gullibility are indicated in *inverse* ratio to the number of Communist affiliations), "American standards of justice and fair play have not deteriorated to the point that our citizens become disloyal on the basis alone of their affiliations with organizations found to be subversive several years after the affiliations, particularly in the case of Communist fronts which are deliberately designed to deceive and hoodwink the unsuspecting."*

However, let us for a moment assume that Judge Kenyon was not even a security risk. What then, were the lessons of the Kenyon case as regards the adequacy of the State Department's loyalty-security apparatus? *The outstanding fact of the Kenyon case is that neither her loyalty nor her reliability was ever explored by the State Department.* When Senator McCarthy expressed surprise at her having been *"cleared* by the State Department Loyalty Board"[25] he was, for once, guilty of an understatement. *The Loyalty-Security Board had never held a hearing on the Kenyon case— had never even sent her a routine "interrogatory"!* We have Miss Kenyon's own word for it that no Department official ever questioned her on the subject of her Communist associations. And her version of this matter was never contradicted by the State Department. In a word, not only did the State Department fail to find Miss Kenyon a security risk; her record of 28 (or, if you like, 24) Communist front affiliations did not even prompt Department security officers to *look into* that possibility!

It can therefore hardly be disputed that, with respect to Dorothy Kenyon, McCarthy presented a *prima facie* case for doubting the adequacy of the State Department's loyalty-security program.

* Note how the Committee, in reaching its conclusions, loads its premises. It speaks of the affiliations "admitted" by Miss Kenyon although it had no evidence other than Miss Kenyon's word that the affiliations which were not admitted by her were erroneously charged to her. And it speaks of affiliations after the organizations were found to be subversive although, as we have seen, the Committee did not *know* the dates of Miss Kenyon's affiliations, except as indicated by the documents provided by McCarthy. It speaks of "loyalty" as though finding a person a security risk required an affirmative finding of *disloyalty*. And so on.

The Case of Haldore Hanson

AT THE time McCarthy named him before the Tydings Committee, Haldore Hanson was employed by the State Department as Chief of the Technical Cooperation Projects Staff, one of the three staffs responsible for the administration of the Point 4 program.* He had come a long way since 1934 when, fresh out of college, he had sailed for China as a stowaway.

For three years Hanson had taught school and had written as a free lancer, mostly while living in Peiping. The turning point in his career had come in 1937, when Japanese and Chinese troops clashed at the Marco Polo Bridge: he then took a job as war correspondent with the Associated Press. Two years later, at the age of twenty-seven, he published a book called *Humane Endeavor*. The book, though it got good reviews, sold poorly and was all but forgotten until Senator McCarthy told the Tydings Committee that *Humane Endeavor* "sets forth . . . [Hanson's] pro-Communist answer to the problems of Asia as clearly as Hitler's *Mein Kampf* set forth his solution to the problems of Europe."[26]

McCarthy was bent on proving that Hanson had *knowingly* relayed Communist propaganda; that he had written favorably about the Communists because of his "pro-Communist proclivities."[27] "This," said McCarthy, "is not a dupe. Here is one of the cleverest, one of the smoothest men we have in the State Department."[28] And later on: "Here is a man with a mission—a mission to communize the world."[29]

In deciding to spear Hanson as a Communist, or pro-Communist, rather than a mere security risk, McCarthy took for himself an unnecessarily hard row to hoe. He was out to make a case against the State Department; and so he had only to prove that the Department was employing persons about whose reliability there was a "reasonable doubt." McCarthy would have been well-advised to confine himself to that single job. But since we seek to throw light not only on government security practices, but also on McCarthy, we must keep in mind the specific accusations he brought against Hanson.

As we say, McCarthy painted an alarming picture of Hanson. "This young man," he said, "was running a Communist magazine

* McCarthy claimed, erroneously, that Hanson's job put him "in charge of Truman's Point 4 program."

in Peiping when the Japanese-Chinese war broke out."[30] He later "spent several years with the Communist armies in China, writing stories and taking pictures which the Chinese Communists helped smuggle out of the country."[31] And, McCarthy told the Committee, "Hanson himself said—they [the Chinese Communists] do not tolerate anyone who is not completely on their side."[32]

Humane Endeavor, McCarthy charged, was a pro-Communist polemic. It exalted the Chinese Communists at the expense of the Nationalists. It awarded to the guerillas the now familiar kudos for having done the only serious fighting against the Japanese, and for having redistributed the land "as fairly as possible."[33] Directly and indirectly, McCarthy went on, it extolled the Communist leaders—indirectly, for example, by quoting from Red apologists of the stripe of Major Evans Carlson.* On Carlson, it hung the following tendentious characterizations: Mao Tse-Tung—"the most selfless man I ever met, a social dreamer, a genius living 50 years ahead of his time"; and Chu Teh, Commander of the Eighth Route Army—the "prince of generals," "a man with the humility of Lincoln, the tenacity of Grant, and the kindliness of Robert E. Lee."[34] McCarthy also cited tributes to Chinese Communist leaders that were Hanson's very own: "I left Yenan with the feeling that Mao was the least pretentious man in Yenan and the most admired. He is a completely selfless man."[35] And (though here he had not done his homework, as we shall see below) McCarthy cited a reference to the Communist leaders as "a group of hard-headed, straight-shooting realists."[36]

On the other hand, McCarthy charged that Hanson had disparaged the Chinese Nationalists, whom he had described as "rightists" who were "fighting the Democratic Revolution as proposed by Mao Tse-Tung and the Communists."[37] Lastly, McCarthy fixed attention on the following excerpt from *Humane Endeavor:* "Leaders of the Communist Youth Corps were arrested by military officers at Hankow. I myself," Hanson went on, "was the victim of one of these incidents and found that local officials were the instigators."[38] On the basis of this, McCarthy told the Committee: "this young man has a criminal record in China where he was arrested, not by the Communists, but by the anti-Communists."[39]

McCarthy cited, in all, only eight or nine passages from *Humane Endeavor.* Even so, and even though they had been written twelve

* Of "Carlson Raiders" fame. In 1950, Louis Budenz named Carlson, now dead, as a member of the Communist Party.

years earlier, they added up to a *prima facie* case against Hanson. On the strength of them, the Committee should have given the book a careful reading and subjected Hanson to a thoroughgoing investigation. It did neither.

Hanson appeared before the Committee fifteen days after Mc-Carthy had testified about him. He was an indignant and persuasive witness, and he made the most of McCarthy's overzealous characterizations of him. "I deeply resent this attack upon my loyalty. I wish to state now, under oath, that I am not a Communist. I have never been a Communist. . . . Senator McCarthy produced no new facts before this Committee which were not available to those [FBI] investigators. In fact, he produced nothing that I hadn't put in a public library. After the FBI investigation I was given a complete clearance by the Department of State."[40]

In speaking of *Humane Endeavor*, Hanson[41] pulled all the stops —from modesty ("It was not a great book. It was published when I was 27 years old. . . .") to patient factual description, to special and didactic pleading ("now it is grossly misleading to take objective journalistic reports about the Chinese Communists in 1938, at the time of a united front with Chiang Kai-shek against Japan, and to deduce from them my attitude toward the Chinese Communists, 11 years later, in the midst of a cold war between the democracies and world communism").*

Senator McCarthy, Hanson went on to say, had not mentioned that, at the time of his contact with the Chinese Reds, he was working for the Associated Press. Moreover, he had been with the Communist armies not for two years, as McCarthy had said, but for only four months; and what he had subsequently written in *Humane Endeavor,* he insisted, he had written as a mere reporter chronicling the facts as they came to his attention. The *Chicago Tribune,* one of the many papers that had carried favorable reviews, treated his book as an objective account of the Sino-Japanese conflict.[42]

Some of the excerpts McCarthy had quoted from *Humane Endeavor,* Hanson claimed, were inaccurate and misleading. Here he

---

* Note that Hanson is saying two things here, each tending to contradict the other. He asserts (a) that his observations in *Humane Endeavor* were objective reporting, and (b) that they were somehow conditioned by the existence of the United Front. Even if we concede the second of these statements, the question remains whether Hanson wrote favorably of the Communists because they were fighting side by side with the Nationalists, or took it somewhat easy on the Nationalists because they were then fighting side by side with the Communists.

thoroughly convinced the Committee, which in its report took great pains to bring to the public's attention McCarthy's "factual inaccuracies." Since so much was made of McCarthy's alleged "misrepresentations" and distortions, we shall pause here to examine the McCarthy quotations which the Committee took exception to.

(1) McCarthy stated that Hanson called the Communist leaders a "group of hard-headed, straight-shooting realists." This was indeed a misquotation since what Hanson had written was that the Reds were "hard-headed, hard-shooting realists."[43] (McCarthy continues to misquote this passage, for example in his own book.) *

(2) McCarthy stated that *Humane Endeavor* showed Hanson had a "criminal record" in China since it revealed that he had been arrested in connection with a crack-down on the Communist Youth Corps. Actually, in the paragraph following Hanson's assertion, "I myself was the victim of one of these incidents," he tells of the seizure of his passport by Nationalist officials when they found him en route from Communist territory.[44] The presumption, then, is that it is this incident, not that of the Youth Corps leaders, in which Hanson was involved as a "victim." It is, therefore, not easy to quarrel with the Committee's conclusion that McCarthy here quoted Hanson out of context. On the other hand, Hanson himself describes the use McCarthy made of the quotation as merely "careless," and as we read the chapter in *Humane Endeavor,* it can indeed be construed as saying that he was involved in both events.

(3) McCarthy told the Committee, as we have seen, that *Humane Endeavor* quoted Major Carlson's eulogies of Mao Tse-Tung and Chu Teh. There was never any question from what McCarthy said but that Hanson was setting forth *Carlson's,* not his own evaluation of the Chinese Red leaders. (Hanson himself did not criticize McCarthy's presentation of this datum.) Yet Senators Tydings and McMahon, for no other conceivable reason than to heckle McCarthy, spent fifteen or twenty minutes on two occasions to "make it clear" that the words were not Hanson's own, implying, in the process, that McCarthy had taken liberties with the text. McCarthy had done no such thing, as anyone can see by looking at the transcript. Nevertheless, the Committee reported the incident as an example of McCarthy's mendacity.[45]

(4) McCarthy attributed to Hanson the statement that the Chinese Communists "do not tolerate anyone who is not completely on their side," implying that since Hanson had been permitted to

* *McCarthyism, the Fight for America,* p. 76.

report on guerilla activities in Yenan, he must have been *persona grata* with the Communists. (McCarthy did not give a source for the quotation.) When Hanson took the stand, he acknowledged that in an article written for *Pacific Affairs* in 1938, he had said "The guerillas do not tolerate neutrality; a man's either for or against them." However, he pointed out that the article referred to the Communists' attitude toward Chinese traders who were not cooperating in the war against Japan, not to their attitude toward American news reporters.[46] If, therefore, McCarthy had the above passage in mind, it does not document the inference he drew. Another possibility, however, is that McCarthy was not dealing with the quotation from *Pacific Affairs,* but was merely giving the drift of certain passages in *Humane Endeavor* in which Hanson (a) intimated that only a very few reporters were granted admission to Yenan, and (b) described his own enthusiastic welcome there by the Communists. Whether he intended to or not, Hanson certainly conveyed the impression in his book that only sympathetic reporters were allowed to visit Yenan. Thus, as regards the issue whether McCarthy misrepresented Hanson, the quotation from *Pacific Affairs* is neither here nor there.

It is indeed characteristic of McCarthy to put into direct quotes what amounts to his own paraphrase of someone's position*—as, for example, his assertions that Hanson had "*said*" such and such, while actually Hanson had said it in some other way, or had clearly implied it. Such interpolations, to be sure, pay scant heed to the rules of scholarship. But to condemn McCarthy on the strength of these rules is to judge him by unusual standards; it is to demand of McCarthy a norm of behavior not subscribed to by other politicians and, for better or for worse, not expected of them. The canons of politics, at their severest, proscribe misrepresentation. McCarthy in the instance we have just mentioned, did not misrepresent Hanson.

The Tydings Committee, in cross-examining Hanson, took a Cook's Tour through the salient points of interest in Senator McCarthy's testimony: Hanson was brought in and simply asked to comment, item by item, on what McCarthy had said. An example of the superficiality of the cross-examination: the matter on hand was completely dropped when, in answer to Senator Hickenloop-

---

* In February, 1953, for example, by way of contrasting Abraham Lincoln's philosophy with Communist doctrine, McCarthy stated: "Lenin said 'The world cannot exist half slave and half free: it must be all slave.'"

er's question why *Humane Endeavor* had referred to the Communists' "Democratic Revolution," Hanson answered that "democracy" means something in China entirely different from what it means in America. "Mao Tse-Tung was using the term 'democracy' —I did not put it in quotation marks; perhaps I should have."[47] The Committee showed no curiosity about any passage of *Humane Endeavor* other than those McCarthy had mentioned, and asked no questions about Hanson's other writings, or about his activities through the years. There is, indeed, no indication from the record that any member of the Committee ever read *Humane Endeavor!* Just so, by the time Hanson left the stand, it was clear, from the attitude of the Democratic majority at least, that the Committee was ready with a verdict.

It was, therefore, thrown for a complete loss when four weeks later a witness, testifying in secret session, *named Haldore Hanson as a member of the Communist Party.*

The witness, Louis Budenz, was presenting to the Committee a list of persons whom he had known to be Party members and who contributed to *Pacific Affairs* at the time it was being edited by Owen Lattimore. He came to No. 6 on his list, Haldore Hanson. "I know him," Budenz said, "only from official reports, to be a member of the Communist Party."

SENATOR MCMAHON. Somebody told you that he was?
MR. BUDENZ. Not gossip around headquarters; official information. I carried his name with me.
SENATOR MCMAHON. Who gave it to you?
MR. BUDENZ. Well, as I recall at the moment, Jack Stachel.[48]

(Budenz went on to say that he had given Hanson's name to the FBI only a week before. Thus, the State Department's security division had had, as yet, no opportunity to reprocess Hanson on the basis of this new development.)

These, then, were the data the Tydings Committee had before it when it made its report flatly stating that McCarthy's evidence against Hanson "fails in credibility, relevancy and competency."*

---

* By way of substantiating its conclusion about Hanson, the Committee said, *inter alia*, "there was *no evidence at all* to uphold the charge that the magazine with which Hanson was so briefly associated in Peiping many years ago was a Communist magazine" (italics supplied). This astounding statement is itself strong evidence that the Committee never read Hanson's book. For Hanson himself tells us in *Humane Endeavor* that the magazine was started by Edgar Snow and Nym Wales, both of whom have been named, under oath, as members of the Communist Party.

"The quotations from Hanson's book," it continued, "had been unfairly presented and grossly misinterpreted in the first instance,"
and had upon examination "failed miserably as proof of any pro-
Communist leanings on his part." Even Budenz' testimony had left
the Committee unimpressed. The revelation of a tested witness to
the Communist conspiracy provoked nothing more than one comment. It "leaves us," said the Committee, "to a degree in wonderment."

The Committee summed up: "On the basis of our record and the
results of the FBI investigation as indicated by the Loyalty Board's
action,* we do not find Haldore Hanson to be disloyal, or a man
with pro-Communist proclivities or a mission to communize the
world."[49]

Before making our own evaluation of Hanson, we shall examine
certain evidence about him which, for reasons unknown, appears
never to have been weighed—or even reviewed—by the Tydings
Committee. In particular, certain observations about the full text
of *Humane Endeavor* will, we believe, prove relevant.

First, Hanson left the readers of his book with the firm impression that he sympathized with the Communist movement in China.
He expressed admiration for the political communities the Communists had established at Yenan and Mt. Wu Tai. He pointed to
the "cooperation" between Communist and "liberal" groups in the
Communist-held areas as a model for the political organization of
China as a whole.[50] He thought the Communists had been unfairly
persecuted.[51] Where apologetics seemed in order, he supplied
them: "the chopping off of landlords' heads" by the Communists,
he reminded his readers, followed upon generation after generation of "man-made famine."[52] In contrast, Chiang's persecution of
students, teachers, union organizations, and others accused of Red
sympathies, was "a heinous crime."[53]

Often, the favorable references to the Communists were en-
closed in quotation marks; for example, when he decided to tack
down the "old bogy that Soviet Russia is directing the activity of
the Chinese Communists," he came up with the following comment from "an editor": "Why should we need the Russians to tell
us what to do?"[54] Again, he dispelled doubts about the "reform"
nature of the Chinese Communist movement by quoting from a

* Why the Committee thought the Loyalty Board's action was reason for
confirming the *correctness* of the Loyalty Board's action, leaves *us* to a degree
in wonderment.

guerilla general: "Our new task was to give the villagers something to fight for. . . . That is why we decided . . . to give each village a democratic council and complete political freedom. . . ."[55] When he considered the future course of the Communist movement, he called in Mao Tse-Tung himself—the "red philosopher." Mao explained that, whereas it had been necessary in the early days of the Revolution to adopt violent methods such as expropriating private property and killing landlords, the forces of reaction had now (1938) become so weak that the Communists were in a position to join with other groups in a democratic coalition, on behalf of social reform.[56]

In short, Hanson's claim to having written an objective book wears thin. His book is an impressive example of a well-known and effective propaganda technique: an author avoids personal responsibility for the opinions he communicates, yet relies on their cumulative effect to advance his own position; and the more objective the presentation *appears*, of course, the more it invests the author's opinion with an aura of authenticity.

In some passages of Hanson's book the veil of objectivity disappeared altogether and Hanson the advocate was clearly visible: "I am convinced," he wrote, "that there are no . . . Russian arms [being used by the Chinese Reds] . . . except a small amount of ammunition Chiang Kai-shek turned over to them."[57] And at another point: "The Chinese Communist leaders are not anti-Christian."[58] On the other hand, Hanson had occasional kind words for Chiang Kai-shek. He cited the Generalissimo's personal courage and spoke of his efforts to wipe out the opium trade and to eliminate corruption from the Kuomintang.[59] Elsewhere, he commended Chiang's military chieftains; for example, his reference to Chang Chun who had a "reputation for integrity, diplomacy and absolute loyalty."[60] But when the cards were down, and comparisons had to be made, the Communists invariably came out on top and the Nationalists on the bottom.

In sum, we believe that *Humane Endeavor* falls short of revealing, definitively, Haldore Hanson's political allegiance.* One person might read *Humane Endeavor* and reasonably conclude that

* Of course, *Humane Endeavor* could, at most, reveal Hanson's political orientation as of 1938, when the book was written. But we must remember that he did not later repudiate the book. Quite the contrary. What is more, the Department's own security regulations insisted that "A former course of conduct or holding of beliefs will be presumed to continue in the absence of positive evidence indicating a change, both in course of action and conviction, by clear, overt, and unequivocal acts."[61]

its author was knowingly peddling Communist propaganda to the American people; another might read it as a book by a man who, not being an experienced student of Chinese or of world affairs, was taken in by the Communists.

What, then, were the obligations of the State Department Loyalty Security Board which, in 1950, was under instructions to dismiss employees about whose reliability there was a "reasonable doubt"?* Can we say that the Hanson case was—as McCarthy claimed—a black mark against the Department?

An evaluation of the Board's performance requires a brief digression. We must consider an aspect of loyalty board decisions which, though of critical importance, has received insufficient attention from students of the loyalty program.

What we have in mind is the *presumption-of-innocence* aspect of loyalty-security proceedings; and our contention is that the loyalty-security program, to date, has operated in terms of such a presumption. Even though loyalty and security boards are instructed to rule against a man about whose reliability there is a "reasonable doubt," the presumption of "innocence"—a carry-over from our criminal law—affects that ruling. To be sure, no such presumption is articulated in any loyalty board opinion we have read; and it is not likely that board members consciously apply it as they go about their work. It is nonetheless *there*—an inescapable consequence of the moral climate in which the loyalty program operates. It has its deep roots in Anglo-Saxon jurisprudence. It is grounded in the basic attitudes about "innocence" and "guilt" which an American absorbs as he grows up, and which an American carries with him into all phases of political and governmental life.

The notion that a man is innocent till proved guilty cannot be set aside by a mere Executive Order assigning to the government the "benefit of the doubt." The presumption of innocence is bound to seep into decisions about the fitness of government employees as long as they are made through quasi-judicial proceedings and as long as an adverse judgment carries with it overtones of moral censure. The very fact that we have loyalty or even security tests— as opposed for example to a "fitness" test—invites analogies with

---

* The nature of the evidence in the Hanson case—i.e., information bearing on his political allegiance—would have put Hanson, initially, in "loyalty" rather than in "security" channels. But, as we have seen, Department officials have insisted that whoever is a loyalty suspect is also a security suspect. Thus, even in 1950, an evaluation of Hanson's case had to be made, at the margin, with reference to the security—i.e., the reasonable doubt—standard.

the sentences handed down by courts. Thus, even if we instruct the boards to fire everyone about whose loyalty or reliability there is "a reasonable doubt," we can expect the decision as to whether there *is* a doubt to be influenced by the unconscious presumption in favor of the "accused's" "innocence."

Just how the members of a loyalty board apply the presumption—how much weight it is given, and at what stage of the evaluation it is interjected—all this, of course, is pure conjecture; the board members themselves would be hard pressed to give a precise answer. But what goes on must be something like this: An employee has written that Mao Tse Tung is promoting a "Democratic Revolution" in China. The Board members thereupon indulge what lawyers call a "rebuttable presumption" that the analysis was made in good faith. That is to say, they take it for granted that the employee was not knowingly parroting Communist propaganda. This presumption can be overcome by other evidence that generates reasonable doubt as to the employee's pureness of motive. But it stands if such other evidence is not forthcoming. And, of course, the presumption attaches to each piece of evidence that comes up for consideration.

In any case, the mechanics of the presumption are not so important as the fact that it is present; and it must remain present and effective until we get rid of the type of security program we now have. We may feel that it *ought* not to enter into the calculation at all; that "innocence" and "guilt" have no business figuring in the adjudication of an employee's fitness. But in evaluating the past performance of the State Department Board, of the Tydings Committee, and even of Senator McCarthy, we must take that overriding presumption into account.

Keeping all this in mind, what was to be concluded from Haldore Hanson's authorship of *Humane Endeavor?* Certainly, in the *absence* of a presumption of innocence, the Board was obliged to find there was "a reasonable doubt" about Hanson's reliability; for reasonable men could, certainly, conclude that he was knowingly advancing the Communist Party line. The innocence presumption, however, alters the picture. If Hanson had been an experienced observer of Chinese politics—as were John Service and Owen Lattimore—the thesis that he was "taken in" by the Communists would have been implausible, and the original presumption of innocence would thus have been rebutted. We feel therefore that the State Department was justified in clearing Hanson, security-wise, *as of the time McCarthy levelled his charges;* and, consequently, that the Hanson case was not, when the Tydings Committee heard it, *prima facie* evidence of derelict security practices in the Department.

It does not follow, of course, that McCarthy was unjustified in questioning Hanson's loyalty, or that the Tydings Committee should have cleared Hanson—or that the Department should have kept him on *after* the hearings. At the time he made his charges, McCarthy was aware of what Budenz would testify to. And once Budenz' information was on the record, both the Committee and the Department were obliged to find against Hanson; for the scales were now tipped against him, the "presumption of innocence" notwithstanding.

Conceivably, Budenz might have fabricated his story. But it is a matter of elementary logic that, if we find (in spite of Budenz' testimony) no reasonable doubt of Hanson's reliability, we are simply saying that Louis Budenz is a liar, *beyond* reasonable doubt. Yet the FBI, out of long experience, has given him the highest rating for reliability and accuracy. Now we may concede that the presumption of the accused's innocence in some cases would justify such a conclusion about Budenz—if the "accused's" previous record were particularly impressive in support of the "innocence" presumption. For example, if Budenz asserted that he had known Senator Taft as a member of the Party, Budenz might be written off as a liar, his own previous record of witness veracity notwithstanding. Haldore Hanson, however, bordered on being a security risk even before Budenz' testimony; consequently, doubt about his security reliability was now reasonable.

Yet the Tydings Committee cleared him, and the State Department kept on doing so through the succeeding months—sufficient justification, in our opinion, for McCarthy's claim that the one "white-washed" and the other went on its way, unregenerate.

Finally, in 1953, the Technical Cooperation Administration, of which Hanson was now an assistant administrator, was moved from the State Department to Harold Stassen's Foreign Operations Administration. On August 16, the *Washington Times-Herald* carried a report that Stassen had demanded Hanson's resignation—as the alternative to summary dismissal. Stassen's explanation for the separation: "Reduction in force."

The Case of Philip Jessup

THE CELEBRATED "Jessup case," second only to McCarthy's attack
on George Marshall, has become for the Liberals the symbol and
the definitive proof of the evils of McCarthyism. Before McCarthy
went after him, Philip Jessup—like Marshall—was in the front
ranks of those "great Americans" whose patriotism and integrity
were simply not open to question. Unlike Marshall, however, Jessup achieved martyrdom. A year and a half after McCarthy brought
his name before the Tydings Committee—at a time when he had
risen to be United States Ambassador-at-Large—Jessup was for all
intents and purposes forced out of public life; a tragic victim, we
are frequently told, of the Great Witchhunt.

What finished Jessup was, of course, the Senate's refusal in the
fall of 1951, to confirm his appointment as U.S. Ambassador to the
UN. But, according to the Liberal view, McCarthy, not the Senate,
is to be blamed for the loss to the nation of Jessup's invaluable
services. The fact is generally ignored that prominent members
of both Senate parties vigorously opposed the appointment, and
that a majority of a Senate Committee declared Jessup's past performance to be such as to disqualify him as our national spokesman
at the UN. But McCarthy it is who captained the attack; and it is
McCarthy who planted doubts about Jessup's loyalty in the minds
of his Senate colleagues. So Jessup remains McCarthy's victim.

Our concern here, however, is not with the alleged consequences
of McCarthy's campaign but with the Jessup *case*, and the light it
throws on McCarthy's battle with the Tydings Committee.

The Jessup case, in view of its subsequent notoriety, made a para-
doxically unpretentious entrance onto the Committee stage. A
quarter of the way through his statement about Dorothy Kenyon,
McCarthy paused for an aside—so casual that a number of the reporters present assumed they probably hadn't heard right:

Although I shall discuss the unusual affinity of Mr. Philip C. Jessup,
of the State Department, for Communist causes later in this inquiry, I
think it pertinent to note that this gentleman, now formulating top-flight
policy in the Far East affecting half the civilized world, was also a sponsor of the American Russian Institute. . . .[62]

This reference to Jessup's affiliation with the American-Russian Institute is all McCarthy told the Committee about Jessup.* Before evidence could be heard in support of the charge that he had an "unusual affinity for Communist causes," Jessup had flown in from Pakistan to make his reply. Once the "accused" had entered on the stage, the case became Philip Jessup's own show, and the Committee, as impresario, was content to listen to a soliloquy. After hearing it, the Committee never asked McCarthy to state his case.

As he stood before the Committee, Jessup was a model of confidence, dignity and restraint. "I am not a Communist and never have been a Communist sympathizer. I have never knowingly supported or promoted any movement or organization which I knew had as its objective the furtherance of Communist objectives. Although I cannot claim to have any detailed knowledge of the process, I wholeheartedly support the efforts of those whose official responsibility it is to see that Communist sympathizers are kept out of our Government."[64]

Since McCarthy had not yet presented the evidence against him, Jessup had no occasion to answer specific charges. Instead, he offered the Committee a detailed account of his public career, especially his anti-Communist speeches and public statements as delegate to the UN and, later, as roving Ambassador. On no less than nine occasions, he pointed out, the Communist press in Russia and elsewhere had attacked him as the "responsible executor" of American aggression and imperialism. And if his own word was not enough, Generals Marshall and Eisenhower, no less, had sent him warm letters of support. "It does not read," he said in concluding the recital of his anti-Communist activities, "like the record of a Communist, a pro-Communist or a fellow traveler."[65]

Meaningful cross-examination of Jessup was, of course, out of the question. For one thing, since the "prosecution" had never presented its case, there was nothing to cross-examine him about. For another, the "prosecutor," though permitted to be present as the witness spoke, was forbidden to ask questions. And the Committee members' own curiosity was at one of its frequent rock-bottom lows.

The following abstract from the hearings is as good a commentary as any on the attitude of the Tydings "investigators." Senator

---

* On only one other occasion did McCarthy mention Jessup's name. While discussing Owen Lattimore's connection with the Institute of Pacific Relations, McCarthy said, "The familiar pattern starts again with Messrs. Lattimore, Hanson, Bisson and Jessup."[63]

Hickenlooper had just been turned down once more on his recurrent demand that the personnel files be made available to the Committee.

SENATOR HICKENLOOPER. One other thing, Mr. Chairman. I think it is very important, in the interests of complete examination of this matter at this moment—and ineffective as I think any examination of this kind can be without full access to the files—that a decision be made on whether or not Senator McCarthy, who is the moving force in connection with Mr. Jessup, be permitted to interrogate Mr. Jessup at this time, when they can confront each other. . . . Senator McCarthy is here. . . . I don't know Mr. Jessup. I have never seen any information on him of any kind. I think it is very important that Senator McCarthy, who has generated this matter, be permitted to bring up whatever matters he has with Mr. Jessup. . . .

SENATOR TYDINGS. We will lay this question before the Committee and decide on procedure. I do not want to be precluded from passing on it in the committee. However, I think this is a fair observation that Mr. Jessup . . . might be entitled to interrogate Senator McCarthy. . . .

SENATOR MCCARTHY. Mr. Chairman, I will be glad to let Mr. Jessup ask me any questions he cares to.

SENATOR TYDINGS. Just a minute. We haven't asked you as yet, Senator McCarthy. . . .

SENATOR HICKENLOOPER. I take it that the Committee at this time says that Senator McCarthy cannot confront Mr. Jessup.

SENATOR TYDINGS. Not until we pass on it as a committee. . . .[*66]

Armed only with some notes and documents he had received from McCarthy, Hickenlooper then tried, on his own, to go into Jessup's alleged Communist front affiliations. But he was like a child in Jessup's hands. He had only to mention the name of a front organization, and Jessup would suddenly be off again, explaining that his association with that organization had been peripheral and had, in any case, occurred at a time when he had had no knowledge of its Communist complexion.**

The Committee's majority members, clearly unhappy about what Hickenlooper was up to, sat impatiently, each, no doubt, studying the arrangement of the furniture with an eye to being the first to wring the Ambassador's hand when his ordeal was over. Hickenlooper did not presume upon their good nature. He soon gave up, and Senator Green won the race to the Ambassador's

* The matter was never put to the Committee. Subsequent requests by McCarthy that he be allowed to question witnesses were ignored.

** See Appendix A for an account of Jessup's comments on his front affiliations.

hand. "Dr. Jessup," he said, ". . . let me congratulate you on the way you have so thoroughly cleared whatever charges, so-called, have been made against you"[67]—although only one charge had been made, and the evidence with which it might have been supported had not been heard. Senator McMahon, when his turn came, effused an encomium, even warmer, for his was a special privilege: "Dr. Jessup, I am proud to have you as a constituent of mine. I am delighted that you are a fellow-citizen of the State of Connecticut."

Nothing remained for the "investigators" to do except to work out appropriately handsome words for inclusion in the report. This was finally accomplished by the suggestion that the prestige of Philip Jessup and the prestige of the United States are one and the same thing: "This subcommittee feels that the accusations made against Philip C. Jessup are completely unfounded and unjustified and have done irreparable harm to the prestige of the United States."[68]

McCarthy had in the meantime determined to specify his case against Jessup before a forum where he could not be so easily silenced. In two speeches made on the Senate floor, on March 30 and June 2, 1950, he catalogued his evidence against Jessup; and although the speeches are not, strictly speaking, a part of the Tydings Record, the Committee report did advert to them in discussing Jessup. Partly for this reason, and partly because they are documents to which the student must turn in his attempt to test the Committee's conclusion, we will summarize them here.

To support his charge that Jessup had an "unusual affinity for Communist causes," McCarthy reported:

That Jessup had been affiliated with five Communist fronts;[*][69]

That Jessup had been a leading light in the Institute of Pacific Relations at a time that organization was reflecting the Communist Party line; and that he had "pioneered the smear campaign against Nationalist China and Chiang Kai Shek" and propagated the "myth of the 'democratic Chinese Communists'" through the IPR magazine, Far Eastern Survey, *over which he had "absolute control;"*[70]

That Jessup had associated with known Communists in the IPR;[71]

That the IPR's American Council under Jessup's guidance had

* The fronts are listed in Appendix A, along with an indication of the nature of Jessup's affiliation with them.

received more than $7,000 of Communist funds from Frederick Vanderbilt Field;[72]

That Jessup had "expressed vigorous opposition" to attempts to investigate Communist penetration of the IPR;[73]

That Jessup had urged that United States atom bomb production be brought to a halt in 1946, and that essential atomic ingredients be "dumped into the ocean";[74]

That Jessup had appeared as a character witness for Alger Hiss, and that later, after Hiss's conviction, Jessup had found (as McCarthy put it) "no reason whatever to change his opinion about Hiss's veracity, loyalty and integrity."[75]

A Committee seeking a sober and impartial judgment on State Department security practices might at least have had to think twice before dismissing McCarthy's case. The Tydings Committee did not in fact think once.

In the matter of Jessup's alleged front affiliations, this is what the Committee said in its report: *"Only a casual review of the record is required to demonstrate the erroneous and misleading character of the charge that Dr. Jessup had been affiliated with five Communist front organizations. . . . The true facts . . . are that Dr. Jessup is shown to have been associated with only two organizations, in both cases prior to the date they were cited as Communist fronts."*[76]

With just which two fronts the Committee was prepared to concede Jessup's affiliation it is impossible to discern from its jumbled recapitulation of Jessup's testimony. But the inaccuracy of the statement is, in any case, easy to demonstrate. Uncontroverted evidence showed Jessup to have been affiliated with *four* groups, all of which have since been officially cited or designated as fronts: the American Russian Institute; the National Emergency Conference (and its successor, the National Emergency Conference for Democratic Rights); the American Law Students Association; and the American Council of the Institute of Pacific Relations.*

The fifth affiliation charged by McCarthy, he did not establish. The Coordinating Committee to Lift the Spanish Embargo (a Communist front, to be sure), did publish a statement by Jessup on the embargo in one of its pamphlets. But the statement appeared along with statements from some thirty other persons, and there is no evidence that Jessup had given the Coordinating Committee

---

* It should be noted that the citation against the IPR's American Council was withdrawn in 1951. But at the time of the Tydings Report, the citation was in effect.

permission to use it. Moreover, the pamphlet in question seems, on the face of it, to have been a catchall for public statements from pretty much any and everyone in favor of ending the embargo, which the organization turned to its own uses. It is difficult to see how McCarthy could have mistaken it for anything else.

To the extent the Committee was willing to concede that Jessup in fact *had* front affiliations, it rationalized them in familiar terms: the organizations were cited as fronts after the date of Jessup's association. Yet let us repeat that one cannot make any general inference from the date on which a subversive organization is *cited* as to when intelligent people should have been able to *spot* it as Communist-dominated. Official proscription occurs only after lengthy and painstaking investigation and it is evidence of Communist activity *in the past*.*

If the Committee had bothered to investigate the public files of the House Committee on Un-American Activities, it would have found that each organization with which Jessup had been connected was engaging in pro-Communist activities *at the time of Jessup's association*. And if it had bothered to question some of Jessup's prominent colleagues in the various fronts he had belonged to, it would have discovered that the Communist complexion of the organizations was not very difficult to spot. It would have found, for example, that Senator Paul Douglas, a co-sponsor with Jessup of the National Emergency Council for Democratic Rights, had resigned from the group in September, 1940, precisely on the grounds that the Council was "a Communist front."[77] Jessup, though a member at that time, took no such action.

A word is in order about the one Jessup affiliation McCarthy charged and did *not* establish—i.e., that with the Coordinating Committee to Lift the Spanish Embargo. The facts are, as it happens, vastly more damaging to Jessup than a substantiation of his alleged affiliation could possibly have been. For they add up to this: Jessup, having advocated lifting the embargo, later opposed lifting it, and chose as the time for his about-face the month of

---

* The attitude of some observers on this matter, we may note in passing, reflects the normal Liberal tendency to have it both ways. On the one hand, they challenge the right of the Attorney General to cite an organization as "subversive" at all; and on the other, when it suits their purpose, they imply that the Attorney General feels a peculiar afflatus on the subject and is hence the first individual to become aware that an organization is subversive—from which it readily follows that all organizations are all right until the Attorney General says they aren't.

September, 1939—after the Hitler-Stalin Pact had been signed. So much McCarthy proved, beyond the shadow of a doubt, at the Senate Foreign Relations Committee Hearings in the fall of 1951 by citing (1) a letter Jessup had written to the *New York Times* on September 21, 1939, *opposing* repeal of the embargo and (2) a letter he had written to the *Times* eight months earlier when he had contended that lifting the embargo would

mark a return to our historic policy of avoiding intervention in European civil wars, following a strict hands-off policy instead of taking affirmative action which, as events have demonstrated, inevitably affects the outcome of a struggle in which we profess not to be concerned.[78]

The September letter, by contrast, insisted that repeal of the embargo would be "unneutral" and would be

contemptuous of the legal duty which the law of nations imposes upon every neutral sovereign. Such conduct is . . . a specious form of interposition sought to be disguised under a cloak of professed equality of the opposing contenders.[79]

Jessup's interest in the matter, one may legitimately suspect, was political rather than professional.* Jessup, of course, knew that maintaining the embargo in January meant unofficial American intervention on the side of the Spanish Loyalists (by that time Communist-dominated), and that lifting the embargo in September

* To both of his arguments Jessup lent the force of his *expertise* in International Law. And like any resourceful lawyer, he was full of arguments with which to justify drawing a distinction between two apparently similar situations. He argued on the one occasion that General Franco's status as a "belligerent" during the Spanish Civil War had not been officially recognized by the United States; and that therefore legal precedent would be against an embargo on shipments to Spain. On the other occasion he started out from the existence of the general European war and argued that repealing the embargo *after* the conflict had begun would be unneutral conduct; thus, illegal under the law of nations. Most learned persons would dismiss such talk as sophistry, and recognize that, practically speaking, Jessup had, in the name of neutrality, urged diametrically opposed policies in essentially similar situations. But even within the strict confines of legal reasoning, Jessup proved too much. For, if precedents were to be his guide, he should have started out by noting that America has traditionally opposed embargoes against belligerents as well as against rebels; which would have ended him up opposing the embargo in September as well as in January. Or, if he was saying that no alteration of the *status quo* after the commencement of hostilities is to be the controlling consideration, how could he justify a repeal of the Spanish embargo at a time when the Spanish Civil War was nearly three years old?

meant unofficial American intervention on the side of England and France against Germany and its ally of the moment, Soviet Russia. Now there may be other common denominators in the two positions Jessup took; but the one that stands out is the interests of the Soviet Union. This the Tydings Committee, if it meant business, could not ignore. Nor is it any answer here to say that McCarthy did not present the two letters in time for Tydings' consideration: the letters, printed in the *Times,* were available to any one prepared to conduct a probe of Jessup's past.

In the matter of Jessup's alleged influence in the Institute of Pacific Relations at a time it was promoting Communist interests, the Committee reported as follows: *"His connections with the Institute of Pacific Relations do not in any way reflect unfavorably upon him when the true character of the organization is revealed."*[80]

Just what the Committee conceived the IPR's "true character" to be it did not undertake to say beyond noting that only a small portion of IPR funds had been contributed by Communists. Ascertaining the real significance of Jessup's association obviously required a conscientious inquiry into IPR activities; and that the Committee, characteristically, deemed beyond its call of duty. It was left for the McCarran Committee to do the job a year later, and to report, "The IPR was a vehicle used by Communists to orientate American Far Eastern policy toward Communist objectives."[81]

To be sure, the IPR, as the McCarran Committee Hearings clearly show, was not a Communist "front" in the sense that experts on organizational Communism use the term to describe an organization either "created" or later "taken over" by Communists. But the hearings also show that the IPR had a Communist "cell" that succeeded in putting the organization's official organs at the service of Communist imperialism; and that this was done by "manipulating" the IPR's policy-making officials.

Philip Jessup certainly was among the policy-makers whom the Communists "manipulated." It is quite true that among the IPR's sponsors, members, and contributors, there was an impressive list of "irreproachables"—publishers, diplomats and industrialists whose anti-Communism is beyond question; but who, be it noted, had very little to do with the actual management of the Institute. The McCarran investigation makes it abundantly clear that IPR policies were controlled by a closely-knit brotherhood. While there is nothing sinister about operational autocracy in an organization of this character, the small group which does run it must accept responsibility for its conduct and policies, and not attempt to deflect criticism by citing the respectability of its uninvolved front men.

If Jessup had remained merely a member of the Institute's Board of Trustees (on which he sat from 1933 to 1946) he could lay claim to having, like the irreproachables, played a relatively unimportant role. In 1939 and 1940, however, he was chairman of the Institute's American Council, and from 1939 to 1942 chairman of its Pacific Council, both of which are policy-making bodies. Moreover, he was a member of the American Council's Executive Committee during most of the years in which he was not its chairman. And in 1944, he was chairman of the IPR's Research Advisory Committee—this being, of all the IPR hats he wore, the one to which McCarthy attached the greatest significance.

All this does not prove that the IPR was "Jessup's organization," as McCarthy had put it at one point. But it does, unmistakably, establish his membership in the IPR's policy-making echelon during the crucial years of its exploitation by the Communists. Judging from the McCarran Committee Hearings, it seems probable that Jessup's power during this period exceeded that of any other IPR officer. In a word: it is difficult to see how the Communists could have "used" the IPR as a propaganda instrument without having "used" Philip Jessup in the process.

Specifically, McCarthy charged that Jessup had "pioneered the smear campaign against Chiang Kai-Shek" in the American Council's official organ, *Far Eastern Survey.* As to this, the most electric of all McCarthy's charges against Jessup, the Committee reported: "*We also cannot find any evidence to support the allegation that Dr. Jessup was in control of the publication* Far Eastern Survey *or that that magazine took part in a smear campaign against Chiang Kai-Shek.... The evidence in support of the so-called 'smear campaign' is non-existent.*"[82]

A charitable explanation for this astounding statement is that the Committee (a) failed to inquire into the organizational setup of the IPR; (b) did not read *Far Eastern Survey;* and (c) deemed judicial notice of the brazen propaganda war against Chiang to be beyond the scope of its inquiry. We need not waste time on the Committee's denial of the *existence* of the smear campaign against

Chiang; this—unquestionably the most successful job of political huckstering in our time—has already been so thoroughly documented that we may regard it as *res adjudicata*.* The *Far Eastern Survey's* role in that campaign is, however, worth looking into, as is the question of Jessup's precise connection with this influential magazine.**

We have studied the issues of the *Far Eastern Survey* over the years 1943-1946 and are satisfied that anyone who does likewise will immediately recognize the *Survey's* pro-Communist bias. The skeptic we invite to look for himself.

The McCarran Committee tried to make the point by examining articles in the *Survey* from 1931 to 1951, on a statistical basis, classifying their authors as "pro-Communist," "anti-Communist," or "neutral," respectively. (Into the "pro-Communist" group they put only persons who had been named under oath as Communist Party members and/or members of officially-cited Communist fronts in the Asiatic field;[83] as for the other two groups they trustingly allowed IPR Secretary-General W. L. Holland to do the classifying himself.)[84] The results: 33.73% were contributed by "pro-Communists," 15.18% by "anti-Communists," and 51.09% by "neutrals."[85] If we confine our attention to the years 1943-1946, the McCarran-type breakdown yields approximately the same results.

Yet such an analysis is inadequate for it fails to reveal how much of the material submitted by each group had any *political* significance. Much of the magazine's space was devoted to highly technical discussions of economic and social problems, which had no particular bearing on the conflict between the Communists and the

---

* The most conclusive proof for this assertion is to be found, of course, in the books, articles, and book reviews on China that appeared during that incredible decade. The political reporting of Chinese affairs was then virtually monopolized by a left-wing cadre of writers closely connected with the IPR, notably Owen Lattimore, Edgar Snow, Lawrence Rosinger, Agnes Smedley, John Fairbank, Theodore White, Israel Epstein. The story was subsequently told by Mrs. Irene Kuhn (in the *American Legion Magazine*, 1951); by Senator Owen Brewster (in a speech to the Senate, 1951); by John T. Flynn (in *While You Slept*, 1952); by Victor Lasky and Ralph de Toledano (in *Seeds of Treason*, 1950); by de Toledano (in the *American Mercury*, 1951); and, most authoritatively, in the IPR Hearings, 1951 and 1952.

** The influence of the *Survey* is not to be measured by its circulation, which was small, but by its unchallenged domination—in company with *Pacific Affairs* (IPR) and *Amerasia* (an offshoot of the IPR)—of the field. Expert discussion of Far Eastern problems was for many years the exclusive domain of these three political "trade journals."

free world; and most of the articles by the "anti-Communists" were of this character. On the other hand, *every article* dealing with the Chinese Communists painted a favorable, often an ecstatic picture of the Reds; and not a single article on the internal policies of the Nationalist government, from 1943 on (when the Communist Party line turned against Chiang), refrained from severe criticism of the Kuomintang.

The *Survey's* campaign against Chiang was touched off by T. A. Bisson's now famous "China's Part in a Coalition War" which appeared in the issue of July 14, 1943. The Bisson article, which explained the differences between "Democratic China" (the Communists) and "Feudal China" (the Nationalists) was, according to Louis Budenz, planned and planted by the American Communist hierarchy to keynote the switch in the international Party Line on China. The revised party line was clearly visible in the subsequent numbers of the *Survey*. Criticism of Chiang came to be a dominant theme in the magazine. Article after article posed the question, "Is China [the Nationalist government] really a democracy?" Of course, not even Chiang's greatest admirers would have contended that his government was democratic in the western sense. But the *Survey's* repeated asking of the question and its manner of asking it, carried the suggestion, tacitly or explicitly, that everything would be enormously improved once Chiang "broadened the base" of his government "to include other groups"—meaning, of course, the Communists. Significantly, the *Survey* never once indicated similar misgivings over the internal political conditions of the Soviet Union, although such observations would have had a place in a magazine that devoted a good deal of space to rhapsodical accounts of life in Soviet Asia.

By the end of 1944, such "constructive" criticism of Chiang was giving way to an openly hostile treatment of the Nationalists. In a lead piece called "Report on China," *Survey* editor (Lawrence Salisbury) wrote that "a number of Americans with varying backgrounds have obtained first-hand knowledge of the Chinese 'Communists,' enough for us to realize that the term can be used correctly only in quotation marks. The 'Communist' areas are in fact primarily agrarian communities intent on driving the Japanese from China. In those areas private property is respected and private enterprise encouraged. Reports which have come out of China recently by, for example, American correspondents indicate that a comparison of conditions in the 'Communist' and Kuomintang areas inclines heavily in favor of the former."[86] And so the campaign progressed. Not one article during the entire 1943-46 period suggested the possibility that China's "Communists" were sure-enough Communists.

In analyzing a magazine that has no editorial page, the most indicative index of editorial bias is the book-review section. During the years in question, the *Far Eastern Survey's* pro-Communist batting average in that area was a cool 1.000. Every book critical of the Soviet Union or the Chinese Communists was reviewed unfavorably; and every book praising the Communists, or dressing them up to look like non-Communists, was reviewed favorably. As everyone in the trade knows, book reviewers are invariably selected with the editors' foreknowledge that the opinions they will express do not differ substantially from those which the editors themselves hold.

This brings us to our other question: How did Philip Jessup figure in the "smear campaign" against Chiang's government? Jessup was chairman of the American Council's Research Advisory Committee in 1944, *which, on Jessup's own showing, was responsible for the policies and activities of the "Far Eastern Survey."* In December, 1944, Jessup and three other members of the IPR hierarchy answered Alfred Kohlberg's charge that Communist writers dominated the magazine. How could the *Survey* be accused of pro-Communism, they replied, when its contributors, after all, were not in control of the magazine's policies?

The research conducted by the American Council is under the direction of its Research Advisory Committee. . . . *This Committee formulates and approves the research programs, and it approves the research personnel who are engaged for their competence to undertake the special assignments required in the research program.* Having hired competent research workers, it is not the policy of the Committee or of the American Council to censor these findings, but to publish them as the research results of the authors themselves.* [Italics added.]

Let us not be put off by the statement that it was not the "policy" of the American Council to "censor these findings." The questions remain: Why were the results *not* censored (i.e., rejected on account of their patent partisanship)? And why—among the research

* Letter to Alfred Kohlberg, December 19, 1944, signed by the Chairman of the American Council of the IPR, Robert G. Sproul; by Robert D. Calkins, G. Ellsworth Huggins, and Philip C. Jessup. See McCarran Committee *Hearings,* Vol. 14, p. 4938.

personnel that the Advisory Committee by its own admission had approved—was the incidence of Communists and fellow travelers, unqualified, on the face of it, to carry on objective research, so very high?

Jessup did not become head of the Research Advisory Committee until several months after the *Survey's* anti-Chiang campaign was launched. Whether or not he had a hand in casting the magazine's policies in 1943 is not clear. Mr. Alfred Kohlberg (whose credentials we discuss below) believes he did. He cites, in particular, the fact that he (Kohlberg) learned, in the course of preparing his analysis of IPR publications in 1944, that the touchy situation created by Nationalist objections to Bisson's opening shot at Chiang was referred to Jessup; and that Jessup arranged to have the Nationalists' protests printed in the form of a letter to the *Survey* and to have the protest answered by a letter from Bisson running in an adjoining column of the same issue. If Kohlberg's information is correct, it appears that Jessup was pretty close to the magazine even in 1943. But even if Kohlberg's information is wrong, it would be difficult to exculpate Jessup for the *Survey's* 1943 policies. For, as one of the most influential and hence most responsible members of the IPR hierarchy, Jessup was certainly obliged to speak out against the magazine's increasingly blatant pro-Communism, and decline, in the circumstances, to take over as its impresario the following year.

In summary: while the available evidence does not substantiate McCarthy's statement that Jessup "*pioneered* the smear campaign," McCarthy's indictment of Jessup was decidedly closer to the mark than the uninformed yet categorical denials of the Tydings Committee. For the record shows that Jessup, wittingly or not, did give the Communists valuable assistance in their propaganda war against Chiang's government. And though McCarthy, in crediting Jessup with "pioneering" the campaign, over-stated his case, his general charge—that Jessup had an "unusual affinity for Communist causes"—was, in the light of the evidence, remarkably shrewd and apt. What McCarthy should have said, specifically, is that but for the active cooperation of Jessup, the *Far Eastern Survey* could not have developed into a militantly pro-Chinese-Communist magazine. Jessup apparently had the power to flush out the fellow travellers. And if he did not have this power, he could at least, by resigning and publishing the reason for his resignation, have frustrated the American Council's efforts to further the Communist Party line under the cloak of scholarly impartiality.

In the matter of McCarthy's charge that Jessup had associated with known Communists in the IPR, the Tydings Committee said nothing in its report, absolutely nothing. Two years later, the McCarran Committee reported that 46 persons connected with the IPR had been named under oath as members of the Communist Party; and that at least eight others had collaborated with the Soviet Intelligence apparatus.[87] While this does not establish that they were all *known* Communists, and certainly does not show that Jessup knew them to be Communists or that he was personally responsible for their connection with the IPR, Jessup's *association* with them is beyond doubt. Either, therefore, he was the victim of incredibly elaborate deceit, and thus had the poorest nose for Communists in all the world; *or* he knew he was associated with Communists. Those who are prepared to accept the first of these possibilities are conceivably entitled to regard him as a first-rate dupe but a sound fellow security-wise. If, however, the second is correct, he was a bad security risk as Ambassador-at-large.

Of course, since Communist infiltration is normally a covert operation, it does not follow as a matter of course that Jessup was aware of the political allegiance of these persons—any more than it follows as a matter of course that Dean Acheson and Felix Frankfurter were aware of Alger Hiss' ideological commitments. On the other hand, there are certain facts that put the burden of proving the "dupe" or "poor nose" thesis on Jessup and his supporters. For example, ten of the thirty-three individuals whom Jessup recommended as delegates to the IPR Hot Springs Conference in January, 1945, have since been named, under oath, as members of the Communist Party; and it would be difficult to argue that the bias which most of these ten would carry into the deliberations was hard to predict.* Jessup may not have known what he was doing when he recommended these men; but this is to contend that he was abysmally ignorant in the fields of activity in which he was supposed to be, and indeed never pretended *not* to be, an expert.

A special word is in order about Jessup's association with Fred-

* The ten: Benjamin Kizer, Lauchlin Currie, John Carter Vincent, Owen Lattimore, Joseph Barnes, Frederick V. Field, Alger Hiss, Harry Dexter White, Len de Caux, and Frank Coe.[88]

erick Vanderbilt Field. Field was secretary of the American Council in 1939 and 1940, when Jessup was its chairman. Field's sympathies were perfectly evident in those years.

In the summer of 1940, the Communist Party created a new front—the notorious American Peace Mobilization—to oppose U.S. aid to the Allies. Field was selected to head it. When Field, anticipating a busy time, requested that he be relieved of some of his duties with the IPR, Jessup sent a memorandum to the Board of Trustees of the American Council that read in part as follows:

I cannot acquiesce in his complete separation from the direction of the affairs of the American Council. I have therefore appointed him Staff Adviser with the understanding that he is to be on leave without salary for the next six months. . . . *We consider that it is in the best interests of the American Council that Mr. Field should remain as closely associated with it as possible.* We should therefore like to see him continue as secretary of the Council, *exercising the maximum amount of guidance in the determination of policy* consistent with his desire to be relieved of the burden of administrative work and financial promotion.[89] [Italics added.]

It was left to the Communist Party to tell Field later that he would have to drop his work with the IPR altogether (see below) and devote full time to his new job. Louis Budenz' testimony before the Tydings Committee throws further light on Jessup's attitude toward Field at the time:

MR. BUDENZ. Well, Dr. Jessup was working very close, on very close and friendly terms, with Frederick Vanderbilt Field, and his name came into Field's report [to the Communist Party].
SENATOR McMAHON. As a member of the Party?
MR. BUDENZ. No, sir; not to my knowledge. I never heard him mentioned as a member of the party. . . . I dare say, however, that Mr. Field did declare at the time—and I don't know whether this ought to be on the record or not—
SENATOR McMAHON. This is an executive record.
MR. BUDENZ. The thing is that, well, I am saying this in justice to Dr. Jessup. I do not know him as a Communist. I repeat, Mr. Field reported that Dr. Jessup felt that he [Field] could serve better in the Institute of Pacific Relations. Now, you must understand, I do not know whether Dr. Jessup knew fully what Mr. Field intended to do. . . . The Political Bureau decided nevertheless that Mr. Field should become the head of the American Peace Mobilization, which he did.[90]

The light becomes more illuminating still if we place beside Budenz' statement what Jessup had to say when the time came to arrange a public announcement of Field's resignation from the IPR. Writing on October 29, 1940, to IPR head E. C. Carter, Jessup spoke of Field as follows:

Dear Ned: I don't really think we can use Fred's statement as is, *much as I would be glad to help him with his cause.* How about a combination of the two, something like this:

"Frederick V. Field, who has been on the staff of the American Council since 1928, has resigned in order to become Executive Secretary of the American Peace Mobilization. *'The American Peace Mobilization is a mass organization of progressive trade unions, farm, church, youth, Negro and fraternal groups, dedicated to preserving the interests of the United States through the strengthening of American democracy and through non-participation in the war between England and the fascist powers.'* Mr. Field had a deep conviction that he was obligated to accept this new responsibility and felt that in view of the acceptance of his new position, it was not possible for him to continue his official connection with the IPR. *The Executive Committee . . . expressed the hope that when his new task was completed, it would be possible for him to resume active leadership in the work of the IPR."*[91] [Italics added.]

Are we really to believe that Professor Jessup was uninformed as to the nature of Field's "cause" which he professed to be "glad" to "help"? Are we to believe that Jessup, who was active in the America First Committee,* thought of Field as merely a fellow-isolationist? Hardly, since it was public knowledge that the American Peace Mobilization was first and foremost a Communist mouthpiece. It had been exposed as such at the time of its organizational rally in Chicago, late in August, 1940, *before* Jessup produced the encomium quoted above. The Executive Committee of the New York Young Democrats, for example, had declared on August 31 that the APM was "one more Communist-lead 'fifth column' attempt to weaken national unity."[92] And a few days earlier, Jessup's America First colleagues, Senators Gerald Nye and Bennett Clark, had refused to address the rally because of its Communist inspiration.[93] If, in the light of all this, one still wants to conclude that Jessup, though an expert student of public affairs, was unaware of

* Jessup continued on the America First Committee even after the invasion of Russia by Hitler's armies, when the Communist Party was clamoring for American intervention.

Field's "cause," it must at least be admitted that the odds are heavily against this assumption.[*]

In response to McCarthy's charge that the IPR's American Council had received over $7,000 in Communist funds from Field, the Tydings Committee reported as follows: *"Of the many thousands of dollars received by the Institute as contributions only a few thousand are shown to have come from Communist contributors."*[95] Jessup had already driven that point home in a statement incorporated in a State Department press release:

... in the years when these donations were made, 1942 and 1943, I had ceased to be Chairman of the American Council. . . . At that time, Dr. Robert Gordon Sproul, president of the University of California, was chairman. . . . Mr. Francis Harmon was treasurer; and Mr. William R. Herod, now president of the International General Electric Company, was chairman of the finance committee. During that period, Mr. Juan Trippe, president of Pan American Airways, and Mr. Henry Luce of Time and Life, were sponsors of a drive for funds on behalf of the American Council. Surely, these gentlemen would never have acccepted payments from Mr. Field or anyone else for "selling the Communist Party Line." Neither would I if I had been in control. These contributions, according to Senator McCarthy's own figures, total only $3,500[**] as compared with total expenses for the 2-year period of approximately $200,000. About half of the amount was met by contributions from the Rockefeller Foundation and Carnegie Corporation. Generous donations by large industrial concerns made up a large portion of the remainder.[96]

Resolutely resisting the temptation to reflect upon the enthusiasm with which American capitalists dig their own graves, let us simply note the fact that Jessup's statement here crowds dishonesty—and that the Tydings Committee's endorsement of it, if not dishonest, was at least premature. McCarthy's evidence consisted of a number of cancelled Field checks he had somehow laid hands

[*] E. C. Carter, then the IPR's Secretary General, and not a man to be lightly accused of helping to expose Communism, made no attempt to conceal from the McCarran Committee how open Field had been about his political sympathies:

SENATOR EASTLAND. When did he [Field] take that position with the Peace Mobilization? . . .

MR. CARTER. It was in the autumn of 1940 . . . .

SENATOR EASTLAND. . . . you knew that Field was a Communist, did you not?

MR. CARTER. I know at that time he was behaving like a Communist.[94]

[**] This was the figure McCarthy had given in his March speech; by June he had uncovered additional checks from Field for $3,500, bringing the total to $7,000.

on, made out to the IPR during 1942 and 1943 on behalf of the
American People's Fund.* Now on what grounds did the Committee and Jessup (the latter obviously knowing better) blithely
assume that McCarthy's desultory discoveries had told the *whole*
story of Communist money going into the IPR? Certainly McCarthy was suggesting that a great deal more of this sort of thing had
been going on than was proved by the few checks he had been able
to dig up. Once again, it remained for the McCarran Committee
to get at the truth.

Mr. Morris [Counsel for the Committee]. Mr. Carter testified yesterday that the total of your contribution to the Institute through the
years that you were associated with it approximated $60,000.
Mr. Field. I am perfectly willing to accept that. . . .[97]

From here it is a short step to an educated guess that a considerable part of the $60,000 (since Field was especially active in the
IPR at the time) was contributed during Jessup's tenure as Chairman of the American Council during 1939 and 1940. But educated
guesses are, happily, not needed. For on June 3, 1940, Carter,
writing to his colleague, W. L. Holland, about the need to cut down
the American Council's expenditures, let the cat out of the bag:
*"It is impossible for Field to go on paying each year's deficit. I
think he now feels contraction should have been effected years
ago."*[98]

Now it beggars belief that Jessup, as chairman of the organization, was unaware of Field's role with respect to its financial situation. Why, then, did he see fit to evade the truth by implying that
the few 1942 and 1943 checks uncovered by McCarthy, told the
whole story of Field's donations?

The reader however may concede the point as to Jessup's lack
of candor, yet object to McCarthy's underlying argument here,
i.e., that acceptance of Communist funds is indicative of Communist sympathies. After all, an organization may take money from
Red sugar daddies, provided no visible strings are attached, and
use it for anti-Communist purposes—just as an organization may
take money from the anti-Communist Rockefellers and use it for
Communist purposes. This is a cute objection, but not a valid one.

* The American People's Fund was organized and directed by Frederick
V. Field "as a repository for funds to be distributed to Communist enterprises." (California Committee on Un-American Activities, *Report,* 1948,
p. 168.)

The Communists, on the record, are much more inclined than the Rockefellers to carry into politics the habits formed in meeting the payroll: the Communists, notoriously, hold on to their money until they know they are going to get for it something they want worse than they want it. Any political expert is on notice that, when he gets gifts from the Communists, the Communist cause is getting something in return. This notice, together with what it implies in terms of sympathies, must be imputed to Jessup. For while it is possible that the distinguished and preoccupied businessmen who served on the IPR's Board of Trustees were unaware of Field's political leanings, the same cannot be said for one of Field's closest associates.

To McCarthy's charge that Jessup opposed attempts to investigate alleged Communist penetration of the IPR, the Tydings Committee replied: *"It has been shown that this reference is to an attempt made by Alfred Kohlberg to wrest control of the Institute. The dispute was primarily a private feud between the controlling group and the faction supporting Kohlberg which resulted in overwhelming defeat for Kohlberg and his faction. While we do not pass on the merits of the contest, it is apparent that this is a correct explanation of the incident in contradiction of the erroneous interpretation given by Senator McCarthy."*[99]

How the Committee figured it could thus endorse the IPR line (that Mr. Kohlberg's personal ambition and not his anti-Communism* was at the heart of the "feud" in question), and *not* "pass on the merits of the contest," it did not explain. The facts about the Kohlberg controversy, as it relates to Jessup, appear to be as follows: Kohlberg opened the "feud" in November 1944, when he submitted to the trustees of the IPR an 88-page report showing, with chapter-and-verse citations from IPR publications, the Institute's pro-Communist bias, and demanding a self-administered housecleaning. Kohlberg's allegations, we may note in passing, were fully corroborated by the McCarran Committee.

---

* Alfred Kohlberg is to many people the "China Lobby" incarnate. His sinister motives for supporting Chiang (i.e., concern over his financial investments in China and his personal ambition to run the IPR) are now a cliché— thanks to one of the most vicious and successful smear campaigns ever visited upon a private citizen of this country. This is not the place to review Mr. Kohlberg's record, except to note that, had his counsels been heeded in 1944, the IPR would have been saved; and Chiang's China might have had a fighting chance to survive.

The IPR's answer came in a letter signed by Jessup and three other members of the American Council's Executive Committee: "The Executive Committee and the responsible officers of the American Council find no reason to consider seriously the charge of bias."[100]

Kohlberg then requested a copy of the organization's membership roster, so that he might put his brief in the members' hands. The request was refused. Kohlberg brought suit—which some two years later resulted in a court order compelling the IPR to provide facilities (at the IPR's expense) for circularizing its members. Heartened by this minor triumph, Kohlberg sent out his 1944 analysis, together with a proposal that an impartial board of investigators be appointed to test the validity of his charges; and he requested that supporting proxies be sent to him for the next members' meeting. The IPR administration, not to be outdone, also requested proxies with which to fight "*any and all proposals made by Alfred Kohlberg.*" "For over two years," so read the administration's letter, "Mr. Alfred Kohlberg, a former member of the American Institute of Pacific Relations, and an importer with substantial business interests in China has been carrying on [his] ... campaign. ... The Executive Committee of the Board of Trustees *has investigated Mr. Kohlberg's charges,* and found them inaccurate and irresponsible."[101] (Italics added.) The letter was signed by Jessup and six other members of the Board of Trustees.

Kohlberg's request for an investigation was turned down by a vote of 1163 to 66.

Kohlberg clearly showed good faith in suggesting that an independent group adjudicate the issue. As for the assertion by Jessup and the IPR administration that the Executive Committee had already conducted an objective investigation (the ostensible reason for opposing an inquiry by outsiders), this excuse appears to have been far from the truth, as an excerpt from the McCarran Committee hearings indicates:

MR. MORRIS. Mr. Dennett, were you secretary of the American Council of the IPR when Alfred Kohlberg brought his charges that there was Communist influence in the Institute?

MR. DENNETT. I was. ...

MR. MORRIS. Mr. Dennett, was there ever any thorough investigation made of the so-called Kohlberg charges?

MR. DENNETT. I would say "no." I would say an answer was prepared, which is somewhat different.

Mr. Morris. Who prepared the answer?

Mr. Dennett. Marguerite Ann Stewart.*

Mr. Morris. Did she make any objective investigation of the so-called charges?

Mr. Dennett. I am not really in a position to judge that, Mr. Morris. I would be inclined to think not.

Tydings investigators could easily have got hold of the facts of the Kohlberg controversy and of Jessup's part in blocking an objective investigation of the IPR. Instead, they chose to authenticate the version of the incident that nervous IPR apologists were then telling to anyone who would listen. The facts, of course, would have gotten in the way of exonerating Jessup.

To McCarthy's charge that Jessup in 1946 urged the United States to stop its atom bomb production, the Tydings Committee retorted: *"Dr. Jessup admitted signing the letter of February 16, 1946, which appeared in the New York Times, and stated that among the signers were prominent professors who were leading physicists working on atomic energy. Dr. Jessup testified that the letter was a conscientious effort to make a useful suggestion with respect to control of the atom bomb through the United Nations. He added that in view of the changed attitude of the Soviet Union and its failure to cooperate with free peoples, the proposal is no longer applicable, and that his views have changed completely."*[102]

This seems to be a fair treatment of the episode in question. Jessup's atom bomb proposal has a probative value of exactly zero as regards his political orientation. For, besides Jessup's affinity for Communist causes (of which halting U.S. atom bomb production was certainly one), we must also reckon with Jessup's infinite capacity for reading the future wrong and arriving at unwise judgments—a capacity he shares with some of the most impeccable American patriots.

Finally, McCarthy charged that Jessup had supported Alger Hiss even after his conviction. The Tydings Committee was right in saying that McCarthy's statement ("Jessup said he can see 'no reason' . . . to change his opinion about Hiss' veracity, loyalty and

---

* Dennett's testimony that Mrs. Stewart prepared the answer to Kohlberg's charges is contested by Messrs. Holland and Carter, who claim she merely edited the staff report—that is, a report by the very same staff that was the primary object of Mr. Kohlberg's accusation! See *McCarran Hearings*, pp. 5345, 5366.

integrity") was inaccurate and misleading.[103] The following testimony appears to have been all that McCarthy had to go on:

SENATOR HICKENLOOPER. Are you of the same opinion about Mr. Hiss that you were when you testified as a character witness for him at his trial?

AMBASSADOR JESSUP. The testimony which I gave in his trial, sir, as you properly pointed out, was as a character witness, in which I testified to the reputation. I see no reason to alter the statements which I made under oath as a witness in that case.[104]

Assuming the above was his reference, there is no excuse for McCarthy's having read into Jessup's words the meaning he attributed to them. As a lawyer, McCarthy must know that the function of the character witness is not to testify as to his own opinion, but to the "opinion of the community"—i.e., to the general reputation of the accused. And the fact that Hiss had fooled his associates so completely as to win for himself an excellent reputation has been confirmed by many persons who had even more opportunities than Jessup to penetrate Hiss' disguise. And Hiss' conviction has nothing to do with his reputation at the time Jessup knew him.

Before we turn to an evaluation of the "Jessup case" as a whole, we should examine one more incident in Jessup's career, namely, the notorious State Department Policy Conference of October 1949 over which Jessup presided.* Jessup's activities in connection with it certainly cannot be taken as proof of disloyalty to the United States; but they do have some bearing on the question whether he was fit for government service "beyond a reasonable doubt."

As chief advisor to Acheson, Jessup personally arranged the conference—ostensibly a gathering of non-government Far-Eastern experts held for the purpose of eliciting their advice on Pacific and Asiatic policy. Some of the persons present had a sound claim to the title of expert on the Far East; but some of them did not; and many conspicuous experts were missing. Their absence has yet to be explained by Jessup or his defenders.

Explanations from other quarters, however, have not been wanting; and they all point in one and the same direction. Mr. Harold

* The conference was mentioned in McCarthy's case against Lattimore; which means that at the time the Tydings Committee was sitting, zealous investigators could have uncovered the story, including Jessup's role in it.

Stassen, who was there, testified[105] how he saw from the first that a decisive majority of those present held quite similar views on policy, views, moreover, that he (Stassen) did not share—his implication being, of course, that the persons constituting a decisive majority had not got there by accident. Stassen noted further that the principal spokesmen of the "prevailing group" were Owen Lattimore and Lawrence Rosinger (both of whom have been named under oath as members of the Communist Party).* The Lattimore-Rosinger "plan," as Stassen recorded it in his notes, covered ten points:

1. Europe should be given priority over Asia.
2. Aid to Asia should not be started until after a "long and careful study."
3. Russian Communists should be viewed as "not as aggressive as Hitler" and as "not apt to take direct military action to expand their empire."
4. Communist China should be recognized by the U.S.
5. Britain and India should be urged to follow suit in recognizing the Chinese Communists.
6. The Chinese Communists should be allowed to take over Formosa.
7. The Communists should be allowed to have Hong Kong "if they insisted."
8. Nehru should not be given aid because of his "reactionary and arbitrary tendencies."
9. The Nationalist "blockade" of China should be broken and economic aid sent to the Communist mainland.
10. No aid should be sent to Chiang or to the anti-Communist guerillas in South China.[107]

Stassen's report of Lattimore's and Rosinger's views is supported by the memoranda the two men drew up in preparation for the conference.[108] Moreover, the official transcript of the conference proceedings clearly shows that a substantial majority of those present approved their program, more or less as Stassen had set it forth.[109] The McCarran Committee, on the basis of the transcript, summarized the results of the conference as follows: ". . . the prevailing [majority] view at the conference advocated (a) the recognition of Communist China; (b) normal trade relations between the United States and Communist China; (c) encouragement of trade

* Lattimore by Louis Budenz; Rosinger by Budenz, Karl Wittfogel, and William Canning.[106]

between Japan and Communist China; (d) economic assistance to Communist China; (e) recognition that Communist conquest in Asia was a natural and inevitable consequence of revolutionary ferment in Asia with its Communist nature being incidental."[110]

There are grounds, quite aside from the fact of his having chosen the experts, for believing that Jessup shared Lattimore's and Rosinger's views. Stassen reports that between sessions he repeatedly urged Jessup to reject the advice of the Lattimore-Rosinger group, only to be told that the "greater logic was on their side."[111] And General Joseph Fortier, Chief of General MacArthur's Intelligence Staff, has testified that Jessup, while on an official mission to Japan in early January, 1950, told him that United States recognition of Communist China was due in "about 2 or 3 weeks," and that he (Jessup) personally was in favor of it.[112] (Jessup has denied Stassen's and Fortier's statements of his position.)

Yet far more informative on the matter of Jessup's political orientation than what he may or may not have said is the fact that the 1949 conference was his personal enterprise; and that the participants were, to a man, personal acquaintances of Jessup. *Every one of the 25 participants was a past member of the IPR, and seventeen of them were still active in it.* Jessup must therefore have known beforehand which faction in the conference would carry the day; and thus, which ideas would be pressed upon those responsible for American foreign policy.

Now there is nothing particularly sinister about one IPR old boy inviting the gang down to Washington to do in direct fashion what it had been doing behind the scenes for many years. But the fact that in 1949 Jessup was still turning to the IPR for advice surely seals the case against his statecraft, and leaves him on the defensive as regards more serious charges. For here was a man presiding over the wake of Free China and calling upon accomplices to her murder for suggestions as to which would be the most suitable funeral arrangements.

Let us now attempt to answer the questions posed at the beginning of this chapter: Is there evidence here of dereliction on the part of State Department security officials? Was McCarthy justified in raising the loyalty issue in Jessup's case? Did the Tydings Committee, in this instance, go into McCarthy's charges competently and impartially?

The Tydings "investigation" of Jessup was, any way you look at it, a fraud. Even if it had done the rest of its work well (which it did not), this phase of its inquiry should have discredited it in everyone's eyes.

The Committee's task was roughly similar to that of a Grand Jury. A Grand Jury is asked to make a preliminary determination as to whether sufficient grounds exist for indicting an individual. The Tydings Committee was asked to weigh all the evidence on persons "against whom charges [of disloyalty] have been made" and to report its findings to the Senate. This it certainly failed to do in the Jessup episode, where its preoccupation with clearing the State Department and discrediting Senator McCarthy was particularly obsessive and where, therefore, it ignored, with consummate arrogance and astonishing self-assurance, any evidence that tended to get in the way of the realization of these objectives.

What of Senator McCarthy's role in the Jessup case? McCarthy went no farther than to label Jessup a man with an "unusual affinity for Communist causes." This label, in our opinion, was fully justified by the evidence—all readily available. What *else* can we conclude about a man of proven intellectual stature who belonged to Communist fronts; who helped to frustrate an investigation of Communism in the IPR; who spoke approvingly of the American Peace Mobilization; who relied upon the "guidance" of Frederick Vanderbilt Field; who accepted, on behalf of his organization, money from Field; who associated closely with a number of Communists over a period of years; and who allowed an organization in which he had great influence to become an instrument of Communist propaganda? Certainly not that such activity is "usual" or that it does not amount to making, wittingly, or unwittingly, common cause with Communism.

But, someone may say, to accuse a man of an affinity for Communist causes, in context of the loyalty investigation, is, in effect, to call him disloyal or, at least, a loyalty risk. But, surely, we must not put words in McCarthy's mouth. Nor should we read into Resolution 231 more than the Senate put there; or if we do, we must not hold McCarthy responsible for doing so. *Jessup, simply, was one of the individuals whose cases, McCarthy thought, should be examined in an "investigation as to whether persons who are disloyal to the United States are . . . employed by the Department of State."* In other words, McCarthy made it clear he thought Jessup's loyalty was worth *looking into,* but he withheld—and with-holds to this day—any personal judgment as to what the results of such investigation would be.

Was McCarthy justified in pointing to Jessup's case as one that wanted looking into? In our opinion, he was, and we reject the premise that underlies the objections to this phase of McCarthy's behavior; namely, the premise that certain citizens occupying positions of respect in the community are by definition not par-ticipants in the Communist conspiracy, and that no one must sug-gest they may be unless he has the real goods on them. This is an age of surprises, and at our peril we neglect the meaning of the few revelations as to the dimensions of the conspiracy that providence has granted us. In this age, the beginning of political wisdom is to learn the lesson of the Hiss case. And when McCarthy spoke up, Jessup's case was a good deal more suspicious than Alger Hiss' had been when, two years earlier, Whittaker Chambers appeared in a dusky chamber of the House Office Building and said softly but resolutely that he had known Alger Hiss as a member of the Communist underground.

Jessup's pronouncements, as a diplomat, had been vigorously anti-Communist; yet his record is barren of any conspicuous af-front to the Communist cause before he became an official spokes-man for the government and had to make such pronouncements in the line of duty. Jessup's admirers frequently remind us that we are dealing with a noted scholar, wise in international affairs—forgetting that precisely this conversance with the world we live in, and the tensions that threaten to pull it apart, taxes the thesis that every time Jessup lent himself to a Communist cause he did so because he was "duped." To be sure, Jessup was an America Firster and remained one until Pearl Harbor; but he was concur-rently involved with pro-Communist organizations, and his re-maining with America First after July of 1941 *may* have been pro-tective coloration.

The essence of Jessup's record is that he was not unsympathetic either to Communists or to their policies from 1939 to 1944. This is not to assert that Jessup's allegiance was to the Soviet Union dur-ing this period. But if today's security standard had governed eligibility for State Department employment in 1944, and if Jessup had been screened under it then, the Department's security office would have had to disqualify him *as a security risk.*

This brings us to the third question: was the Jessup case evidence of dereliction on the part of the State Department security officials in 1950? Jessup's past record was sufficient reason for asking the Tydings Committee to inquire into his loyalty. But it does not follow that he was a loyalty risk as of 1950. In our opinion, the evidence turned up as a result of McCarthy's leads was not sufficiently incriminating to justify such a finding. It was not incriminating enough to rebut the "presumption of innocence";* and this presumption was fortified by Jessup's consistent anti-Communist statements after 1946.

Yet this is not to say the State Department's security division was on the job.

In 1950, on the basis of the evidence now available, Jessup may not have been a loyalty risk. But the only way to find this out was to explore the questions raised by McCarthy. If the Department had not gone into these questions, it stands indicted under the same test it failed to pass in the case of Dorothy Kenyon. And whether or not the Department had investigated Jessup at all the Tydings Investigating Committee did not even try to find out.

In fine: it is our judgment that under the prevailing understanding of the reasonable doubt standard Jessup was not a security risk in 1950. It remains to be said that given a security program of the sort we did not have in 1950, and do not yet have—that is one that does not in effect invite an adjudication as to whether an employee is "innocent" or "guilty"—Jessup would have been disqualified for duty with a sensitive agency of government, even in 1950. The sort of program that is required by the exigencies of the day we discuss in a later chapter; let us note here simply that it would eliminate the Jessups. It would operate without reference to a "presumption of innocence"; and thus would permit a comparatively cold-hearted evaluation of Jessup's past contributions to Communist causes. Moreover, it would encourage security officers to take a skeptical view of Jessup's anti-Communist pronouncements as a diplomat in the late 'forties *as long as he persisted in his explicit refusal to acknowledge that during the late 'thirties and early forties he had contributed, actively and passively, to the Communist cause.* For this would emerge as the crucial consideration in determining Jessup's fitness under such a program. Not because it is im-

---

* The presumption of innocence in the particular sense we use it here is discussed at some length above, in the section on Haldore Hanson, and again below, in Chapter XII.

portant to extract abject self-denunciations from the dupes of yes-
teryear, but because the absence of such self-denunciations can,
and definitely does in Jessup's case, raise questions of credibility.
And because it indicates an intransigent spirit and an invincible ignorance about the nature of Communism which the government
cannot indulge its lieutenants in time of war. Under an effective
security program Philip Jessup would be quietly but firmly removed from the combat areas, and sent back to his books. Happily,
this is where he has gone.

The Case of Esther Brunauer

ESTHER CAUKIN BRUNAUER was at the time of the Tydings hearings Assistant Director of Policy Liaison of the UNESCO Relations Staff of the Department of State. She had served the Department in various capacities, including a tour of duty as Division Assistant in the Department's critical Division of Internal Security.[113]

"I think," McCarthy told the Committee, "this definitely should be the very first case [you investigate]."[114] Undoubtedly McCarthy considered the Brunauer case to be explosive ("This is one of the most fantastic cases I know of");[115] but we should note at the outset that he took as his primary theme—more explicitly than in any other case—*the need for further investigation*. Except for venturing, on one occasion, the further opinion that Mrs. Brunauer was not a "dupe,"[116] he simply relayed the information in his possession, invited the Committee to uncover such further facts as it could, and to draw its own conclusions. In spite of their anxiety to keep the American people informed about his methods, McCarthy's critics have had little or nothing to say about the statement—in our opinion a model of senatorial sobriety and restraint—to which his testimony in the Brunauer case was geared: *"I urgently request that this committee give serious consideration to the details of this case and act immediately to ascertain the facts."*[117]

Were, however, McCarthy's data sufficiently unfavorable to Mrs. Brunauer to warrant a full-fledged investigation? We propose to canvass the implications of each item of evidence, including both McCarthy's statements and Mrs. Brunauer's comments; and, where possible, to take note of the Committee's reaction to each.

The Brunauer case had been No. 47 in McCarthy's Senate speech of February 20. The information about Mrs. Brunauer which he disclosed at the time (and which he repeated for the benefit of the Tydings Committee) was taken from the so-called "Lee Report" of 1948.* An excerpt from the Brunauer file, as prepared by the investigators of the House Committee on Appropriations follows:

A CSA [State Department Security Agency] report on August 15, 1947, indicated as a result of contact with seven associates and former

* The Lee Report is discussed below in the chapter, "Warmed-Over Charges."

supervisors of subject that she reportedly was a Liberal. Her husband, according to the informants, has a highly confidential position with the Navy Department and was possibly present at the Bikini Atom Bomb test.

The House Un-American Activities Committee advised [the Department security division] on August 18, 1947, [that] X-9, an admitted former Communist Party member, was formerly associated with the subject in Communist Party activities in Washington, D. C. Interview with this informant by the CSA Agent indicated that the subject's husband had admitted to him in 1929 or 1930 that he was a member of the Communist Party in Baltimore, Maryland. The informant also advised that the subject had associated with a group of known Communists. The informant said he had not seen the subject in over ten years.

On July 16, 1947 it was ascertained that, in 1941, a Senate Investigating Committee had stated the subject and her husband were members of the Communist Party. On September 15, 1947, a Government Investigative agency advised that early in 1941 a reliable informant reported the subject as a Communist. Further, that the subject had been recently contacting a subject of a Soviet Espionage case. [Italics added.]

This investigation is in a pending status.[118]

The significance of this file information to a committee investigating the State Department is self-evident. For the adverse data, *as long as they were not discredited,* certainly added up to a presumption that Mrs. Brunauer should have been declared a security risk under the "reasonable doubt" standard; and that the agency that had failed so to declare her was sleeping on the security problem.

But the Committee did not see it that way. Its only reference to the file summary in its Report is the caustic and totally irrelevant observation: "The allegation taken from the Government report of July 16, 1947, was obviously lifted verbatim from the case memoranda from among the so-called 108 list of the subcommittee of the House Appropriations Committee of the Eightieth Congress which list was based on State Department loyalty files." "We have," the Report says, "of course, reviewed the entire loyalty file of Mrs. Brunauer."[119] Presumably, the Committee intended this enigmatic remark to suggest to its readers that the complete files had not borne out the House Committee's summary of them; or, failing this, that the derogatory information in the summary had been satisfactorily explained away. But precisely the opposite inference is in order. For, if the Committee had found that, for example, X-9 and the other "reliable informant" referred to in the summary, are deranged mischief-makers who busy themselves besmirching the reputations of Liberals, it most certainly would have brought this out. We know enough about the Committee to be sure that it was in no mood to pass up any such opportunity to make McCarthy look bad. Thus, the presumption is that the Committee simply wished this item away.

In addition to the file information, McCarthy presented new evidence purporting to show that Mrs. Brunauer had engaged in Communist front activity:

1. Mrs. Brunauer [McCarthy said] was for many years Executive Secretary of the American Association of University Women. . . . Mrs. Brunauer was instrumental in committing this organization to the support of various front enterprises, particularly in the so-called consumer field. One such instance of this activity was reported in the *New York Times* of April 27, 1943. In that case, The American Association of University Women joined with the Consumers Union, the League of Women Shoppers, and other completely communist-controlled fronts.[120]

Actually, however, the *Times* article in question shows that the AAUW merely joined with 15 other organizations, only two of them Communist fronts, in urging grade-labelling of canned goods in order to implement price control regulations governing such foods.[121] Moreover, the AAUW (not itself a Communist front) promptly informed the Committee that Mrs. Brunauer had never been its "executive secretary" (she had been "international relations secretary" and, later, "associate in international education"), and that she "at no time . . . [had] any connection with the association's consumer program."[122] Here, pretty clearly, McCarthy hadn't a leg to stand on: not only was he in no position to prove that the combine the AAUW had joined was in any sense a Communist front, he also had no evidence that Mrs. Brunauer had in fact been "instrumental" in committing it to the combine.

2. Exhibit 21 indicates that Mrs. Brunauer presided at a Washington meeting of the American Friends of the Soviet Union [in 1936]. The principal speaker at this meeting was Myra Page, long an avowed leader of the Communist Party and frequent writer for the Daily Worker and other Communist periodicals.[123]

Here McCarthy came off a great deal better. For Mrs. Brunauer acknowledged, in her prepared statement to the committee, that she had indeed presided at the meeting in question and later, under

cross-examination by Senator Hickenlooper, she further acknowledged that she had addressed a similar meeting in 1934. Her explanation, moreover, was not altogether satisfactory: "... [It] was
part of my job [as associate in international education with the
AAUW]," Mrs. Brunauer testified, "to attend and preside on occasions at meetings of numerous organizations in this field. In 1936,
the attitude of most Americans toward the Soviet Union was friendly and hopeful. I had no way of ascertaining then that the organization . . . would at some later time be declared subversive. I was
never a member of that organization, and it was not considered
reprehensible or a sign of disloyalty for American citizens to attend
lectures on conditions in Soviet Russia, even if made by Soviet
sympathizers."[124]

The Committee's report on this aspect of the case was, it will be
seen, simply a paraphrase of Mrs. Brunauer's own verbal testimony.
She had, the Committee reported, "attended" two meetings of the
Friends of the Soviet Union, but each "for perfectly legitimate
motives. . . . [No] inference of Communist sympathies can be
raised therefrom."[125] What this proves, more than anything else, is
that the Committee had not studied the extensive literature on the
Friends of the Soviet Union, prepared by various legislative Committees.* These findings make it abundantly clear that the organization was, from its founding in 1921, among the most notorious
as well as the most important Communist groups in the United
States. (It was succeeded during the Hitler-Stalin pact by the
National Council for American-Soviet Friendship.) They make
it virtually impossible *not* to draw an "inference of Communist
sympathies" from the facts about Mrs. Brunauer which the Committee had before it.

3. Exhibit 22 shows Esther Brunauer was a signer of the call to the
annual meeting of the American Youth Congress of 1938.* *[126]

Mrs. Brunauer did not deny having signed the call in question,
but stated that she had been joined in doing so by a number of "irreproachables," among them a spate of U.S. Senators, Representatives, and Governors. "My recollection of this call," she testified,

---

* See *Special Committee on Un-American Activities, Report,* January 3,
1939, p. 78; *California Committee on Un-American Activities Report,* 1948,
pp. 65, 244, 321; *Massachusetts House Committee on Un-American Activities Report,* 1938, pp. 77 and 129.

** July 1–5, *1939*, is the correct date for this meeting of the AYC.

"is that it represented an attempt of the liberals to capture the leadership of the American youth organizations. The fact that the American Youth Congress had been cited by the Attorney General as a subversive organization is an indication that we failed, but if we are to be criticized it is perhaps because we are not active and aggressive enough to succeed, but at least we tried."[127] Mrs. Brunauer did not, however, present any evidence that she had fought against or denounced the Communist leadership of the AYC at that time, or later.

The Committee reported: ". . . the announced principles of the meeting were entirely proper and the list of the signers *conclusively refutes* an implication of Communist sympathy because of this act. *In addition, there is no evidence before the sub-committee that this particular meeting was under the domination of the American Youth Congress, as alleged.*"[128] (Italics added.)

This statement is unwarranted on two counts. The isolated act of sponsoring this particular congress is, indeed, not very persuasive evidence of Communist sympathies; for, notwithstanding its blatant Communist history, the AYC had at that time managed to inveigle persons of every political coloration—most notably political bigwigs*—into endorsing its "calls." But the Committee's talk here about "conclusive refutation" is a thin piece of nonsense. The respectability of one's fellow-signers is, at most, a factor to be weighed in appraising a front affiliation, and in some situations it weighs less heavily than in others. Here, for example, we must be wary of thinking that a Senator with a natural appetite for publicity will have the same motives for sponsoring a nationally known organization, as, say, an Esther Brunauer, who, we may assume, is more interested in helping the organization than in getting helped by it.

With its further statement that it had "no evidence that this particular meeting [The Congress of Youth] was under the domination of the American Youth Congress," the Committee only proved its incompetence. The Congress of Youth *was* the American Youth Congress—same people, same program, same organization. Indeed, the official report issued by the 1939 Congress is a part of the Tydings Committee's record, and therein, under a list of the officers elected "at this particular meeting" is the statement:

---

* For example, Senators Capper, Logan, Murray and Wagner; Cabinet members Ickes and Farley. Mrs. Roosevelt supported the AYC even after it endorsed Stalin's somersault of August, 1939.

"Elected officers listed above constitute the Cabinet of the American Youth Congress"![129] (Italics ours.)

4. Esther Caukin Brunauer was very active in launching an organization called the American Union for Concerted Peace Efforts. . . . [The AUCPE] was cited as a Communist-front organization, the leader of which was the editor of the Daily Worker. [130]

Mrs. Brunauer admitted that she had been active in the American Union for Concerted Peace Efforts; indeed, she was "proud of the fact." Hotly denying it was a front, she pointed out that the Union had favored collective security before and after the Hitler-Stalin pact, and was the predecessor of the (William Allen White) Committee to Defend America by Aiding the Allies.[131]

Neither the Tydings Committee nor McCarthy handled this point creditably. The Committee, surprisingly, found here the only evidence of Mrs. Brunauer's membership in a Communist front. It stated, quite rightly, that Mrs. Brunauer had been a member of the *Committee for Concerted Peace Efforts*, which after three months became the American Union for Concerted Peace Efforts (the organization mentioned by McCarthy). But it went on to imply that the CCPE was a Communist front. The Committee made this mistake because it misinterpreted a reference to the CCPE in the files of the House Committee on Un-American Activities.[132] The House Committee had *not* cited the CCPE—or the AUCPE—as a Communist front.

McCarthy had made a different mistake. He had confused the AUCPE with (if the reader can stand it) a *third* organization, the Union of Concerted Peace Efforts, which *had* been cited as a Communist front, "a leader of which was Clarence Hathaway, then editor of the Daily Worker."[133] There is no evidence that Mrs. Brunauer was ever affiliated with this group.

So much for McCarthy's allegations concerning Mrs. Brunauer's front activity.

McCarthy also told the Committee,

[T]his woman, Esther Caukin Brunauer . . . was the first assistant to Alger Hiss in the San Francisco Conference. This is set forth in her biographical sketch issued by the State Department.[134]

Yet the State Department register does not show that Mrs. Brunauer was Hiss' first assistant; and no other documentary evidence has come to light to support McCarthy's statement, which must accordingly be set down as unfounded.

One further question came up regarding Mrs. Brunauer's activities while representing the State Department at an international conference. Senator Hickenlooper asked Mrs. Brunauer whether she or her husband had been visited by "the Communist member of the Hungarian Delegation to UNESCO" on his way back from UNESCO's Mexico City Conference of December, 1947.[135] Yes, she said, she and her husband had received such a visit; and, if the Committee cared to listen, here was how it all came about:

While attending the Mexican Conference, she said, she had been invited to lunch by a Mr. Ferenczi, who was a member of the delegation from Communist Hungary. Ferenczi, it turned out, wanted to know whether Hungary could expect to receive "education reconstruction aid" from the United States. "I gave him no encouragement whatever," Mrs. Brunauer told the Committee. She went on to say that Ferenczi then changed his tack. En route back to Hungary, he proposed he stop in Washington to see *Stephen* Brunauer and discuss with him aid for Hungary's "scientific institutions" from the Rockefeller Foundation, with which Mrs. Brunauer was associated. Ferenczi had claimed to have letters of introduction from "two or three people . . . whom my husband knew as anti-Communist." But when he arrived in Washington he had "lost" his letters. He nevertheless saw Mr. Brunauer and put to him the question of Rockefeller aid for Hungary. "My husband said that under the circumstances [the existence of a Communist regime in Hungary] he could not do anything about it."

Sometime later, Mrs. Brunauer continued, Ferenczi and a Mr. Florian, a member of the Hungarian Legation who was subsequently ordered to leave the U.S., "discussed very seriously the possibility . . . as a matter of something that they could use as revenge on my husband, of revealing to the public my husband's long ago Communist connection." But they were "dissuaded" from harassing Brunauer by another member of the Legation who raised "the point that when a man had worked hard and achieved as much as my husband had done, there was no reason, and it was unfair, to bring up something that existed long ago in his past, and that had no influence whatever on his present life—quite the contrary."[136]

Mrs. Brunauer's account of the Ferenczi incident left several questions to be answered. Why had a Communist diplomat sin-

gled the Brunauers out in the first place? Mrs. Brunauer intimated
it was because, Hungary being her husband's native land, they
were well acquainted with Hungarians in Washington, most particularly with the diplomatic representative of the pre-1947, anti-
Communist regime.[137] But if the Brunauers were well known for
their sympathies with the *ancien* regime, why would representatives of the *Communist* regime turn to them for help? And again,
are we to believe that two Communist diplomats were swerved
from their purpose by being reminded that persecution of a Party
apostate was "unfair"?

The Committee did not see fit to pursue any of these lines of
inquiry. Its Report noted, perfunctorily, the salient points of Mrs.
Brunauer's testimony about Ferenczi, and let it go at that.[138]

The Committee also refused to pursue a line of inquiry suggested by Senator McCarthy in his concluding remarks on the
Brunauer case:

I ask that the Committee immediately seek to learn whether or not
Stephen Brunauer had: 1. Been the subject of a constant investigation
by government agencies over a period of 10 years. 2. [Been] a close
friend and collaborator of Noel Field, known Communist who recently
and mysteriously disappeared behind the iron curtain. 3. . . . recently
admitted to associates that he was [had been?] a member of the Communist Party.[139]

To be sure, it was Mrs. Brunauer, not her husband, who was an
employee of the State Department; and thus it was only she who
fell within the scope of the investigation authorized by the Senate.
But McCarthy was invoking the principle of "security risk by association"—quite legitimately, in our opinion: if persons with whom
an employee is in "habitual or close association"* are Communists
or Communist sympathizers, then these facts are pertinent in determining security reliability. Stephen Brunauer's sympathies were
therefore relevant; more so since Mrs. Brunauer had testified that
"on matters of this sort my husband and I see completely eye to
eye, and inform each other completely."[140]

The Committee, nevertheless, did not subpoena Mr. Brunauer.
But it did hear Mrs. Brunauer testify about her husband:

He dropped out of the Young Workers League early in 1927 and has
not been a member of any Communist group since that time . . . The

* As the State Department's own security regulations put it.

Young Workers League was organized and run by the Communist Party. There is no attempt to deny that my husband for a short time supported the Communist ideals.[141]

With respect to her own political ideals, Mrs. Brunauer stated:

I am a loyal American. I am not a Communist and never have been a Communist. I have never engaged in Communist activities. I am not a Communist sympathizer and have never been a Communist sympathizer. I do not have, and never have had, any sympathy for any doctrine which conflicts with the basic principles of our American democracy. I support the President's loyalty program and have been cleared under that program.[142]

Whereupon she handed the Committee a batch of supporting letters, headed by tributes from Dr. Milton Eisenhower and former Senator Joseph Ball, which the Committee cited as one reason for clearing her.[143]

McCarthy's evidence against Esther Brunauer—aside from the data he cited from her loyalty file—must be set down as weak and inconclusive. But this is not to say that McCarthy should not have *raised the question* of Mrs. Brunauer's reliability—or of her "loyalty," if you will. He was justified in bringing her name to the attention of the Committee even if there had been nothing against her save that *"a reliable informant" had testified in 1941 that he had known her to be a member of the Communist Party.* This datum alone made it not only his right but his duty to do so. For McCarthy's task, we must remember, was to hand over to the investigating committee information he possessed about persons whose loyalty or reliability he thought should be *looked into.* And as long as the adverse information in her loyalty file stood unrebutted, Mrs. Brunauer was worth looking into. Her file was *prima facie* evidence that the Department's security precautions were inadequate: any such case required immediate investigation as a matter of course.

Should the Committee, then, have declared Mrs. Brunauer a security risk? No. In the absence of further investigation, the Committee was in no position to find either that she was or that she was not a security risk. Though the unrebutted loyalty file data were sufficiently grave to constitute a *prima facie* case against her, they also required further careful inquiry into their authenticity. Just what conscientious investigators would have uncovered, had they undertaken an investigation, no one save possibly the FBI and the State Department security officers can say. What *can* be asserted, however, is that the Tydings Committee undertook no investigation at all. It accepted at face value Mrs. Brunauer's own account of herself. It shrugged off not only the loyalty file matter, but also the Ferenczi affair and Mrs. Brunauer's involvement with the Friends of the Soviet Union. Instead of investigating, the Investigating Committee handed down an oracular clearance: "The conclusion is *inescapable,* on the basis of our inquiry, that there is no evidence that Mrs. Brunauer is disloyal, a Communist sympathizer *or a security risk.*"[144] (Italics added.)

There is an epilogue to the Brunauer case. A year after the Tydings Committee heard McCarthy's evidence against Mrs. Brunauer, the Navy Department announced that Stephen Brunauer had been suspended from his post as a chemist in the explosive research division—for security reasons. Brunauer resigned from the Navy before his case was adjudicated by the Navy's loyalty board. And Esther Brunauer was dismissed from the State Department as a security risk on June 16, 1952—two years after McCarthy suggested to the Committee that hers be the first case it investigate.

We may ask, then, whether the firing of Mrs. Brunauer in 1952 constitutes an indictment of State Department security practices in 1950. Security standards, we must remember, had not changed between 1950 and 1952. There is, of course, no way of knowing whether the evidence considered by the Loyalty Security Board in 1952 was identical with the evidence before the Board in 1950. If new data had been uncovered in the interim, then the reversal of the case in 1952 obviously cannot be cited as evidence that the Board was negligent in 1950. On the assumption that *no new data* came to light, two explanations for the Department's reversal on Mrs. Brunauer are commonly advanced. One of them—that the Department had decided to appease McCarthy—is implausible. For even after Mrs. Brunauer's suspension, General Conrad Snow, chairman of the State Department Loyalty Security Board, was making speeches around the country about "Demagog McCarthy," and State Department publicists continued to churn out their contempt for him—hardly evidence that State Department officials were intimidated by McCarthy. And anyway, the Department did not set out to fire other McCarthy targets. There must have been a reason, it would seem, for firing Mrs. Brunauer and not, say, Haldore Hanson. The other explanation, and this one seems to fit the circumstances, is that the agency which had in the past trumpeted its confidence in Mrs. Brunauer had begun, in 1952, to take a somewhat harder look at the nation's security requirements, and, on more mature reflection, decided that its earlier decision in the Brunauer case had, after all, not been in the national interest.

The Cases of Frederick Schuman and Harlow Shapley

ALTHOUGH McCarthy included them among his public cases, neither Frederick Schuman nor Harlow Shapley has ever worked for the State Department on a regular-employment basis. Both had been, at the time McCarthy discussed their fellow-travelling records, and are now, full-time professors at Williams and Harvard, respectively—their connection with the Department having been strictly extra-curricular.

Dr. Schuman had been a "consultant" to the Department, in the sense that that term is commonly but unofficially used to describe a private person asked on occasion to attend or to address policy conferences and training classes. The record shows only one instance when he actually served: in 1946 he lectured to Foreign Service officers under a program called "Orientation Conferences and Training Programs for Personnel of the Foreign Service and the Department of State." All but three of the fifty-seven instructors who participated in this particular orientation program were government officials—the interesting exceptions, besides Schuman, being Edward Acheson (Dean's brother) and Owen Lattimore.[145]

As for Dr. Shapley, he was for three years (1947-1950) a member of the United States National Commission for UNESCO (a State Department "job" in the sense that members are appointed by the Secretary of State, and compensated on a *per diem* basis by the Department).

Given the peripheral nature of Schuman's and Shapley's relations with the Department, it might seem that McCarthy's evidence against the two men, no matter how devastating it might be, could not add up to a serious indictment of the State Department's loyalty and security program. Yet this is very definitely not the case. The American people can be assumed to want a State Department security program that is choosy not merely as to whom the Department employs, but also whom it lets ride on its coat-tails. The investigators might have been entitled to point out, as they did, that the two cases did not come within a literal construction of Senate Resolution 231; but it is another question whether they should have omitted entirely a discussion of the cases. The question was (and remains): Did these two cases shed enough light on the larger issues involved in the Committee's study to warrant an investigation, as thorough as, say, that accorded McCarthy's activities at Wheeling, West Virginia?

Schuman and Shapley both boasted spectacular records of joining Communist fronts and supporting Communist causes. Read side by side, their cases suggest a personal contest between the two to see which of them could help the Soviet Union more while hanging on to his academic reputation.

Schuman's accomplishments were barely hinted at in McCarthy's testimony. McCarthy's documents showed him to have been affiliated with a mere twelve Communist fronts, eight of them on the Attorney General's list.[146] But the files of the House Committee on Un-American Activities show over fifty front citations after Schuman's name. Even so, McCarthy had enough to prove that Frederick Schuman was a fellow-traveler's fellow traveler, a Grand Master of the lodge. As far back as 1932, Schuman had signed up with the League of Professional Groups for Foster and Ford, which supported the Communist Party ticket in that year's elections.[147] He played along with the Popular Front movement of the 30's and, just nine days before the Hitler-Stalin Pact, signed one of the truly great documents in the anthology of party-lining. On August 14, 1939, four hundred "leading Americans" proclaimed that "reactionaries are attempting to split the democratic front. . . . With the aim of turning anti-Fascist feeling against the Soviet Union, they have encouraged the fantastic falsehood that the USSR and the totalitarian states are basically alike. . . . "[148]

Though Schuman seems to have had certain difficulties with the party-line after Hitler and Stalin signed their 1939 agreement,[149] he was a prominent rider on the pro-Soviet bandwagon during the war and after it. He joined numerous new Communist fronts, urged the presidential candidacy of Henry Wallace, and wrote learned apologetics for Stalin's regime. A typical Schuman value judgment, found in his book *Soviet Politics at Home and Abroad*, appeared just about the time the State Department enlisted him to help out with the orientation of Foreign Service officers: "The Russian adventure," Schuman wrote, "marks a long forward stride toward human mastery of man's fate. . . . "[150]

Harlow Shapley took up party-lining in a big way only after the outbreak of the European war in 1939—that is, *after* the Communists had ceased to employ the deceptive blandishments of Popular

Frontism. Once involved, however, Shapley achieved real distinction in that field. Unlike other fellow travelers who were sensitive to the company the Soviet Union was keeping in 1939–41, Shapley joined up with at least six Communist fronts during the German-Soviet honeymoon. By the time McCarthy presented his name to the Tydings Committee, Shapley had no less than twenty-one front-affiliations to his credit, eight of them with organizations proscribed by the Attorney General. McCarthy's documents also showed that Shapley had stayed on with at least ten fronts *after* they had been officially cited as subversive by one or more legislative investigating committees. Moreover, at least fourteen of the affiliations were active even after the cold war had begun in 1946.

Shapley attained his chief notoriety as chairman of the National Council of Arts, Sciences and Professions, the organization that in 1949 sponsored the "Waldorf Peace Conference." In open contempt of public opinion, now relatively informed and aroused on the Communist issue, Shapley insisted that the Stalinist extravaganza over which he presided was seeking "cultural understanding" between East and West. Senator McCarthy drew attention in his testimony to the irony of the fact that at the very moment the State Department was denouncing the Waldorf Conference as a "sounding board for Communist propaganda," it had on its payroll the Conference's chief organizer!

Both Schuman and Shapley refused to "dignify" McCarthy's charges by appearing before the Committee. Both professors wrote to Senator Tydings denying (1) that they were or had been employed by the State Department, and (2) that they had ever belonged to an organization they had known to be a Communist front. The second of these denials seems brash beyond compare in the light of the facts. To say that these two men are inaccurately labelled if called fellow travelers, one would have to take the position that *no one* can legitimately be called a fellow traveler. The public facts prove beyond dispute that, over the years, Frederick Schuman and Harlow Shapley have given expansive support to the policies of the Soviet Union.

Ought the Tydings Committee, then, to have advised the Senate and the American people about Schuman and Shapley?

The Committee was entitled to point out, as it did, that the two professors were not technically within the purview of its mandate. Schuman apparently was never paid by the Department; and though McCarthy implied that he was regularly used as a lecturer, he appears to have lectured only once. As for Shapley, the Committee correctly stated that his appointment by the Secretary of State was a routine confirmation of the recommendation of a private organization, as the law on the subject provides. However, Congress was on record as opposing the expenditure of government funds to pay the salary of anyone involved with a subversive organization. During the years when Shapley served with the National Commission for UNESCO and received compensation from the government, the prevailing understanding *in the State Department* was that a Rider to the Appropriations Act forbade the paying of funds to persons actively affiliated with any organization on the Attorney General's list. And Shapley, according to the evidence before the Tydings Committee, clearly was such a person.

The Committee, however, let the matter go with its comment on Schuman's and Shapley's employment status; and thus a significant piece of evidence that the State Department had been tolerant of pro-Communists went by the boards. Yet a responsible committee, with the issue before it whether or not the Department had maintained adequate loyalty and security precautions was, as McCarthy insisted, obligated to take cognizance of the Department's doing *any* business with Schuman and Shapley.

The Case of Gustavo Duran

GUSTAVO DURAN is a Spanish immigrant to the United States, a onetime employee of the State Department and, in recent years, a high ranking member of the United Nations Secretariat.* He came to McCarthy's notice because of his allegedly Communist activities as an officer of the Republican Army in the Spanish Civil War. These activities McCarthy regarded as sufficient to warrant the judgment that Duran was a "possible bad security risk."[151] Let us note that the only significance McCarthy attached to the Duran case was in the lessons to be learned from it about the Department's *past* (pre-1950) record in protecting itself against Communist infiltration.

The Tydings Committee seized upon the fact Duran had left his position as assistant to Spruille Braden in October 1946 as an excuse for not even discussing Duran. In flat violation of its mandate, it refused to go into the case at all—on the spurious grounds that his employment by the Department antedated President Truman's Loyalty Order. The Senate, let us remember, had directed it to ascertain whether disloyal persons "are *or have been* employed" by the State Department; and had not even mentioned the Loyalty Order, much less confined the Committee's investigation to the period following its promulgation.

Was Gustavo Duran a loyalty or security risk? If so, was evidence of this available to the State Department in 1946? If so, why was he cleared, and how did he subsequently get by in his UN post?

To begin with, Duran had been a target of Senate investigators long before McCarthy documented the case against him. The Senate Appropriations Committee, for example, questioned Secretary Byrnes about Duran in April, 1946, expressing grave concern over the employment in the State Department of a man who allegedly had been a member of the Communist secret police during the Spanish Civil War. Ah, Byrnes told them, but you're all mixed up.

---

* The State Department announced at the time of the Tydings Hearings that Duran was currently employed as Chief of the Cultural Activities Section of the Department of Social Affairs, United Nations. McCarthy, however, charged—and continued to charge—that his own "physical check" revealed that Duran was with the International Refugee Organization, "engaged in work having to do with screening refugees coming into this country."[152]

The Duran about whom the Senators have incriminating information, he said, is not the same Duran who is working in the State Department as an assistant to the Assistant Secretary, Mr. Spruille Braden; and taking Byrnes' word for it, the Senators let the matter drop. But some weeks later, members of the Committee were advised of a new intelligence report from the U.S. Military Attaché in Madrid[153] which (a) strengthened the charges against Duran, and (b) dispelled all doubt that the suspected Duran was the man then enjoying the intimate confidence of Mr. Braden. Senator Wherry promptly wrote to Byrnes requesting that he "immediately discharge Gustavo Duran"[154] but received no answer to his letter for several months. In September he finally heard from Assistant Secretary Donald Russell. There was no more talk about "mistaken identity"; there was, instead, news that "the Security Committee [has] recommended favorably on Duran ... and I have approved their recommendations. ... " "While I recognize," Russell's letter went on to say, "that the above conclusions are at variance with your own feelings, I have to do my duty as I see it. ... "[155] A few weeks later, Duran voluntarily resigned.

Senator McCarthy's evidence, presented some four years after these events, consisted exclusively of intelligence reports and other documents which had been in the State Department security officer's possession at the time they cleared Duran.* These documents reveal that U.S. intelligence officers became interested in Duran in 1943. At that time, Military Intelligence warned Spruille Braden, then our Ambassador to Cuba, that Gustavo Duran, a member of his staff, had been a Communist before emigrating from Spain. McCarthy quoted from Braden's answer to this warning, contained in a memorandum to the Military Attaché in Havana, of December 21, 1943:

Mr. Duran has now served as one of my immediate associates for more than a year. His work has been excellent and outstandingly useful to the United States Government. From my personal knowledge based on close association, Mr. Duran is not a Communist, but a liberal of the highest type.[156]

* These reports were also in the possession of *Time* magazine when it cited McCarthy's charges against Duran as an especially good example of McCarthy's mendacity (*Time*, October 22, 1951). Even so, *Time* told its readers that "Duran, never a Red, was definitely and clearly anti-Communist," implying that McCarthy's story was sheer fabrication. See "Time Marches on McCarthy," *American Mercury*, February, 1952.

A week later, Intelligence replied to Braden's rebuff, emphatically confirming what it had previously said about Duran's Communist record. The letter was written by Edward J. Ruff, U.S. Assistant Military Attaché in the Dominican Republic, and read as follows:

I cannot see . . . how our report can be branded as "absolutely incorrect." *Our only statement in the report on Duran is that he was a member of the Communist Party in Spain. From further reports received, this information can now be evaluated as A-1.* . . . I, myself, am convinced that Duran was a Communist and consider Ambassador Braden's statement that he is a "liberal of the highest type" to be a euphemism. . . . The Ambassador here is *inclined to concur in my report, but has asked that* [in view of Braden's attitude] *no further official correspondence on the subject be sent up.* Hence this personal letter from me.[157] [Italics added.]

In response to Braden's intervention, the heat was taken off Duran for the duration of the war. He moved to Washington with Braden when the latter became Assistant Secretary of State for Latin American Affairs.

McCarthy's next document was a confidential report dated June 4, 1946, from Colonel Wendall Johnson, Military Attaché to the American Embassy at Madrid, marked "for general use by any U.S. Intelligence Agency." Most of the information it contains, Colonel Johnson noted, had been furnished (on request) by the Spanish Intelligence Service. Duran, the Spanish Intelligence reported, went to Madrid sometime during the twenties. He then drifted for several years in various European capitals and eventually turned up in Paris as an agent of the Soviet Secret Service. "Upon [the] proclamation of the Spanish Republic," the report continues,

the "Porcelana" [as Duran was nicknamed] returned to Madrid. His identity papers indicated that he was the representative of Paramount Film Co. However, his true mission was service of the GPU. Duran was greatly successful in his activities due to the political protection he enjoyed. He soon became one of the leading members of the Youths of the Communist Party. . . . [After the Franco revolution began], he was one of the principal leaders of the popular militia created by the Communists . . . and soon became captain, major, and lieutenant colonel of the "Red" Army. . . . When the international brigades were brought into the Madrid and Aranjuez fronts, Gustavo Duran formed part of the High Russian General Staff with headquarters at Tarancon.[158]

Turning from Colonel Johnson's report, McCarthy produced testimony that Duran had been a regional chief of the SIM, the Spanish counterpart of the GPU. Duran's role in the SIM was described by Socialist Minister of Defense Indalicio Prieto in his pamphlet *Why and How I Left the Defense Ministry in the Intrigue of Russia in Spain,** the relevant passages of which McCarthy laid before the Committee. One of them:

Because of insistent pressure [from the Russians] I created the SIM. Regional chiefs of the SIM were designated, and they [apparently the Russians] proposed to me a certain Gustavo Duran for the Madrid zone. It was not concealed from me that the person proposed was a Communist. I knew this, but in spite of that, he was appointed by me.[160]

Prieto went on to say that Duran then usurped power by appointing agents in the Madrid organization without the authorization of his superiors (i.e., Prieto). "Some hundreds" of the appointees, says Prieto, "were Communists and only four or five were socialists. I faced an intolerable situation. . . ." Duran, a commissioned officer in the regular Spanish Army, was later gotten rid of by being sent to active duty in the field. Prieto concludes by saying that a Russian agent subsequently put heavy pressure on him to reinstate Duran in the SIM.[161]

So much for McCarthy's evidence.

Like all other persons publicly named by McCarthy, Duran was invited to appear before the Tydings Committee and answer the charges. Duran declined to do so, citing Article 100 in the UN Charter, which provides that members of the UN staff "shall refrain from any action which might reflect on their position as international officials responsible only to the organization."[162] But he did dispatch a lengthy memorandum to Senator Tydings in which he set forth his side of the matter. He was not, he said, and never had been a Communist. He had "never held any command in any international brigade." He had indeed been an officer in the Spanish regular army; and though he had been assigned to the SIM it was against his will. "I had a deeply rooted aversion toward the proposed type of activity." His "actual tenure of office" was "about

* Lest the title suggest to anyone a political confession designed to appease the Franco regime, note that Duran himself says this work was written by Prieto as a report to the Spanish Socialist Workers Party on August 9, 1938.[159]

two weeks," during which he had made a "few temporary appoint-
ments. . . . at the recommendation of the experts." After the war,
through the intervention of British and American diplomatic officials, he had been evacuated to England, and had proceeded from
there to the United States.[163]

By way of comment on McCarthy's documents, Duran described
the 1946 intelligence report from the U.S. Military Attaché in
Madrid as a "literal reproduction of a scurrilous attack on me published in the April 9, 1946, issue of the newspaper *Arriba,* which is
the mouthpiece of the Falange Party of Franco Spain. The article
. . . was part of the campaign of the Franco Government to counter
the disclosures that had been made by the United States State Department on the relations between Nazi Germany and Franco
Spain during the last World War. . . . The Franco Government,
which had paid no attention to me for seven years, suddenly undertook to make me an agent of Moscow and to smear my character in
the vilest possible way."[164]

As for Prieto's pamphlet, Duran went on to say, he had not even
heard of it until 1946, eight years after it was written. In the course
of these eight years, Prieto had been his house guest, and relations
between them had been "cordial." Upon first hearing of the report,
therefore, he had written to Prieto, demanding an "explanation,"
and had received the following statement in reply: "I have never
accused you of being *an agent of the Russian police* nor a *member
of the Comintern. . . .*"[165] (Italics added.) (Note that, even on Duran's showing, Prieto did *not* repudiate his pamphlet in which he
had simply stated that Duran was a "Communist" and that he had
appointed "hundreds of Communists" to the SIM.) In fine, Duran
dismissed the intelligence reports to Ambassador Braden as "merely repetitions of the charges that have been previously answered in
this memorandum."[166]

The gist of Duran's defense, then, was that he had been the victim of a calculated smear by the Franco Government. There are,
however, several difficulties here. For one thing, the 1943 U.S. intelligence report stating that Duran had been a Communist in
Spain was written at least three years before the Franco government (according to Duran) "suddenly undertook to make . . .
[him] an agent of Moscow." Secondly, there is Prieto's pamphlet
to corroborate vital points in the indictment allegedly concocted
by the Fascists eight years later. And Prieto's later "explanation"
to Duran does not retract a single one of the charges in the pamphlet.

But the central question in the context of the Tydings investigation was this: Had the State Department, at the time it cleared Duran in 1946, bothered to find out how accurate Colonel Johnson's information was? Or had it simply discounted it, perhaps to please Mr. Braden? The fact is that Duran was not suspended, pending an investigation of the adverse data, and that his clearance came down less than three months after the information was received (hardly enough time for a full investigation). It is difficult to avoid a suspicion, in short, that the State Department simply took Duran's word. The alternative hypothesis is one that reflects even less credit on the Department's security procedures: namely, that the Johnson Report *was* taken seriously but that Duran was kept on in spite of it.

The Department, naturally, must consider the possibility that foreign governments with which we have tense relations will use the facilities at their disposal to discredit Department employees known to be inimical to their interests (as Duran certainly was to Franco Spain's). But this does not justify security officers in dismissing unfavorable security information about an employee just because its source has reason to wish him ill. The State Department was obliged to look into the Johnson report with all possible care. Apparently it did not. And if it reacted much as Ambassador Braden did in 1943, when adverse information was brought to his attention, the Department was truant to its obligations.

This was, in effect, McCarthy's point throughout his testimony. "According to all existing rules, [the Johnson report] . . . called for Duran's immediate dismissal—*unless the facts were proved to be wrong.*"[167] (Italics added.) And again: "It would be interesting to know what, if any, investigation was made by State Department officials as to his conduct while in a responsible, confidential capacity in the Department."[168] Even the committee seemed to agree at first flush that the case would bear looking into. (Senator Tydings: "We will investigate the case. . . . ")[169] McCarthy also asked the Committee to find "who has gotten [Duran] . . . the important task of going to the UN." "I have received," McCarthy added, "a confidential report that Duran was recommended for his UN post by a member of the President's [Truman's] Cabinet."[170] Said Tydings: "Senator McCarthy, I would like to say that your . . . [request] that we should find out who got him the job in the United Nations . . . will be a part of our inquiry. We don't know who he is, whether innocent or guilty, but we will find out anyway."[171]

In spite of Tydings' pledge, the Committee failed to look into this or any other question raised by McCarthy's testimony. And this failure constitutes the gravest possible indictment of the Committee. McCarthy, to say the very least, had presented *prima facie* evidence of gross negligence on the part of Department security officials, involving, perhaps, the complicity of a Cabinet officer. Evidence existed that a highly situated employee had been cleared by the Department in 1946 while charges were outstanding which raised serious questions as to his loyalty, and that he was currently presiding over an important UN department. In short, the Committee had in hand a striking example of what McCarthy had been talking about these last months—the entrenched apathy of the State Department toward Communist infiltration. If the Committee hoped to impress the people that McCarthy's charges were a "fraud and a hoax," it would have to do some fancy footwork to divert attention from the implications of the Duran case. And with this in mind, it hit on the shabby expedient we noted above: "In view of the fact that [Duran's] . . . employment in the Department ceased before the loyalty program was instituted, we do not feel that a discussion of him is merited in the body of our report."[172]

The Case of John Stewart Service*

In the aftermath of the war, United States political and military influence, in effect, swung to the side of the Chinese Communists and helped to establish them in power. The overriding question at issue in the Service case was, quite simply: had Service helped to bring about that shift of U.S. foreign policy; and, if so, had he done it out of honest confusion or out of partisanship for Communists?

The Tydings Committee was determined to avoid this question. Why? Because its hearings took place at a moment when all but the incorrigibly naive were beginning to see that the shift in U.S. Far Eastern policy had been produced neither by chance, nor by the might and cunning of the USSR, nor by sheer blundering on our part; but, to some extent at least, by conspirational forces operating on the highest levels of the U.S. government.

The burden of McCarthy's charge was that Service was "one of the dozen top policy makers in the entire State Department Far Eastern Division"** and "part of the pro-Soviet group" which advocated that the United States overthrow Chiang Kai-shek "because the only hope of Asia was communism."[173] The charge rested mainly on Service's reports from China.

In his Report No. 40, of October 10, 1944, for example, Service had written the following comment on Chiang and the Kuomintang Government:

> We need not fear the collapse of the Kuomintang Government. . . . any new government under any other than the present reactionary control will be more cooperative and better able to mobilize the country. . . . The example of a democratic, non-imperialistic China will be much better counterpropaganda in Asia than the present regime. . . .

* For reasons given at the beginning of this section, we shall not present a blow-by-blow account of the Service case, or of the Lattimore case, which follows.

** McCarthy's charge related to a particular division (the Far Eastern) of the State Department. The Committee disposed of it with the remark that it is doubted whether "the *entire* State Department" (italics added) was in conspiracy with Service. It observed also, that at the time in question (1944-1945) Service was only a junior grade Foreign Service officer. The premise here, that the grade occupied by a man determines the extent of his influence on high policy is, of course, absurd: all available evidence supports McCarthy's argument here that the policy makers in the State Department lean heavily on the judgment of on-the-spot experts.

The key to stability must be a strong, unified China. This can be accomplished only in a democratic foundation. . . . Chiang's main supports are the most chauvinist elements in the country. . . . We need feel no ties of gratitude to Chiang. . . . We cannot hope to deal successfully with China without being hardboiled; secondly, we cannot hope to solve China's problems (which are now our problems) without consideration of the opposition forces, Communist, Provincial and Liberal. . . . It is impractical to seek Chinese unity without the use of the Communist forces. . . . *We should not be swayed by pleas of the danger of China's collapse. . . . There may be a period of some confusion, but the eventual gains of the Kuomintang's collapse will more than make up for this . . .*" [Italics added.]

The Tydings Committee denied, in effect, that this report revealed any pro-Communist bent on Service's part. But it did not really argue the questions it raised. Instead, it pontificated about the impropriety of "singling out" one report from a series of reports. It simply ignored what the report "singled out" uncontestedly proved: Service had urged that America should transfer its support to the Chinese Communists.[174]

Besides, the Committee's own record makes it clear that no matter *what* Service report might be "singled out," one was likely to find pro-Communist bias. Note the following excerpts, all available to the Committee: "This widespread popular support must, under the circumstance in which it has occurred, be considered a practical indication that the policies and methods of the Chinese Communists have a democratic character" (September 4, 1944). "The Communists have used their influence in a democratic way and to further democratic ends" (September 10, 1944.) *"Politically, any orientation which the Chinese Communists may once have had towards the Soviet Union seems to be a thing of the past. . . .* The Communists have worked to make their thinking and program realistically Chinese, and *they are carrying out democratic policies which they expect the United States to approve and sympathetically support"* (September 28, 1944). (Italics added.)

The most casual reading of these reports would convince an impartial observer that Service in fact recommended the "change of policy," which was one of McCarthy's charges. This, however, does not dispose of the possibility that Service, rather than entertain pro-Communist sentiments and a wish to serve the Communist cause, made his recommendation with the best of patriotic intentions. One must—so argues the defense—take into account the circumstances in which Service's reports were written.

The issue here seems to boil down to two questions: Are we retrospectively entitled, in view of Service's experience in China and his position as a U.S. official observer in the field, to demand of him an informed account of what was going on in China? And: Did his reports present an accurate picture of what was going on?

The answer to the first question is inescapable: Service was ideally situated to know whereof he spoke. He was a man of rare experience in China, having spent most of his life there; and, as the U.S. Government's accredited representative, he was in constant contact with the Nationalist and the Communist leaders. He was thus one of the few American officials in China (Owen Lattimore, Oliver Clubb and John Vincent being three others) whose *expertise* as American advisors on China was of the sort that evoked special confidence in their acuity and reliability.

The answer to the second question—did Service's reports present an accurate picture of what was going on?—depends on whether or not Communism in China *was* an indigenous democratic movement at the time Service said it was—or, to put the issue in a way that takes into account the Communists' talent for disguising their proximate objectives, it depends on whether Chinese Communism, at the time in question, really *looked* to seasoned experts on Chinese affairs like a democratic movement.

This second question, of course, is by no means so easy to answer as the first. Service's defenders are in position to say: "If Service's picture of the Chinese Communist movement was so obviously wrong, then other experienced observers of Chinese affairs would surely have been giving a different picture at that time. Give us some reference to the official and/or scholarly literature of the day that will produce a different picture, the one you now say to be the correct one—or else give up your point that Service must have deliberately lied."

And indeed, the China literature that "informed" this country in the forties predominantly supported Service's contentions. But no one who has read the McCarran Committee report has any reason to be surprised at that, for the Far East literature of the day was largely written by active participants in the cabal surrounding Owen Lattimore. Moreover, the whole argument ("everybody was saying it, so why deny that Service could honestly have believed it?") is a logical trick calculated to transfer the burden of proof from where it belongs, on Service, to where it does not belong, on Service's accusers. For the relevant question is not, What did the Far East literature of that time say about the Far Eastern situation of that time; but rather, What does the competent Far East literature, of today, no longer monopolized by Lattimore *et al.* show to have been the Far East reality of the forties. And that literature does *not* say that China, when Service wrote his reports, looked as he said she looked. It does *not* say that the Chinese Communist movement, *after* the Service reports were written, underwent a sea-change, ceasing to be what Service then said it was and becoming what we know it to be. The reliable literature says it then *was* what we know it to be now. Thus the presumption must be that Service misrepresented what he was seeing. For all agree that he is a sane man with his wits about him.

This being the case, why did he not report what he saw? What were his motives? One possible explanation is that he was trying to sell the Communist line to his superiors in Washington. The facts, in other words, inexorably raise (though they do not necessarily answer) the question of loyalty. And the burden of proof, once the loyalty question is raised, falls on the "accused."

Service's China record, as it stood, provided grounds under the "reasonable doubt" standard for his dismissal from the Department. His activities on returning to the United States, far from dispelling the doubts that had arisen, made things a great deal worse. For he got caught transmitting classified government documents to the editors of *Amerasia*, a Communist magazine.

His having done so rocked the Tydings Committee: "We must conclude that Service was *extremely indiscreet* in his dealings with Gayn and Jaffe. . . ."[175] (Italics added.) (To be sure, the Committee did not lose its sense of balance by acknowledging the logical upshot of this evidence, i.e., that a government employee cannot possibly be "extremely indiscreet" with classified government documents and not be a security risk.) But the question of Service's guilt in the *Amerasia* affair had, after all, been laid to rest by the 1945 grand jury which had voted not to indict him. Apparently lost on the Committee was the fact that some of the most incriminating evidence against him, e.g., that obtained by wire-tap, could not, because of legal insufficiency, be considered by the grand jury. Here is an example of the evidence Tydings could weigh, but which was not before the grand jury. The FBI had recorded a conversation between Service and *Amerasia's* editor, Philip Jaffe. Service had said at one point: "Well, what I said about the military plans is, of course, very secret." When questioned by the Committee about this remark, Service's reply was: "I chose my words very unwisely, because I was not revealing any military plans." The suggestion was made to him: "You think you misspoke?" He answered, "I think I misspoke, yes."[176] The Committee pressed the matter no further.

McCarthy also charged that Service had "Communist associations," and cited the *Amerasia* case in proof of them. Though the grand jury had no-billed Service, his "association" with those who were indicted was never denied. Service claimed, however, that he had not known they were Communists. Yet since Service testified that he *was* acquainted with many prominent and militant Communists, the "conclusion" of the Tydings Committee ("the charge that Mr. Service had well-known Communist associations, *is completely unfounded*")[177] is fantastic; as, indeed, are all the Committee's broadsides concerning Service and the *Amerasia* affair.

One of Service's most vocal defenders was Mr. John Peurifoy, then Deputy Under Secretary of State. His following statement on Service captures unerringly the sentimental confusion and invincible ignorance of the Department's security division:

In the person of J. S. Service we have an able, conscientious, and a *demonstrably* loyal Foreign Service officer. . . . On the basis of *implied "guilt by association,"* that has been used in most of the other "cases" thus far presented to the Senate Sub-Committee, he underwent a grand jury investigation back in August 1945 in connection with the charges that he had transmitted classified material to unauthorized persons. . . . Mr. Service's file has been reviewed three times during the ensuing five years, and in each instance the findings of the reviewing agents have been completely favorable. . . . But now, as a result of Senator McCarthy's resuscitation of these *dead, discredited, disproven charges* against him, Mr. Service finds his character once more called into question . . . and his *brilliant* career as a diplomat once more interrupted so that he can be defended, and can defend himself, against such *baseless* allegations all over again. . . . It's a *shame* and a disgrace. . . . I would like to say that the sympathy and good wishes of the entire Department go out to them [Mr. Service and his family].* [Italics added.]

* Later, to be sure, Peurifoy was somewhat more cautious. He made the quoted statement on March 16. On June 21 he was asked by the Tydings Committee whether he still held the opinion he had expressed earlier. Peurifoy replied: ". . . that statement was probably misinterpreted; maybe I went too far." Mr. Morris insisted: "Did you know at the time, that Mr. Service had passed secret documents to Mr. Gatley, the Soviet secret agent?" Mr. Peurifoy answered, "At that time, I did not know it." (Tydings Hearings, p. 1246.) (The mysterious Mr. Gatley has never, to the authors' knowledge, been identified.)

The Tydings Committee evidently thought much the same way about Service. It ultimately reported that his case was one of "complete innocence"—"not disloyal, pro-Communist, *or a security risk*"[178] (Italics added). And with this the matter ended—not with exposure or remedy, but with a routine denunciation of "McCarthyism."

But McCarthy was to be vindicated in a way that even the Tydings Committee, had it still existed, would have understood. After Service's clearance by the Tydings Committee, the State Department's Loyalty Security Board had him up four more times, and each time cleared him. But in December of 1951, Service was dropped from the State Department "as the result of an adverse finding as to his security qualifications by the Loyalty Review Board of the Civil Service Commission."

The Case of Owen Lattimore

On June 27, 1952, the Senate Subcommittee on Internal Security, in detailing the IPR's impact on American foreign policy, announced several corollary findings:

"The IPR possessed close organic relations with the State Department. . . . Owen Lattimore and John Carter Vincent were influential in bringing about a change in United States policy in 1945 favorable to the Chinese Communists."

"Owen Lattimore was, from some time beginning in the 1930's, a conscious articulate instrument of the Soviet conspiracy."

"Owen Lattimore testified falsely before the subcommittee with reference to at least five separate matters that were relevant to the inquiry and substantial in import."[179]

In due course, a Grand Jury indicted Owen Lattimore for having testified falsely under oath with respect to seven separate matters.*

Two years before, the Tydings Committee had written its findings on Owen Lattimore. Everything that McCarthy had said about Lattimore, the Committee reported, was false. Lattimore was not a spy, not a State Department employee, not the architect of our Far Eastern policy, not a Communist or a witting associate of Communists. Rather, he was a victim of "promiscuous and specious attacks upon private citizens and their views." Furthermore, the Committee recorded its regret that it had gone into the Lattimore case: such inquiries should rather be conducted by "the duly constituted agencies of our Government that are equipped to handle such matters by intelligent and proven methods designed to obtain the truth without injustice, character assassination and a prostitution of the American concept of fair play."[180]

To be sure, McCarthy had got off on the wrong foot in the Lattimore case—by assuring the Committee (in closed session) that Lattimore was "definitely an espionage agent . . . one of the top espionage agents . . . the top Russian spy . . . the key man in a Russian espionage ring."[181] The words had hardly left McCarthy's mouth when Drew Pearson leaked these charges to the nation. Thus McCarthy was immediately put on the defensive in the Lattimore case. But the fact is that here indeed was his "best" case, i.e. the

---

* A U.S. District Court subsequently dismissed four of the seven counts. (Its ruling is, at this writing, being appealed.)

most sensational, and the one with respect to which McCarthy was in a position to adduce the most damaging evidence. "I am willing to stand or fall on this one," he told the Committee in turning over Lattimore's name. And for this he had excellent reasons.

Soon after making the "top espionage" charge against Lattimore, McCarthy modified it on the floor of the Senate. "I fear," he said, "that I may have perhaps placed too much stress on the question of whether or not he had been an espionage agent. . . . "[182] It soon became clear, however, that no matter how precisely or how moderately McCarthy might have put his indictment of Lattimore, the Tydings Committee had no intention of making an exception to its policy of clearing everyone on whom McCarthy put the finger.

Though Lattimore was not an employee of the State Department in the orthodox sense, McCarthy started off, he was nevertheless "one of the principal architects of our Far Eastern policy." [183] This allegation was important. For one thing, the technical propriety of the Committee's investigation of Lattimore hinged on whether or not Lattimore was, or had been, pertinently connected with the State Department. For another, Lattimore emphatically denied having had any relationship whatever with the Department. And as for being influential, said Lattimore, ". . . I am the least consulted man of all those who have a public reputation in this country as specialists in the Far East."[184] Much, then, turned on whether McCarthy could prove that Lattimore had played a quasi-official role in the preceding years.

He started in: In 1941, he said, Lattimore was chosen by President Roosevelt to be the personal political adviser of Chiang Kai-shek. He stayed with Chiang until the end of 1942.

From 1942 to 1944, Lattimore was the chief of Pacific operations for the Office of War Information which, McCarthy inferred, naturally worked hand-in-hand with the State Department.

In 1944, Lattimore accompanied Vice-President Henry Wallace on his trip to Siberia and China.

In 1945, Lattimore was appointed by Truman as a member of the Pauley Reparations Mission to Japan.

In 1949, Lattimore attended a State Department conference on China policy.*

Throughout this period, Lattimore had been extremely active in the IPR, whose "organic relations" with the State Department

* See above, "The Case of Philip Jessup."

were demonstrable well before the McCarran Committee began its investigation.

What is more, added McCarthy, Lattimore at one time even had a desk in the State Department.

All of this (except for the "State Department desk") was a matter of record. Yet Lattimore hotly resisted the implication that the data added up to a firm connection between him and the State Department. "I told the newspapermen," he wrote in *Ordeal by Slander,* "that Senator McCarthy was crazy if he had got me mixed up with the State Department. I had never been in the State Department."[185] The Committee consulted the Department on the matter, and concluded that Lattimore was right.[186]

Two years later, during the McCarran Committee's interrogation of Lattimore, the Committee counsel, Mr. Morris, showed Lattimore a photostatic copy of a letter Lattimore had written to Benjamin Kizer on June 12, 1942. The last paragraph of the letter read:

My home address is as typed above, and my home telephone is Towson 846-W. I am in Washington about 4 days a week, and when there can always be reached at Lauchlin Currie's office, room 228, State Department Building; telephone National 1414, extension 90.
Yours very sincerely,
OWEN LATTIMORE

At the time he gave evidence to the Tydings Committee, McCarthy had no intimation of the close relationship between Lattimore and Lauchlin Currie (named a Communist under oath), whose office was put at Lattimore's disposal. Lattimore testified before the McCarran Committee as follows:[187]

MR. MORRIS. Mr. Lattimore, isn't it a fact that when Currie went away for a period of time he would ask you to take care of his mail at the White House?
MR. LATTIMORE. No. . . .
MR. MORRIS. Tell me this, Mr. Lattimore. Is it your testimony that you did not at the request of Lauchlin Currie take care of his mail at the White House when he was away?
MR. LATTIMORE. That certainly is my statement.

Morris subsequently adduced a letter written by Lattimore to E. C. Carter of the IPR, on July 15, 1942, the first paragraph of which read: "Dear Carter: Currie asked me to take care of his correspondence while he is away and in view of your telegram of today [addressed to Currie, presumably], I think I had better tell you that he has gone to China on a special trip. This news is absolutely confidential until released in the press. . . . "

After reading the letter, Morris continued:

. . . Did the top official of the State Department—

MR. FORTAS [Lattimore's lawyer, interrupting]. Excuse me just a moment, Mr. Morris.

(Mr. Lattimore conferred with counsel.)

MR. LATTIMORE. Mr. Morris, I should like to add to what I have just said that this refreshes my recollection and that I believe that Currie told his secretary to open his mail and to pass on to me anything that might be of concern to me.*

Another matter, flippantly dismissed by Tydings, was caught up and made to stick by McCarran. McCarthy told the Tydings Committee, to show Lattimore's influence on American policy, that Lattimore had visited Truman shortly before the Potsdam Conference to urge upon the President his views on Far Eastern policy. Lattimore admitted having gone to the White House. "Our conference lasted about three minutes," he later told the McCarran Committee. But it developed that, however long Lattimore had actually conferred with Truman, he had left with the President a memorandum detailing his recommendations on Far Eastern policy.

SENATOR FERGUSON. Did you show the exhibits that we have now on the record, of your visit to the White House, that is, the memorandum and the letter, to any member of the Tydings Committee?

MR. LATTIMORE. No.

SENATOR FERGUSON. Or the staff?

MR. LATTIMORE. No.

SENATOR FERGUSON. How do you account, Mr. Lattimore, for not making that part of the record? Did you not think that was material on the question as to whether or not you ever had anything to do with the foreign policy of the Far East, as far as the President or the State Department was concerned?

MR. LATTIMORE. I did not think it was material. The question of whether the committee wanted to see it was up to them.

SENATOR FERGUSON. How would they know that it existed? You did not disclose it to any of them.

MR. LATTIMORE. . . . as a citizen I would not take the initiative in

* Lattimore was subsequently indicted for having committed perjury in this matter.

revealing the details of a citizen asking to see the President of his country. . . . the responsibility lies with the Committee. *I see no obligation to volunteer anything of that kind.*[188] [Italics added.]

Thus, with Lattimore seeing no obligation to volunteer any information that might throw light on the points at issue, and with the Tydings Committee seeing no obligation to press Lattimore for such information, it was only left for the two parties to recognize their obligation to expose McCarthy's blackhearted mendacity, and this cause mobilized them both—above and beyond, even, the call of duty. We are not implying, to be sure, that the Tydings Committee was in a position to bring to light the data on Lattimore which at that time reposed peacefully in an old barn in Lee, Massachusetts. We *are* saying, however, that McCarthy demonstrably fulfilled his function of giving to the Tydings Committee enough leads to justify its going into Lattimore's record. McCarthy, in fact, gave the Committee more; he gave it enough leads to enable it to blow sky-high Lattimore's pretensions to being a disinterested and sedentary expert on the Far East, enough data to put the State Department on warning against further traffic with Lattimore, and enough, even, to have spared the intelligentsia the lasting embarrassment of taking Lattimore's snivelling book, *Ordeal by Slander*, to their bosom, and of martyrizing its author, who now succeeded Alger Hiss as the First Lady among American witches.

For McCarthy had not confined himself to "document-snitching-type" charges;* he invited the Committee to inspect Lattimore's *writings*, and on his insistence Miss Freda Utley was called in to analyze them out of her *expertise* on the Communist Party line on the Far East. Miss Utley summarized her testimony:

Soviet Russia, in all of Lattimore's writings, is always sinned against and is always represented by Lattimore as standing like a beacon of hope for the peoples of Asia, even when she is collaborating with the Nazis or aggressing on her own account. Russia is never in the wrong and if he is forced to take cognizance of a few slight misdemeanors on her part, he excuses them as only a reaction to American imperialism or some other country's misdeeds.[189]

* We borrow Miss Utley's shrewd observation on McCarthy's "top spy" charge against Lattimore: "To suggest that Mr. Lattimore's great talents have been utilized in espionage seems to me to be as absurd as to suggest that Mr. Gromyko or Mr. Molotov employ their leisure hours at Lake Success, or at international conferences, in snitching documents."

And if the views of Miss Utley (as a premature anti-Communist) were suspect, the Committee might have turned for a summary of one of Lattimore's books to his own publisher. This blurb had appeared on the jacket of his *Solution in Asia:*

He [Lattimore] shows that all the Asiatic people are more interested in actual democratic practices such as the ones they can see in action across the Russian border, than they are in the fine theories of Anglo-Saxon democracies which come coupled with ruthless imperialism. . . . He inclines to support American newspapermen who report that the only real democracy in China is found in Communist areas.

Yet the Committee declared, simply, that Lattimore's writings "obviously cannot be declared to approach Communist dogma."[190]

McCarthy then charged that Lattimore had associated with known Communists. To mention a few: Frederick Vanderbilt Field ("As far as I knew," Lattimore told the Committee ". . . he was rather a liberal young man. . . ."); Philip Jaffe (". . . one of those Americans who had a very bright and open view of the democratic nature of the Communists in China, but I had no reason to believe that he was himself a Communist"); Agnes Smedley (". . . she is not and never could be a Communist"); Nym Wales ("I have no reason to believe that she is or was a Communist"); T. A. Bisson (no grounds "whatever" for believing him to be a Communist); and Chao-ting Chi ("I don't know that he is in fact a Communist [even] now." "Is there any doubt in your mind," retorted Senator Hickenlooper, "that he would be here as the proposed representative of Communist China to the UN if he is not a Communist?" "It is possible, Senator. The Communist government in China appears to have taken over the services of a considerable number of non-Communists especially where they were men of specialized training of various kinds. . . .")[191]

The Committee concluded that Lattimore was not a witting associate of Communists.

McCarthy charged that Lattimore was a Communist and under Party discipline. Louis Budenz corroborated McCarthy's charge in what was perhaps the Committee's most dramatic session. For he testified that, in 1937, Communist leader Earl Browder, in the presence of Frederick Vanderbilt Field, had agreed with him (Budenz) that Lattimore should take over the general direction of the move to depict the Chinese Communists as "agrarian reformers"; that in 1943 he (Budenz) had heard Field report at a Communist

Party meeting that Lattimore had been instructed of a change of the party-line on Chiang Kai-shek; that in 1944 he (Budenz) had been instructed by Jack Stachel, one of the highest Communist Party functionaries in the United States, to consider Lattimore a Communist; that in 1945, Stachel, at a session at Communist headquarters, had indicated that Lattimore had been of service to the Communist Party in the *Amerasia* case.[192]

". . . The whole story is a plain, unvarnished lie,"[193] said Lattimore.*

The Tydings Committee caught its cue and dismissed Budenz's evidence as "hearsay."[194]

As we have said, we shall not be treating the Lattimore episode in detail. Those who want more—and there is a great deal more—will find a near-definitive exposure of Lattimore in the hearings of the McCarran Committee. These hearings** should be read side-by-side with *Ordeal by Slander*.

Suffice to note here, simply, that in addition to the evidence we have briefly treated here, McCarthy gave the Committee a number of additional leads, none of which the Committee undertook to follow up with anything like the perseverance necessary to trip up those whose occupation implies, after all, a considerable talent for throwing investigators off the scent.

McCarthy exposed one of the most important political operators of our time. Owen Lattimore's skills, energies, and single-mindedness enabled him to play a dominant role in a movement that dispossessed our allies in the Far East of their homeland, enslaved four hundred million people, and doubled the perimeter of the Iron Curtain. Owen Lattimore had moved discreetly throughout the period. His name was not known—except in academic and Far Eastern circles—until McCarthy attacked him. But in his unobtrusive way, Lattimore was serving the Roosevelt and Truman Administrations as the oracle on all matters Asiatic. His books were standard in American colleges and graduate schools. He and his votaries dominated the book review sections of the metropolitan

---

* "Listening to Budenz," wrote the disingenuous Mrs. Lattimore in *Harpers* (September, 1950) ". . . describe his sordid life in the Communist underworld in which he spent 10 years was a gruesome experience. He built up a picture of a sinister, murky world of Communist conspiracy which for all I know may exist."

** Mr. John T. Flynn has written an excellent condensation of the hearings. See *The Lattimore Story* (New York; Devin-Adair, 1953).

press. If a new book on China followed the Party line, it won their endorsement. If it so much as intimated the tragic folly of our Far Eastern policies, it was doomed either to denunciation or to oblivion.

Yet despite all Lattimore's precautions, some Americans had got on to him. Shortly after McCarthy connected with Lattimore, *Time* magazine commented on three figures in the week's news—Joliot Curie of France, John Strachey of England, and Owen Lattimore.

All formed their political consciousness in the years of World War I, when a generation was assaulted by the century's most vicious fallacy, i.e. that communism was akin to progress. All were affected by the fallacy in varying degrees, and all, being gifted with brilliant intellects, did a great deal to spread this paralyzing poison through the West's thinking.

The fact did not make any of them a traitor, either in law or in morals. . . . But the legal right to be wrong had somehow gotten distorted into a lazy translation that assumes all ideas to be created equal, part right, part wrong—and who is man to try to judge between them? It was this same public negligence about ideas that made wrong ideas dangerous. . . .

The fact that Lattimore is no Soviet agent* does not clear him of having had, in less dramatic ways, a disastrous influence on the foreign policy of his country. . . . [Lattimore's memorandum to the State Department on Far Eastern policy] paid lip service to the idea that Asiatic Communism must not be appeased, but it was in effect a thorough and detailed program for appeasement. . . . Lattimore's ideas did work to thwart the development of an effective program of U.S. help to anti-Communist forces in China."

And yet, if one looks through the *Reader's Guide to Periodical Literature* for the years preceding McCarthy's exposure of Lattimore, not a single article is found warning America against Lattimore's insidious influence—not even in *Time* magazine.** This job was left to the junior Senator from Wisconsin, who for his pains met with the damnation of the intelligentsia that had countenanced Lattimore and in fact had been bewitched by him for so many years.

* It should be recalled that this article was written on April 17, 1950, *before* the IPR investigation was undertaken.

** *Columbia Magazine,* an organ of the Knights of Columbus, published an article by the Reverend James K. Kearney attacking Lattimore in September of 1949. References to Lattimore's party-lining had also appeared in *The Chicago Journal of Commerce,* and in the *New Leader.*

CHAPTER VIII

"Warmed-Over Charges"

T HE foregoing nine public cases must be viewed as McCarthy's earnest money towards the investigation he had been promised. For that reason we have taken a detailed and perhaps laborious look at them; for on that basis alone we have to decide whether McCarthy had a *prima facie* case against the security practices of the State Department. We believe that, on the whole, the record here vindicates McCarthy.

Notwithstanding, the Tydings investigation of the State Department, to all intents and purposes, ended with its hearing of the nine cases.

Yet there is more to the Tydings saga. More must be said about certain things the Committee purported to do, and did not do, in the process of discrediting McCarthy; and about things that it did not even purport to do but *had* to do under its mandate to investigate the State Department. For the Tydings Committee's most obvious obligation was, of course, to undertake a thorough study of the eighty-one cases McCarthy had presented in his Senate speech of February 20 (only two of which—Philip Jessup and Esther Brunauer—were "public cases").

Over and over again, the anti-McCarthy literature bears down exultantly on the "fact" that a subcommittee of the House Committee on Appropriations of the Republican-controlled 80th Congress had already investigated *all* of McCarthy's cases in the winter of 1947-1948; and had cleared them all. There is no more fundamental—or more pervasive*—inaccuracy in this field.

---

* Even the shrewd and ungullible British author, Miss Rebecca West, is ensnared by this legend. See her otherwise admirable article in *US News and World Report*, May 22, 1953.

Here is how the Tydings Committee put it:

There is no factual information relative to any one of the February 20 cases which does not have its identifiable counterpart among the "108 list." . . . The subcommittee of the House Appropriations Committee of the Republican-controlled Eightieth Congress which considered the 108 memoranda *did not regard them of sufficient significance even to submit a report concerning them or the loyalty of State Department personnel generally.*[1]

Here are the facts: In the fall of 1947, the subcommittee in question, through its chief clerk, Mr. Robert E. Lee, conducted an investigation of State Department security practices. The aim was an evaluation of the Department's security program, its standards and its administration. Lee's investigators prepared summaries of the loyalty files of "108 present, former, and prospective" Department employees. The subcommittee studied these summaries, interrogated responsible State Department officials, and reported its conclusions, early in 1948, as follows:

The Committee held extensive hearings on the security phase of the Department [of State] and the employment of individuals that were considered poor risks from the security angle. Committee investigators disclosed and reproduced from Department files the employment histories of 108 present, former and prospective employees. Files on the prospective employees were active, and the individuals, at the time of the investigation, were being considered for employment, even though information of record pointed to their being poor risks. *The Committee does not feel that the Department has been as diligent as it might have been in the selection of its personnel and has not sufficiently exercised the prerogative given it under the so-called McCarran Rider,* contained in appropriation acts for this Department for the past several years. . . . It would seem to the Committee that any doubts in connection with employment of personnel in the Department of State should be resolved in favor of the United States, and officers or employees who are suspected in the slightest degree should be encouraged to resign.* [Italics added.]

The members of the subcommittee, in other words, made no secret of their belief that the State Department had been lax in its security practices. Moreover, committee members did not always express their feelings in the matter with such restraint.

* *House of Representatives Report No. 1433,* 80th Congress, 2nd Session, February 27, 1948, p. 3. The report, presented to the House by Congressman Karl Stefan, was unanimous.

During the Committee's questioning of Mr. Hamilton Robinson (the Department's director of the Office of Controls), Congressman Karl Stefan's exasperation became uncontrollable. "I am just a man from the prairies of Nebraska," he blurted out, "just asking you why it is that these people are on the pay roll when the people of the United States are trying to get behind the Government to fight communism and the encroachment of communism in this country and all over Europe. And here we find them employed in the State Department."[2]

When the House Committee concluded its interrogation of Mr. Robinson, the Chairman remarked:

I have no other questions at this time. However, I would say this to you, that it makes me disturbed as to whether we have any representation of the United States in the State Department. I have not been as much disturbed in a long time. . . . here are 100 cases and many of them are still on the payroll and the people are going to ask us, what are we going to do about it.[3]

Yet on the basis of such facts the Tydings Committee and its camp-followers dared conclude that the Subcommittee *had cleared* the State Department!

Only a few weeks after the House Appropriations Committee had questioned the Department about the 108, another House Committee—Expenditures in the Executive Department—was asking Deputy Assistant John Peurifoy to bring it up to date on the Lee list. He stated that 9 of the 108 were still being considered for employment, that only 57 of the 108 were currently employed by the Department and that, of the employed group, 22 were being checked by the FBI. He added that the resignation of one of the 57 was pending. Thus, 42 of the 108 were by this time already separated from the Department.

Then, on March 3, 1948, Representative Stefan again focused attention on the 108—"concerning most of whom," he said, "there was some doubt as to loyalty."[4] In no way did he, any more than the Committee that had heard Peurifoy, express satisfaction with the State Department's handling of personnel security.

The 108 came up for notice on several other occasions in the ensuing months. On March 25, for example, Representative Busbey sharply criticized the State Department Director of Controls, Mr. Hamilton Robinson, and particularly emphasized the derelictions revealed by the investigators who compiled the list of 108.[5]

In short, there was indeed a list of 108 cases. Drawn up in the last days of 1947, it did receive a great deal of public attention; and the testimony before the Expenditures Committee to the effect that only 57 of the 108 persons on it were currently employed did serve to assuage Congressional anxiety. *But there is no record of any Congressional "clearance" for the entire list of 108 or any part of it; rather, there is clear evidence that the House Appropriations Committee, which gathered the data on the 108, expressed marked dissatisfaction with the State Department security after examining them.* To pursue the matter any further was impossible for *any* Congressional committee because, on the 13th of March, 1948, Truman banned the release of security data to Congress; and that information was absolutely indispensable to any comprehensive evaluation of security practices in the State Department.*

The Tydings Committee "found" that *all* numbered cases presented to it by Senator McCarthy were "old and stale." Its Report said that "there is not one of the cases discussed [by McCarthy] on February 20, 1950, on the Senate floor which is not to be found among the '108' list"—implying that all McCarthy's (non-public) names were taken from the Lee list. Nowhere in its report did the Committee comment upon the fact that McCarthy had given it a number of names which had not appeared on the Lee list. In short, the Committee consciously attempted to persuade the public (and in this it was successful) that McCarthy furnished no names—or evidence—that had not already been reviewed by Congressional committees in 1948.

Let us be very clear about the relation between the Lee list and the McCarthy list. It is quite true that the two lists overlap. But the Lee list did *not* include the entire McCarthy list. What is more, a State Department document in the Appendix to the Tydings *Hearings* (pp. 1814-17) reveals that much!**

---

* Two other committees of Congress are often said to have cleared the State Department in 1948 and, in the process, the 108. One is the Senate Committee on Appropriations of the 80th Congress, and we have noted the explicit denial of any such clearance by one of its most active members, Senator Homer Ferguson. The other—the House Committee on Foreign Affairs—delegated the task of checking on State Department security to a committee-of-one, Congressman Bartel Jonkman, whose amusing "report" we mentioned in a previous chapter.

** This document is not, however, either completely accurate (e.g., it fails to note that McCarthy's Case No. 14 corresponds with Lee's No. 10) or exhaustive (it makes no mention of any of McCarthy's cases after his 81st).

McCarthy gave to the Tydings Committee 110 persons to be investigated.* Of these, 37 were not on the Lee list. And of the 37, 26 were still employed by the State Department at the time McCarthy brought his charges.

Yet in the teeth of such facts, countless books and editorials have stated, and continue to state, that McCarthy did nothing more than renumber the Lee list!

As we say, McCarthy gave the Committee 110 names. Of these, 62 were employed by the State Department at the time of the Tydings hearings:**

> 6 had been cleared by the State Department before February, 1950, and were not being reprocessed as of June, 1951;
> 19 were cleared between February, 1950, and June, 1951;
> 29 were being investigated under the President's Loyalty Order as of June, 1951;
> 7 had never been investigated as of June, 1951;
> 1 resigned in December, 1950, while under investigation.

Total: 62

In short: within one year after Tydings had unambiguously cleared all persons on McCarthy's list, and the State Department had indignantly affirmed their loyalty and reliability, the Department saw fit to reprocess† no less than 49 (out of 62!), 29 of whom were still "in channels" as of June, 1951.

The high incidence of "reprocessings" cannot be explained away on the grounds that President Truman's Executive Order of April

---

* This excludes duplications and unidentified persons, and *includes* McCarthy's public cases. For a detailed breakdown of these and ensuing figures, see Appendix C.

** Information on the balance of McCarthy's cases, those who were working for the State Department at the time he brought his charges, is derived primarily—though by no means exclusively—from one fairly comprehensive and absolutely authentic document, dated June 13, 1951, to which the authors have had access. For that reason, and that reason alone, that date appears in the ensuing breakdown.

† We say "reprocess" because, in the light of the age of the derogatory evidence against them, it is virtually a foregone conclusion that the 49 were back in loyalty-security channels they had already weathered in the days before Tydings.

28, 1951, changing the loyalty standard from "reasonable *grounds*" to "reasonable *doubt*," had forced the State Department to reprocess *all* employees against whom derogatory information had ever been received. *As we have shown above, the Department had been operating for years under the "reasonable doubt" standard in the security category.* Neither the Department nor the apologists for its security program can take refuge here in the plea that the rules of the game had been changed. What had changed was the Department's disposition to observe them.

Eighteen of the 49 McCarthy cases reprocessed after the Tydings hearings had left the Department as of the first of January, 1953. We do not know whether they all were classed, or were about to be classed, as loyalty or security risks. But the presumption lies in that direction with respect to a number of them; if for no other reason than that the turnover among McCarthy cases (18 out of 62) is a good deal higher than that of the Department as a whole.

To sum up: During the Tydings hearings, State Department officials time and again asserted that all of McCarthy's cases had been "thoroughly investigated" and, on the strength of these investigations, cleared. The Committee itself reinforced this verdict with its own across-the-board clearance. Yet a year later, 80 per cent of McCarthy's cases had been put into loyalty or security channels; and before long, 29 per cent of them were separated. The Department, in other words, by its decision to take a new hard look at the 49, tacitly admitted what McCarthy had been saying all along: that an important number of State Department employees had not been given an adequate security screening. It is evident, then, that we are indebted to McCarthy's campaign for jolting Department officials into reopening the question to see whether their investigations had been thorough enough or their evaluations stern enough.

mendacious . lying

CHAPTER IX

Some Unanswered Questions

WE HAVE by now learned enough to pass judgment upon the Tydings "investigation." "Fraud" and "hoax" are pretty good words for describing not McCarthy's charges, but Tydings' conclusions about them, i.e., (1) that the persons McCarthy had accused were patriots beyond a reasonable doubt, (2) that the State Department's security division had been efficient and effective when, according to McCarthy, it had been lax and futile, and (3) that Senator McCarthy was a charlatan.

We must remember, however, that investigation of McCarthy's specific charges was but the first item on the Committee's agenda— and could not be interpreted as anything more in the light of the Committee's mandate to *investigate the State Department*. The Tydings Committee's tacit assumption that if it could discredit McCarthy's charges it was automatically justified in endorsing the total loyalty-security program of the Department, was entirely unwarranted. The Committee's mandate, though ambiguous in some other respects, was quite clear in this one regard: the State Department was to be thoroughly investigated.

Senator Lodge apparently sensed that, in deference to the wishes of American Liberaldom, his Democratic Committee colleagues were about to hand down a blanket endorsement of the State Department. For he read into the record no less than 19 specific questions which had been raised by persons *other* than McCarthy; and Lodge argued that the Committee had no business reporting that the State Department's security program was satisfactory while they remained unanswered.

To none of these 19 questions did the Tydings Committee address itself either in its investigation or in its report. Lodge's list, to be sure, by no means exhausted the available supply of such questions; it did not purport to be more than a sampling of questions relevant to State Department security that then wanted asking (and that, for the most part, want asking today). Yet it was sufficiently revealing to merit citation in full. Senator Lodge asked:

What State Department officials were responsible for placing Hiss and Wadleigh in the State Department?

What person or persons were primarily responsible for sponsorship for employment of the 91 sexual perverts who were in the State Department and who were reported as having been dismissed beginning with January 1, 1947?

Were those State Department officials who opposed United States recognition of Soviet Russia and who thereafter warned against any appeasement of the Soviet regime in any way discriminated against or unfairly treated by the State Department?

What were the procedures whereby Communists gained entry into the United States upon the basis of visas obtained through our consular service abroad?

What are the facts with reference to the release of the Soviet spy named Gaik Badalovich Ovakimian on July 23, 1941?

What are the facts with reference to the release of the Soviet spy named Mikhala Nickolavich Goran on March 22, 1941?

What is the significance of the statement by Adolph Berle to the House Un-American Activities Committee that Alger Hiss belonged to the pro-Russian clique in the State Department?

Who in the State Department was responsible for obtaining the services of Frederick Schuman and Owen Lattimore as speakers for the Department's indoctrination course for Foreign Service employees?

What are the facts of the charge that a State Department security officer's decision that 10 members of the Department be discharged was subsequently reversed by higher authority?

What State Department officials were responsible for advice given higher officials that the Soviet Government would allow free elections in Poland and Czechoslovakia, Hungary, Rumania, and the other satellite countries?

What are the facts surrounding the case of Arthur Adams, an alleged Soviet spy, who was permitted to leave the United States in 1946?

It is reported that the FBI had prepared a chart which purported to show the number of "agents," "Communists," "sympathizers," and "suspects" in the State Department as of May 15, 1947. Who are these Communists and agents and sympathizers and suspects? What are their names? Why are they there?

In the Lattimore case, there are a number of questions to which answers were not obtained. For example:

There is no authoritative and detailed presentation in the record from the State Department setting forth the precise facts, dates, etc., concerning Mr. Lattimore's relationship with the State Department.

The persons mentioned by Mr. Budenz as having had relations with

Mr. Lattimore have not been examined. There were some 16 in number.

Those who headed the China desk in the State Department have not been questioned to determine whether Mr. Lattimore gave advice on United States policy on China and whether this advice was followed.

The United States Ambassadors to China who held that office during Mr. Lattimore's period of activity have not been questioned along the same lines.

The subcommittee has not discovered whether any new information has come into the possession of the Department of Justice respecting Mr. Lattimore since March 24, 1950, when the members of the subcommittee were allowed to see a summary of Mr. Lattimore's file.

On April 25, Mr. Budenz stated that he would furnish the subcommittee with names of Communists whom he knew to be in the State Department. That list has not come to the subcommittee.

Investigation has not been made of all those whom Mr. Lattimore is supposed to have brought into the Institute of Pacific Relations.[1]

The Tydings Committee chose not merely to ignore all these matters, it attempted also to conceal their existence from the reading public: *some member of the Committee, or someone on its staff, saw to it that the portion of the transcript containing Senator Lodge's questions was deleted from the published record of the hearings.*

Lodge detected the omission several days after the Committee submitted its Report. He expressed his indignation to the Senate in no uncertain terms. "Is the Senator [Tydings] aware . . . of the fact that in the printed copy of the hearings of the subcommittee on disloyalty, there are omitted, beginning at page 1488, about 35 typewritten pages of the transcript of the subcommittee meeting on June 28? . . . Permit me to say that I shall not attempt to characterize those methods and the tactics of leaving out of the printed text parts of the testimony and proceedings. . . . I shall not characterize such methods, because I think they speak for themselves."[2]

Senator McMahon hurried to the rescue: someone had slipped up, he said; but, happily, there was a remedy, namely, to run the omitted portions in an amended version of the hearings.

No, Lodge retorted, the explanation would not do. "The omission . . . could not have been a mistake, in the sense that by mistake the entire latter part of the proceedings was omitted, because after the omission of the large number of pages to which I have referred, in the printed copy of the hearings appear the last several sentences shown in the typewritten transcript, including the statement about the adjournment."[3] In other words, *someone** had simply moved the closing sentences in the original transcript back some thirty pages, evidently in a desperate and childish attempt to shield the Committee from the embarrassment to which such adroit questions from one of its own members might expose it.

The thirty-five omitted pages contained, besides the Lodge questions, other testimony that put the Committee in an extremely poor light. Siding with Lodge, Senator Hickenlooper had protested against the inadequacies of the investigation: "We have 20 or 30 names [that have come up in the course of the investigation] that I think we ought to look into."[8] If the Committee would reconsider its decision to close the hearings that day, he continued, he would draw up a list of the "20 or 30" names, and "you can have it tomorrow afternoon." But the majority was adamant. Senator Tydings: "I think our work is pretty well concluded, if you want my opinion." It is not hard to see from the ensuing dialogue, why the Committee majority elected to suppress those thirty-five pages:

> SENATOR HICKENLOOPER. I don't think it has even started, Mr. Chairman.
> SENATOR TYDINGS. You disagree with me?
> SENATOR HICKENLOOPER. I disagree with you.
> SENATOR TYDINGS. But I disagree with you, so there we are.
> MR. MORRIS [Minority counsel]. Senator, may I mention just one case here?

* The identity of the culprit(s) has never been revealed. Note, moreover, that this is not the only indication that the Committee was underhanded in preparing its Report. Senator Hickenlooper has branded the Report "a mysterious and a mysteriously prepared document."[4] And Senator Ferguson, speaking four days later, went still further: "I really feel that the subcommittee . . . should resume its work and undertake an investigation of its own staff. . . ."[5]

Nor is even that all. Senators Lodge and Hickenlooper had intimated during the hearings that they would not sign the sort of report the majority apparently had in mind to submit to the Senate. They were not even given an opportunity to see it before it was sent to the Senate and copies had been given to the press.[6] And Senator Mundt detected yet another bit of sharp practice. The report was at first "labeled a 'subcommittee report' and . . . after the [parent] Committee on Foreign Relations had disavowed paternity of the report, it was finally printed, and, in the process of printing, the jacket was changed from 'subcommittee report' to indicate that it was a report of the full committee. . . ." "I wonder," Mundt concluded after hearing Senator Ferguson list some of the more patent derelictions of the Committee, "Whether the Senator from Michigan [Ferguson] will agree with the Senator from South Dakota that this whole business of a report and censored set of hearings comes very close to being a hoax and a fraud, to use the words of the original report."[7]

SENATOR TYDINGS. Mr. Morris, we can mention cases from now until doomsday.

MR. MORRIS. It is in the record, Senator. May I just finish?

SENATOR TYDINGS. Of course, you are not a member of the Committee. When we want counsel to speak, we will ask them, but I am going to let you speak. However, that is a matter for the Committee to decide.

SENATOR LODGE. I would like to hear what he has to say.

MR. MORRIS. There is a case of a man named Theodore Geiger. He has been an employee of the State Department. He is now one of Paul Hoffman's top assistants. He is doing work that is quasi-State Department in character. I have gone and gotten some witnesses together who will testify that he was a member of the same Communist Party unit as they were, and I think that we would be delinquent if in the face of this evidence that is now on the record—

SENATOR TYDINGS. Why didn't you tell us this? Why did you wait until this hour to tell me?

MR. MORRIS. I am not waiting, Senator. One day Senator Green made me a witness and I put it all in the record.

SENATOR TYDINGS. You haven't told me about it. This is the first I have heard about it.

MR. MORRIS. Senator, I assume that you are aware of everything in the record.

SENATOR TYDINGS. No, there are some things in the record I haven't been able to read.

MR. MORRIS. Certainly Mr. Morgan [the Committee's chief counsel] knows it. I have mentioned it several times to him. . . .

SENATOR TYDINGS. Turn it over to the FBI or do something with it. I would like to get a decision here. We don't want to waste this afternoon. . . .[9]

Such are the facts. Yet it is still being claimed that the Tydings Committee found nothing left to investigate once it had gotten at the "truth" behind McCarthy's specific charges!

The Committee's investigation of the loyalty files (which Truman finally consented to hand over to it) was a farce. This is so for a number of reasons that will be detailed in the Appendix, where we will also consider McCarthy's charge that the files had been skeletonized. Suffice to quote the first sentences of Senator Lodge's estimate of the futility of the Committee's review of the files:

After having read a representative cross section of the 81 loyalty files [he told the Senate], the conviction was reached that the files alone did not furnish a basis for reaching firm conclusions of any kind and that to attempt to conclude with respect to an individual case on the basis

of the files alone would be a most half-baked and superficial procedure. . . . The files which I read were in such an unfinished state as to
indicate that an examination of each file would be a waste of time. . . .

Two possible avenues of investigation the Committee *did* consider. Both merit only brief treatment here since the salient facts
about one of them, the *Amerasia* case, are widely known; and those
about the other, the mysterious "FBI chart," are still unavailable—
thanks largely to the inertia of the Tydings Committee.

AMERASIA

The Tydings Committee would almost certainly never even have
glanced at the *Amerasia* case but for the public pressure the
Scripps-Howard newspapers generated in the spring of 1950 with
a series of articles by Fred Woltman. These articles demanded that
the questions left unanswered by the Hobbs Committee inquiry of
1946 be cleared up once and for all.

The major facts of the case appear to have been these. In February, 1945, OSS agents discovered a number of highly confidential
State Department documents in the offices of the Communist *Amerasia* magazine. The FBI undertook a physical surveillance of persons who appeared to be involved in the theft of the documents.
On June 6, arrests were made and 1069 additional documents
seized at the *Amerasia* offices (540 of them classified).

Of the six persons who were arraigned on charges of conspiracy
to steal government documents relating to the national defense,*
four went scot free; the two others were let off with fines of $500
and $2500, respectively. And at least two questions had seemed to
cry out of those facts. First, did they mean that someone had
stumbled into a network of spies whose tentacles extended into
the State Department? And, second, had the conspirators and their
sponsors exercised influence on the government to short-circuit investigation of the affair's ramifications?

The first step in seeking answers to these two questions was, of
course, to look into the handling of the case by the Justice Department. The Tydings Committee turned to that very Department
for *judgment* on the matter, and ended up taking the Justice Department's word that all charges levelled against the Justice De-

---

* Three of the six defendants, John Service, Mark Gayn and Kate Mit-
chell, were no-billed by the Grand Jury; it indicted Andrew Roth, Emmanuel
Larsen and Philip Jaffe.

partment, in connection with the case, were unfounded. Had hidden forces masterminded a whitewash of the *Amerasia* case? The Justice Department said no. Had the Justice Department, despite the fact that the case seemed of the open-and-shut variety, pressed it with something less than its usual vigor? Certainly not, said the Justice Department. Was there evidence that at least three of those arrested (Jaffe, Larsen and Roth) had put classified State Department documents at the disposal of the Communists? As far as it went, yes, that was correct, said the Department. Had the Justice Department nevertheless let the Roth prosecution drop altogether and made deals with Jaffe and Larsen (that it would recommend only nominal fines if they would agree to enter pleas of "guilty" and "nolo contendere," respectively)? Yes, said the Department; but there were legal obstacles that made the case against the *Amerasia* defendants weaker than it seemed to the layman.

The above is no caricature of the minuet between the Tydings Committee and the Justice Department. The Committee called before it the Department officials who had been involved (Mr. James McInerney, head of the Department's Criminal Division, and Mr. Robert Hitchcock, the Department prosecutor in charge of the *Amerasia* case) and asked them to recite, as they had done to the Hobbs Committee four years before, the Department account of the matter. And having heard what the Justice Department had to say, the Committee published over its imprimatur a lengthy memorandum on the legal points involved—not, as one might have expected, a canvass of the legal pros and cons, but a venture in advocacy that pleaded the case against the prosecutor as passionately as the accused's attorneys would have dared to plead it. But the Committee was at least honest enough not to conceal the sources from which the memorandum was obtained: it was conceived and executed in the Justice Department itself!

In the circumstances, it was the clear obligation of the Tydings Committee to obtain an impartial verdict on the tenability of the Justice Department's legal premises, and write that verdict into its report. And the place to go for such a verdict was not to the Justice Department, but to a body of disinterested legal experts brought together *ad hoc* under the Committee's auspices. Let us note some of the issues such a panel would have been in a position to consider; and then we shall leave the *Amerasia* case as the Tydings Committee has left it—a deep and disturbing mystery.

First: Were the *Amerasia* defendants prosecuted under the right law? The original complaints charged violation of a statute that dealt with conspiracy to steal government documents *relating to the national defense*. This charge was subsequently dropped, and the cases were finally prosecuted under a law that deals simply with conspiracy to steal government property. The reason for this change, as stated by the Department attorneys, was their uncertainty about being able to prove that the theft was "for the purpose of obtaining information respecting the national defense." Was this a reasonable explanation in view of the nature of the stolen documents? The documents included, to identify just a very few of them: a report on the disposition of the Japanese fleet prior to the Battle of Leyte; a report on the development of the Chinese Nationalist armies, giving the location, strength and armament of all Nationalist troops, division by division; a report on the Navy's schedule for bombing Japanese strategic targets; the Navy's counter-intelligence "organization plan"; a report on the location of 25 American submarines in Pacific waters; an "Eyes Only" message from President Roosevelt to Chiang proposing that General Stilwell be given supreme military command in China. As we say, when it drew up the original indictment, the Justice Department felt it might possibly convince a court that such documents related to the national defense.*

Beyond this, there was the question, Why did the Department fail to add to its complaint a still further account, namely, espionage? In its memorandum to the Tydings Committee, the Department attorneys did not even mention this possibility; and we must assume they had felt they could not prove that transmitting government documents to a known Communist (Jaffe), and to a magazine that could easily be identified as Communist, amounted to transmitting them to a foreign power. And it may be true that such a charge could not have been made to stick in 1945. But this does not dispose of the question, Were the possibilities of making it

---

* The Department attorneys pointed out that, since the maximum penalty provided by each of the statutes in question was the same, i.e., two years in jail, it was a matter of indifference which law was used; the Tydings Committee obediently reported that the issue was, therefore, "academic." Any reasonably imaginative person should be able to see why the choice of the law under which the case was to be prosecuted was crucial: If the "national defense" statute had been used, the Department would have had a "spy" case on its hands, and Congressional investigation would very likely have resulted from the attendant publicity. Thus, the national Administration stood to avoid considerable embarrassment if the case could be passed off as small-time pilferage.

stick good enough to warrant an *attempt* to make it stick? We must remember that the overriding issue here is not whether the Government would have *won* its case had it vigorously pressed the prosecution, but whether the chances of its winning it were good enough to warrant the old school try.

Secondly: Was it advisable for the Government to conceal from the court the Communist element in the case? The Department attorneys advanced two rather different theories for having kept Roth's and Jaffe's Communist connections, as well as *Amerasia's* political coloration, out of the case. They told the Tydings Committee (a) that to have brought in the Communist angle would have *weakened* the case, since the Communists were friends and allies at the time; and (b) that to bring it in would have been *"prejudicial"* to the defendants and thus grounds for a mistrial since Communism was *anathema* at the time! Mr. Morris, minority counsel for the Committee, took the position that such evidence certainly would have been admissible, and most certainly would have strengthened the case (even though the charge was simply theft of government documents), since it would have helped establish a motive for the crime. At any rate, let us note how this aspect of the Jaffe case had been handled before Judge Proctor of the U.S. District Court:

MR. ARENT [Jaffe's attorney]. Your Honor, this indictment charges the defendant and others with conspiring to obtain various Government papers. *The Government does not contend that any of this material was used for any disloyal purposes. . . .* If Mr. Jaffe has transgressed the law, it seems he has done so from an excess of journalistic zeal. . . . We recognize, technically, the violation—and not from any desire to enrich himself, as demonstrated by the character of the publication, or any intent to jeopardize the welfare of his country. . . .

THE COURT. I think it would be well, perhaps, if, in view of the statement that has been made, which I understand you [the Government attorneys] approve of as a correct statement—

MR. HITCHCOCK [the prosecutor] (interposing). In substance, yes, Your Honor. . . .

THE COURT. Let me ask you this question, please: Is there any evidence that the use to which these documents were put would be a use whereby injury or embarrassment would come to the Army or the Navy in the conduct of the war?

MR. HITCHCOCK. We have no evidence of that, Your Honor, and, furthermore, no evidence that they were intended to.

THE COURT. Was there anything in the nature of publication that had that tendency?

MR. HITCHCOCK. There was not, Your Honor, as far as we know. So far as we know, there was nothing in the use put of these documents that had that tendency nor is there anything that we have in our possession that would indicate—in fact quite to the contrary—that the defendant intended that they should have that tendency. To us, it was largely to the purpose of lending credence or variety to the publication itself, and perhaps increase its circulation and prestige. . . .

THE COURT. . . . I accept without any doubt the assurance both of your [Jaffe's] counsel and of the Government attorneys that there was no thought or act upon your part which was intended or calculated or had a tendency to injure the Government or the military forces in the prosecution of the war. *It would make quite a difference to me if I did not have that assurance and did not know, confidently, that that was true.* . . .[10] [Italics added.]

Third, and most important, What of the "evidentiary" problem that lies at the heart of the dispute about the Justice Department's handling of the case? The Department argued—and this argument has ever since been the mainstay for its defenders in what has amounted to a legal hot stove league—that the documents seized in *Amerasia's* offices were "tainted evidence," and thus would have been inadmissible in a trial. Specifically, the Department maintained that it had been compelled to make a "deal," and to do so in a hurry, since one of the defendants (Larsen) had discovered that illegal searches and seizures had been undertaken by the OSS and the FBI prior to the arrests, and thus might have moved, successfully, to quash the indictment.

The argument by which the "tainted" or "polluted" evidence theory is applied to the *Amerasia* case runs as follows: The OSS raid and several FBI searches prior to the arrests were conducted without search warrants. But knowledge obtained from these illegal raids led to the procurement of the warrants that authorized the arrest of the defendants and the seizure of 1,069 *Amerasia* documents. Therefore, under the theory that evidence is inadmissible which has been discovered through illegal means, the Department argued that *none* of the *Amerasia* documents would have been admitted in evidence at trial, and thus that the success of the prosecution depended upon the defendants' not finding out about the illegal searches. And once Emmanuel Larsen had got wind of the illegal entry, the case was jeopardized—and deals had to be made.

There were indeed legal precedents supporting the Department's position. On the other hand—and this is the crucial consideration in evaluating the handling of the *Amerasia* case—there was also authority for the view that the evidence *was* admissible. Six weeks before the Tydings Committee made its report, on June 2, 1950, Senator Ferguson submitted to the Senate a lengthy and detailed analysis of the legal considerations, and he came to the conclusion that, at the very least, the evidentiary issue involved in the *Amerasia* case was moot. According to Ferguson, at least six separate arguments supporting the admissibility of the government's evidence—all of them backed by legal precedent—would have been available to the Department attorneys had they elected to press the prosecution:

a) The tainted evidence rule does not apply where the prior illegal seizure involves the recovery of stolen Government property;

b) The Government's procurement of the arrest warrants and thus the seizures of June 6 did not depend *exclusively upon knowledge obtained in the course of the illegal searches and seizures that preceded the arrest.* The Government had grounds for the arrest in the knowledge it had obtained from other sources; for example, from the discovery, prior to the OSS raid, that one of the restricted documents had appeared almost verbatim in the pages of *Amerasia;*

c) Since they were necessary in protecting national security in wartime, the OSS and FBI raids were legal, even in the absence of warrants, under an implied exception to the Fourth Amendment;

d) The protection of the Fourth Amendment, at the most, extends to the magazine *Amerasia* (whose premises were violated by the original OSS seizure) not to the individuals involved;

e) The "tainted evidence rule" is, simply, not good law in situations of this kind. As a U.S. District Court said in a case involving the Government's seizure of certain machinery parts: "[the contention that the seizure is illegal] . . . would have to rest on the single fact that the Assistant U.S. Attorney knew where the parts were [due to a previous illegal raid]. If we so held, we would say in effect to [the defendant:] . . . since the first seizure was illegal, you now have a chance to spirit away the evidence, for no search can be made until some time after the FBI has lost track of its whereabouts. The protection of the Fourth Amendment is not to be secured by adopting rules of hide and go seek."[11]

But if the evidentiary question was moot—and it is the authors' opinion that the panel of impartial experts would have so found— then, of course, the Justice Department is left without a leg to stand on. For the prosecution, particularly in a case as important as the *Amerasia* case, is obliged to test the law when there are rea- sonable grounds for believing that a conviction can be obtained.*

THE FBI CHART

On June 6, 1950, Senator McCarthy made, on the floor of the Senate, a profoundly disturbing revelation. It was based, he said, on "information which has never before been brought to the atten- tion of the American people"—information, moreover, that had been elicited from a report on the State Department by one of its own officials, a Department security officer named Samuel Klaus. This report, McCarthy continued, contained a chart prepared by the FBI, showing the size of the Soviet task force in the State De- partment. As of May 15, 1946, the chart allegedly revealed, there were 20 "Communist agents," 13 "Communists," 14 "Communist sympathizers," and 77 "suspects" working in the Department. The chart also contained, according to McCarthy, an amended count made two and a half months later; by that time, as a result presum- ably of Department personnel action, there were 11 "agents," 10 "Communists," 11 "sympathizers," and 74 "suspects" left.

"Can the Senators conceive of it?" McCarthy asked. "Eleven Communist agents were left in the State Department two months after the FBI had labeled them and said, Our files show these men are Communist agents."[13]

Nor, let us note, has anything been done, seven years later— as far as we have been able to learn—by way of ascertaining how many of the employees in question, if any, are still around. But a

---

* This view of the matter is the more convincing because the Department itself adopted it in another case that arose at about the same time. A man named Harris was caught trafficking in U.S. draft cards, and there was some question whether the charge could be made to stick, it being far from clear that the incriminating evidence had been legally seized. The Government attorneys might easily have persuaded themselves, "on the basis of prece- dent," that the weaknesses in their case were fatal. But they went ahead all the same and, in a United States Supreme Court decision that marked a mile- stone in the evolution of U.S. Constitutional law, they finally won out. How explain the Department's zeal in putting behind bars a small-time offender, and its apathy (with much the same legal issues involved) in prosecuting Communists who had stolen secret government documents?[12]

year after McCarthy's revelation, steps were being taken to punish him for having brought the matter up! In September, 1951, Senator Benton announced to the Gillette-Monroney Committee that McCarthy's "FBI chart" was one of the occasions on which McCarthy had deliberately deceived the Senate. How so? By telling it that the FBI had prepared the chart; whereas J. Edgar Hoover has denied that the FBI had done any such thing.

True, *after* McCarthy's speech, Hoover asserted that Mr. Klaus' statement attributing the chart to the FBI was erroneous. But McCarthy, without claiming any personal knowledge of the matter, had merely relayed to the Senate a piece of information from a report that he had had every reason to regard as authentic; which lets him off, but certainly not his accusers, to whom the chronology of McCarthy's claim and Hoover's denial was readily available. (To be sure a contradiction remains on the record: some one—maybe Klaus, maybe Hoover—either misrepresented the facts or misunderstood them. Mr. Hoover has a reputation for undeviating honesty; but so does Klaus. Which appears to be all that can be said about the matter—except to note one hypothesis that lets both men off the hook: namely, that FBI personnel had prepared the chart, but without the authorization or knowledge of Mr. Hoover.)

In any case, no one has ever questioned that the chart existed or that it was available to the Tydings Committee—which should have made it its business to find out who drew it up and what the State Department had done about the state of affairs the chart described. Here, certainly, was something for the Committee to move in on, and interesting questions should not have been hard to think up. Who were the "Communist agents," the "Communists," the "sympathizers," the "suspects," referred to in the chart? How many of them had continued in the Department's employ? For how long? Were some of them, by any chance, still in the Department in 1950? If so, had the security division acted wisely in clearing them?

The Committee squared off to the chart in characteristic fashion: *"While these charges are not before us,"* its Report stated, ". . . it is believed proper that the reader should have the facts in the matter."[14] Whereupon it reprinted Hoover's letter denying FBI authorship of the chart, and a letter from John Peurifoy, the State Department's Deputy Under Secretary, which declared that "the conditions mentioned by Mr. Klaus do not exist today. . . . none of these persons are now employed by the Department, except those who

have since been investigated and who have been checked and evaluated under the loyalty program."[15]

Once again, the Committee had signed up the State Department
to find out whether the State Department was delinquent in its
handling of loyalty and security cases. The Committee's explanation as to why it was not going into the matter itself ("these
charges are not before us") is, in the light of its mandate, simply
unintelligible. What we must conclude is that, as its hearings
moved into their fourth month, the Committee decided to narrow
its arbitrary and unwarranted interpretation of Senate Resolution
231 even further: not only would it limit its investigation to
charges made by McCarthy before the Committee; charges made
outside its chambers were to be ignored—even if they were made
on the floor of the Senate.

The reader, having examined this much of the Tydings Committee's performance, will perhaps agree that McCarthy's general
charge that shocking security conditions prevailed in the State Department was not disproved, but merely set aside. And why did
the Committee refuse to do the job that had been assigned to it?
Some say the Committee's shortcomings were due to the incompetence or the inexperience or the ignorance of its members, or a
combination of the three. But this answer is more recommended
by its charitableness than by its plausibility. Incompetence was a
factor, all right; but it leaves too much unaccounted for. *The Committee's hearings and its Report demonstrate beyond reasonable
doubt that the Tydings Committee—determined from the first to
vindicate the State Department—consciously set out to destroy Mc-
Carthy and make of him an example for all who, in the future,
might feel tempted to agree that the Democratic Administration
was jeopardizing the national security by harboring loyalty and security risks in sensitive agencies.* The record is there; and it shows
that the Committee's majority never had any intention of conducting an objective investigation of the State Department; that, from
the day the Senate adopted Resolution 231 to the day McCarthy's
charges were pronounced to the Senate and the nation at large to
be a "fraud and a hoax," Senators Tydings, Green and McMahon
played the role of Administration hatchetmen.

This explains a great many things that would otherwise remain
incomprehensible. For one thing, it explains the Committee's harassing of McCarthy before he was even allowed to begin his presentation, of which the usually imperturbable Senator Lodge spoke as

follows: "a perfectly extraordinary procedure. I have never seen anything like it, and I have been here since 1937. . . . I do not understand what kind of a game is being played here."[16]

It explains, also, the Committee's dogged refusal to allow the man presenting the charges, and the only person present who had made prior study of the evidence, to cross-examine the witnesses. Time and again McCarthy requested the routine privilege of interrogating persons before the Committee—a courtesy that traditionally is extended by any Senate Committee to any Senator.[17] He was turned down every time. At first, Tydings ruled, unprecedentedly, that the courtesy would be extended to McCarthy only if he were willing to be cross-examined in turn by the witnesses. When McCarthy consented to this arrangement, Tydings changed his mind, and refused to let him cross-examine at all.[18]

Our hypothesis also explains the Committee's consistent refusal to go beyond the evidence McCarthy had presented, and its repeated acceptance of a denial by the "accused" as the conclusive refutation of the allegation. It explains the Committee's insulting treatment of all witnesses whose testimony pointed to laxity on the part of the Department's security division; and, by the same token, its lickspittle bearing towards any and all, including Communists, whose testimony tended to discredit McCarthy's charges.

Consider its treatment of Louis Budenz, whose reliability as a first-hand source of detailed information about the Communist conspiracy was by then firmly established. He told the Committee that Lattimore and Hanson were Communists. The Committee used on him every known technique for humiliating a man. The following is an instance of its effort to discredit him by ridicule.

[Budenz had just finished itemizing the sources from which he had learned that Owen Lattimore was a member of the Communist Party.]

SENATOR GREEN. Do you know Mr. Lattimore?

MR. BUDENZ. Do you mean personally?

SENATOR GREEN. Yes.

MR. BUDENZ. I do not.

SENATOR GREEN. Have you ever seen Mr. Lattimore?

MR. BUDENZ. No, sir; I have not. As a matter of fact, however, I did not see Mr. Alger Hiss, either, and I knew him to be a Communist and so testified before the House Committee on Un-American Activities.

SENATOR GREEN. *But you are not reasoning that everyone you have never seen and never heard may be a Communist. Is that your argument?*

MR. BUDENZ. No, sir; that is not.[19] [Italics added.]

Or consider the Committee's behavior toward Miss Freda Utley, a woman with an international reputation as a courageous and knowledgeable anti-Communist. She had known Lattimore personally, and had given years of study to the Communist Party line in the Far East; so she ought to have merited attention in connection with the Lattimore case. When, however, she attempted to demonstrate, passage by passage, how Lattimore's writings had tallied with the Communist line, Tydings scornfully and impatiently cut her short: "We don't want opinion evidence here. We want facts, f-a-c-t-s. We are getting very few of them. We are getting mostly opinion."[20] (If ever a group of men needed some expert opinion, o-p-i-n-i-o-n, on how to spot party-lining in the area of Chinese policy, this one certainly did.)

After Miss Utley had finished her prepared statement, the Committee, instead of questioning her about Lattimore and his writings, plied her with impudent queries about herself. It wanted to know (a) whether she was Alfred Kohlberg's stooge, (b) whether she was being subsidized by the Chinese Nationalists, and (c) whether she had been a Nazi sympathizer.*

Consider now, by way of contrast, the Committee's demeanor in the presence of, first, Earl Browder, and second, Frederick Vanderbilt Field.

Let us look in on the Committee at the moment when Senator Hickenlooper has been asking Browder whether he knew this or that person to have been a member of the Communist Party. Browder has refused to answer ("I want to declare to the Committee that I consider it outrageous that this hearing should be devoted to the development of new smear campaigns," etc., etc. "I refuse to take part in such proceedings"),[21] and Senator McMahon is moved to intervene:

SENATOR McMAHON. . . . there are two names Senator Hickenlooper has presented to you. . . . Miss Kenyon and Mr. Hanson were named

* These questions were asked by the Committee's counsel, Edward Morgan. But they had been prepared, and placed in Morgan's hand, by Abe Fortas, Owen Lattimore's lawyer. The innuendo regarding Miss Utley's Nazi sympathies was based on one of her books, *The Dream We Lost* (1940), in which she urged a negotiated peace with Germany, so as to avoid Soviet domination of Europe, and predicted that a war of "unconditional surrender" against Germany would open the way to such domination. The insinuation that she was a pawn of Kohlberg was based on the sole fact that she was a member of the China Policy Association, of which Kohlberg was chairman of the board. The insinuation about her receiving financial support from Nationalist China was based on heaven only knows what.

openly and charged openly by Senator McCarthy. . . . It occurs to me that whatever your answer may be, that to withhold an answer to Miss Kenyon and this other gentleman, if you are sincerely interested in not contributing to a smear campaign, that your withholding of an answer on them, if the answer is in the negative, is contributing to that smear.

On the other hand, if the answer is in the positive, since those cases are before the Committee, I believe you should answer. . . .

SENATOR TYDINGS. Allow me to talk to the witness a moment. . . . The chairman would like to bring this matter to your attention and in the interest of fairness and truth, and in pursuing the investigation which we are ordered to make, to ask you if you will not reconsider on those two names, and tell us whether or not you know or do not know they are members of the Communist Party.

Browder is not to be outdone in courtliness by a mere democratic Senator:

MR. BROWDER. I am quite willing to answer the question about those two persons, and I refused to answer before only because . . . [the question] was obviously the beginning of a fishing expedition for new names to smear by association. . . . I would say, without the slightest hesitation, that neither one of them ever, in my period of leadership in the [Communist] organization . . . had any organized connection as members or friends.

SENATOR TYDINGS. Thank you very much for cooperating. . . .[22]

Several moments later it is called to Tydings' attention that Browder has refused to answer with respect to two other "McCarthy cases." He moves in to clear up the record:

SENATOR TYDINGS. . . . To your knowledge is Mr. John Carter Vincent or Mr. Service, members [sic] of the Communist Party? Those are the only two names I shall present to you.

This time, however, Browder gets cantankerous and puts the chairman on warning that, at some point, enough gets to be enough:

MR. BROWDER. Yes—before it was two other names. Now, it is two, maybe one by one we will get into a list of thousands.

Senator Tydings now plays his trump card—an appeal to Mr. Browder's natural wish to strengthen the State Department, to help Congressional committees, and to gain the chairman's gratitude.

SENATOR TYDINGS. . . . I see your point of view. I am not arguing at the moment, *but I do think you are defeating the purpose of this in-*

quiry in a way that you perhaps do not realize, if you allow this to be obscured, and if you felt that you could answer, in the cases of Mr. Vincent and Mr. Service, I would be very grateful to you. . . .

MR. BROWDER. . . . I would say that regarding the two names you mentioned, to the best of my knowledge and belief, they never had any direct or indirect connection with the Communist Party.

SENATOR TYDINGS. Thank you, sir.[23] [Italics added.]

As for Field, who appeared the next day, he too, at first, but only at first, refused to take the Committee into his full confidence. Then Tydings reminded him, as he had reminded Browder, that a refusal to answer would damage the persons involved more than it would help them. Field's better nature promptly asserted itself:

MR. FIELD. Yes, Mr. Chairman. I would be glad to state I have no— to the best of my knowledge—Mr. Vincent is not and never has been a Communist. . . .

SENATOR TYDINGS. I want to thank you for your cooperation, and I hope, after the conference with your attorney, you can go into other areas. . . . I would like to ask you whether or not these three men— Haldore Hanson, John S. Service, and John Carter Vincent, or any of them, insofar as you know—have committed any act of disloyalty to the Government of the United States, including the State Department, of course?

MR. FIELD. No, Mr. Chairman; to the best of my knowledge, none of these three men have committed any act of disloyalty.

SENATOR TYDINGS. Thank you.[24]

Our hypothesis explains the Committee's startling decision to deny Senator McCarthy, *and even the minority's counsel, Mr. Robert Morris,* access to the Committee's chambers while Louis Budenz was testifying in executive session—despite the presence in that chamber of both Owen Lattimore and his lawyer Abe Fortas!*

Our hypothesis explains why the most important of McCarthy's witnesses was made the victim of an unspeakable venture in character assassination on the floor of the Senate—with, it seems, the connivance of the Committee's majority. Let us listen to Mr. Morris as he relates this phase of the story in an article in *The Freeman* magazine (October 30, 1950):

. . . A high point in calumny was reached when Lattimore introduced into evidence a sealed copy of the transcript of the Santo deportation proceedings, at which Budenz had been the principal government wit-

---

* Only after strenuous protests by McCarthy did the Committee finally ask the Lattimore people to leave.

ness. It included a record of what the Communists through their attorney, Harry Sacher, had thrown at Budenz in that hearing.* The Immigration authorities, sensing its vileness, had decreed that only one copy be made, a fact that was verified in writing by the District Director of Immigration in New York, who asserted that this one copy had been given to Sacher in the event he had to use it on appeal. Santo never appealed; he voluntarily went behind the Iron Curtain. But Lattimore received (obviously from Sacher) that one copy of the transcript.

Then, surprisingly, Senator Dennis Chavez (Dem., New Mexico) revealed its contents on the Senate floor, even though it was sealed and the contents were never made known to Senators Hickenlooper and Lodge or myself. Senator Tydings, as Chairman of the Subcommittee, and Senator Lucas, as Democratic floor leader, officially joined Chavez in this attack. It was but one of many instances pointing to a secret liaison between the Communists, Lattimore, the Subcommittee and the Democratic Administration. . . .

The Tydings Committee, moreover, *published the entire Sacher transcript in the Appendix section of its hearings.*

Our hypothesis explains the Committee's vicious smearing of private citizens who had supported McCarthy—who, indeed, had anticipated him—in demanding an investigation of the State Department. We have in mind, specifically, *Plain Talk* editors Isaac Don Levine and Ralph de Toledano, and Mr. Alfred Kohlberg, whom, along with General Patrick Hurley, the Committee identified as the three "well-defined sources" of the charge that U.S. China policy had been undermined by saboteurs.

Plain Talk had published, in 1946, an article by *Amerasia* defendant Emmanuel Larsen entitled "The State Department Espionage Case." Larsen, however, attempted to repudiate his article, asserting that Levine and de Toledano had completely rewritten the original draft of his piece and had exerted financial pressure on him to authorize publication of the revised version. The Committee, though conceding that Larsen's "credibility generally is open to serious doubt,"[25] nevertheless proceeded to print his story as the authoritative version of the incident, without so much as putting in a telephone call to Levine or de Toledano for a check on the facts. And as if this were not enough, the Committee levelled a disgraceful and cowardly libel at the two editors: *"The fact that these persons have been reported to us as professional*

---

* Sacher had attempted to discredit Budenz by submitting him to smutty questioning on his personal life prior to his conversion from Communism.

'anti-Communists,' whose incomes and reputations depend on the developing and maintaining of new Communist fears, while not deemed necessarily significant, has not been altogether overlooked by the subcommittee."[26] (Italics added.)

Several days after the publication of the Committee's Report, Levine and de Toledano requested Tydings to repeat the statement without the benefit of immunity. Tydings promised to repeat outside the Senate anything from the Report, if pressed for satisfaction by allegedly injured parties. Yet he never repeated this charge.*

We have already told how the IPR smeared Alfred Kohlberg. The Tydings Committee went ever further than the IPR: "[Mr. Kohlberg's] wealth appears to have stemmed from contracts with representatives of the Nationalist Government of China." This "individual behind the scenes," the man "responsible . . . [for] a great deal of Senator McCarthy's assertions," is "reported," to have a "financial stake in the eventual victory of the Nationalist Government."[27] But there is not a single shred of evidence in the Committee's records (or anywhere else, to our knowledge) to support the implications of this charge—unless it be the two undeniable facts that Mr. Kohlberg was (a) an importer of Chinese textiles, and (b) an anti-Communist American, and as such certainly had "a stake" in the "eventual victory of the Nationalist Government."**

Some other things our hypothesis can explain are:

—The Committee's failure to hear the testimony of the "20 or 30" witnesses described by Senator Hickenlooper as persons "to whom the trails in this thing lead."

—The Committee's refusal to go into the numerous (Senator

---

* Levine and de Toledano also forwarded to the Committee their account of the handling of the Larsen article—which Senator Tydings did not circularize or, as far as is known, examine.

** The facts on Kohlberg are: (1) He has never had a financial transaction of any character whatever with the Nationalist Government, any of its subsidiary or affiliated organizations, or any individual who has ever been connected officially with the Chiang regime; moreover, he has formally offered to so testify under oath; (2) he is on record as having favored a China policy detrimental to his own financial interests: in February of 1949, when the Communist conquest of China was a foregone conclusion, Kohlberg made an energetic effort to persuade the Far East–American Council of Commerce and Industry (a "Chamber of Commerce" for American business interests in Asia) to adopt a stand *opposing all trade with China.* Only one other member of the Council was willing to go along. He, in short, was one of two persons doing business with China who were prepared to put their anti-Communism *above* their commercial interests.

Lodge, as we have seen, listed nineteen) questions that arose in the course of the hearings and that remained unanswered at the time the Report was written.

—The Committee's manipulation of the portion of its transcript that dramatically revealed the inadequacies of the investigation.

—The Committee's consistent practice of passing to the public the State Department's answers to charges brought against that very agency.

—Some of Tydings' more shameless ventures in sideshowmanship—for example, his turning his formal presentation to the Senate of the Committee's Report into burlesque.

Of that last item, more must be told. When the Senate convened on July 20, to hear what its investigating committee had found out, Senator Tydings had a stage act prepared for his colleagues, props and all. He pointed to a large chart set against the chamber wall. It purported to show that eight Congressional committees had previously reviewed and cleared McCarthy's 81 cases.* ". . . I love this little chart," said Tydings, "I call it Behind the 8 Ball. . . . Some time I hope it will earn merit in the National Gallery of Art. (Laughter.) I have titled this futuristic design and paint 'Whitewash.' I have seen whitewash before, but it is the first time I have ever seen it applied with eight coats on any political fence in America."[28]

But the act had just begun. On a stand in front of the chamber Senator Tydings ceremoniously placed a phonograph. "I wonder," he asked, "if I could get unanimous consent to play a radio recording of the Senator's [McCarthy's] own voice on one of these occasions?"** Tydings was determined to make the point once and for all that McCarthy's version of the Wheeling speech was a bald lie. "I am not asking the Senators to take my word, but to hear the Senator's own voice, who says he has not made a statement of this character."

Senator Wherry rose at this point, not to make a formal objection, but to observe that for the sake of decorum the record might better be played "some place else than on the floor of the United States Senate."

* The Committee's report made the more modest claim that *four* committees had processed and cleared McCarthy's cases; as we have seen, even this claim is patently false.

** Tydings referred to McCarthy's Wheeling speech and the raging controversy as to whether he had said he had "in hand" the names of 205 Communists in the State Department or simply 57.

Tydings promptly withdrew his request, although Wherry insisted that he had not actually objected. Tydings was adamant: "If the unanimous-consent request is to be denied, I withdraw it. I withdraw the unanimous-consent request and retain the floor. . . . I will play this record off the Senate floor in due time, but admission will be by card only. [Laughter.]" He went on referring again and again to the recording that would "once and for all" settle doubts as to whether Senator McCarthy was a truthful man. In summing up, he hammered the point home a final time: "Then what is there," he asked, "other than a fraud and a hoax and a deceit about this whole matter? It ought to make the blood of Americans boil, that they have been told these foul and vile charges—and here is a record to prove it. And if that is broken, I have duplicates. [Laughter]"[29]

Next morning, newspapers all over the land headlined Tydings' "proof" that McCarthy had lied. But when a number of newspaper reporters asked Tydings for a private audition of the Wheeling recording, he put them off. He had to put them off. *For Tydings had no such recording, and did not have one when speaking before the Senate!* The only recording made of the Wheeling speech had been destroyed the day after the speech was made—a fact discovered by the State Department investigators who reported on the Wheeling episode to the Tydings Committee—and this was well known to Tydings.*

So much for the things our hypothesis explains—a hypothesis, we may note, which is confirmed by a story that had appeared in

---

* Tydings later admitted, at a deposition hearing pursuant to McCarthy's libel suit against Senator Benton, that he had never possessed the Wheeling recording. Why, then, did Tydings so expose himself? Was it sheer bravado? Perhaps; but leavened with the cool calculations of a parliamentary veteran. Tydings unquestionably counted on the objection of a Republican Senator to his prepared stunt—in which case he would proceed, as he in fact did, to draw precisely the same inferences about McCarthy's truthfulness as if he had actually played the record and it had proved McCarthy a liar. As for the next day and the press, he would simply put them off—as he did—and the issue would sooner or later simmer down—as it did; but McCarthy would have been damaged all the same. And in the unlikely event that no one in the Senate should have objected to the playing of the recording, Tydings was prepared for this contingency, too. For he did have a record—of the *Salt Lake City* broadcast. A careful reading of Tydings' speech bolsters this hypothesis; for, until the time Wherry "objected" and Tydings "withdrew" the request to play the record, Tydings had spoken ambiguously on the point whether it was a recording of the *Wheeling* speech or of the *Salt Lake City* broadcast that he proposed to serenade his colleagues with. And only after Wherry had unwittingly obliged did Tydings firmly settle into the Wheeling groove.

Newsweek six weeks prior to the Tydings extravaganza of July 20. The story (a *Newsweek* scoop, later confirmed by Tydings himself) told of a strategy meeting held at Tydings' apartment on May 7, 1950, at which the course of the Administration campaign against McCarthy was charted. Present at the meeting were Tydings, Committee Counsel Edward Morgan, and Deputy Under Secretary of State for Administration, John Peurifoy, the Department's front-man in the McCarthy controversy. "The time had come, said Tydings [in the *Newsweek* account], to expose McCarthy. He had discussed it with the President and advised him that the counterattack would be launched on the floor of the House and the Senate."

Thus, the chairman of a Senate tribunal, in league with the tribunal's chief of staff, and the representative of the defendant, plotted together *even before the tribunal had completed its deliberations* to discredit the prosecutor!

In Summary:

McCarthy's own behavior during the Tydings episode was far from exemplary. He showed himself to be inexperienced, or, worse still, misinformed. Some of his specific charges were exaggerated; a few had no apparent foundation whatever. All his transgressions we have recorded in detail, so that those whose concern it is to remind him and his countrymen about his past sins may at least know what sins he committed, and what sins he did not commit.

McCarthy never redeemed his unredeemable pledge to reveal the names of "57 card-carrying Communists." He did, however, unquestionably redeem his promise to expose shocking conditions with regard to State Department security administration. And if the Tydings Committee was unimpressed, the State Department as we have seen, was not; for it "reprocessed" 46 of the 59 "numbered" McCarthy cases who were still in its employ—and before long, 18 of them were gone and then there were 41. Besides the 59, there were those former State Department employees named by McCarthy who had found their way into other federal agencies or into the staff of the United Nations. The Tydings Committee, in the teeth of its mandate to investigate present and past evidences of Communist infiltration in the Department, let slip through its fingers the chance to track down fellow travellers and loyalty risks so situated as to do hurt not merely to U.S. foreign policy, but also to U.S. governmental programs in general, and to the international organization on which, wisely or unwisely, the government has put its bets.

The statement is interminably made that "McCarthy did not present evidence on one single Communist working in the State Department." McCarthy himself, with his famous three days of orgiastic speeches and radio broadcasts, made it possible for his enemies to beat that particular drum. No doubt, McCarthy did not establish that his "57" were card-carrying Communists. Whether he *named* 57 Communists is another matter. We must remember that McCarthy was dealing with men and women who had compromised themselves by joining Communist organizations, maintaining Communist associations, making and writing statements of such a nature as to arouse legitimate suspicions. The available information on the technique of the crypto-Communist has evoked a healthy respect for his elusiveness and ingenuity. Alger Hiss was able to fool intimate friends and such seasoned men of affairs as Dean Acheson and Felix Frankfurter. And who would today believe Hiss was a Communist but for the tenacity and foresight of Whittaker Chambers and his uncanny prescience in preserving the pumpkin papers? We dare not assume that for every Alger Hiss providence will give us a Whittaker Chambers.

Thus, a precise verdict on McCarthy's charges would be as follows: McCarthy did *not* present conclusive evidence that there were 57 *card-carrying* Communists in the State Department; and he should not have made the specific charge he made. It does not follow that none of the persons he named was a Communist; nor that in the light of their records they should have been permitted to remain employees of the State Department. Franklin Roosevelt is not widely remembered as the American President who repudiated virtually every plank of the platform on which he was elected. Just so, McCarthy should not be remembered as the man who *didn't* produce 57 Communist Party cards but as the man who brought public pressure to bear on the State Department to revise its practices and to eliminate from responsible positions flagrant security risks.

After Tydings' Report, the odds were against McCarthy's political survival, and certainly against his being remembered in this way. We must not, however, lodge the Tydings Committee with too great a share of the responsibility for the scandalous public misinformation about McCarthy. All that the unscrupulous authors of the Tydings Report could do was write a smear Report and file it. The fate of the Report was placed, as all such things are placed, in the hands of opinion-molders throughout the land.

There was that Report—a palpable fraud. They could expose that fraud; or they could become accomplices after the fact. For the most part, they chose the latter course. And this—not McCarthyism, not even the performance of the Tydings Committee—is the nation's living shame.

CHAPTER X

A Vindication

IT IS hardly possible to examine State Department security without having access to data that are as readily available as the latest statistics on the hydrogen bomb. Still, an authentic (as distinct from a complete) appraisal can be made by piecing together the scraps of information that *have* become public and by searching out a few others. In our examination of the Department's performance we have concentrated on the *evaluative* division of its security apparatus; that is to say, we have at all times assumed that the *investigative* arm has done its job thoroughly and in good faith. We then asked whether, given the information available to it, the Department acted in the national interest.

The document of primary importance in evaluating the Department's security program is the transcript of Loyalty Security Board hearings. This is the Board before which a suspect employee appears (if he so wishes) to answer charges made against him. But the transcript is highly confidential and its release to the public can only be authorized by the employee under investigation. These minutes would reveal the extent to which the "government's case" is pressed before the Board. They would indicate whether suspect employees are being subjected to artful and penetrating cross-examination, and whether the Board evidences initial prejudice for or against the employee. They would expose any tendencies to stray from justice in the direction of either Kangarooism or whitewashing. Finally, they would throw light on the quality of the working judgment of the Board's panel members. For they would indicate whether these men are intelligently and rigorously applying the loyalty and security standards set by Department directives. The minutes would, in fact, be the best evidence as to whether or not the internal security of the United States is being adequately protected in the State Department.

But only one set of Board minutes has, to our knowledge, been released. It deals with the case of John Stewart Service.

John Stewart Service appeared before the State Department's Loyalty and Security Board in May of 1950. Even then, Service was a strong contender for the title, "most frequently cleared man in all Washington." He had been cleared by the Board on January 18, 1949. After McCarthy made his charges, Service's case had been reprocessed, and a new clearance had been given him on March 1, 1950. He had been called up again, and cleared again, on October 6, 1950. He had been cleared a fourth time on March 7, 1951. Three months after that, a fifth time; and on July 31, 1951, a sixth time. Several months later, however, the Civil Service Loyalty Review Board took the Service case out of the State Department's hands and found, on December 31, 1951, that there was "reasonable doubt" as to his loyalty. Mr. Acheson immediately suspended Service (as is mandatory under the Executive Order) and subsequently fired him.

The charges against Service were based on two separate counts. Between 1942 and 1945, Service was stationed in China as a Foreign Service Officer. From there he submitted memoranda to his superiors in Washington enthusiastically praising Mao Tse Tung and the Chinese Communists and avidly supporting the contention that their movement had its roots, not in Leninism, but in an aspiration for indigenous agrarian and democratic reforms. The Service memoranda were also severely critical of the Chinese Nationalists, whom they described as an effete, corrupt, and unreliable force. The question arose whether Mr. Service's judgment, as expressed in these memoranda, was influenced by a devotion to Communism, or whether he simply suffered from a severe case of politico-ethical astigmatism. With this question we have dealt in an earlier chapter.*

The second count was more dramatic and perhaps also more important. On June 6, 1945, Service was arrested by the Federal Bureau of Investigation for having transmitted, without authority, classified documents to the editors of *Amerasia,* a Communist magazine. Other factors in the case, together with a précis of Service's defense, are discussed in the foregoing chapter on the Tydings Committee. Here we concern ourselves only with a few security aspects of the case. And the following questions warrant careful attention:

1. Having at least *prima facie* evidence against Service (there

* See "The Case of John Stewart Service."

was no disputing his breach of security regulations in 1945), why did the State Department wait several years* before presenting his case to a loyalty tribunal?

2. Having been cleared on the *loyalty* count ("reasonable grounds"), why was he not dismissed as a *security* risk where action would have been governed by the "reasonable *doubt*" standard? Is not the transmission of classified material to a Communist** enough to create reasonable doubt of an employee's reliability?

3. What about the two of Service's six trials that were held *after* the 28th of April, 1951, and hence under the revised, "reasonable doubt" loyalty standard?

4. How many members of Congress, had they been ruling on the case, would have exonerated Service under the security standard? Which brings up the further question. Does it matter *how* members of Congress would have ruled?

5. Why (see Service's published loyalty hearings) did not a security officer assume a function analogous to that of the public prosecutor in a trial? Service was represented by an able and convincing lawyer. The government was not. Government cross-examination and rebuttal were, therefore, ineffective, unresourceful, and diffident. (This procedural deficiency confers a formidable and often crucial advantage on the "accused." To be sure, members of the Board are permitted to cross-examine and even to contradict witnesses. But, by definition, as a panel of judges, they are expected not to show bias. Certainly they cannot legitimately do for the government the sort of job Charles Rhetts did for John Service.†)

6. Does not the Civil Service Loyalty Review Board's reversal of previous determinations indicate that its conception of what constitutes a "reasonable doubt" of loyalty differed from that of the State Department Board? Which of the two—the Civil Service Board or the State Department Board—exercised the sounder judgment on this point? Is it not perplexing—and significant—that, while the Civil Service Board ruled *adversely* even in the *loyalty*

---

* During which time he was promoted.

** By an officer who had given evidence, a few months before, of a distinct understanding of security regulations when he *refused* to reveal classified material to Mr. Brooks Atkinson of the *New York Times*.

† The same deficiency prevailed on the appellate level, where the defendant and his lawyer were entitled to plead before the Secretary of State (or his designee), while no one was allowed to argue for the other side. At the suggestion of Senator McCarthy (*Senate Appropriations Committee Hearings* [fiscal] 1953, p. 435), the State Department revised this procedure in the summer of 1952.

category, the State Department had cleared Service on loyalty *and* security?

McCarthy pressed the case against John Stewart Service before the Tydings Committee, which, as we have seen, cleared him.

No other Board minutes, that we know of, have been released. For the most part, therefore, scattered data on particular cases must be leaned on to arrive at a judgment regarding the performance of the State Department in the field of security. In discussing these cases in the following pages, we shall mention by name the persons concerned—but only if their loyalty has been publicly questioned elsewhere. What is more, we shall not reveal damaging information that sits, undiscussed, in the raw files of some of them; for some of the information may be false, or may be explainable, and may, for those reasons or others, have remained suppressed.

WILLIAM T. STONE

William T. Stone left the Board of Economic Warfare to join the State Department as director of its Office of International Information and Cultural Affairs on the 12th of November, 1945. On the 22nd of March, 1946, the Bannerman Security Screening Board of the State Department concluded a report on him as follows:

. . . it is recommended that action be instituted to terminate subject's services with the State Department. It is suggested, to achieve this purpose, that an appropriate officer of the Department should inform [Stone] that his continued presence in the Department is embarrassing to the Department and that he be given an opportunity to resign. If [Stone] should not resign voluntarily, action should be instituted under Civil Service Rule 3 to terminate his services with the Department.[1]

The case against Stone was based on the following information:

1. From 1937 to 1941, Stone was a member of the editorial board of *Amerasia*. *Amerasia* was not captured by the Communists; it had been pro-Communist from the outset.

2. On December 10, 1941, Frederick Vanderbilt Field wrote to the head of the Institute of Pacific Relations, Edward C. Carter, as follows:

I have just had a conversation with Bill Stone over long distance. He was speaking from the office of the Economic Defense Board and indicated that we should go into the problem of my getting a job more fully in personal conversation. Nevertheless we had enough of a talk to convey a pretty clear picture.

Bill said that there would be very formidable obstacles indeed to my getting a Washington job.[2]

Subsequently, Stone endorsed Field for a job in military intelligence.[3] Whether Stone knew Field to be a Communist, only he can say. Certainly he had reason so to regard him. (See "The Case of Philip Jessup" for a discussion of the notoriety of Field's Communist activities at the time.)

3. While Stone was Assistant Administrator of the Board of Economic Warfare, an adverse security report arrived from military intelligence on Communist spymaster Nathan Gregory Silvermaster, also employed by the BEW. Stone advised Silvermaster of the report—in fact, turned it over to him for his perusal.

MR. STRIPLING [Counsel, House Committee on Un-American Activities]. Mr. Stone, of the Board of Economic Warfare, gave you a copy of the Naval Intelligence protest against you?
MR. SILVERMASTER. Yes.
MR. STRIPLING. He gave it to you?
MR. SILVERMASTER. Yes.
MR. STRIPLING. You answered that report yourself?
MR. SILVERMASTER. I answered the report.
MR. STRIPLING. You *yourself* answered it?
MR. SILVERMASTER. That is right.
MR. STRIPLING. Where was your report submitted?
MR. SILVERMASTER. . . . to Mr. Stone.[4] [Italics added.]

4. A report prepared for the House Appropriations Committee in late 1947 noted that "subject [Stone] has also since recommended two former employees of the *Amerasia* Editorial Board to positions with the State Department."

On June 18, 1947, after the replacement of Panuch, Bannerman, and other members of the relatively hard-hitting security staff of 1946, a State Department official summarized the case of Stone as follows:

It is not believed by this office that the information at hand raises a reasonable doubt as to the subject's loyalty to the United States, and accordingly, security clearance is recommended. However, this office intends at a later date, when the personnel is available, to review the issues of *Amerasia* Magazine from 1937 to 1941 and to determine if the contents of the articles are such as to have a bearing on the security status of subject.

Four months later, the State Department had not yet reviewed these issues of *Amerasia*. It is not known whether the promised bit of research was ever accomplished; though it *is* known that even the very first issue of *Amerasia* satisfied the American Politburo on its faithfulness to the Party Line.

And it is known that in the summer of 1950 Stone's case was in the State Department's loyalty and security channels, awaiting adjudication. He was cleared. A year later, in November or early December, 1951, presumably as a result of further investigation, he was again cleared. On January 31, 1952, the records of the case went to the Civil Service Loyalty Review Board for the customary post-audit. The Board expressed its dissatisfaction with the handling of the case and indicated it would take charge of it (as it had done with that of John Stewart Service). On the 2nd of February, 1952, William T. Stone resigned from the State Department, so that the reviewing Board never decided his case.

It is quite possible that Stone has satisfactory explanations for having served on the editorial board of *Amerasia;* for having recommended Frederick Vanderbilt Field for a job in military intelligence; for having tipped Silvermaster off on his dossier in the Naval Intelligence files; and for having recommended other *Amerasia* editors for positions in the State Department. Still, it was the view of the Civil Service Board, as of January of 1952, that despite his State Department clearances there were still questions about Stone worth investigating. And if Stone *was* a loyalty or a security risk, he had six years time, while occupying an influential position, to damage the United States—even though his dismissal was recommended in the first of these six years. His unexpected and untimely resignation, of course, does not inspire confidence in either him or the State Department officials who handled his case.

William T. Stone's name is one of those given the Tydings Committee by Senator McCarthy. He was McCarthy's Case Number 46.

JOHN CARTER VINCENT

John Carter Vincent's case is in some respects similar to the Service case.

The doubts about Vincent rest, first, on his energetic activities in behalf of the Chinese Communists while occupying various important positions in the State Department. Vincent joined the State Department in 1924, and he rose rapidly after the beginning of the war. In 1943 he was appointed Assistant to the Chief of the Far Eastern Division of the State Department, under Joseph Grew. Later the same year he was appointed Special Assistant to President Roosevelt's Administrative Assistant for Foreign Affairs, Lauchlin Currie, whom former communist Elizabeth Bentley named as a member of the Silvermaster communist spy group. During the ensuing years, most particularly after he took over the Division of Chinese Affairs, Vincent had an important hand in U.S. diplomatic activities that hastened Mao Tse Tung's conquest of China.

The report of the McCarran Committee, based on fourteen volumes of testimony concerning the Institute of Pacific Relations, concluded that "over a period of years, John Carter Vincent was the principal fulcrum of IPR pressures and influence in the State Department."

But in addition to doubts that reasonably arise concerning the reliability of a Far Eastern "expert" who so consistently misinterprets vital data and misdirects American policy in favor of our enemies, the case against Vincent has been substantially reinforced by the testimony of Louis Budenz who stated in the summer of 1951 that he had known Vincent to be a member of the Communist Party.[5]

Yet on the 19th of June, 1952, Mr. Carlisle Humelsine, Deputy Under Secretary of State for Administration, testified that John Carter Vincent had been cleared three times by the Loyalty Security Board of the Department of State.[6] And Vincent was cleared twice again during the next six months.

On December 12, 1952, the Civil Service Loyalty Review Board reversed the State Department by finding that reasonable doubt existed concerning Vincent's loyalty.

This, then, is another instance in which a subordinate board repeatedly clears a man on loyalty *and* security, and a superior board finds against him even on *loyalty*. If the Civil Service Review Board's judgment was the sounder one, then the State Department's security setup was such as to enable a loyalty risk to occupy crucially important posts indefinitely. During Vincent's stay in the State Department, the Communist cause in the Far East was dramatically advanced; and since a reasonable doubt about Vincent in

1952 presumably constitutes a reasonable doubt about him in 1947 (though the critical Budenz testimony was not elicited until 1951), Vincent *may* have been instrumental in this advance. The McCarran Committee came to just this conclusion.

Notwithstanding the Loyalty Review Board's recommendation, Dean Acheson (although he suspended Vincent) did not fire him. Instead, he persuaded President Truman to repudiate, in effect, his own loyalty program. Truman set up a board, headed by Judge Learned Hand, to review the findings of the Review Board. Secretary Dulles dissolved this novel piece of machinery when he assumed office in January, 1953.

But shortly thereafter, *without authority and in clear violation of the regulations of the federal loyalty program,** Dulles reversed the findings of the Loyalty Review Board. He went on to "request" Vincent's resignation—on the grounds that he had shown bad judgment—but he publicly stated that, in his view, Vincent was neither a loyalty nor a security risk and, by implication, that any doubts as to whether he was either, were unreasonable.

The refusal of the State Department Loyalty Security Board—and of Secretary Dulles—to declare Vincent either a loyalty or a security risk, commits them, incidentally, to the curious position concerning Louis Budenz' veracity that, as we noted above, the Tydings Committee took in the Hanson case:

Louis Budenz declares that John Carter Vincent was a member of the Communist Party.

Concealed membership in the Communist Party constitutes reasonable doubt as to a man's loyalty.

The State Department and Secretary Dulles find the loyalty of John Carter Vincent to be beyond reasonable doubt.

---

* It is curious that Secretary Dulles was never censured for his cavalier disregard of the rules. The State Department's *Manual of Regulations and Procedures* governing loyalty and security clearly implies that the Secretary of State has no power to overrule the Civil Service Loyalty Board. (See sections 396.11 and 366.41, May 4, 1951). Carlisle Humelsine of the State Department stressed the sovereignty of the Loyalty Review Board early in 1952 before a Senate Committee:

"SENATOR MCCARTHY. Am I correct in saying that Mr. Acheson [i.e., the Secretary of State] has the final say on both loyalty and security cases in the State Department?

"MR. HUMELSINE. He has the final say in the Department on security cases, *but in loyalty cases* [Vincent's was a loyalty case], *he does not have the final authority. The final authority rests with the Review Board.*" (Italics added. *Senate Appropriations for 1953,* p. 982.)

Therefore: The State Department and Secretary Dulles find no reasonable doubt but that Louis Budenz lied.

This conclusion assumes especial interest if we bear in mind that Budenz' contributions to the work of the Federal Bureau of Investigation have been warmly applauded by Mr. J. Edgar Hoover, and that an official of the Justice Department has said of Budenz, "His evidence has been worth 20 divisions to the United States."

The question arises: If sworn testimony from the former managing editor of the *Daily Worker* (a witness whose reliability has been frequently tested), to the effect that a State Department official was known to him to be a Communist, is not sufficient evidence to satisfy the State Department that *reasonable doubt* exists concerning that official's loyalty—much less reliability—what, then, does it take to arouse "reasonable" doubts? Secretary Dulles' unthinking reversal of the Civil Service Board has thrown a wrench into the security operation of the federal government.

John Carter Vincent's name was given to the Tydings Committee. He was one of McCarthy's numbered cases.

OLIVER EDMUND CLUBB

The public case against Clubb, a career Far Eastern expert in the State Department, rests principally on his associations with such Communists and Communist sympathizers as Agnes Smedley, Michael Gold, Lawrence Todd, Philip Jaffe, and others.*

There are scattered references to Clubb in the McCarran Committee hearings on the IPR; and there is a note in Whittaker Chambers' book, *Witness,* which tells of Clubb's visiting the editorial offices of the *New Masses* in 1932. All the above does not, in the opinion of the authors, justify a "reasonable doubt" as to Clubb's loyalty; nor does it justify an adverse security finding. It seems a safe guess, then—though a guess just the same—in the light of what follows, that the State Department or the FBI had assembled further and more conclusive evidence against Clubb. (An employee is presented with a transcript of his hearings before a loyalty board, and is privileged to release them. Clubb has not done this.)

* The minutes of Clubb's hearing before the State Department Loyalty and Security Board have not been released. The House Committee on Un-American Activities, however, interrogated Clubb on March 14, August 20, and August 23, 1951, and its hearings are public.

On June 27, 1951, he was suspended from his job—an unusual step. The Department does not, as a matter of course, suspend an employee when he is put in channels, pending final action on him by the Department's security division.

On February 11, 1952, the State Department called in the press and announced that Clubb had been cleared.

Q. [By a reporter] Did you say he was cleared of these charges?
A. Absolutely cleared,—cleared on loyalty and security.
Q. If there were loyalty charges, this new standard [reasonable doubt] was used and he was judged innocent?
A. That is right.
Q. Mac, [Assistant to the Secretary for Press Relations, Michael Mc-dermott] you say he was cleared on both loyalty and security charges,—then there were both charges against him?
A. He was cleared on both loyalty and security. It doesn't say charges. There is no question about either one and he was re-stored to duty.

This, it turned out, was not quite the whole story. Senators Ferguson and McCarthy discovered (1) that the State Department Loyalty and Security Board had, by unanimous vote, decided that Clubb's retention in the State Department constituted a security risk; (2) that Mr. Carlisle Humelsine, Deputy Under Secretary for Administration and top official in the security field, had concurred in the Board's judgment; (3) that Clubb had appealed to Secretary Acheson, who appointed a retired diplomat, Mr. Nathaniel Davis, to review the case; and that on Davis' recommendation Acheson had overruled the Board and restored Clubb to duty; (4) that Clubb had promptly resigned—whether by prearrangement or not, it is impossible to say.

On March 5, 1952, Mr. Acheson admitted to the press that Senators Ferguson and McCarthy were correct.

Oliver Edmund Clubb had been an employee of the State Department since 1928. He had held responsible posts in Hankow, Peking, Peiping, Tientsin, Nanking, Shanghai, Saigon, Chungking, Kunming, Tihwa, Mukden, Harbin and Changchun, prior to his appointment as chief of the China Desk in 1950. If the State Department's Board and the State Department's chief security officer were correct in adjudging him a security risk his presence in the Department through the years that cost us China becomes (like the presence of Vincent and Service) highly significant.

Why was the State Department so tardy in investigating Clubb? Was the evidence against him unavailable until 1951? Or did the State Department satisfy itself with the blanket clearance given him by the Tydings Committee?

Although Clubb was not one of McCarthy's "numbered" cases, McCarthy gave the Committee Clubb's name and some of the evidence against him.

Edward G. Posniak

On July 6, 1948, the FBI transmitted to the State Department an eleven-page report on Edward G. Posniak who had been one of its employees since October 26, 1945. He was then working as an international economist in the Division of Investment and Economic Development, Central and Eastern European Branch.

Posniak, born in Russia, emigrated to the United States in 1935 and was naturalized in 1939. Except for a few months he had spent with a manufacturing concern in Stamford, Connecticut, in 1937, and a short period under contract with the Brookings Institute, Posniak had always worked for the government. Before entering the State Department, he had been employed, in that order, by the Department of Justice, the Federal Public Housing Administration, and the Office of Strategic Services. He enlisted in the Army in August, 1943, and remained in the service for two years, doing work for the OSS. Then he joined the State Department.

His State Department post was important. It is described in the FBI report as follows:

In this capacity, he [Posniak] works with the Assistant Chief and other ranking officers in the drafting of final policy determinations regarding various forms of economic assistance, investment and development programs. He also makes policy recommendations in connection with questions of public and private investment and effect on industrial organizations, economic stability and development of the central and eastern European areas and their relationship to the broad objectives of the United States "foreign policy." For the past several months [i.e., in early 1948] he has been working on the question of exports to Russia and the satellite nations.

With respect to Posniak's ideological affiliations, the report had this to say:

An FBI agent who joined the Communist Party at the request of the Bureau in 1936 and was expelled from the Communist Party in 1948 and whose record as an informant was one of complete reliability, stated that Posniak was a member of the Communist Party and personally known to him as such. . . .

According to this informant . . . Posniak came to a lot of "open unit" meetings and to all recruiting meetings of the Communist Party from 1938 to sometime in 1942. This informant said he had no contact with Posniak since 1942, stating further that Posniak was horrified at the Russo-German alliance of 1939.

Another reliable FBI informant recalled Posniak as a member of the Communist Party in the late 1930's. [Italics added.]

In the summer of 1938, while—according to the testimony of an FBI agent—Posniak was an active member of the Communist Party, he was engaged by the Brookings Institute to work on one of its studies. Before hiring him, the report goes on to say, his superiors "specifically questioned Posniak as to any Communist connections he might have had in Russia or Europe, and Posniak said he had none, and expressed himself against Communist Party principles."

Furthermore, an associate in the Federal Public House Administration, who had known Posniak "from 1938 to 1941 and had worked under him for one year," "highly regarded Posniak and stated [that] during the time he had known Posniak, Posniak had exhibited nothing reflecting on his loyalty."

In short, Posniak appears to have had something of Hiss' talent for persuading his associates that he was loyal to the United States.

The FBI also included an affidavit from a responsible scholar who had been associated with Posniak for some time in the State Department. (In reproducing it, we withhold only the name of the informant, the names of other persons, and some identifying data.) The affidavit shows impressively how the presumption that State Department personnel had been thoroughly screened helped pro-Communists to influence the conduct of foreign affairs.

I served [the informant stated, in] . . . the Czechoslovakian Committee in May and June of 1946. My acquaintance with the person in whom you are interested is limited to this period. At the first meeting and at all meetings thereafter, I noted that he approached each problem from the standpoint "How will this help Czechoslovakia?" . . . As I recall, such questions as German transit rates, the settlement of the Army's debts, and further loans to Czechoslovakia were under consideration. I know nothing about the person in question, but the bias displayed was so marked that I queried [Miss X] and found she had reacted in a similar fashion. I assumed he was of Czech origin and checked the register as a matter of curiosity, only to discover that his origin was Russian. Since he had worked in other agencies and his origin would naturally have caused him to be thoroughly investigated, I did nothing further at the time.

I recall two other episodes. He requested me to have reproduced, as a Committee document, an article by . . . which had appeared in the Congressional Record. (I believe at the request of Congressman Sabath, but am not certain.) The article was a eulogy of Benes' policy of friendship and cooperation with the Soviet Union. Apart from the contents of the article (about which I had grave questions), the request to publish it as a Committee document was peculiarly out of order. I spoke with [Y] and [Z] of the Secretariat about it, but they took the position that the Secretariat couldn't question a Committee member's request. I then spoke with . . . the Committee Chairman, stressing the inappropriateness and the expense (the article was lengthy). He directed me not to issue it as a document, but to obtain a few copies of the Record and circulate them for information. That was done.

At that stage I was beginning to have doubts of the nature of the pro-Czech bias—was it pro-Czech or pro-Soviet?—particularly since the reports from our Embassy were to the effect that Czechoslovakia was over the hump and that we might be building up Czech industry for Russia. All the information coming into the Department during that period was certainly opposed to the position taken by the person under consideration, and policy in line with the reports was established by the Secretary shortly thereafter. Toward the end of June I attended a meeting of the Russian Committee under. . . . , Secretary of the Committee, at which the individual under consideration was present. After the meeting, which was on a highly secret matter [X] commented that he considered the individual dangerously pro-Soviet and that he intended to discuss the question of his further attendance with the Chairman of the Russian Committee.* I do not know what subsequently transpired, since I went on detail to . . . early in July. . . .

It was considerably later, when all connection with the Committee and the individual had been terminated, that I recommended an investigation.

The determining factor was the realization, from facts emerging in another case, that the assumption of thorough investigation in view of background was not necessarily valid. I still hesitated since I am totally opposed to "red-smearing" and other forms of harassment. I was questioned about another individual both by the Department security officers and by FBI agents and was impressed by their ability and by their sincerity in trying to search out the truth. With that assurance of a thorough investigation and fair hearing for the individual, I felt that

---

* The person in question substantially corroborated this account of his reaction.

I dared not refrain any longer from recommending an investigation. This is the only instance in over six years with the Department when I have felt that I had to take such action. [Italics added.]

The FBI report stated that Posniak had continued to associate with at least three Communists and fellow travelers into 1948, that is, up to the latest moment the report covered.*

On the other side of the ledger, the FBI report contained a dozen or so statements from former associates and employers to the effect that they believed Posniak to be loyal.

With this evidence before it, the Loyalty Security Board of the State Department cleared Posniak in 1948 on both loyalty and security and he resumed his duties with the Department. In the minds of the Board's members there were no grounds for believing Posniak to be a loyalty risk, and no grounds for justifying even a reasonable *doubt* that he was a security risk!

Two years later, on November 15, 1950, the State Department wrote to the Loyalty Review Board that Posniak "elected to resign rather than accept suspension pending investigation and adjudication of certain charges bearing on loyalty."

Evidently, the FBI had had information on Posniak's Communist allegiances as early as 1938. Did it communicate this information to the OSS and to the State Department? If so, how was Posniak able to get jobs in those sensitive agencies? Why did the State Department Loyalty and Security Board wait until 1948 before processing him? And how, in the face of the FBI agent's testimony, did it persuade itself Posniak was clearable? Why—with the same security standards valid in 1950 as in 1948—did Posniak get cleared in 1948 and find himself suspended in 1950?

Edward C. Posniak's case was submitted by McCarthy to the Tydings Committee (Case No. 77).

* Also included in the report is a bizarre affidavit from a confidential informant who volunteered his opinions about Posniak's loyalty because he had distributed literature of the America First Committee (during 1939 and 1940)—"which at that time I considered to be a group which were [sic] disloyal to the United States." "I believe Mr. Posniak was a member of the America First Organization," the informant went on, "because he tried to sell the principals [sic] of the organization to two of the elevator operators which he intimated to the operators as being better than our American way." Messrs. Roger Baldwin and Alan Barth will be pleased to note that true to its claims, the nonevaluating FBI passes along *all* its information, no matter how ridiculous.

DAVID ZABLODOWSKY AND STANLEY GRAZE

David Zablodowsky resigned from the State Department on July 7, 1946, having served as chief of its Editorial Branch. (He then became Director of the United Nations Publishing Division.)

Six years passed. On October 23, 1952, Whittaker Chambers testified before the McCarran Committee that he had known Zablodowsky as a member of an underground espionage ring in 1936. This Zablodowsky admitted, though he denied ever having been a "member" of the Communist Party (which, in the circumstances, is neither here nor there).

Zablodowsky was McCarthy's Case No. 103. Like everybody else, Zablodowsky was cleared by the Tydings Committee.

Stanley Graze worked for the State Department until 1948. On April 20, 1948, he was cleared by the Loyalty Security Board. He resigned from the State Department ten days later to go to work at the United Nations.

On October 14, 1952, Graze refused to answer the following question put to him by the McCarran Committee: "Are you now or have you ever been a member of the Communist Party?" He also refused to answer the question: "Are you now engaged in espionage activity against the United States?"

How, in view of these refusals, are we to explain his having survived his hearing before the State Department Board? Did the Board ask him whether he was a member of the Communist Party? If so, did he on that occasion (as before the McCarran Committee) refuse to answer—and win a clearance notwithstanding? If he did answer and denied Communist Party membership, how explain his refusal to answer the same question four years later? Is the State Department in a position to furnish the Justice Department with a transcript of the Graze hearings, with a view to determining whether perjury has been committed?

Graze (McCarthy's Case Number 8) was cleared by the Tydings Committee.

ESTHER BRUNAUER

Dr. Esther Caukin Brunauer (for a full discussion see Chapter VII) joined the State Department in November, 1944, and rose to the position of policy liaison officer for UNESCO (July 1, 1947).

Immediately after her husband's suspension by the Navy for security reasons in April, 1951, Mrs. Brunauer was suspended by the State Department—where suspension of an employee pending adjudication of a security proceeding was by no means a common practice. There is reason to believe that the evidence against her prompted this unusual action.*

On June 16, 1952, Mrs. Brunauer was dismissed by the State Department, as a security risk.

Senator McCarthy submitted the Brunauer case to the Tydings Committee. She was McCarthy's Case Number 17.

The following cases, briefly summarized, throw light on one or another of the points at issue in this book. In most instances, the persons listed below were members of the State Department who brushed up against its security division. They are not all—by any means—transparent security risks. In one way or another, however, their experiences add to the picture of a fumbling and insensitive security program.

Herbert Fierst was hired by the State Department in September, 1946. In 1951, he got into the loyalty-security channels of the State Department. The Civil Service Loyalty Review Board expressed dissatisfaction with the handling of his case, and sent it back to the State Department Board for readjudication. In short, a judgment was handed down by the Central Board (as the Civil Service Loyalty Review Board is often called) that a State Department officer's loyalty status had not been explored with sufficient thoroughness even after seven years. Fierst was one of McCarthy's numbered cases.

❖

John Paton Davies had been processed at least four times by the State Department Board on the strength of charges of pro-Chinese-Communist activity. In December, 1952, the Civil Service Board (whose jurisdiction extends only to loyalty, not to security cases) ruled that no reasonable doubt existed as to Davies' loyalty.

* Senator Ferguson: ". . . your board has already decided in the loyalty channel that there was sufficient evidence to suspend [Mrs. Brunauer]?" Mr. Humelsine: "There was." (*Senate Appropriations for 1953*, p. 457, March 27, 1952.)

However, in April, 1953, Davies was transferred by the new administration from an important post in Germany to a relatively unimportant post in Lima, Peru. In the meantime, the McCarran Committee had found that Davies had "testified falsely before the subcommittee in denying that he recommended the Central Intelligence Agency employ, utilize and rely upon certain individuals
having Communist associations and connections. This matter was
. . . substantial in import."[7] Davies was one of McCarthy's numbered cases.

❖

Hans Lansberg had left the State Department before the Tydings Committee began its work, to take a job with the Department
of Commerce. As a former State Department employee, however,
he came under the purview of the Tydings Committee, which
cleared him. A year later he was ruled a loyalty risk by the Commerce Department, a ruling which the Civil Service Loyalty Review Board upheld on May 25, 1951. In other words, the State
Department's loyalty-security machinery failed to apprehend a
loyalty risk whom a less sensitive agency disposed of as such at a
later date. And here, as elsewhere, the Tydings Committee not only
slept on a tip from McCarthy that was to be vindicated in due
time, but actually gave the individual a further "clearance" to
point to. Landsberg was one of McCarthy's numbered cases.

❖

Val R. Lorwin joined the State Department in December, 1945.
He became chief of the Department's European division of international labor, social and health affairs; subsequently, he worked
for the Department as a labor economist. A year after the Tydings
Committee cleared Lorwin, the Department suspended him—on
February 5, 1951. He was restored to duty by the Department on
March 28, 1952, and in June was formally cleared of all charges
bearing on loyalty or security. Shortly after, he resigned, and went
to work for the University of Chicago as an assistant professor of
social sciences and industrial relations.

On December 4, 1953, a Federal Grand Jury handed down an
indictment of Lorwin, charging that he had lied under oath in
claiming (1) that he had never been a member of the Communist

Party, (2) that he had never carried a Communist Party card, and (3) that he had never held a Communist Party meeting in his home.

Lorwin was McCarthy's Case Number 54.

❖

Peveril Meigs joined the State Department in September, 1945, and resigned in 1948, to go to work for the Department of the Army. He was cleared by the Tydings Committee. Several months later he was suspended by the Army Loyalty Board and, subsequently, was discharged. Meigs was one of McCarthy's numbered cases.

❖

[Writes Whittaker Chambers:] The treasurer of the Ware Apparatus, Henry H. Collins, Jr., Princeton and Harvard, and a scion of a Philadelphia manufacturing family, was my personal friend. He also served, voluntarily and, in fact, irrepressibly, as a recruiting agent for the Soviet apparatus among members of the State Department. It was he who recruited *one of the Bykov apparatus' State Department sources, a man of much more glittery social background than Alger Hiss.*[8] [Italics added.]

The person referred to in the italicized portion of the above paragraph (his name has never been publicly discussed) joined the State Department in 1940, and resigned in December of 1948. At that time the State Department had had in its possession *for over two years* a memorandum stating that he was a "recognized leader" of the Communist underground in the State Department. He was McCarthy's Case Number 53.

❖

Dorothy Kenyon* was hired by the State Department in 1947 to act as United States Delegate to the United Nations Commission on the Status of Women. Three years later, the Tydings Committee was given documentary evidence of her participation in at least twenty-four Communist fronts during the thirties and forties. Judge Kenyon's appointment with the State Department expired

* For a full discussion of the Kenyon case, see Chapter VII.

the last day of December, 1949. She had never been so much as investigated by the State Department during the years of her employment.

Judge Kenyon was one of McCarthy's cases.

⋄

Haldore Hanson* wrote an allegedly pro-Chinese-Communist book, *Humane Endeavor*, in 1939. Before that, he was associated with Edgar Snow and Nym Wales, named communists, on a magazine in Peiping. Hanson was employed by the State Department in 1942, and rose to the position of Chief of the Technical Cooperation Project Staff shortly before the time the Tydings Committee convened. Louis Budenz testified to the Committee that he had known Haldore Hanson to be a member of the Communist Party. The Committee—and the State Department—cleared** Hanson. It was not until September, 1953, that he was dismissed from federal service.

He was one of McCarthy's public, unnumbered cases.

⋄

William Remington is in jail, having been convicted of perjury for denying his membership in the Communist Party. McCarthy cannot be given the credit for exposing Remington; he did, however, give his name to the Tydings Committee at a time when Remington was widely considered guiltless. Remington had been cleared by the Civil Service Loyalty Review Board. Remington was not an employee of the State Department, but he held a job with the Commerce Department in which he worked closely enough with the State Department to be of interest to its security office.

He was McCarthy's Case Number 19.

⋄

Robert T. Miller joined the State Department in June, 1944, and resigned on the 13th of December, 1946. State Department security officers under Panuch urged his dismissal as early as July 24,

---

* For a full discussion of Haldore Hanson, see Chapter VII.

** The implications of this clearance in the face of Budenz' testimony are identical with those discussed above in connection with John Carter Vincent.

1946, and the investigators for the House Committee on Appropriations classified him, in 1948, as "in all probability the greatest security risk the Department has had." Former Assistant Secretary of State, William Benton, in whose office Miller worked, has testified[9] that Assistant Secretary Russell, even with the McCarran Rider in hand, did not feel he had enough evidence to fire Miller. In 1951, Elizabeth Bentley testified before the McCarran Committee: "Robert Miller was one of the Communist Party members that I took on as an espionage agent way back in 1941. . . . He was one of the people I dealt with directly, collected his dues and got his information."[10]

Robert T. Miller was McCarthy's Case Number 16.

It would be comforting to state, at this juncture, that we have mentioned every security dereliction in the State Department during the period from 1947 to 1950. But we have not. Indications are that what we have pieced together is but a tiny, though horrifying representative fragment of the whole security picture—much of it brought to the attention of an unresponsive public by the irrepressible efforts of one man.

CHAPTER XI

Confrontation

. . . a lot of people get the idea that this particular program [the State Department's security program] *is not under Congressional scrutiny. I have to go up and get the budget of the Department of State each year, and I go before two appropriations subcommittees, one in the House and one in the Senate . . . and they are satisfied that we are running this program in the proper way.*—CARLISLE H. HUMELSINE, Deputy Under Secretary of State for Administration, on "Meet the Press," August 19, 1951.

McCARTHY'S "terrorization of the Department of State" has for several years now been the central preoccupation of our intelligentsia. They see in it conclusive evidence that the new Age of Conformity is upon us. The Department, they allege, is petrified: unable to go about its normal business because it must forever be warding off a new McCarthy offensive, unable to recruit the talented young men it needs because no self-respecting young man would hazard the indignities McCarthy will subject him to, powerless in dealing with foreign nations because it is known around the world that McCarthy has undermined public confidence in the State Department.

To be sure, at least until the change of administration in 1953, the State Department often behaved as if McCarthy were its Number One problem. The public work on that problem was normally left to Mr. Acheson's low-echelon operators—in part, no doubt, because it would have been *infra dignitate* for Mr. Acheson himself to engage in such sordid encounters. In any case, these underlings, especially those responsible for the operation of the security program, went at the job lustily and certainly not in the manner of men terrorized by the mighty McCarthy.

In October of 1951, for example, General Conrad E. Snow, Chairman of the State Department's Loyalty Security Board since its inception, had this to say about the State Department's troubles in a speech delivered at George Washington University: "What, then, is all the shouting about? . . . The old saying is—where there is so much smoke, there must be some fire. There is, however, no excuse for mistaking dust for smoke. The dust in the present case is created by one man, tramping about the Nation and making, over and over again, the same baseless and disproved accusations. The one man is able to raise so much dust only because (1) he is a Senator of the United States, and (2) he speaks in a loud and determined voice and waves in his hand a bunch of photostats that nobody takes the trouble to examine."

Two months earlier, on *Meet the Press,* Carlisle Humelsine, whom moderator Martha Rountree introduced as "the man who is responsible for the security program in the State Department," faced a battery of newspaper men and welcomed their questions. "Senator McCarthy," one reporter asked, "has been quite active in this field [loyalty in government]. How many new leads would you say he has given you for investigation of people in the Department?"

Very few indeed [Humelsine answered]. The Senator picked up an old list that was furnished to the 80th Congress. A couple of new names were provided by him. Those have been carefully investigated, and as a result of that investigation they have been cleared. Now, it might be of interest . . . to tell you a story of one of those investigations because he charged—among these various lists of names he gave one particular name. We looked into this case. The FBI had a very careful investigation. They found nothing wrong with the man but they did find something wrong with his dad. They found that his dad when a young man had been accused of drunken driving and the drunken driving had occurred on a bicycle. Now, is that the type of man that you want us to get rid of in the State Department?

The consensus of the reporters present and of the national television audience was, presumably, No, that's *not* the type of man we want you to get rid of. "Most of these investigations you are talking about, at least those which grew out of Senator McCarthy's charges beginning in February, 1950," asked another reporter, "have occurred while you have been in charge of the security work of the Department, haven't they?" Humelsine:

Well, most of the investigations growing out of Senator McCarthy's charges occurred before I even got in this business because he has taken old names that have been gone over and dredging [sic] them up anew. I mean, he is riding piggy-back on the 80th Congress committee that made the investigation and *cleared* the State Department. [Italics added.]

When asked whether anyone in the Department was furnishing McCarthy with material, Humelsine went out of his way to issue a warning to all State Department personnel: "I don't know . . . [but] if I catch anyone that is feeding him information, I am afraid they won't be in the State Department any longer."

On March 25, 1952, a few months after this broadcast, the principals in the controversy, excluding only Mr. Acheson, met face to face. A subcommittee of the Senate Committee on Appropriations had taken up the question of loyalty and security in the State Department. Humelsine and Snow and various of their associates had appeared to represent the Department. The Committee, composed of Senators McKellar, Ellender, Hill, Kilgore, McClellan, Bridges, Saltonstall, Ferguson and McCarthy, was headed by Senator McCarran.

The Committee's hearings on loyalty and security in the State Department runs to several hundred pages and, even including the *ex parte* hearings of the Tydings Committee held some two years earlier, they constitute the most exhaustive inquiry into State Department security practices that any Committee of Congress has ever conducted. We shall, therefore, examine them here at some length.

The interrogators did not neglect the early phases of the State Department's security program. What, asked Senator McCarthy, had become of the employees whom Secretary Byrnes, in his 1946 letter to Congressman Sabath, had described as unfit for continued employment with the State Department because their loyalty was questionable? Humelsine did not have the information at hand, and had to set his researchers to dig out the facts. He later summarized the findings as follows:

Investigations by the screening committee [under Byrnes], including those spot checked and those reviewed after full investigation, resulted in 341 disapprovals. *Of these 341 cases, 46, as stated above, after receiving full clearance, are still employed by the Department.* Of the remaining 295 cases two were discharged under the McCarran rider.

The remaining 293 persons *were removed* through various types of personnel action.[1] [Italics here and throughout this chapter are added.]

This makes especially interesting reading if we go back two years and examine a State Department memorandum to the Tydings Committee. The memorandum summarized the fate of the Byrnes' board findings as follows:

Investigations by the screening committee, including those spot checked and those reviewed after fuller investigation, resulted in 341 "disapprovals." *Of these 341 cases, 58, after receiving full clearance, are still employed by the department.* Of the remaining 283 cases two were discharged under the McCarran rider, referred to hereafter. The remaining 281 persons *were removed* through various types of personnel action.[2]

After two years of denouncing McCarthy, and touting the efficiency of its security division, the State Department, in other words, gave the Senate Committee a paragraph from an old memorandum, freshened up a bit with some new arithmetic—and even failed to notice that its manicured figures proved how truly its security program had been defective. Consider what the two paragraphs, taken together, say: In 1950 the Department assures the Tydings Committee and the American people that the entire Byrnes list has been thoroughly investigated; that the security risks have been weeded out; and that of the persons in question only 58 remain—completely trustworthy employees who have received "full clearance." Two years later it tells another Senate committee that the entire Byrnes list has been thoroughly investigated; that the security risks have been weeded out; and that of the persons in question only 46 remain—completely trustworthy employees who have received "full clearance." At the very outset of his campaign against the State Department, McCarthy had asked for a full report on the Byrnes list. Nothing to worry about there, the State Department had explicitly answered: Only 58 of them are still around and they are all right, take our word for it. But the Department was apparently prompted to go back and take a second look; and twelve of the 58 did not survive that second look. Needless to say, the State Department did not acknowledge its admitted twelve delinquencies; it did not even bring in a new phrasemaker to plead its case.

The Committee asked: Had the State Department in the entire history of the President's loyalty program ever found against, and

separated, anyone as a loyalty risk? Answer: No.* However, for
the first time in its history, the Loyalty Security Board had gone
so far as to rule that somebody—three employees, to be exact—was
a loyalty risk. But the three were not out yet: the adverse decisions
were being appealed. What is more, a veritable purge was in the
offing. For before the year (1952) was over, the Board was to find
ten security risks; and the preceding year it had found six security
risks.** The Department had found only one security risk—McCarthy's Case No. 53 incidentally—in 1948, one in 1949, and two in
1950.

Since the President's ban on security information does not preclude the furnishing of statistical—as opposed to personal—data,
the authors requested the security division of the Department to
release the dates on which the persons dismissed as loyalty or
security risks between 1948 and 1952 had been *hired*. The information is, to say the least, startling.

The one employee separated in 1950 had joined the Department
in 1944. Of the five persons separated in 1951, one had been hired
in 1933, two in 1946, and one each in 1948 and 1949. Of the nine
separated in 1952, one each had been hired in 1935, 1942, 1944,
1945, 1947, 1948, and 1949, and two in 1946. In other words: *all
15 were employed by the Department at the time McCarthy began to criticize Department security practices!*

Now what are we to think of this? That the employees in question joined the Communist Party in 1951 and 1952, having been,
up to that moment, unimpeachably patriotic Department employees? That the FBI had neglected, over a period of years, to transmit
available derogatory evidence to Department security officials? Or,
that the Department was finally prompted *to act on evidence it
had possessed all along?* Clearly, the last of these hypotheses is
the only convincing one.

One thing, at least, is certain: In 1950, when State Department
officials were so vociferously asserting the Department's inviolable
security, at least 15 persons whom it was itself finally to classify as
of doubtful loyalty or reliability, were still in its ranks. It is impossible, due to the President's ban, to ascertain just how many of

---

* John Stewart Service had, to be sure, recently been fired as a loyalty
risk; but only after the Civil Service Loyalty Review Board had overruled the
Department board and ordered his ouster.

** There is no way of telling how many of these loyalty and security risks
were among the twelve on the Byrnes list who, according to Humelsine's
report, had been removed between 1950-52.

these persons McCarthy had named to the Tydings Committee. We do know, however, that he had named some of them.*

In any case, what clearly stands out from these statistics is the softness of the Department's security attitude at a time when it was pretending to be hard. And this is confirmed by what we learn from other sources.

Hiram Bingham, former Republican Senator from Connecticut, replaced Seth Richardson as head of the Civil Service Loyalty Review Board on the 3rd of January, 1951. On February 13 and 14, he convened the Board to discuss, among other things, the State Department. The minutes of this meeting reached Senator McCarthy, who brought them to the attention of the Appropriations Committee:

"I think it is fair to say," Bingham observed, "that the State Department, as you know, has the worst record of any department in the action of its Loyalty Board. . . . The Loyalty Board, in all the cases that have been considered in the State Department, has not found anyone—shall I say, 'guilty' under our rules. It is the only Board which has acted that way."

It quickly became clear that Bingham was not alone in this view. Said one of his colleagues:

. . . I don't understand their position at all, because although their board has not held their people ineligible under the loyalty test, who should have been held ineligible under that test, they have plenty of power to remove them as a security risk. Why haven't they exercised it? They haven't exercised it, in spite of all the searchlights that have been turned upon them.

The following exchange, initiated by a fourth member of the Board, further clarifies the picture:

BOARD MEMBER. What are you going to do when the attorney who is presenting the charges acts as though he were the attorney for the incumbent? I read 100 pages of a record where the three members of the Board were acting as attorneys for the employee. . . .

EXECUTIVE SECRETARY. Oh, you're talking about the State Department. They're taking the attitude that they're there to clear the employee and not to protect the government. We've been arguing with them since the program started.

ANOTHER MEMBER. That brings up a question that has been on my mind a little. . . . I have been disturbed about the State Department— their remarkable record of never having fired anybody for loyalty, and

* See "A Vindication."

yet we do nothing about it as far as the Board is concerned. I have been troubled about whether or not we owe the duty of having somebody call the attention of the President, for example, to the fact that the program simply does not work in that Department and let him worry about it. It seems to me we assume more responsibility when we sit back (as we have done) for three years and know that the country rests in a false sense of security that we are looking after their interests here when we know darn well that it is completely ineffective in one of the most important departments of the Government, and I wonder whether we ought to say anything to anybody about it.

Mr. Bingham reminded his colleagues that he had recently spoken to the Secretary of State and had said to him: "You've got to tell the Loyalty Board members [of the State Department] to behave themselves." And Mr. Acheson, he reported, had promised to do something about this.

When the Committee confronted Humelsine with this judgment of his division's performance by members of the President's Central Loyalty Board, he answered in effect: If the Board indeed felt that things were all that bad, why had it not pre-empted jurisdiction over the alleged loyalty risks in the Department and—as it was entitled to do under its own regulations—ordered their ouster? Since they had done so in only one case (that of John Stewart Service),* didn't this mean that the situation was not quite as serious as it had been painted by a bunch of overwrought gentlemen?

Not, let us note, a bad answer. The Civil Service Board did unquestionably have the authority to overrule the Department; and the question *does* arise why, given the vehemence with which the Board members spoke of the Department, they did not regularly invoke that authority. McCarthy, however, was ready with an answer. For one thing, until 1951 the Board had been restricted by Presidential decree to the "reasonable grounds" standard; for another, it had a millstone around its neck: Seth Richardson was its chairman.[3]

Neither of McCarthy's points here was by any means idle. The reasonable grounds formula saddled the administrators of the program with difficult problems, as we have submitted in an earlier chapter. For that reason, a few days after he succeeded Richardson

---

* Six months later, the Loyalty Review Board acted again, reversing the State Department on John Carter Vincent. In 17 instances, the Board expressed dissatisfaction with the Department's handling of a case, and ordered them reopened (*Hearings*, p. 462).

as Board Chairman, Bingham requested President Truman to revise the standard. As for the attitude of Richardson's Board—and McCarthy's point about Richardson himself—it is difficult to quarrel with. During his tenure, the Review Board overruled a great many decisions of subordinate boards.* But the fact that the decisions reversed were decisions *against* employees suggests precisely the kind of bias McCarthy attributed to the Review Board while Richardson was Chairman. (There were of course no reversals of State Department decisions, because none of them went against employees while Richardson was chairman.)

"I regret the destruction of any government employee," Richardson once told an editor of the *New Republic* (February 4, 1952). "It's a terrible penalty to be called disloyal. *That's why the Board has leaned back in the way it has.*" Thus it is not surprising to find him writing to Mrs. Roosevelt, on December 6, 1949, that the "penalty of a disloyalty discharge is so disastrous that *the Loyalty Review Board has inclined toward resolving all doubts in favor of an involved employee.*" Or consider how the Director of Personnel of the Government Printing Office testified in August 1953 (before the McCarthy Committee) as to why Edward Rothschild, a GPO employee, had been cleared despite abundant evidence that he was a member of the Communist Party:

THE CHAIRMAN. Let me ask you this: the other day [in executive session] as I recall you said your board operated under the general rule—I think that is an exact quote—the general rule that mere membership in the Communist Party was not sufficient to bar a worker under your loyalty program. Is that the general rule under which you operate?

MR. HIPSLEY. That is true. I went further, sir, if I may take another moment, and told you that Seth Richardson gave us the philosophy behind that. He gave us a long-winded story about the fact that some time ago he wanted to become a member of the IOOF [Odd Fellows] and he had no knowledge of the charter and bylaws, and he wanted to be a member of the IOOF not because of its charter and bylaws, but because it has a nice library of books he wanted to read. He said [therefore that] it was the *purpose* of the membership [i.e., in the Communist Party], *why* you belonged, that was important. That was his explanation. He was our guide.[4] [Italics added.]

---

* See *The Federal Loyalty-Security Program*, by Eleanor Bontecou (Cornell, 1953), p. 57. Notorious among the employees so rescued was William Remington, whom the Board exonerated in 1949, reversing an agency determination.

Seth Richardson was perhaps always a little terrified with his authority. "You know," he once said, "the State Department is the first department in the government. When Truman walked up to Congress the other day Acheson was there next to him. . . . Well, I always felt that they felt chagrined that anybody else—especially just a board in the Civil Service Commission—should have the power to check up on State. They always seemed to say: 'You let us run the State Department.'"[5]

No wonder that Senator McCarran's Judiciary Committee decided to sit on Richardson's suggested appointment as chairman of the Subversive Activities Control Board set up under the McCarran Act, and thus eased him along toward retirement from public life.

There is, however, a further explanation of the Central Board's record: it never had jurisdiction over security (as distinct from loyalty) risks. Thus, it could legitimately interest itself only in the more blatant cases; and these, of course, it had to review under the "reasonable *grounds*" standard. Richardson reminded Mrs. Roosevelt of this in the letter mentioned above: ". . . as you may be aware, the Loyalty Review Board was not clothed with any power whatever in relation to security matters. Our own hairshirt, is the question of loyalty. . . ." Hiram Bingham understood this. In answer to the question, "Why isn't your Board empowered to consider the security risk?" Bingham answered,[6] "Because the President, in the last paragraph of Executive Order 9835, says, 'You will have nothing to do with security cases.' . . ."

"Wouldn't it be better if [your Board did both] . . . ?"

"It would be much better, in my opinion. . . ."

In sum, then, it appears that Bingham's Central Board, to the extent it was not engaged in throwing stones from a glass house, was criticizing the State Department's practices in the *security risk* field in which (as Humelsine well knew) it was powerless to intervene. But it appears further that the Board, even with Bingham as chairman, and with the revised standard, and despite its avowed alarm over Department loyalty practices, simply let things slide—except, of course, in the cases of Service and Vincent. That the Board did not move to oust either Edward Rothschild or Haldore Hanson is evidence of its lethargy. Bingham, who after all was a Truman appointee, seems to have been a little on the diffident side when it came right down to overruling (as distinct from simply criticizing) the State Department—although there is no evidence of the kind of obsequiousness on his part that his predecessor showed toward the State Department.

The Civil Service Board did not (for a number of reasons we have mentioned, and perhaps for others we know not of) force the Department to act on all its loyalty risks. Still and all, there is no getting around the fact that various Board members, including its chairman and its executive secretary, felt strongly in 1951 that the State Department was jeopardizing America's security. And it is significant that, in the two years following the Board's indictment of the Department, the Department's security division did root out four times as many security and loyalty risks as during the preceding three years.

Just as light is thrown on the Central Board's activities by what we know of Seth Richardson, so light is thrown on the Department's Loyalty Security Board by what we know of the mind and manners of its chairman, General Conrad Snow. His statements before the Appropriations Committee, and elsewhere, show him up as a well-meaning blunderer, without any clear idea of what the whole thing was about.

Take his speech at George Washington University on October 25, 1951, and his speech before the Harvard Club on November 17, 1951. His topic on both occasions was "Loyalty in the State Department"; his clear purpose, on both, was to discredit McCarthy and to reassure his listeners about the Department's security division.*

When Snow came before the Committee, Senator McCarran wanted to know whether the speeches put forward merely the personal views of General Snow, or whether they argued the official "line" of the State Department. "You were speaking as an individual in this case?" McCarran asked. "Yes, sir," Snow answered.

But it developed that the State Department had printed and circularized the speeches; that General Snow's staff had helped him prepare them; and that the Department had cleared both manuscripts for delivery. Snow had said in one of the speeches, "I can speak only for the Department of State and for the period 1947 to the present." And this seemed to the Committee difficult to square with what Snow was now telling it. "You state there," said McCarran, "that you are speaking for the Department of State." "Yes; that is right." But had he not just testified, asked Senator Ferguson, that he spoke only as a private citizen? Snow: "That is right." Senator McCarran and his colleagues became curioser and curioser:

---

* The two addresses are printed in full in *Senate Appropriations, Hearings for (fiscal) 1953*, pp. 502-12. The page references that occur below in the body of the text refer to these hearings.

SENATOR McCARRAN. You say that you are speaking as an official of the Department of State?

MR. SNOW. I do not want to get confused with the issue that you have just raised.

SENATOR McCARRAN. You told your people—

MR. SNOW. I was saying that I was speaking *about* the Department of State.

SENATOR FERGUSON. That is not what you say. You say: "I speak only *for* the Department of State for the period 1947 to the present."

MR. SNOW. That is right. The word "for" in both cases has the same implication. I was not speaking *for* the Department of State in any different sense than I was speaking *for* the period 1947 to date.

SENATOR FERGUSON. Now, wait a minute. You are a lawyer, are you not?

MR. SNOW. Yes sir.

SENATOR FERGUSON. And you use words in their proper meaning?

MR. SNOW. I try to.

SENATOR FERGUSON. Now, when you say that you speak *for* the Department of State, you are the *spokesman* for the Department of State?

MR. SNOW. I might be so construed. What I meant there was—when I said that I speak *for* the Department of State, in that particular case I meant that I was speaking *about* the Department of State and *about* the period 1947 to the present. The word "for" there—

SENATOR FERGUSON. I am not speaking about the period. You say that you are speaking *for* the Department of State for a certain period of time.

MR. SNOW. I am speaking in relation to the Department of State only.

SENATOR FERGUSON. That is not what you said.

MR. SNOW. I said "for," but what I meant was "with relation to."

SENATOR McCARRAN. And this speech was evidently censored, passed upon, and approved before you gave it?

MR. SNOW. I think it was; yes sir. [pp. 477-78.]

And so on—until the Committee concluded that Snow had indeed been speaking as a representative of the Department; and this, of course, gave the speech added significance.

Snow's two addresses differed only slightly. In his first speech, Snow had said:

Since December 17, 1947, when the President's loyalty program was implemented . . . the Loyalty Security Board of the Department of State has had before it over 500 cases of State Department employees who have been investigated for loyalty by the Federal Bureau of Investigation—the FBI—and not one case has been found of a present Communist working in the State Department. Over that period eight employees have been held to be security risks. . . . I cannot discuss individual cases. [p. 502.]

In short, General Snow revealed on October 25, 1951, that in a period of three and one-half years, the Loyalty Security Board had found *no* loyalty risks and *eight* security risks.

In his second address (November 11, 1951), he dealt rather differently with this aspect of his Board's record:

> During the whole period—June 1947 to the present, the Board of which I am Chairman has adjudicated 594 cases; and has found adversely on both loyalty and security grounds in numerous cases—I cannot give statistics. [p. 508.]

Now in the first place, General Snow *could* have given statistics, just as he had done three weeks earlier: President Truman's ban does not extend to statistical information. What is more, far from finding adversely on "both" loyalty and security grounds in "numerous cases," the Board had yet to make its *first* adverse loyalty determination! It was two months *after* this speech was delivered (on January 24, 1952) that a loyalty risk was uncovered by the Loyalty Security Board.

But how should one account for Snow's radical change in emphasis? In the first speech, he tells his audience (citing statistics) that security risks in the Department have been few and far between. In the second, he tells his audience (withholding statistics) that the adverse findings of his Board have been "numerous." Had Snow discovered that the public reaction to his first speech was different from what he had anticipated? That, far from inspiring confidence by citing the *small* number of adverse determinations the Board had made, the speech caused widespread dismay to a public conversant with the success of Communist penetration of the State Department? Whereupon, in his second effort, he abandoned this line in favor of something less accurate but bigger sounding? The Senators, regrettably, did not spot the anomaly; and General Snow was not questioned about it. Hence it is possible only to guess what caused him to swing around so abruptly.

Let us consider another aspect of the two speeches. General Snow had made it clear in both of them that he was speaking of the period since 1947, i.e. the period during which he had been head of the Department's Loyalty Security Board. This, among other things, permitted him to exploit the Hiss case (under him, said Snow, Hiss would not "have been employed by [the Department] . . . for a day after [his] . . . acts were discovered"), and yet give it a wide berth.

I should like to limit the field of inquiry to the limits of my own competency. . . . I am sure that you would much prefer that I speak of matters within my own knowledge, rather than speculate on what may or may not have occurred in the State Department during the hectic days of war, under Hull, Stettinius, and Byrnes, and under security programs previous to that set up by Secretary Marshall in June, 1947. . . . I mention this particularly because every time I discuss the program which I have helped administer for over 4 years, someone wants to argue the case of Alger Hiss, and I know no more about the Hiss case than anyone else who has read the newspapers. . . . [p. 508.]

Hiss was a bad customer, all right, but, General Snow concluded, "My point is that one swallow does not make a summer, nor does this Hiss case make out an infiltration of the State Department by Communists." The Committee, on the other hand, tacitly adopted another view, namely, that the chairman of the State Department's Loyalty Security Board *ought* to know more about the Hiss case than what had appeared in the newspapers, and certainly ought to know *as much* about it as was public knowledge. Yet the more Snow talked, the more evident it became that he knew less about it than a well-informed newspaper reader. When reminded that reports about Hiss had been submitted to the Department by Berle and by the FBI years before 1947, his recollections were vague. When pressed about Hiss' contacts in the Department and about the persons with whom Hiss had most closely associated, he had nothing to contribute. And the demonstrated fact that there had in fact been a second, a third, and even a tenth swallow to help make the summer had never crossed his mind.

And if none of this was calculated to quell the Committee's anxieties, Snow's estimate of the implications of the Hiss case (as expressed in the first of his two speeches) could only multiply them: *"The Hiss case and the case of Judith Coplon in the Department of Justice,"* he had said, *"have done more harm in terms of public confidence than any harm Hiss or Coplon ever did in the delivery of classified papers."*

To judge from a few scattered comments, public reaction to this statement was not favorable. The *New York Journal American,* for example, in an editorial entitled, "Strange Theory"[7] commented, "If this [statement by Snow] means anything at all, it means that the man charged with determining the loyalty of men and women employed at the highest level of Federal responsibility believes there is more harm in catching criminals than in letting them have complete freedom to do their utmost to destroy the country."

Nothing of the sort, said Snow in his second speech; nothing he had ever said could be construed to mean that he "deplored the prosecution of Hiss. Nothing could be further from the fact. While I deplore the undoubted harm, in terms of loss of public confidence in the Department that the public disclosure of Hiss' acts has done, I am, of course, entirely in favor of public prosecution of illegal actions." (p. 508.)

The Committee duly noted General Snow's amplifications in his second speech, but it persisted in asking the General the still unanswered question, Which has done *more* harm—Hiss' exposure or Hiss' treachery? Senator McCarthy took the lead:

SENATOR McCARTHY. You say: "The Hiss case and the case of Judith Coplon in the Department of Justice has done more harm in terms of public confidence than any harm Hiss or Coplon ever did in the delivery of classified papers." Now, by that you mean that the exposure of them did the damage rather than their spying?

MR. SNOW. No, sir. What I meant by that was that the damage which they did by being traitors to their country had done more damage.

McCarthy, baffled, turned to a colleague: "Senator Ferguson, I think we have different speeches." Senator Ferguson: "I *know* we have different speeches." General Snow tried again: "What I meant to emphasize was the infinite damage that both Hiss and Coplon did by being traitors to their country. That is what I intended to emphasize, that the infinite damage which they did by becoming traitors to their country was greater than the damage they could have done by being spies."*

Senator McCarran took a deep breath: ". . . Is it not clear that what you were saying there was that the harm was done by the public *exposure* of Hiss and Coplon rather than by their *spying* activities?"

Snow finally capitulated:

MR. SNOW. I must admit, Senator, that the language that I used must have been subject to misinterpretation because it was misinterpreted not only by you, sir, but by the public.

* General Snow now serves the Eisenhower administration as the State Department's legal adviser to the Bureau of Far Eastern Affairs.

SENATOR McCARRAN. Anyone would construe it the way the Senator is construing it. A 6-year-old child would. . . .

MR. SNOW. . . . I had no such intention.

SENATOR McCARTHY. Would you not think that the normal person would so interpret that?

MR. SNOW. I am afraid that the normal person might, because it has been so interpreted.* [pp. 475-76.]

The Committee came finally to the animadversions about Mc-Carthy and McCarthyism in Snow's speeches, but soon found itself dealing with matters of far greater moment than whether or not McCarthy had been maligned.

General Snow had defined McCarthyism in his speech as follows:

This is McCarthyism—the making of baseless accusations regarding the loyalty and integrity of public officers and employees, by a person who is himself in high public office and who uses his office at one and the same time as a platform from which to shout his accusations and as a screen to protect himself from action for defamation. The purpose of it all is, of course, not the public interest, but political advancement in a period of public tension and excitement. [p. 503.]

Against whom, McCarthy wanted to know, had he made baseless accusations? Snow ran for cover. "I cannot," he replied, "discuss individual cases under the prohibition I labor under. [sic]" McCarthy then tried a different approach. You have just finished telling us in another connection, McCarthy reminded Snow, that 54 disloyal cases were allowed to resign under investigation and that three other individuals had been found to be disloyal or are in the process of appeal. That, by a strange coincidence makes 57, does it not? (p. 481) Could it be, McCarthy wondered out loud, that these 57 tally with the 57 on the original McCarthy list? No, answered General Snow, they were "not the same individuals"—which might have been well enough had he not, a few seconds later, confessed that he did not know the *names* of the 54 who had resigned!

McCarthy pounced:

. . . Mr. Chairman, I want to call the chairman's attention to the statements made by this witness. [Turning to Snow] I think you should

* In finally acknowledging that a "normal" person would so interpret these remarks, General Snow had come a long way. For he had written to the editors of the *Journal American* (pp. 540-41) a few months before: "Just how you could torture my speech . . . to mean [what you wrote about it] . . . is a mystery to me."

be sworn now. . . . He made the statement a minute ago that the 57 individuals whose names [I gave] . . . were not the same as the 57 who either resigned or were found disloyal. Now he says, "I do not know who the 54 were. I do not know what their names were."

Now, either you are lying Mr. Snow, when you said that you did not know who they were, or you were lying to us when you said they were different from the 57 that McCarthy names. You cannot be telling the truth at both times. Does not that follow as the night follows the day?

MR. SNOW. No, it does not.

MR. HUMELSINE. [interrupting] I do not think that is fair . . . General Snow . . . would not know anything about the 54 who resigned when under loyalty investigation. He would not have anything to do with the 54 resignations.

SENATOR MCCARTHY. Then he must not lie to us if he does not know anything about it. Mr. Snow just got through saying that the 54 were not the 54 on McCarthy's list, and now you say you could not possibly know.* [p. 481.]

McCarthy reverted to his request that Snow mention an instance from McCarthy's Tydings list in support of his charge that McCarthy had made "baseless accusations." And this time Snow attempted momentarily to meet the challenge:

MR. SNOW. As I recall, Haldore Hanson was on that list.
SENATOR MCCARRAN. What is that?
MR. SNOW. As I recall—
SENATOR MCCARTHY. Mr. Snow says that Haldore Hanson is on that list.

But immediately, General Snow retreated.

MR. SNOW. Now, I cannot answer questions about his case.
SENATOR MCCARTHY. Your position is that I made baseless accusations against Haldore Hanson. Have you ever read what I said about Haldore Hanson?
MR. SNOW. I think so, yes.
SENATOR MCCARTHY. You have?
MR. SNOW. Yes.
SENATOR MCCARTHY. [What I have said about Hanson] . . . is here in the document. Will you take that and tell me what in it are baseless accusations?

* As it happens, General Snow was correct in his guess that the two sets of names were not identical: we have seen in the section on the Tydings Saga, that only 18 of McCarthy's cases had been separated from the Department as of January, 1953.

MR. SNOW. I cannot do that, I say, without discussing the individual case. . . . I cannot discuss the case of Haldore Hanson, Mr. Chairman, without going into the substance.

SENATOR MCCARTHY. . . . Let us forget your files and look at this and see if you can tell us anything which is baseless on the basis of the information available to the public. In other words, take the public information.

MR. SNOW. I don't know of any information available to the public. I do know something about the files and I cannot discuss them.

SENATOR MCCARRAN. Now, there is a peculiar situation here, Mr. Snow. You can go out to the public and accuse a member of the Congress of the United States of falsifying and you can call him by a certain name. You call it McCarthyism. Now, you come before this committee, and when you are confronted with the situation you go under cover that you cannot disclose.

MR. SNOW. . . . The only information I have about Hanson is from my files. I do not know him personally. The only information that I have about him is from my files.

SENATOR MCCARTHY. . . . Mr. Humelsine, may I ask you a question? . . . Let me ask you this: In view of the fact that Mr. Snow has publicly stated and now before the committee states, that the charges . . . against Hanson are baseless, do you think he is competent to act as chairman of the board to hear the evidence and decide whether the charges are valid, or not, keeping in mind that the Hanson case is now pending before Mr. Snow's Board? Do you think that he is disqualified from his job as the result of this?

MR. HUMELSINE. Obviously, I think the general is competent to perform the duty or I would not have him in that particular assignment.

SENATOR MCCARTHY. Will you try to answer my question?

MR. HUMELSINE. What is your question again?

SENATOR MCCARTHY. Let us narrow it down. When Mr. Snow says that the charges against Mr. Hanson are baseless, was Mr. Hanson's case pending before the Board as of [that day?] . . . does not that disqualify him from sitting on that case and determining whether or not the charges actually are baseless?

SENATOR MCCARRAN. In other words, it is a preconceived conclusion.

SENATOR MCCARTHY. Yes.

SENATOR MCCARRAN. Is that what you mean?

SENATOR MCCARTHY. Yes. You are a lawyer, Mr. Humelsine. Would you not say that Mr. Snow is disqualified?

MR. HUMELSINE. I would have to look into that question further and give you an answer to it, Senator. I cannot on that basis give you an answer.

SENATOR MCCARTHY. You mean that when a man publicly states that the charges against Mr. X of Communist affiliations or connections— when he publicly states that those charges are baseless, and condemns the man who makes them, can you now tell us whether or not you think that disqualifies him from sitting on a board and making a decision on it?

MR. HUMELSINE. I would have to decide whether he is right, or not; whether the charges are baseless.

SENATOR McCARTHY. All right.

SENATOR McCARRAN. [Snow] is the one who decides. He has already decided that they are baseless. Do you not see the position you are in?* [pp. 482-87.]

Snow began reading a summary of McCarthy's indictment of Hanson, and agreed that the first few charges were not, in point of fact," baseless." But after a few minutes' reading, Snow objected: "The next allegation is that he [Hanson] spent several years in the Communist army in China writing stories and taking pictures which the Communists helped him smuggle out of the country. I cannot comment on that without a reference to the files."

SENATOR McCARTHY. You can answer that by referring to his [Hanson's own] book [*Humane Endeavor*], Mr. Snow. Have you read his book?

MR. SNOW. I have not read his book.

SENATOR McCARTHY. And you are passing on him?

MR. SNOW. That is right. [p. 491.]

At last Snow finished his perusal of the précis of McCarthy's statements about Hanson. He was not able to single out one charge that was clearly "baseless."

The Committee moved to other matters. What, it asked, about Snow's statement that there were no known Communists in the State Department? Had there been, General Snow answered, "the FBI would have found out about it. The FBI reports would come to my board, and my board would pass on it."

"Just a minute," McCarthy said: "Let us not start giving the FBI the blame for this. You have the Posniak case, Mr. Snow, before you. That case was called to your attention by me. I sent you copies of 12 FBI reports. I put those reports in the Congressional Record. Your board cleared him by a split decision of 3 [2?] to 1. . . . You

---

* It was subsequently revealed (p. 493) that the Hanson case no longer lay, as of this moment, before the Loyalty Security Board. But the question remains whether it was Hanson's case that Snow had in mind on October 25, 1951 when he made his first speech on McCarthyism and whether the case lay before the Board at that time.

had before you evidence that he had been a member of the Communist Party. You have had before you evidence that he was living in the same apartment with a man known to the FBI as an individual who was recruiting Communist spies. That is in your file, Mr. Snow. Now why do you tell us that no evidence has ever come before your board that you had a Communist in the State Department? . . . Now, you just got through saying that if there was a Communist, the FBI would notify you."

MR. SNOW. That is right.
SENATOR MCCARTHY. Now, what more notification can the FBI give you than what they gave you in the Posniak case where there were 12 investigations, I cannot say.
MR. SNOW. I cannot discuss the Posniak case, I am sorry. I would have to have the file before me.
SENATOR MCCARRAN. You always come to a dead end. You come to the point where we cannot go further.
MR. SNOW. That is right. [pp. 489-90.]

After a luncheon recess, General Snow returned. He came back with a definite plan of action. He would outline, he told the Committee, five statements that had been made over the years by McCarthy, on the basis of which he felt entitled to call McCarthy, in effect, a liar. He had cited these statements in his second speech.

The first of these, it turned out, was Senator McCarthy's statement at Wheeling on February 9, 1950: *I have here in my hand a list of 205—a list of names that were known to the Secretary of State as being members of the Communist Party and who nevertheless are still working at shaping policy in the State Department."* (p. 494.)

SENATOR MCCARTHY. Mr. Snow, you are aware of the fact that the investigators for the Gillette-Monroney committee went to Wheeling, West Virginia, and completely disproved what you have said?
MR. SNOW. I am not aware of that.
SENATOR MCCARTHY. Did you not read that in the paper?
MR. SNOW. No, sir.
SENATOR MCCARTHY. . . . You say "baseless"; that my statement was baseless. . . . I would like to read two paragraphs into the record from the statement by the Investigator for the Gillette-Monroney committee. He said: "My job in Wheeling I thought was to find the facts, to find whether, as Senator Benton charged, McCarthy had said that he had lists of 205 Communists in the State Department, or whether, as Senator McCarthy maintained, he had said he had a list of 57 individuals,

either members of or loyal to the Communists [sic]. While in Wheeling, I thoroughly interviewed a large number of witnesses who were in a position to know what Senator McCarthy had said. Every one of those witnesses save one supplied information which cast grave doubt and suspicion on Senator Benton's story and substantially corroborated Senator McCarthy's account of the facts." [pp. 488, 532. The investigator was Mr. Dan Buckley. See above, "The First Charges."]

General Snow went on to the second of McCarthy's five allegedly false statements—i.e., a statement that, said Snow, McCarthy made on the Senate floor on February 9, 1950: *"I have in my hand 57 cases of individuals who would appear to be either card-carrying members or certainly loyal to the Communist Party, but who nevertheless are still helping to shape our foreign policy."*

Actually, McCarthy had made no such statement on the Senate floor on the date Snow mentioned. Snow presumably had in mind the Wheeling speech (McCarthy's version), which McCarthy repeated on the floor of the Senate on February 20, 1950. In any case, Snow was not familiar enough with the history of the McCarthy controversy to nail the Senator down on his most vulnerable statement, that made at Salt Lake City on February 10, 1950, to the effect that he knew of 57 "card-carrying Communists" in the Department. McCarthy challenged Snow (whose assistants, at least, knew the identity of McCarthy's cases) to name names by way of showing that the statement ("57 . . . individuals who would appear to be either card-carrying members or certainly loyal to the Communist Party") was baseless. Snow again declined, on the grounds that the regulations forbade him to discuss the persons concerned.

"The third statement [General Snow continued] *was made on May 6, 1950, in Chicago, that the loyalty files in the Department were 'skeleton,' 'purged,' and 'phony.'"* "That was further developed on May 15, at Atlantic City, [Snow continued] when he [McCarthy] said they had been 'rifled'; on June 9 at Milwaukee, when he said they were 'raped,' 'denuded,' and 'tampered with'; and on July 12, 1950, when he said they had been 'stripped.'"

These allegations of McCarthy are discussed in some detail in the Appendix. For present purposes, we can content ourselves with excerpts from the resulting give-and-take between McCarthy and Snow:

SENATOR McCARTHY. [You say that my] statement that the State Department files had been rifled is one of the "baseless" and "unproved" charges. Are you aware of the fact that there were submitted to the Tydings Committee the statements of four State Department employees, one of Burney Threadgill, who is in the FBI; another one of Paul Sullivan, who is in the Foreign Service School at Georgetown, and two other State Department employees?

They state that they personally had been engaged over a period of months in stripping from the State Department files any material which would adversely reflect upon a man's loyalty or his morals.

Are you aware of the fact that those statements have been put in the record?

Mr. Snow. I am not aware of the statements to which you refer.

Senator McCarthy. . . . Are you aware of the fact that we have those statements?

Mr. Snow. No, sir.

Senator McCarthy. You never heard of them?

Mr. Snow. Never heard of them; never saw them.

Senator McCarthy. As chairman of the Loyalty Board, do you not think you have the duty to check those affidavits?

Mr. Snow. First, I would have to know about them to have the duty to check them. I knew nothing about them, as I say.

Senator McCarthy. You never heard of them?

Mr. Snow. Never heard of them.

Senator McCarthy. Before you made the speech which was O.K.'d by the State Department did you try to find out what evidence I had given that the files were rifled?

Mr. Snow. I still don't believe the files were rifled.

Senator McCarthy. I do not care what you believe. I asked you a question. Before you make the statement such as you made in the speech, that McCarthy was a liar because he claimed the files were rifled, do you not think you have a duty to check and see what evidence I had presented of rifling?

Mr. Snow. How could I find what evidence you had, Senator?

Senator McCarthy. What evidence I had publicly presented to the Tydings Committee.

Mr. Snow. I didn't know anything about it and didn't know you presented it.

Senator McCarthy. You did not answer my question. You went out to Chicago and said McCarthy is a liar because he said the files were rifled.

Mr. Snow. Yes, sir.

Senator McCarthy. My question is this: Before you call me a liar on that, do you not think you had a duty to check with the Tydings Committee and see what evidence I had presented of the rifling, and check on the veracity of the men who gave the statements?

Mr. Snow. . . . I was so confident that the files had never been rifled that I had no presentiment [sic] of any duty to investigate what the basis of your speech was. [pp. 495-97.]

General Snow's answers are extraordinary in more ways than one. They reveal not only the wantonness of State Department criticism of McCarthy, but also General Snow's total ignorance of an important aspect of the Tydings investigation—which was held several years *after* his 1947 point of recall. And the Tydings inquiry was certainly a strategic event in the history of the State Department's security division.

The fourth "lie" Snow had in mind (and the last one we shall discuss)* was "[McCarthy's charge] made on April 20, in his address before the American Society of Newspaper Editors in Washington, in which he said: *'The President's own Security Board,'* which, he said, had listed 205 persons as bad security risks, was gotten rid of by Secretary Acheson 'in favor of a weaker board.'"

SENATOR McCARTHY. One of the men on that original board was [Robert] Bannerman; is that right?

MR. SNOW. I don't know who was on the original board. It was before my time.

SENATOR McCARTHY. Do you know whether [J. Anthony] Panuch was on it?

MR. SNOW. I don't know.

SENATOR McCARTHY. Do you know who got rid of Bannerman?

MR. SNOW. I don't know anything about that except the board went out of existence before we came in under Secretary Marshall.

SENATOR McCARTHY. But Bannerman and Panuch were the men having to do with security in the State Department. You know that, do you not?

MR. SNOW. That was before my time.

SENATOR McCARTHY. You are talking about things before your time. You know those are the men who named the 284 and they said they are unfit to serve. You know that, do you not?

MR. SNOW. Yes, I know they had prepared a list that they said would not be employed continuously [sic] by the State Department.

SENATOR McCARTHY. And you know that those men did disappear from the Department before your board took over, do you not?

MR. SNOW. No; I do not know that.

SENATOR McCARTHY. You do not know whether they did, or not?

MR. SNOW. No; I do not know that.

SENATOR McCARTHY. Do you say I lied when I said Acheson had gotten rid of them?

* The fifth: McCarthy, said Snow, had falsely claimed that a recommendation by Alger Hiss had in "dozens of cases" been enough to "completely clear" Department employees. But Snow chose not to press this point—perhaps because he was at all times adamant about his ignorance of all events prior to June of 1947 (by which time Hiss had left the Department).

MR. SNOW. Yes.

SENATOR McCARTHY. Acheson was in the State Department in 1946, was he?

MR. SNOW. I believe he was Under Secretary.

SENATOR McCARTHY. Do you know?

MR. SNOW. I can find out.

SENATOR McCARTHY. You made the statement that you are objecting to my statement that Acheson had gotten rid of them. Do you know what his job was at that time?

MR. SNOW. He was the Assistant Secretary at that time.

SENATOR McCARTHY. You know that Bannerman and Panuch are no longer there, do you not?

MR. SNOW. I don't know that; no.

SENATOR McCARTHY. In other words, your testimony now is that you do not know *who* was on that board; you do not know *whether* Acheson got rid of them; you do not know *who* fired them; nevertheless, you say, McCarthy lied because McCarthy said Acheson fired them. Is that a correct resume of your testimony?

MR. SNOW. Yes. [pp. 499-500.]

Here then is a short summary of what General Snow did *not* know: (1) The security board in question did not complete its mission in 1946; it continued to operate until June of 1947, when it gave way to General Snow's Board—which developed in December, 1947, into the present Loyalty Security Board. (2) Bannerman was not only a member of that Board but its executive officer, and continued in this function until his separation from the Department in the spring of 1947. (3) Acheson was Under Secretary—not Assistant Secretary—of State until he resigned in June of 1947. (4) Marshall became Secretary of State in January of 1947 when the so-called Bannerman board had not yet ceased to operate. (5) Until January 1947, the entire security program of the State Department was under the direction of J. Anthony Panuch.

On the point whether or not Bannerman and Panuch were fired—the crux of the matter at issue—Carlisle Humelsine intervened to assure the Committee that neither of them had been dismissed. "I would not want the record to show that, because that is not a fact. Neither Mr. Panuch, who happens to be a very close personal friend of mine, nor Mr. Bannerman, for whom I have the highest regard—he is well and favorably known to me—neither of those was fired. They both left of their own accord."

Now just to keep the record straight, and to check *en passant* on Humelsine's knowledge and/or veracity, we may pause to note why this question seemed to the Senators worth pondering; and whether, in fact, Bannerman and Panuch *were* fired. Bannerman was separated from the State Department early in 1947; and while it is not known whether he was fired, his departure certainly coincided with a considerable exodus or reassignment of people who entertained views like his own on the loyalty-security issue; and his departure was later associated with the sudden paralysis of the Department's security division. But with respect to the departure of J. Anthony Panuch, the facts are available. On the 25th of June, 1953, he presented to the Senate Internal Security Committee his own account of his separation.

MR. CHAIRMAN. Will you tell us about your departure from the State Department, when that was consummated?

MR. PANUCH. I was dismissed instantly. I will give you the data on it. . . . Mr. Byrnes resign[ed] in January. My superior, Mr. Russell, immediately tendered his resignation, which was accepted, to clear the decks for General Marshall, and I tendered my resignation to Mr. Byrnes. I told him I wanted to get out because my life wouldn't be worth a nickel after the new team took over.

MR. CHAIRMAN. Why do you say that, Mr. Panuch?

MR. PANUCH. I was a very unpopular man in the State Department.

MR. CHAIRMAN. Why?

MR. PANUCH. Well, on account of the issues that I have testified about.

However, Panuch went on, Byrnes persuaded him to stay on in the Department to guide General Marshall on the Departmental matters of which he had expert knowledge. Panuch consented, though he went through the formality of submitting his resignation:

MR. PANUCH. . . . .When General Marshall came from Hawaii, Secretary Byrnes did talk to him and I was told that "General Marshall wants to see you, talk to you immediately, and he wants to have you stay on."

The next day I was told by a newspaperman that I was slated to get the full treatment, and I found out that Secretary Acheson, who was then Under Secretary Acheson, who was expected to be Under Secretary for George Marshall during an interim period until Under Secretary Lovett could come over from the War Department, would not tolerate my being around the Department.

SENATOR WALKER. Who was this? Dean Acheson would not tolerate your being around the Department?

MR. PANUCH. If he were Under Secretary under George Marshall;

yes. . . . Under Secretary Acheson called me into his office, and we had a conversation and he said, "Joe, you and I haven't gotten along very well," and he said "Now General Marshall has asked me to take over here as Under Secretary until Mr. Lovett comes over and I told him that I would do so only on condition that I would have complete charge of the administration of the Department and, as you and I don't see eye to eye on various matters, I would like your resignation."

So I told him I had already tendered my resignation to Secretary Marshall, and he said, "Really?" And I said "Yes." . . . It was one of the simple ones: "I resign at your pleasure, Acting Secretary for Administration."

. . . Acheson . . . reached out a (prepared) letter accepting my resignation, signed by General Marshall, effective as of the close of business that date, which under Department rules, was 10 minutes later.

Such were the tribulations of General Conrad Snow. He had shown himself to be ignorant of data that had a crucial bearing not only on his specific charges against McCarthy, but on the work of the division in which he was playing a vitally important role. His humiliation could hardly have been more complete. "Would you make this speech over again?" Senator Ferguson asked him. "Oh, no; certainly not," he answered. Senator McCarthy volunteered his own summary, which included some of the most penetrating remarks he has made on the loyalty-security problem:

I may say, in fairness to Mr. Snow, I think I understand his reasoning better than some of his friends do. He is the son of a judge; his grandfather was a judge. I understand they were kindly men. I think that he feels that he is in effect trying criminal cases; that he must give everyone the benefit of the doubt, and if there are any doubts which can be resolved in favor of the employee, he resolves them in favor of the employee.

It is the kindly thing to do, but makes him completely incompetent to act as head of that board.

I do not accuse you of being an evil man, Mr. Snow, but watching the results that come from your board, I am trying to find out what prompts you. And I have talked with some of your friends. The general report that we get is that you are a kindly individual who just dislikes seeing a man lose his job.

The bulk of the Committee's questions, however, were directed not at Snow but at Carlisle Humelsine. Humelsine proved a difficult witness—not because he was arrogant (few bureaucrats are when dealing with an appropriations committee), but because of his remarkable capacity for misunderstanding every question put

to him by the Committee, and for coming up with answers so oblique as to puzzle all within earshot. His testimony is an example
of the sort of Washingtoniana that once caused Senator Douglas
to weep noisily on the floor of the Senate after struggling with
the President's budget.

Senator McCarthy attempted to find out from Humelsine
whether the State Department Board had followed the practice of
"sitting on" loyalty cases—i.e., postponing almost indefinitely a
final adjudication of them—so as to prevent the Central Board from
assuming authority over them. McCarthy knew pretty well that
Humelsine would never admit any such thing; so he tried to get at
the problem from a different angle: Did the Central Board have
the *power* to pre-empt jurisdiction before final adjudication of a
case by an agency board? And, if so, the significant question arose:
did it *do* so as a matter of practice?

SENATOR McCARTHY. Is there anything to the suspicion on the part
of some that you [the State Department] hold some of these cases
indefinitely after suspension because the Review Board cannot get
them until you get through with them? In other words, if you hold the
Brunauer case indefinitely, the Review Board never can see it, can they?
MR. HUMELSINE. The Review Board cannot post audit [(a) it can;
(b) how is this observation relevant?] but the Review Board could and
has the authority at any time, as I understand it, to take the case out
of our hands and handle it themselves.
SENATOR McCARTHY. Has that ever been done?
MR. HUMELSINE. Yes, sir; it has been done in two cases.
SENATOR McCARTHY. In what cases?
MR. HUMELSINE. They took the Service case and one other case, two
cases.
SENATOR FERGUSON. Before you were through with them?
MR. HUMELSINE. No, sir; after they had been sent over to them.
SENATOR FERGUSON. Why do you not answer the Senator's question?
SENATOR McCARTHY. Why do you not try to answer my question? It
is like pulling teeth. I should not have to ask several questions, in order
to get the truth. I asked you whether the Review Board had ever taken
a case *away* from you.
MR. HUMELSINE. They have in that sense.
SENATOR McCARTHY. Now, you heard my question.
MR. HUMELSINE. Yes.
SENATOR McCARTHY. You said the Brunauer case was pending.
MR. HUMELSINE. That is right.
SENATOR McCARTHY. Was being processed.
MR. HUMELSINE. Yes, sir.
SENATOR McCARTHY. My question was: *Can* the Review Board get

this case until you finish it. You see, there is a serious suspicion on the part of some—will you listen to me?

MR. HUMELSINE. Yes.

SENATOR McCARTHY. There is a suspicion on the part of some, including myself, that you hold some of these cases indefinitely and wait until you get through and make a decision, knowing that the Review Board never does come over and pick up a case until you have finished with it. You said they could do that, and I asked to name one case in which they have done it. You said the Service case.

MR. HUMELSINE. Yes, sir.

SENATOR McCARTHY. But you said that you had *finished* the Service case.

MR. HUMELSINE. It was over there for post auditing. But as I understand rule 14 of the Board, they can take jurisdiction of a case at any time.

SENATOR McCARTHY. Do you know of a single case where they have ever done that?

MR. HUMELSINE [finally!]. They have not taken jurisdiction in a case up to this time until it has gone to them for post audit. [pp. 455-56.]

Or take the effort of the Committee to get to the bottom of the Department's suspension regulations and procedures. Humelsine was asked: Do the Department's rules call for an employee's suspension when the charges are first brought against him, or only after an adverse determination has been handed down by the Loyalty Security Board? In other words, does an accused employee have access to secret material while his case is pending? If so, is this wise?

Suspension, it was learned finally, was not mandatory at any stage of the loyalty-security process.* That is to say, neither the President's Executive Order, nor the regulations of the Loyalty Review Board, nor Public Law 733—as the latter had been construed—required that at such and such a stage an accused employee must be suspended. Only when investigation had absolutely established an employee's present membership in the Communist Party, or in any other organization bent on overthrowing the government by force, did suspension—and, indeed, firing—become mandatory under section 9A of the Hatch Act (and under various appropriations riders forbidding the expenditure of public funds to pay the salaries of employees belonging to such organizations).

So much for the Department's *regulations* on the subject. The

---

* This was established only after interminable wrangling, in the course of which Humelsine admitted his own confusion on the subject. (pp. 447 ff., p. 989).

Committee, however, was more interested in its *practices*. This is what it learned: If an employee fell under suspicion resulting from information or allegations about him that had come to the security office's attention, a full field investigation was ordered, in most cases to be conducted by the FBI. After that field investigation the security officials decided whether or not there was sufficient adverse evidence to warrant further probing. If they were satisfied that certain questions needed clarification, those questions were forwarded to the employee. Upon receipt of his reply, the security office determined whether to let it go at that or proceed to the next step on the security ladder. In the latter event, the employee received a formal "letter of charges," and was afterward given a hearing by the Loyalty Security Board.

Now, General Snow had said in his speech that only when there was "reasonable doubt" of any employee's loyalty or reliability did he receive a letter of charges. McCarthy went on from there:

SENATOR McCARTHY [addressing Mr. Humelsine]. Mr. Snow says that letters of charges are filed *only when there is reasonable doubt* there is a loyalty or security risk.

MR. HUMELSINE. *Yes, sir.*

SENATOR McCARTHY. . . . I am wondering now, if you can tell us, after you have decided there is reasonable doubt of a man's loyalty or security, even though he may be ultimately cleared, why do you not deny him access to top-secret material unless he is at least cleared.

MR. HUMELSINE. *We have not decided at this point whether there is reasonable doubt as to the man's security and loyalty.* At a later stage is where that particular determination might be made. At this stage it is determined that we cannot clear this case up without having a formal hearing.

SENATOR McCARTHY. I just read to you what General Snow had to say. I ask you if you agree with this. He says, on page 6 of his speech, "It is only in cases where there *is* reasonable doubt as to loyalty or security risk that a case comes on for hearing." My question is this: If you have reasonable doubt about a man's loyalty or his security, why do you still give him access to secret material?

MR. HUMELSINE. If we have a reasonable doubt as to a man's security or reasonable doubt as to a man's loyalty, we suspend him.

SENATOR McCARTHY. If you have reasonable doubt, you file charges?

MR. HUMELSINE. At that point you cannot have doubt or you can have doubt. It depends on the situation. . . . [pp. 411, 412.]

All that emerged from the contradictions and tergiversations of General Snow and Mr. Humelsine was this: the Department would not suspend an employee unless there was "reasonable doubt as to the man's security and loyalty"; but neither would it file a letter of charges unless there was "reasonable doubt as to the man's security and loyalty"; thus, according to inexorable rules of logic, the reason for *filing* a letter of charges against a man was *ipso facto* the same reason that required his suspension. Yet it proved impossible to make Mr. Humelsine understand, much less acknowledge, this situation.

Senator McCarthy went back to the subject at a later meeting of the Committee, using this time the directest possible approach. He asked General Snow: "Let us take the three cases that you have found against—you found [on] disloyalty. That is much more serious than being a bad security risk. But after letters of charges have been filed on these individuals, and until your board has held the hearing, I understand that if they are in the State Department they can move around freely, associating with people handling secret material and perhaps having access to classified material themselves. Is that not an extremely dangerous situation?"

General Snow answered this question with perhaps the supreme paralogism of the year:

It might be in some cases. I do not think that in either of the three cases to which you refer that that was so however. *The three cases were quite innocuous-appearing on the surface. It was not until we got into the hearing and heard the cases that we arrived at any conception that suspension was desirable.*

In short, the Committee was never able to squeeze out of the State Department spokesmen an intelligible account of Department policy with respect to the suspension of suspect employees. Yet at the time the Committee met, 90 Department employees had been in loyalty channels "over" two months. Just *how* long over two months? Humelsine was asked. An average of 7.2 months. Of course, there is no way of knowing how many of the employees who were ultimately found to be security risks had been suspended during the long period in which their cases had been pending. But the suspicion is strong that many of them were not; for in the entire history of the Department's loyalty security program, only 29 employees (out of 800 candidates) had been suspended while "in channels"! (pp. 523, 998, 999.)

Perhaps the most important line of inquiry the Committee pursued had to do with the criteria governing the Department's decisions as to whether or not an employee was a loyalty or a security risk. What, the Committee asked, were the operating standards in determining whether "reasonable doubt" existed as to the loyalty or reliability of an employee?

Senator McCarthy led off. "Let us assume," he said,

that a man is affiliated with four or five or six Communist fronts. Would you consider that sufficient grounds to hold against him under the loyalty procedure?

MR. HUMELSINE. That would place him in the loyalty channels.

SENATOR MCCARTHY. You did not get my question. Would you hold against such a man under the loyalty procedure?

MR. HUMELSINE. I don't know how I can answer that question. What you do is look at a fellow's record. It may be that he may have been a member of only one front organization, but a sufficient amount of material in connection with that one would make him a loyalty case. I don't think you can go on the basis of the number. It is a matter of degree.

SENATOR MCCARTHY. In other words, you think the number may not be important.

MR. HUMELSINE. It may, or it may not be.

McCarthy upped the ante.

SENATOR MCCARTHY. Let us say that I work in the State Department and that I have affiliations with, say 20 or 25 organizations named as Communist front organizations. *Can you conceive of any circumstance under which I should then be cleared?*

MR. HUMELSINE. I would have to look at the case.

SENATOR MCCARTHY. Even though I belong to 25 Communist fronts you would still look at the case?

MR. HUMELSINE. I think in fairness I would have to look at the case.

SENATOR MCCARTHY. You would what?

MR. HUMELSINE. In fairness, I would have to look at the case. I do not think it would be fair for me to answer that question without going into the facts. On that basis, I would want to look at the case. Maybe the person has gotten into that situation for any one of a number of reasons. I would not know.

McCarthy, of course, was interested in what "reason" would satisfy the Department that a person who had "gotten into that situation" was blameless *beyond a reasonable doubt*. As he put it, what were some of the circumstances which, in the case of an employee who joined 25 Communist fronts, would satisfy the Department's security officers that no risk was entailed in keeping him on?

SENATOR MCCARTHY. . . . You would say that even though you knew I belonged to 25 Communist fronts, that in and of itself would not be sufficient to order me discharged? You would still want to examine the case further?

MR. HUMELSINE. Sure, I would want to examine the case. . . .

SENATOR MCCARRAN. Let me ask you this, Mr. Humelsine: Where the Department of Justice, acting under the law, declares an organization to be subversive, you would not take issue with that?

MR. HUMELSINE. Oh, no, sir: I am not taking issue with that.

SENATOR MCCARRAN. Regarding the question put to you by the Senator from Wisconsin, if a man belonged to 23 subversive organizations as declared by the Department of Justice, you would not clear him for loyalty, would you?

MR. HUMELSINE. I would want to look into the whole case and find out when he got into the organizations and the circumstances surrounding the particular case. I mean it is not a definite case, and it is hard to say.

McCarthy accepted the implied challenge:

SENATOR MCCARTHY. Let us *make* it a definite case. Let us assume that you know that I have belonged to 23 organizations that at the time [I joined them] were subversive and have been declared subversive by the Attorney General. Would you say that you would look into the case before you would discharge me?

MR. HUMELSINE. I would want to see what your motives were and why you belonged to them.

SENATOR MCCARTHY. The mere belonging to 23 subversive organizations at the time they were subversive, and declared so by the Attorney General, you would not consider in and of itself as sufficient for discharge?

MR. HUMELSINE. I would certainly put that case in loyalty channels, and I would want to find out—I would examine the record right away and if the record showed that you were a loyalty risk I would want to suspend you.

SENATOR MCCARTHY. I think it is very important to get your attitude on this. . . . It is very important to know what those of you who are running this program consider [a] disloyalty [risk] or [a] bad security [risk] and for that reason it is extremely important to get your answer to the effect that you would not consider membership in 23 subversive organizations that are declared subversive—you would not consider membership in them in and of itself sufficient to discharge me. If that is your attitude that explains to a considerable extent the unusual workings of the State Department Loyalty Board.

MR. HUMELSINE. That is not my attitude, though, Senator.

SENATOR McCARTHY. You say that you would want to look into the organization.

MR. HUMELSINE. I would say that I would want to examine them. It may be, for example, that someone is charged with having belonged to 23 subversive organizations and maybe he did not belong to any of them. That is quite possible. It is quite possible that that could happen. Now, that is farfetched, but it is possible.

SENATOR McCARTHY. My question did not say that belonging to the 23 organizations was *charged*. My question said that he *belonged* to them.

MR. HUMELSINE. Suppose I made the statement some morning that Mr. So and So belonged to 23 subversive organizations, organizations that had been subversive and that had been so determined by the Justice Department. I have made that statement as a private citizen. Well, the thing I would want to do is to find out whether that is the fact, because you have to operate this program based on facts, not on insinuation or allegation.

SENATOR McCARTHY [wearily, we assume]. Let us assume that you *have* established the fact—I would like to get your attitude on this program—let us assume that you *have* established the fact, it is not hearsay but rather you have *established* the fact that I have belonged to 23 organizations that *have been declared subversive*. I have belonged to them at a time when they *were* subversive. Before you would order me discharged, you would still want to look further into the case?

MR. HUMELSINE. I would want to find out all the circumstances connected with the case before I took action.

SENATOR McCARRAN [intervening with a fourth qualification]. Let us add one more element to the hypothetical situation. If it was established that he *knew* when he belonged to them that they were subversive, would you then—

MR. HUMELSINE. There is no doubt about it, Senator.

SENATOR McCARTHY. You said that there would be no doubt about it. You mean that you would order him discharged?

MR. HUMELSINE. If he *knew* those organizations were subversive, I would certainly discharge him.

SENATOR McCARTHY. Good. [pp. 393-95.]

Senator McCarthy was probably too exhausted to go further into the matter. He did not bring to Humelsine's attention the fact that what he had just finished saying virtually committed him to a standard of eligibility *which the Department had nominally deserted as inadequate seven years earlier!* For Humelsine had implied that nothing short of proof of an employee's evil intentions would bring his dismissal as a loyalty risk. Humelsine had said, in effect, that the Department stood ready to be persuaded that a joiner of 23 Communist fronts, already cited as subversive at the time he affiliated himself with them, had satisfactory reasons for having joined them.*

This may appear to be a hasty indictment of Humelsine. But note that Humelsine did not say, "Nothing short of a discovery that such a person was *instructed* to join 25 Communist fronts by the Federal Bureau of Investigation or by some federal security agency would satisfy us that he was not a loyalty risk," or any such thing. Rather, he stressed again and again that the case would have to be "gone into"—and he persevered with this answer until Senator McCarran broke the camel's back by asking whether or not the discovery that the employee *intended* subversion would bring action from the State Department's security office.

Senator McCarthy might well have asked Mr. Humelsine two pointed questions: (1) In the hypothetical situation described, what sort of evidence is sufficient to persuade the State Department that the employee in question "knew" the 23 Communist fronts he joined to be subversive? (2) What has happened to the "reasonable doubt" standard to which the Department is ostensibly committed? and (3) If that standard *is* operative, must not the employee who had belonged to 23 Communist fronts be presumed to have belonged to them *because* they were Communist fronts? Yet Humelsine comes close to implying that no such presumption guided the Department or at least that no such presumption guided him, the Department's top security officer.

The Department, in short, had evidently not made much progress in the five years that had elapsed since an Assistant Secretary had been confronted by three Senators with evidence that one of his secretaries was a Communist. But "I *know* she is not a Communist," he had told the Senators. "I looked her straight in the eye and asked her, 'Are you a Communist?' and she said, 'No.' "[8]

---

* We are not dealing, of course, with *reformed* Communists, but rather with persons who insist that at no time were they pro-Communist.

CHAPTER XII

Closing Ranks: Some Proposals for the Civil Service

OR NEARLY three decades a handful of prophets—an American Resistance—tried to alert the nation to the Communist threat; and fought a lonely and costly fight. After the Second World War, in the dawn of a new realism about international affairs, these prophets began to get a hearing; for it had become apparent that nothing but the integrity of the United States stood between the Soviet Union and world domination. But it was only when one spy scandal after another rocked the nation that the American Resistance enlisted recruits in sizable numbers and fixed our attention on the problem of Communist infiltration. By 1950, a genuine mobilization was under way. And Senator McCarthy—having fairly recently been mobilized himself—became one of its leaders.

Why have we focused attention on the record of Senator McCarthy rather than on that of the other mobilization leaders? Because it is predictable that, if McCarthy's enemies are successful in discrediting him, the mobilization will lose momentum and, perhaps, grind to a dead halt. Thus we have analyzed McCarthy's performance in generous detail and have tried to evaluate it, commending him where we think he ought to be commended, and censuring him where we think he ought to be censured. But we have pressed our analysis under certain important limitations: We have examined McCarthy, for the most part, in the light of the basic assumptions of the society he is seeking to mobilize.

It is now time to say that, in our opinion, some of these assumptions are inappropriate to the emergency. We do not, we hasten to add, attribute a similar view to McCarthy. He has often *acted* as if he questioned the serviceability of some of our society's premises in the present situation; but he has never *said* so. He has not, at any stage in his hurly-burly campaign against subversion, paused to articulate a new philosophy of national mobilization. The lack of an articulate philosophy of national mobilization is the country's greatest single handicap in its duel with Communism.

For we are not winning this fight. International Communism thrives increasingly with each passing year. Most of the issues involved in our appalling failure the authors leave, willingly enough, to other books by other writers whom the mobilization may in due course enlist. We shall here address ourselves to one problem with which Joe McCarthy has primarily concerned himself: How can the American people make sure that the State Department is manned by personnel able and eager to destroy the enemy? This is by no means a minor aspect of the total problem. For as long as the war against the Soviet Union is a cold war, our first-line troops are the working staff of the State Department; and success or failure in our duel with Communism hinges to a great extent on the ability and eagerness of these men to match the wits and the single-mindedness of their counterparts in the Kremlin.

Those who have been responsible for security in the State Department seem to have formulated programs and regulations with three principal objectives in mind. They have sought to get rid of persons whose employment in the Department might jeopardize the security of the United States. They have sought to shield from social ignominy and from the hazards of unemployment persons whose dismissal was in the national interest. And they have sought in their operations to accommodate the philosophy that the civil servant has, other things being equal, a "right to his job"; and that therefore his job may not be taken away from him without a quasi-legal adjudication of his claim to it.

Now it seems to us that, in seeking to realize all three of these objectives at one and the same time, the security officers have failed to accomplish any one of them. They have failed not necessarily for lack of trying, but because the three objectives are in certain situations incompatible. It is possible, as we shall hereafter be arguing, to achieve the first and the second of these objectives side by side; but they tend to be achieved only at the expense of the third.

PROTECTING THE GOVERNMENT

Security officials invariably preface their public lectures on the Government's security program with such apothegms as "national security must come first" or, "a government job is a privilege not a right"—both of them principles with which we are in agreement. They go on, however, to talk about the present security program (or its earlier version under Truman) as though it reflected these principles; while we submit that, in important respects, it does not.

Another way of saying "national security must come first" is to say: Whenever the interests of government security conflict with the interests of the employee—i.e., his earning power, his vocational preferences—the interests of the employee must give way. The principle does not exclude attempts to reconcile the two interests; and it most certainly does not imply that the interests of the employee are insignificant. But it does hold that the reconciliation must not be achieved at the expense of the government's interest; and that, where reconciliation *cannot* be achieved, the interests of the government shall be given *exclusive* consideration.

Tested this way, the Truman Loyalty Program and (though to a lesser extent) the Eisenhower Security Program are defective in at least three particulars: (a) they assign the decision as to what constitutes the security interest of the government to the wrong people; (b) they stipulate procedures which in and of themselves obstruct a single-minded attention to the government's interest; and (c) they rest on the assumption that a security program deals only with actual or potential traitors. These defects are fundamental.

The correct approach to government security in sensitive agencies like the State Department is, in our opinion, embodied in the McCarran Rider (1946). The Rider flatly authorizes the Secretary of State *"in his absolute discretion"* to terminate the employment of any Department officer or employee *"when he shall deem such termination necessary or advisable in the interests of the national security."*

The Rider embraces the axiom that the government's interest must come first and points the way—explicitly in some respects, implicitly in others—to a suitably hard program for enforcing security in sensitive government agencies. It provides that the Department itself must determine whether an employee satisfies its security requirements. It implies that the dismissal of employees who fail to meet these requirements must be summary in nature, there being no reference to traditional jurisprudential safeguards. And, by focusing on "the interests of the national security," it (again by implication) discourages the notion that disloyalty or suspected disloyalty are the only bases on which employees may be separated.

The President's Loyalty Program is sometimes looked upon as

an implementation of the Rider, because it established certain procedures for adjudicating an employee's fitness. Actually, however,
it repudiated the Rider's approach to the problem. By assigning
to a board of *laymen* the authority to determine an employee's fitness, the President's program called for "judgment by one's peers"
rather than judgment by persons with a claim to the *expertise* such
judgment calls for. The McCarran Rider implicitly acknowledged
the existence of *expertise* in matters of loyalty and security: it conferred upon the Secretary of State himself the power to decide security cases. And by *not* setting up a board of laymen to oversee
the administration of stipulated procedures, the Rider maximized
the likelihood that he will turn for advice to the only persons who
deal, day in and day out, with security matters—i.e., to the Department's own security staff. This staff consists, theoretically at least,
of experts—experts on the nature of the Communist movement and
on its methods of infiltration; experts also in their knowledge of
the particular security requirements of the Department.

On the other hand, the members of the Department's Loyalty
Security Board, as well as those of the Civil Service's Loyalty Review Board, were qualified primarily by their civic respectability.
There is no reason to suppose that these men—lawyers, business
men, diplomats (in the case of the State Department Board)*—are
fit to evaluate with any special acuity information relating to the
Communist conspiracy, or even to adjudge the particular sensitivity of a given State Department post. The rationale for staffing the
loyalty boards with laymen is directly traceable to the common law
notion that the ends of justice are best served when an unbiased
tribunal of average citizens decides whether an accused is guilty
or innocent. But *justice*, we are saying, *is not the major objective
here.*

A second serious deficiency of the traditional loyalty-security
program is its insistence upon quasi-judicial procedures. This tends
to inject factors into fitness-determinations which distract the tribunal from the only task it has any business considering—protecting the national interest.

Let us be very clear about this. We are saying that it is *not* the
function of a security board to give the employee his "day in court";
his "side of the story" should be heard, but the hearing of it has a
limited function of enlightening the government. The function is

---

* Under the Eisenhower program, the "leading citizens" from *other* Departments sit on a Department's Security Board. See below.

to provide the government with *facts,* otherwise unavailable to it, which may help security officers in deciding whether the employee is qualified to retain his job. An employee's case should be "heard," not because he stands to gain by the hearing, but because the government needs the information he possesses.

Now it is clear that formal board hearings are not necessary for the purpose of eliciting information; an interview with security officers will achieve this purpose well enough. But beyond this there are affirmative reasons why formal hearings, at which the employee is permitted to argue his case through legal counsel and through the testimony of friendly witnesses, tend to distract attention from the government's interests. Such hearings, precisely because they suggest analogies with the judicial process, very naturally assume the character of a contest between the Department and the employee. Given the psychological prepossessions of men and women who were brought up on Anglo-Saxon jurisprudence, it is predictable that "justice" to "litigants" will be the central theme of a loyalty board proceeding. And this, in turn, makes the board (as Seth Richardson of the Loyalty Review Board has said himself) "lean over" backwards to favor the employee. The legal paraphernalia, meant to assure fair adjudication of disputes between two parties equally privileged in the eyes of the law, ought not to apply to proceedings whose clear purpose is to safeguard, at whatever cost to the party of the second part, the interests of the party of the first part.

The loyalty-security type hearing also tends to favor the employee because it is, in effect, an *ex parte* proceeding,—i.e., *ex parte* the employee. The "State's case," as Conrad Snow once described the charges against the employees, is not orally argued at these hearings; it consists in written information uncovered by the investigating agencies. While, indeed, the members of the board may direct questions to the employee about this or that item, there is no "advocate" present to press the Department's "case." On the other hand, the employee's case is a "live one": he is there himself; his side of the dispute is presented by legal counsel; and friendly witnesses are called in by him.

But by far the most important consequence of using judicial devices in settling the question of a man's fitness for government service is the "presumption of innocence." We have discussed this presumption and its implications in connection with the Tydings investigation; and we saw there that it may well turn out to be the controlling consideration in determining an employee's fitness under a loyalty-security type program. Philip Jessup, for example, could not be considered a security risk because the presumption of innocence was a factor in the equation. This was unavoidable, for it is unrealistic to assume that an adjudication of a man's "innocence" or "guilt" can be made in this country unrelated to our traditional principle that a man must be presumed innocent until he is proven guilty. Indeed, the presumption arises even where the attempt is made to prevent its intrusion. For even under the confining "reasonable doubt" standard, the decision as to whether there *is* a doubt is influenced by the presumption.

The presumption of innocence will remain the major barrier in the way of an effective security program *as long as fitness adjudications resemble criminal trials.*

The Eisenhower Administration's security program offers little hope of circumventing the hazards we have been discussing. Under it, the State Department has set up a Security Hearing Board; which means that it will continue to hold hearings before a quasi-judicial tribunal which, of necessity, will look after the "rights" of the employee. True, the new regulations contain one considerable improvement: under Truman the Loyalty Security Board (in theory at least) had the last say;* while under the new dispensation, the Board is merely to hand down "advisory decisions." The Secretary of State may now, if he so wishes, turn to experts for guidance as to whether or not to follow the recommendations of the laymen Board. If he does so often enough, the Board, happily, will cease to be functional; and in the course of time its uselessness may even be acknowledged. For, indeed, such a Board must be either abolished or eviscerated if an appropriately single-minded approach to government security is our desire, as it is our need.

The hardness we are urging cannot, of course, be generated by a government edict; a government edict is more likely to *result* from a change in the public attitude to security in government rather than *produce* it. But statute regulations that encourage such hardness can obviously be helpful. If we truly accept the theory that "a government job is a privilege not a right" then we must

---

* Acheson overruled it twice; the Loyalty Review Board overruled it twice. Acheson overruled *adverse* decisions by the Board: the Department's regulations did not provide for an appeal to the Secretary from a decision *favorable* to the employee.

adopt methods for determining an employee's fitness that are better suited to an adjudication of a "privilege" than to an adjudication of a "right."

But there is yet another reason—perhaps the most important of all—why the old approach has not and could not have given us the sort of security program we require. The government has proceeded on the notion that an employee must come under a reasonable suspicion of being, if you will, a wicked man (wicked enough to serve as an agent for an enemy government) before he can properly be separated from the State Department. In other words, by equating bad security with great evil we tend to go after the latter and thus fail to cope with the former.

The nature of the predicament shows up pressingly when you discuss the loyalty programs with the Very Bright Liberal. You have only to state that "John Jones is a loyalty risk," and the pat question is forthcoming, "What *definition of loyalty* have you in mind?" You are, of course, to consider yourself routed unless you come up with an unassailable definition. And a very good definition is, indeed, hard to come by.

Any definition of loyalty that calls for unconditional allegiance to the government of the United States is obviously unsatisfactory: most of us recognize a natural law that supersedes the artifacts of man and even compels us, on occasion, to disobey our government. Nor is the next definition that suggests itself much better: to define loyalty as an attitude that has the "best interests of the United States (as distinct from those of a foreign power) at heart." The difficulties, here again, are obvious: Who is to say Owen Lattimore did not believe that the interests of the United States would be served by allowing Asia to go Communist? Or that William Foster lies when he affirms his belief that the United States will be better off when it is governed by soviets?

The Liberal, in other words, is on his type of "firm ground," and he will take us every time we agree to meet him on that quicksand. But this does not mean he is right and we are wrong. It means, rather, *that the loyalty-security vocabulary is inappropriate to the problem in hand.* The subjective disposition called loyalty is virtually impossible to identify, and is thus a poor yardstick by which to estimate fitness for government employment. The loyalty concept is unserviceable, because it cannot at the margin differentiate the Lattimores and Fosters from, say, the Lodges and Dulleses, and thus it quite obviously fails to distinguish between those who are and those who are not fit to make and execute policy. But beyond being unserviceable, the concept is irrelevant; for when we look closely at the matter, we find we are interested in talking, not about "Who is loyal?" but about *"Who favors those policies that are in the national interest as we see it?"*

In short, when we discuss the need for a tight security program in the State Department in loyalty-security terms, we are apt to forget the basic reason why we need one. We do not, of course, want traitors working in sensitive government agencies. But the reason we don't want traitors working there is that they tend to frustrate America's defense against the Soviet Union. We intend to eliminate traitors not so much because treason is wicked but because it gets in the way of American interests. It is *the advancement of American interests* that a properly conceived security program has to consider and to guarantee. Consequently, the man who frustrates American policy *without* wicked intent is no less objectionable than the man who frustrates it *with* wicked intent. Let us assume that Owen Lattimore, John Stewart Service, John Carter Vincent—or any of a dozen others who come to mind—have had the interests of the United States consistently at heart. Yet is the damage they did to American interests lessened a single bit by our conceding their good intent?

This brings us to some unpleasant truths. When we speak of personnel who frustrate the advancement of American interests we speak of a group that includes some men who are *not* traitors; men whose only fault may be that they are incompetent political analysts, men of bad judgment. And if the ultimate objective of the security program is to remove from government service all who frustrate the advancement of American interests, the merely incompetent men must go out along with the traitors. Let the latter, if they can be identified, pay some stiff price over and above the loss of their jobs. But let us agree that the former will have to lose their jobs.

In a word: our security program must be designed to eliminate personnel who, on the basis of past performance or present attitudes, will predictably hinder our cause, *whether this be their conscious aim or not.* Is the employee, given his past performance, likely to advance the interests of the United States? This is the only feasible standard by which to determine the fitness of a State Department employee to continue in a post in which he can influence policy.

The Liberal's answer to this is easy to anticipate. He will strike a posture of humility, invoke the axiom of human fallibility, and ask, *who*, pray tell, can say which policy is in the national interest? Who is to say that one man's analysis and judgment are sound and another's unsound? Even assuming we *should* dismiss employees whose judgment is predictably bad (he will go on), we would have to be able to say with utmost confidence that Jones has a long record of making "bad" judgments; and this, in the nature of the case, we could never do. For we can say, perhaps, that his judgments have had unfortunate consequences in the long pull; but Jones had to make them in the light of what was known and knowable at another moment in time. In short, the Liberal will have none of our apodictical talk about "bad judgment" because, he insists, it involves the assertion of our own infallibility.

Now the Liberal is quite right in saying that we cannot always pass upon the merits of past judgments with absolute certitude. But to say that, therefore, we cannot evaluate past policy recommendations so as to decide whether we want Jones to draw up future policy is to talk nonsense. We repudiate the notion that the national interest is so vague, and good judgment exercised on its behalf so elusive, that we are never in a position to say which man's judgment endangers the national interest. And we reject the mystification involved in the Liberal's other gambit—namely, the query: *who*, after all, is to say at any particular moment what the national interest is?

Bearing in mind that the Liberal is seldom so demure when asserting his *own* opinions, let us remember that under our system of government decisions as to what the national interest is, and which persons are on the record likely to formulate and execute a foreign policy that will advance it, are made by the people acting through their elected representatives. There would seem to be nothing bizarre in the notion that the men elected to put into effect a certain policy should be the ones to decide what kind of professional workers are equipped to carry out that policy. Yet many who would never challenge a President's right to select his own Secretary of State (or the Secretary's right, in turn, to select his own principal assistants) stop short of what seems to follow as a matter of course: that all employees whose responsibilities touch upon the making of policy, but whose demonstrated views and attitudes on critical issues are athwart the Administration's, should be summarily sent on their way.

Protecting the Employee

President Truman advertised his loyalty program as one designed to achieve two goals—that of protecting the government and that of protecting its employees. The first goal, as we have seen throughout this book, was not achieved. The second was achieved in the sense that government employees were given a high degree of job security—in other words, to the extent the first goal was *not* achieved. But even as regards the protection of employees who did lose their jobs, the program had conspicuous defects. We are speaking of the blighting of personal reputations, which the government is obliged to avoid, wherever possible.

The administrators of the Truman program undoubtedly appreciated the desirability of shielding discharged employees from public exposure. Out of the hundreds of persons separated from government service under the federal loyalty program since 1947, only a handful are known to the public—and some of those identified *themselves* by taking public exception to the adverse decisions of the loyalty boards. Some others became identified in the course of public disputes about the security program. Some leaks, however, did occur; and in some other instances, where the Department was successful in keeping the public uninformed, we must suppose that an employee's friends and close associates were in a position to find out or guess the reasons for his separation. At any rate, some reputations have suffered from the government loyalty program; and the fault lies not so much with the security officials, who tried hard, as with those who drew up the rules of the game.

The first mistake made by the authors of the Truman program is their way of describing a person found unfit to work for the government—i.e., as a "loyalty risk." The loyalty-disloyalty criterion is unserviceable, as we have seen, from the government's point of view; its consequences are even more unfortunate for the employee. The government can, if it sees fit, walk around the philosophical obstacles and use the term "disloyal" as merely meaning "disloyal to the interests of the United States as the government understands these interests." But the employee is not in a position to plead philosophical niceties. The public cannot be counted on to inquire into the semantics of the term "disloyalty." No matter how it is explained, "disloyalty" evokes the most invidious images in everybody's mind; it occupies, quite simply, the top niche in the hierarchy of public sins.

Nor was it particularly helpful to the employee's reputation that the government darkly labelled him a "loyalty risk" instead of affirmatively charging him with disloyalty. For one thing, the public (if it hears of the matter at all) is not likely to distinguish between the "risk" and the "sure" case. For another, the government's standards are such as to invite speculation that the employee was a good deal more than a risk; for to be a "risk" is as bad as you ever can get in the Department. If Georgi Malenkov had a desk there, the worst that the State Department Loyalty Board could call him (assuming it found against him) would be a "loyalty risk."

The loyalty program, in other words, adopted standards for adjudicating an employee's fitness that are alien and repugnant to our jurisprudence. In the interests of national security, it adopted, quite properly, the theory that, although a man may be innocent before the law, he may nonetheless fall short of meeting the much more stringent standards for government employment. But then, having arranged things so that Jones would be found wanting by a loyalty board, although he might easily have survived the same charges in a court of law, it proceeded to pin on him a label every bit as damaging to his reputation as any contained in the vocabulary of crime.

And what worked against the employee in this regard was, ironically, the elaborate procedures that were carefully designed, and expensively executed, to *protect* him. For leaks were normally traceable to the fact that the investigated employee became involved in procedures which could not be concealed from his immediate associates. However tight-lipped and evasive the security officials might be, the procedural mill usually betrayed the fact that an employee was in loyalty or security trouble.

Of course, no security program can so operate as to preclude the possibility that the "security risk" will get publicly identified. But Truman did not go far enough in protecting the employee in this respect. And out of the past performance, certain remedies suggest themselves.

The first is to do away with the formal hearing. And this, as we may have shown, would serve the interests of both—government and employee. But something still more drastic is necessary: *the distinction the Truman program made between employees who are undesirable for security or loyalty reasons, and employees who are undesirable for other reasons must be erased.* The State Department ought to dismiss the security risk and the "policy misfit" the same way it dismisses an employee who is habitually late for work. And, for public consumption, the Department ought to have a stock phrase covering all separations. (The Eisenhower Administration seems, in this regard, to be moving in the right direction. There is reason to suppose that many or all of the 1,456 security risks who had been discharged from executive agencies as of October 1953, were at the time of their separation camouflaged as "riffed" ["Reduction In Force"] cases; and thus, friends and associates of the dismissed employees attributed their separation to government economies. Whether this procedure is to be a permanent feature of the Eisenhower security program it is too early to say.)

But to erase the distinction at the *separation* stage is not to eliminate it altogether, since the security risk will have gone through certain screening procedures that the late-to-work employee has not. Indeed, by advocating that security experts monopolize the handling of security risk cases, we have retained an obstacle to the equalization of security cases and other cases. But we also propose that as early as possible in the process—at the instant the security experts have ruled that an employee should be separated—the risk should be "thrown" into a common channel with all other employees about to leave the Department for sundry reasons.

These proposals have a twofold advantage. Conscientious security personnel are more likely to execute a hard security program *if everything has been done to lighten the consequences for the separated employee.* They feel less tempted to indulge the "presumption of innocence" if they are no longer forced to adjudicate "guilt"; and if the public has no longer a reason to regard separation from a sensitive agency as evidence of such an adjudication. On the other hand, the plight of the separated employee is indeed mitigated.

There remains the argument that some persons deserve to have their reputations blighted: the community *should* be informed that the loyalty of a dismissed department employee was in question—so that he does not land an even more strategic position in American society than that which he has forcibly lost. And the idea that some people deserve to have their reputations blighted is, we believe, widely held. However that may be, we are better off leaving matters of judgment and retribution to Providence. The function of a security program is to get misfits out of government—not to persecute them.*

No doubt, the notion that a security risk ought to be exposed so that the community can protect itself is a notion of some merit. The point is that an adverse security finding should not be regarded as a positive proof of a man's displaced allegiance; and an adverse adjudication of a person's fitness for government employment is not and should not be regarded as a prejudgment of his fitness for participation in normal community life. If we want the government to supply stricter standards in protecting itself than we are willing to incorporate into our jurisprudence generally, we ought to be satisfied to conclude nothing more from the dismissal of a government employee than that he is not qualified for the particular job he was holding.

JOB SECURITY

The protests against the dismissal of government employees on loyalty or security grounds are becoming rare; and not because this is the callous "Age of Conformity," but simply because the public, including many Liberals, began to grasp the elementary fact that the national interest supersedes any individual's job privileges. But the public is not, it seems, prepared to come to the same conclusion about what we have called the "policy misfit," the government employee who gets in the way of the cold war because he holds attitudes and opinions that, however respectable, incapacitate him from contributing to the realization of current United States objectives.

One reason for this bias is clear: in our society, a man's job is deemed one of his most precious possessions. The fact that "job security" has been the underlying theme in one national election campaign after another shows how zealously Americans look upon their job "rights." The passionate attachment of some civic organizations to the idea of a permanent and professional career service in government indicates the same tendency. Nor do we ourselves

---

* The solicitude proper in most classes of security risks is, of course, not indicated when a man has committed espionage or has perjured himself. But such a man is the proper concern of the Justice Department—not the State Department.

wish to appear indifferent to the need for a professional civil service—a career that able young Americans can enter with confidence.

But the essential question is not whether there should be a professional and permanent Civil Service, but whether, in our determination to achieve such a service, we have defeated our own
purposes by giving government employees (a) a kind of job security that few others in our society enjoy, (b) a kind of job security
that goes far beyond what reason can justify, and (c) a kind of job
security that undermines rather than enhances the efficiency and
the professionalism of the civil service. Therefore the question is
worth asking why government workers should not be treated the
same way the community treats other clerical and professional
workers. Why should government jobs not be related to the legitimate day-to-day needs of the consumers of government (i.e., the
electorate), just as other jobs depend on the day-to-day consumer
needs as expressed in the marketplace? Indeed, in discussing the
legitimacy of discharging governmental misfits, the burden would
seem to lie not on those who would do away with special protection for the government employee, but on those who would grant
him extraordinary privileges.

Seventy years ago, the authors of the Civil Service Act advanced
persuasive arguments in behalf of security of tenure for the government employee. Civil servants, they said in effect, are in a different category from other employees in that they can discharge
their obligations to their *ultimate* employers only if they stand in
a peculiar protected relationship to their *immediate* employer.
Their ultimate employers are the nation; but their immediate employer, for whom they perform the manifold clerical, managerial,
and administrative functions involved in the implementation of
policy, is the political party in power. And the latter depends
upon patronage as a means of obtaining and maintaining political
advantage. Thus, if left to its own devices, the immediate employer
will act as though the primary qualification for government employment were party loyalty rather than competence; and as a
result, employees who cannot meet this requirement will, with
each incoming Administration, be discharged—to the great injury
of the nation. If, then, the interests of the ultimate employer—the
nation—are to be given first consideration, the power of the immediate employer (the political party in power) to discharge employees must be restricted. The solution to which all this points,
so the argument runs, is to draw persons of demonstrated profes-

sional competence into the Civil Service and guarantee their tenure.

But this rationale, it will be seen if we recall where the argument started, rests on the assumption that civil servants are not involved in policy but merely perform routine functions. The conclusion to which it leads is, therefore, no better than the assumption; or at least can be applied only where the assumption is valid. Where the responsibilities of a government employee carry him into the policy-making area, the whole argument fails. Permanent tenure for such an employee invites a situation where policies repudiated at the polls by the "ultimate" employer live on forever in the departments.

If things had worked out in, say, the State Department, as our legislators of seventy years ago expected them to work out, policy would be made, exclusively, by the Secretary and his principal assistants, none of whom is a member of the Civil Service or the Foreign Service. But policy is often made and inevitably influenced at much lower levels, and therefore by career personnel. Policy is made by an Edward Posniak, putting the case for Communist Czechoslovakia before a Department liaison committee; or by Oliver Edmund Clubb, drafting memoranda for the Secretary that reflect not only the knowledge and experience in virtue of which Clubb was chief of the China Desk, but also his views on Communism and the future of China. Posniak's and Clubb's personal views are the more likely to influence policy because they are assumed to speak out of *expertise* rather than partisan persuasion. The modern business of the State Department is, in a word, of such character that the traditional line between policy and routine function is difficult if not impossible to draw.

Worse still, many U.S. civil servants are no longer expected, and no longer try, to maintain the attitude of policy impartiality that the traditional view called for. In an era of passionate ideological tensions they become, unavoidably, militant defenders of particular policies. George Kennan, for example, was an "impartial" Foreign Service Officer when his name stood for the Policy of Containment. John Stewart Service and John Carter Vincent were not, in theory, policy makers, yet they supported an identifiable policy toward China; if they were still in the Department, it is clear that they would find it difficult to make common cause with the Eisenhower Administration. Charles Bohlen, also a "career man," is known as a defender of the Yalta Agreement to such an extent that several Senators had legitimate doubts about his ability to serve as Eisenhower's Ambassador to Soviet Russia.

That "it works in England" is no answer at all. British civil servants are far more careful than ours to maintain attitudes of, and a reputation for, impartiality and, in fact, indifference in policy matters. The British foreign officer seems competent and willing, one day to draft measures designed to implement a Conservative government's policy of holding on to India, and the next day, to draft for a Labor government the measures by which India may be turned over to the Indians. It may be desirable that State Department employees act in the British way and acquire the British skill of repressing or avoiding strong convictions. The point is that American civil servants do not do this. And they cannot expect to have it both ways: to act as policy-makers from day to day, and to be treated as impartial janitors when another party comes to power.

Obviously, an incoming administration should be forced, by insistent pressure from public opinion interested in preserving the Civil Service, to go as far as is consistent with its mandate in avoiding the evils of the spoils system. But there is a transcendent commitment postulated in the American philosophy of government: the premises of democracy demand that the electorate be entitled to employ civil servants who will execute policies the electorate wants undertaken. And the premises of republicanism insist that an administration holding the popular mandate must have the authority to implement that mandate.

This is not to suggest, by any means, that the State Department should embark on a wholesale purge of its personnel after each national election. The great majority of Department employees are undoubtedly flexible or dispassionate enough to carry out, most faithfully, the policies of any American administration. But those who are seriously committed to a particular policy must no longer claim tenure immunity.

A final point: all present civil servants are parties to an implied contract that their employment will not be terminated except under standards which were in effect at the time they got their jobs. Thus, and without doubt, compensation is in order for those who are to lose their jobs because the standards have changed: the government must be prepared to make generous financial provisions for employees dismissed under the new security program, and payments from the government should not cease until the em-

ployee finds a new job, with comparable economic return, elsewhere in the community.

It is perhaps not necessary to discuss, in detail, administrative
minutiae of the security program we have in mind. But we owe a
general indication how it would work in the State Department
should the quasi-judicial loyalty-security boards be abolished and
should the Department's security office handle "security risks"
and "policy misfits" solely from the point of view of the government's interest.

1. The preliminary advisory decisions as to whether a State Department employee is a "security risk" or a "policy misfit" would
be made, respectively, by the security and the policy-making officers of the Department. The final decision on security cases would
be made by the chief security officer of the Department, on "policy
misfits" by the Secretary of State or his designee.

2. The men who make the preliminary determination should be
qualified by expert knowledge of both Communism and of current
Department policy. Their up-to-date conversance with the latter
would, of course, be assured only if they received regular briefings
from area offices.

3. Data on security cases would be supplied by the FBI, by Department investigators, and by other investigative agencies; and,
as is the current practice, the discovery of *any* derogatory data
would warrant the attention of the security office. On "policy misfits," the data would be furnished by the relevant Assistant Secretary. The decision as to whether a policy case should be called to
the attention of the security office would be made with reference
to the decisive standard—namely, is there a reasonable doubt that
the employee is capable of working effectively on behalf of the
resolved Department policies?

4. If, having given the benefit of every doubt to the government,
the security officers conclude from the available information that
the person involved may be an "undesirable" from either the security or the policy standpoint, they would notify the employee of this
fact and of the specific reasons which prompted their decision.
The employee should then appear for an interview. In security
cases, suspension of the employee should follow automatically
upon preferment of charges.*

5. The employee would be invited to submit to the security

* This is the recent Department practice.

office any affidavits or documents that may shed light on his security or his policy status.

6. The sole aim of the interview with the employee would be
to elicit information that might shed light on his fitness, security
or policy aptitude, as the case may be.

7. When it has obtained all available information about the
employee, the security office would determine directly whether
the employee retains his job. The sole standard for judging the
security risk: is the employment of this person, beyond a reasonable doubt, consistent with the interests of the national security?
The sole standard for judging the policy risk: is the employee
suited to implement the policies as enunciated by the Secretary
of State?

8. In the event of an adverse decision and subsequent termination of employment, every effort would be made to withhold from
the public the effective reason for the employee's separation.

The Secretary of State should let his chief security officer have
the final say in security cases. We propose this because the chances
are overwhelmingly against the Secretary of State being qualified
to pass judgment on such cases. The Secretary is not, and ought
not to be, chosen by the President for his experience and shrewd-
ness in coping with Communist infiltration techniques, or for his
ability to grasp the complex significance of diverse Communist
affiliations. His qualifications ought to be primarily those of the
statesman skilled in fields altogether different from security en-
forcement. From a practical standpoint, to make the Secretary review every finding of his chief security officer is absurd for he
obviously cannot discharge any such time-consuming duty. He
would, consequently, designate the job to someone else; and since
the person to whom he *ought* to designate it is the Department's
chief expert on security problems, and since the chief expert is
presumably the officer who handed down an adverse decision in
the first place, nothing is to be gained by institutionalizing a round
robin.

These arguments, clearly, do not apply to the policy risks. In
these cases the Secretary is eminently qualified to intervene and
to decide himself.

We have argued that the State Department is the best judge of
the fitness of employees engaged in implementing its policies. But
it does not follow from this that the Department, or any other

sensitive agency, will as a matter of course undertake a hard security program. Nor should the public or Congress take it as a matter of faith that such a security program will take care of itself. The events of the past few years, if they establish nothing else, establish the wisdom of Congressional supervision of security in the sensitive agencies. The stakes are too high, the dangers of lassitude in matters of security too great, for Congress to assume unquestioningly that the executive departments keep their houses clean. The responsibility falls on Congress.

Congress must, therefore, have ready access to the data without which intelligent security evaluation in the sensitive executive departments is impossible. Nothing in recent political history can quite match the futility or the humiliation that Congress suffered when, during the Truman Administration, it tried to live on information scraps tossed to it by arrogant bureaucrats. This is not to overlook the reality of a dilemma the Executive faces as custodian of security data: it cannot release the data indiscriminately, as this could damage both the individuals concerned and the machinery by which the data are obtained; but on the other hand, it cannot withhold data without preventing the Congress from doing its duty.

The Truman way of resolving the dilemma (by disregarding Congress and protecting loyalty-security suspects at whatever price) clearly will not do. Nor is an adequate solution to be found at the other extreme, i.e., by giving *all* Congressmen easy access to *all* security data: this would be tantamount to opening the security files to the general public. Thus, a standing joint committee of both houses should be created, patterned on the Committee on Atomic Energy, which would be furnished copies of all security information in executive files* and would be enjoined by Congress to keep the data confidential.

Such a standing committee's job would be, quite simply, to conduct a continuous survey of security management in government. It would not, of course, be empowered to overrule the findings by agency officers; but it would feel free to discuss loyalty-security actions with them, advocating a change in procedure here, a reversal of a finding there, as the situation indicated.

The Security Committee would make periodic reports to Congress on security practices in the several agencies. Should a report

* Excepting, of course, the names of confidential informants, the identities of FBI penetrators of the Communist Party, and such-like information.

indicate that the security program of a given agency was being conducted unsatisfactorily, Congress should be left to cope with the situation by putting pressure on the President, by exercising its power over the appropriations, or by carrying the issue to the people.

The Congressional Security Committee here envisaged is no fool-proof device for ensuring hard security practices; nor is such a device to be found anywhere else. Perhaps the most notable defect of the committee proposal is that it fails to provide for the sort of situation that harassed McCarthy in 1950. The Tydings Committee (an *ad hoc* Congressional Security Committee not unlike the one we are proposing) ended up *encouraging* lax security practices; and McCarthy's efforts to make it behave proved futile. The Tydings Committee, to be sure, was encouraged to play its obstructive role by the virtual Executive monopoly of security data; but also, as we have shown, it needed no encouragement.

So where is a recourse? Under the American political system, there is no guarantee that a future committee will not betray its mandate, and its responsibilities, other than the force which generated the recent American mobilization: the individual Congressman who has enough devotion to the commonweal to raise some hell when it is being violated—and the sensitivity of the voting public to that kind of hell-raising.

PART THREE

CHAPTER XIII

Senator McCarthy's Method

Introduction

T O APPROVE of Senator McCarthy's "aims" is considered in civilized circles the maximum concession anyone can make to
McCarthyism and still hang on, if precariously, to his virtue.
Everyone, on the other hand, must agree that Senator McCarthy's
"method" is abhorrent, hence the common, stop-loss phrase, "I
approve of Senator McCarthy's aims, but I disapprove of his
method."

An analysis of Senator McCarthy's "method" is not easy, primarily because his method is so variously defined. No single volume
could adequately examine all the characteristics imputed to it,
and all the objections made against it. A great deal of confusion,
what is more, seems to beset McCarthy's critics when they talk
about what they call McCarthy's "method." And since McCarthy's
critics pretty well rule the communications industry, they have
enmeshed the public in their own hectic confusion.

For instance, "damaging the reputations of innocent people" is
talked about as an aspect of McCarthy's "method"; yet it is clear
that while damage to a reputation may *result* from McCarthy's
practice of his method, the result would not appear to be a part
of the *method*. Again, the imposition of "thought control" is often
spoken of as a "method" of McCarthy; but while a measure of
"thought control," or "conformity," is indeed being sought by Mc-
Carthyism (as we shall see in a later chapter), this would appear
to be a proximate *end* of McCarthyism, not a part of McCarthy's
method. Once again, McCarthy's constant urging of the "conspira-
torial view of history" to explain the reversals of the West in its cold
war with the Soviet Union—as well as his imputation of pro-Communist motivations to some of his critics—are characteristic of
McCarthy's method only if it can be established that he does not

believe what he is saying. Thus, should McCarthy tell the American people that Alger Hiss is responsible for the terms of the Yalta Agreement, we would need to ask ourselves, Does McCarthy actually believe this to be so? If he did (as in the absence of contrary evidence we should have to assume), then his saying so would amount to nothing more than his own evaluation of history— to be criticized, perhaps, as ignorant, over-simplified, or simply mistaken—and has nothing whatever to do with his *method*. On the other hand, if it could be shown that McCarthy did *not* himself believe what he said, then his making such a charge would indeed be a part of his method, his immediate end being, let us say, to frighten the American people, or to embarrass the political party that countenanced Alger Hiss.

In other words, an examination of anti-McCarthy literature and journalism reveals that under the heading of McCarthy's "method" there is commonly found a disorderly array of indictments difficult to classify. Lumped together under McCarthy's method are the *consequences* of McCarthyism, the *ends* of McCarthyism and, even, the *spirit* of McCarthyism (suspicion, fear, paranoia, etc.).

To disentangle such rampant confusion calls for nothing less than deep metaphysical therapy. This, let the reader rejoice, we will not attempt. We shall content ourselves with merely indicating the nature of a very, very complex problem. For example: Are the predictable consequences of an act an intrinsic part of that act, or are the two separable? If McCarthy discovers that a State Department official was a member of the Communist Party in 1945, and thereupon exposes that fact, are the ill *effects* of that exposure, as felt by the bureaucrat, a part of McCarthy's method, or are the exposure and the means of exposing alone his method? Is McCarthy's loyalty risk-hunting an end in itself? Is McCarthy like an amateur fisherman whose goal is not so much the selling or the eating of the fish, but rather the catching of it? Or is loyalty risk-hunting the means through which McCarthy seeks to achieve a limited objective (security in government) the achievement of which in turn becomes a means of furthering another end (America's victory in her war against Communism) in turn a means of insuring still a further end and so on? Such questions, and many others like them, are pertinent to a definitive discussion of Senator McCarthy's or anyone else's method. But they do, as we say, involve a philosophical treatise on method; and this is not contemplated here.

We will, rather, having acknowledged the complexity of the subject, discuss only those characteristics of McCarthy's *modus operandi* which constitute, invariably, the staples of the anti-McCarthy diet. It is charged that (1) McCarthy impugns people's loyalty on the basis of insufficient evidence; hence he "smears innocent people" (he has impugned Lattimore's loyalty); that (2) McCarthy exaggerates the evidence and regularly makes unwarranted *specific* accusations; thus, also, he is guilty of "smearing" (he has accused Lattimore of being the "top Soviet espionage agent"); that (3) McCarthy publicizes charges that ought to be kept secret (he runs around the country questioning Lattimore's loyalty); that (4) McCarthy hides behind his Congressional immunity, thus giving his victims no legal come-back (he sees to it that those of his charges against Lattimore that are actionable are made on the floor of the Senate); that (5) McCarthy calls all his critics Communists in an effort to discredit them (he turns on those who disagree with him about Lattimore and calls them pro-Communists).

These charges form the hard core of contemporary criticism of McCarthy's method. They will be examined in an attempt to throw light on two questions: (1) How has McCarthy *in fact* operated? and (2) Does he deserve censure or praise for the way in which he has operated?

The Smearing of Innocent People

IT IS CERTAINLY not characteristic of McCarthy to come forward with dispassionate recitations of the facts. Rather, like an attorney summing up his case for the jury, McCarthy emerges as an *interpreter* of the fact: he assumes the role of the government advocate.

McCarthy, characteristically, seizes upon information that tends to point to disloyalty on the part of a government employee, raises the broad issue of the employee's loyalty, and makes certain charges against the employee—i.e., he characterizes the employee as a "loyalty risk," as a "pro-Communist," as the "pioneer of the smear campaign against Chiang Kai-shek," or what have you. McCarthy's critics insist that it is a part of his method to do all these things without sufficient evidence to back him up. They insist, that is to say, that in almost every instance McCarthy has insufficient factual data, either to call into question the employee's loyalty, or to justify his particular characterization of the employee. Thus they conclude that he "smears innocent people."

We propose to survey McCarthy's record with a view to answering these two questions: Does the evidence he presents justify him (a) in raising the loyalty issue, and (b) in using the particular words that he uses in making his charges? Let us, however, be very clear as to why these are different questions, and why they both need to be asked.

To be sure, McCarthy does not commit separately the two sins with which he is charged. Obviously he does not accuse an employee of being a "pro-Communist" without at the same time (directly or indirectly) raising the question of the employee's loyalty. But clearly, while in certain situations McCarthy ought to be censured for having used certain words in describing his target, he may nevertheless have been justified in raising the question whether his target is a loyalty risk.

McCarthy's friends may feel we are wasting time in fastidiously recording the precise language in which McCarthy couches his charges. After all, they will say, the particular words that McCarthy used do not, anyway, stick in the public's mind; the public recalls merely that a man's allegiance has been called into question. So why hold him to account for the exact wording of his accusations? And, as a matter of fact, McCarthy's most violent critics appear to take precisely this position—except, of course, where it turns out that McCarthy has a particularly good case, in which event they hold McCarthy to the exact phrase he used. (For example, after Owen Lattimore was clearly shown to be at best a loyalty risk, they would not let McCarthy forget that he had called Lattimore "the top Soviet espionage agent," not simply a "loyalty risk.") For the most part, however, Liberal talk about "smearing" focuses not so much on McCarthy's language as on the contention that, however he happens to phrase it, McCarthy manages to put a person's good name under a cloud, and this on the basis of insufficient evidence. Be that as it may, we intend to analyze McCarthy's method under both tests, harkening again to Lord Acton's counsel that one should try to make out for one's opponents an even stronger and more impressive case than they present themselves.

But before we do this, a word needs to be said about two other fashionable tests by which we are invited to judge the sufficiency of McCarthy's evidence. What might be called the *absolute* test of whether McCarthy has "smeared" people is proposed by the Liberal's question: Is there a discrepancy between what a man has actually done, or what a man has actually thought, and what McCarthy has charged that man with having done or having thought? If this test could be applied, it would surely be the final word as to whether a "smear" has been levelled; but it is obviously unserviceable for purposes of evaluating the charge that a man is pro-Communist. In most other situations the test is indeed serviceable, and of course advisable. If, for example, a man is charged with being a member of the Americans for Democratic Action, we can tell whether a smear has been born simply by finding out whether he *is* a member of the Americans for Democratic Action; and this we can do easily enough because members of the ADA do not, as a rule, conceal their membership. But one of the Communist movement's greatest single strengths lies in the skill and determination with which it *prevents* society from finding out which citizens are loyal Communists, and thus disloyal citizens. Thus it becomes very difficult indeed to determine whether X, in calling Y a Communist, has smeared him. The best we can do in the circumstances is to ask whether the charge (by which we mean both the specific accusation and the general impugnation of the person's loyalty) *is justified in the light of necessarily circumstantial evidence.*

In addition to the "absolute proof" test, we must reject what might be called the "legal sufficiency" test. Many of McCarthy's critics are given to pointing out that his evidence in nearly every case is insufficient to establish that the accused has broken the law, which is usually true. But they are also given to saying that this is evidence of McCarthy's irresponsibility, which is foolishness. Only in the rare exception does McCarthy even *accuse* his targets of having broken the law. But he does insist, as a general thing, that the evidence he offers is sufficient to warrant the dismissal of his targets from government service. Thus, those who quarrel with McCarthy on this score (taking the position that only proven law-breakers should be dismissed from the government) should address their grievances to those who drafted the rules for government employment—not to McCarthy, who merely plays by these rules. For by 1947, at the very latest, Congress and both political parties had explicitly endorsed the notion that government service is a privilege, not a right; and that therefore government personnel must meet standards a good deal more exacting than those set forth in the criminal code. Job security for civil servants was therefore to depend not only on their staying outside the law's reach, but also on their satisfying their superiors that their employment was in the national interest.

All this appears to be obvious; but it apparently is not, else we would not hear, so frequently, that McCarthy is to be damned because he goes after government employees without adhering to the standards of proof required of a district attorney going after a thief.

Let us go on now with a review of McCarthy's record, keeping in mind the two questions: Is the evidence he presents sufficient, typically, to justify what McCarthy says about his targets? And is it sufficient, typically, to warrant his calling their loyalty into question?

On the whole, McCarthy's attacks have followed a pattern. Most often he has gone after government employees, or former government employees. If the target of his attack is still employed, McCarthy calls for his dismissal. If he is no longer employed, he calls for an investigation of the security agency of the Department in which he worked. If he finds the employee has not even been processed (which is often the case), he lets the world know that he is flabbergasted. If he finds the employee has been processed and cleared (which is also often the case), he also lets the world know that he is flabbergasted.

McCarthy's critics have so effectively popularized the notion that McCarthy smears a half dozen Americans every week that the statistics may be surprising: the Grand Inquisitor of the Twentieth Century has publicly accused, as of questionable loyalty or reliability, a total of 46 persons.* Of these 46, McCarthy mentioned twelve** only once, and then only to point out that their security status was pending in the State Department and that eleven of them had nevertheless not been suspended from their work.

With respect to ten† others, McCarthy merely quoted from derogatory reports developed by other investigators, with a view to persuading the Senate that at least a *prima facie* case existed for questioning the operating standards of a loyalty program that had cleared them. With one exception (Remington), little public attention was given to these ten. They do not, in short, classify as "McCarthy cases" for purposes of shedding light on his method.

It is, consequently, on the basis of charges against twenty-four persons, whose cases he has especially dramatized, that McCarthy has earned his reputation as "a wholesale poisoner, a perverted destroyer of innocent reputations."‡

To get down to cases: McCarthy has never said anything more

---

* Forty-six is as close a figure as diligent research will bear out. It is possible, though not likely, that McCarthy has accused someone or several people—perhaps in an unpreserved campaign speech here or there—and that we are unaware of the accusations. We naturally exclude McCarthy's frequent references to such established Communists as Alger Hiss, Earl Browder, Gerhart Eisler, Carl Marzani, George Shaw Wheeler *et al.* We also exclude, for the sake of accuracy, accusations made after the first of January, 1953. This procedure is clearly not calculated to tilt the scales in McCarthy's favor; for no one will dispute that McCarthy had been branded a smearer of innocent people well before January of 1953 and that, if anything, his conduct and language have mellowed since Eisenhower's inauguration.

** Gertrude Cameron, Nelson Chipchin, Arpad Erdos, John T. Fishburn, Stella Gordon, Victor M. Hunt, Esther Less, Val Lorwin, Franz L. Neumann, Robert Ross, Sylvia Schimmel, and Francis Tuchser.

† Robert Warren Barnett, Herbert Fierst, Harold Glasser, Marcia Ruth Harrison, Paul Lefantieff-Lee, Daniel Margolies, Ella Montague, Olga Osnatch, Phillip Raine, William Remington.

‡ The incident most often singled out as the outstanding example of McCarthy's "reckless smearing" is that involving George Marshall. Hence we include Marshall in this figure. However, the Marshall episode, while it tells us something about McCarthy's judgment, tells us very little about his method. In the circumstances, we will deal with it in the Appendix, where, by virtue of the unique factors involved, it belongs.

damaging about Lauchlin Currie, Gustavo Duran, Theodore Geiger, Mary Jane Keeney, Edward Posniak, Haldore Hanson, and John Carter Vincent, than that they are known to one or more responsible persons as having been members of the Communist Party, which is in each of these instances true. The fact that this charge against Hanson and Vincent is underwritten exclusively by Louis Budenz is not the basis of legitimate criticism of McCarthy; he cannot be called a smearer because he chooses to rely on the integrity of Budenz. Nor is McCarthy guilty of reckless character assassination because he chooses to take the word of the Spanish Government as against Gustavo Duran's; nor because he finds the testimony of the FBI undercover agents on Posniak's membership in the Party more persuasive than Posniak's denials. Mr. Robert Morris, assistant counsel for the Tydings Committee, offered to present to the Committee "some witnesses . . . who will testify that [Theodore Geiger] . . . was a member of the same Communist Party unit as they were. . . ." Elizabeth Bentley has testified that Lauchlin Currie was a member of a Soviet apparatus. Mary Jane Keeney, having been named as acting as a Communist courier, was dismissed from her post with the United Nations after adverse loyalty reports on her were submitted by the State Department, and has since been cited for contempt by the Internal Security Committee of the Senate.

In short, McCarthy cannot, in our opinion, be indicted as a character assassin for circulating the above facts and for turning them into an accusation against the person concerned. And it readily follows that, in the light of such data, he was fully entitled to call their loyalty into question.

Lattimore has been identified as a member of the Communist Party by Louis Budenz, and as a member of Russian Military Intelligence by Alexander Barmine; and the McCarran Committee classified him, in a unanimous report, as a "conscious articulate instrument of the Soviet conspiracy." There can be no denying, then, that McCarthy was justified in calling Lattimore's loyalty into question.

But McCarthy's specific charges against Lattimore went a good deal further than publication of the evidence that was available; and for this exaggeration he is indeed censurable. He told the Tydings Committee (in executive session, to be sure) that Lattimore was the "top Soviet espionage agent in America"—a daring allegation in the light of our notorious ignorance of the hierarchy of the

Soviet espionage apparatus. A few days later, McCarthy modified this charge, in a speech from the Senate floor.

(It was not McCarthy, one must remember, who publicized Lattimore as the "top American espionage agent"; Drew Pearson broke the story that McCarthy had so described Lattimore in a *closed* session of the Tydings Committee. It was thus a friend and admirer of Lattimore who set in motion Lattimore's "ordeal by slander.")

Though McCarthy's exaggeration is deplorable, it can hardly be maintained that it has been responsible for severely damaging Lattimore. Our society (as distinct from our laws) does not appear to attach much importance to the distinction between membership in the Party, and espionage in behalf of the Party. J. Peters is not more despised in America than Frederick Vanderbilt Field.*

To return to the instances in which McCarthy did *not* misinterpret or exaggerate: McCarthy's insistence that John Stewart Service was a loyalty risk is supported in every respect. Service *was* named by General Hurley as a member of the State Department cabal that was attempting to undermine Hurley's influence in China and urging a policy essentially pro-Chinese-Communist. And Service *was* arrested by the FBI on charges of releasing classified material to unauthorized persons. Nor is that all: the Civil Service Loyalty Review Board ultimately concurred in McCarthy's judgment—to the extent, at least, of ruling that there was a "reasonable doubt" as to Service's loyalty.

Thus it cannot be said that McCarthy smeared Service either in the way he framed the charges against him or in the fact that he called into question Service's loyalty.

The same verdict holds with respect to Professors Schuman and Shapley. McCarthy merely accused them of inveterate party-lining and Communist-fronting. Of these activities they are unqualifiedly guilty (as we have seen in the chapter on the Tydings Committee.)

Of William T. Stone, McCarthy has said that his "Communist activities are legion." What McCarthy refers to is set down in a previous chapter. An extremely cautious man might have said "dubious" instead of "Communist." But let us remember that the State Department security office, after studying Stone's record as far

---

* There is, of course, a great deal of difference between membership in the Party and espionage as far as the *law* is concerned. The law, however, does not distinguish between smear and non-smear, but between what is proved and what is not proved.

back as March, 1946, had recommended that "action be instituted to terminate his services with the State Department immediately." Held to strictest account for the phraseology of his charge, McCarthy probably "smeared" Stone; but if he did, he smeared a man who through the years had taken little pains to protect himself from such charges as were levelled against him. As for the second question we are asking (was McCarthy entitled to call Stone's loyalty into question?), the Department security division's own recommendation provides the obvious answer: Yes.

John Paton Davies has been a target of McCarthy ever since 1950. McCarthy quoted General Hurley as having accused Davies of encouraging, behind his back, a policy favorable to the Chinese Communists. "Davies has been suitably rewarded by Dean Acheson for his sell-out of an ally," said McCarthy to the Senate. "Davies [is now] . . . in Washington as a member of the State Department's Policy Planning Committee, where he is strategically placed to help further the betrayal he began in Chungking." Hard talk, certainly. But "betrayal" is a word that American political lingo was using generously long before McCarthy appeared; and we cannot demand of McCarthy greater verbal precision than is considered par in his métier. But we must not beg the question: McCarthy unquestionably considers Davies a security risk. He is at least not alone in questioning Davies' reliability; the McCarran Committee found that Davies "testified falsely" on a matter "substantial in import"[1] (i.e., concerning his alleged recommendations that the CIA retain certain persons known to be Communists). We do not believe, therefore, that either McCarthy's specific charges against Davies or his calling Davies' loyalty into question were unreasonable.

McCarthy's charges against Philip Jessup, Dorothy Kenyon and Esther Brunauer have been treated amply in the chapter on the Tydings Committee, where we reached the conclusion that McCarthy was justified in bringing their names into a loyalty probe. However, we also saw there that, in the Jessup and Kenyon cases, McCarthy was guilty, in two instances, of gratuitous sensationalism—e.g., his singling Jessup out as the "pioneer" of the anti-Chiang conspiracy, and his calling Miss Kenyon's Communist-front colleagues her "fellow-reds."

Summarizing the security file on Peveril Meigs, McCarthy said in February, 1950, "So far as I know, everything in this individual's file indicates that he is actively working with and for the Communists." Whether this is so, and therefore whether McCarthy is guilty of having smeared Meigs, we do not know, not having had access to the file in question. It is public knowledge, however, that subsequent to McCarthy's charges against Meigs, he was discharged from the Army under the loyalty program. Therefore, the presumption is that McCarthy's questioning of Meigs' loyalty was reasonable.

Drew Pearson definitely *was* smeared by McCarthy on both counts; and the only defense McCarthy could possibly make (which we do not propose to encourage) would run in such terms as, "Those who live by the smear shall perish by the smear." (Pearson's case is treated in another section of this chapter, where it is particularly relevant.)

This, then, is McCarthy's record.* As regards one of the two fundamental questions we have been asking (are McCarthy's specific charges warranted in the light of his evidence?), it is clear that he has been guilty of a number of exaggerations, some of them reckless; and perhaps some of them have unjustly damaged the persons concerned beyond the mere questioning of their loyalty. For these transgressions we have neither the desire to defend him nor the means to do so. Measured against the moral command that proscribes every witting divergence from the truth, they are reprehensible. It remains only to be said that *McCarthy's record is nevertheless not only much better than his critics allege but, given his métier, extremely good.*

As regards the other standard for determining whether smearing has been a characteristic of McCarthy's method (Does the evidence McCarthy presents justify calling into question his targets' loyalty?), the case-by-case breakdown clearly renders a verdict extremely favorable to McCarthy. With the two exceptions of Drew Pearson and George Marshall, not a single person was accused by McCarthy whose loyalty could not be questioned on the basis of a most responsible reading of official records. And this is the only test that seems to be relevant for deciding whether McCarthy "habitually smears people." When a man's loyalty is questioned, more often than not it makes little difference to him just *how* and in what terms it is questioned.

---

* Five of McCarthy's cases are not discussed because the information on them is too scanty to make possible even a preliminary judgment as to whether they were smeared. We refer to Stephen Brunauer, Leon and Mary Keyserling, David Demarest Lloyd, and Philleo Nash.

We may be wrong. But if we *are* right in insisting that this is the apter test, then the record clearly exonerates McCarthy of "habitual character assassination" and of "smearing of innocent people."

"Character assassination" is, of course, a part of McCarthy's method only if we so choose to call the exposure of past activities and associations of government employees. McCarthy has tirelessly combed the records of public servants; and, when the evidence has warranted it, and Administration intransigence blocked other alternatives, he has publicly disclosed their past activities and associations and has raised the question whether, given their records, they merit public confidence. In this, McCarthy has served, so to speak, as a public prosecutor. His concern has not been with establishing "guilt," but with seeing to it that security personnel apply standards stringent enough to give this country the protection it needs against well-camouflaged Communists.

The role of public prosecutor is never an enviable one. His competence is usually judged, unfortunately, on the basis of the number of convictions he wins. The counterpart of the public prosecutor in the security field cannot hope for such clean-cut vindications. At most he succeeds in persuading the "jury"—the Loyalty Security Board—that the doubt as to Jones' loyalty or reliability is "reasonable." And even then, he must face the vituperation of those who not only deem the doubt *unreasonable*, but openly challenge the competence of *any* tribunal to adjudicate such a question.

Let us remember in this connection that it is never particularly difficult to offer a plausible explanation or defense for any stand— or association—that raises doubts as to loyalty or reliability. How often we find ourselves sympathizing, spontaneously and warmheartedly, with the witness who accounts for his participation in a Communist front in terms of a deeply felt identification with the humanitarian objectives with which that front was ostensibly concerned. And how often we fail to remind ourselves that, if the organization was in *fact* a Communist front, *somebody* concerned with it wasn't so much concerned with social reform as with furthering the interests of the Soviet Union, and that therefore the function of security agencies is precisely to look skeptically at explanations commonly accepted as plausible. The layman is perhaps entitled to accept the accounting of the front-joiner, and to despise the "morbid" suspiciousness of the person who does not accept it. But *not* the security agencies—and *not* a United States Senator who feels a vocation to see to it that they do their job. For the hard fact of the matter is that the suspicious person may be the wiser person. And because of bitter experience, we have adopted a national security policy which instructs security personnel to *be* suspicious, and to find against the individual if so much as a reasonable *doubt* exists as to his reliability.

The case of John Stewart Service, if we may drag it up again, illustrates the problem. McCarthy has been severely castigated for imputing disloyalty to a man "whose only crime has been bad judgment." Service, an experienced China hand, dispatched from the field report upon report to his superiors in the Department of State. These reports are of such character as to discredit the hypothesis that their author was both (a) a shrewd reporter, familiar with China, and (b) an anti-Communist. Two alternative hypotheses suggest themselves: (a) Service is not a shrewd reporter; i.e., he is congenitally naive, or else he was temporarily bamboozled; or (b) he was shrewd but not an anti-Communist. The first explanation is the more attractive, but the second is not unthinkable. Then, on top of it all, John Service gets himself arrested by the FBI for turning over classified information to unauthorized persons who, as it happened, were Communists. Two explanations again arise: (a) Service did not deem the information to be in any way critical, and hence he granted himself the authority to reclassify classified information (sometimes exercised by public servants); or (b) Service *wished* to supply the Communists with information to which they might not otherwise have access. Either explanation could account for Service's action. But in the context of an international emergency, McCarthy steps forward to argue that there is at the very least *a reasonable doubt* of Service's loyalty, and that the State Department should therefore dismiss him. McCarthy was perhaps not acting generously, but he certainly was acting reasonably.*

This, then, is "McCarthy's method." Notwithstanding the hectically promoted public impression, McCarthy does not make a

---

* Note the polarization of viewpoints on such men as Owen Lattimore, who is acclaimed by some of his admirers as a "noble man, an earnest, fearless and industrious scholar," and denounced by McCarthy as the "top Soviet espionage agent in America." There is, perhaps, room for disagreement about Lattimore, but the area of controversy, at least, is clear: we must choose between the two propositions: "Lattimore-innocently-swallowed-the-Communist-bait, hook-line-and-sinker," and "Lattimore-consciously-was-out-to-further-Soviet-imperialism."

practice of fabricating evidence. He does, however, make a practice of acting on the proposition—on which he insists the government also act—that Alger Hiss was not the last of the Soviet agents in our midst, and that Hiss' comrades do not publicly parade their allegiance to the Soviet Union.

We have likened McCarthy's role to that of the prosecutor; but let us keep in mind the hazards of carrying the analogy too far. The greatest psychological propaganda victory the Communists and the Liberals have scored in this whole area has been to force everyone to discuss the loyalty-security issue in the terminology of law. The authors of this book are themselves guilty of having used, in the preceding pages, the organically inappropriate imagery of the law, because otherwise they could not join issue with the opposition. But it is palpably foolish to speak, in the area of government security, of "defendant" and "prosecutor," of "guilt" and "innocence," of "proof," of the "presumption of innocence," of the "right to confront one's accuser," of the "right to cross-examination," of "judgment by one's peers," and the rest of it. So long as we continue to use this terminology we can hardly hope to understand the problem at hand, much less to cope with it. We have, in fact, understood and coped with it just to the extent that we have fought ourselves free, at some points, from the legal imagery and its misleading implications.

It is all to the good that we make the district attorney respect the rights of the accused and depend, for a verdict of "guilty," upon the unanimous approval of the jury. Only at our peril do we abandon such revered customs. But let us not be deceived by certain similarities between the role of a public prosecutor and the role of a McCarthy, or between the position of the accused in a murder trial and the position of a Vincent in a security proceeding. The differences between the two are far greater than the similarities, and they reflect all the wisdom we have acquired about how to deal with the Communists in our midst.

The essence of McCarthy—and McCarthyism—lies then in bringing to the loyalty-security problem a kind of skepticism with which it had not been approached before. Others took it for granted that Service backed the Chinese Communists and gave away classified material because he was fooled. McCarthy was prepared to suppose he did so because he was pro-Communist. Others explained Shapley's party-lining in terms of devotion to world peace; McCarthy recognized that devotion to world Communism was an alternative hypothesis that merited equal treatment. And he keeps on being skeptical: if, as so often happens, the evidence does not conclusively establish either hypothesis, McCarthy is there to insist that we cannot afford to *act* on any but the hypothesis that favors our national security. McCarthy would unquestionably admit that Service *might* be innocent; but he would never consent to reinstate him in a position of public trust.

This is the heart of McCarthy's method. It is in many respects as revolutionary as the Communist movement itself—and so it is unlikely to commend itself to people so short on knowledge, or even instincts, as to the nature and resources of the Soviet conspiracy as not to realize that we live in an unbrave new world, in which certain cherished habits of mind are not only inappropriate but suicidal.

The Publicizing of His Charges

ANOTHER aspect of Senator McCarthy's method lies in his demonstrable preference for "carrying to the people" certain controversial issues that others wish to see handled in the absence of public debate. This, of course, is not how his critics put it. They say that McCarthy merely seeks personal publicity. They say that the issues McCarthy concerns himself with are best settled by "cold, silent professionals" working in an atmosphere of secrecy.

As big government has evolved, a greater and greater share of the nation's business has indeed been conducted in secret. Also, an ever-growing number of policy decisions have been made by the Executive and the bureaucracy rather than by Congress. The people and Congress, acquiescing over the past twenty years as the Chief Executive, his Cabinet, and the executive agencies have taken over functions and authority normally reserved to the state governments and the national legislature, have largely renounced active supervision of the affairs of state. The Liberals, in general, have watched this trend with a good deal of satisfaction.

We shall not argue—or attribute to McCarthy the view—that *all* transactions of the government must at *all* times be made public. There are of course situations in which certain information is best withheld from the citizenry. An example, perhaps, is that of informed estimates as to the striking power of our air force, the deliverability of the atom bomb, and the evaluated intentions and capabilities of the enemy.

But not all the withholding nowadays is of this character. The State plays what James Madison called "the old trick of turning every contingency into a resource for accumulating force in the government"; and, in so doing, denies to the people (and their elected representatives) essential information that is legitimately theirs. Truman's press censorship order of 1951 is perhaps the most blatant example of this sort of thing; another, more relevant to our present inquiry, is President Truman's Executive Order forbidding Congressmen access to data on the loyalty of government personnel.

The President's order, in effect, instructed Congress that in the future it will have to take blindly for granted that the executive departments administer the loyalty and security program competently and thoroughly. Truman rationalized his action in terms of an admittedly laudable objective. For it *is* desirable, in most cases, to insure privacy in the proceedings of loyalty and security panels: even if an employee is exonerated by such a panel, he is saddled with the stigma of having had to appear before it; and if he is discharged, he has no recourse, as State Department security regulations point out, to "an outside tribunal which can positively affirm his loyalty."

But what all this proves is merely that the less information that leaks out about the identity of persons processed by the loyalty board, the better for *them*. It certainly does not dispose of the question whether we, as a people, are not entitled to know whether our security program is effective, whether it is the proper concern of Congress to check on the Administration's handling of the security program, and to speak up when there are reasons to believe it is being mishandled.

These questions cannot be dismissed by pointing out that the Chief Executive must himself appear before the people, for a vote of confidence, every four years. The people cannot possibly decide whether the President has done a satisfactory job in the security field without *knowing* about the job he has done. If a fleet of our own B-50's, piloted by our own aviators, carrying our own atomic bombs, attacks Detroit, and then lands in Siberia, the people will deduce that the President's security program has been slipshod. But in the absence of such clues, they are without data to make relevant judgments about government security except as their representatives are in a position to evaluate security performance on the basis of spot checks and some periodic investigations of a more exhausting nature. Yet the people's representatives cannot do their duty without examining the minutes of loyalty and security hearings on specific individuals.

Early in 1950, Senator McCarthy concluded that, on the available evidence, the security program, most particularly in the State Department, was being irresponsibly administered. As it turned out his conclusion was unquestionably and unanswerably correct. But almost immediately after McCarthy made his first charges, in February, 1950, the President, the State Department, and the majority leader of the Senate, publicly and categorically denied them. McCarthy persevered, and the public sentiment he aroused undoubtedly contributed to the decision of the Democratic majority to arrange an investigation.

Moreover, let us remember that McCarthy *refused*, at first, to release to the public the names of the loyalty risks he had in mind. Only when the Tydings Committee had revealed its intention of investigating not State Department security but Joe McCarthy, did he begin in earnest to pound names, dates and figures into the consciousness of the people. And later, with the Tydings Committee's unbelievable report in his hand, McCarthy toured the country insisting that the Truman Administration was protecting loyalty risks in the government, and that something ought to be done about it. The people responded. As a starter, they retired Scott Lucas and Millard Tydings.

Those who, knowing all the circumstances, still denounce McCarthy's method, must be prepared to argue that he should have kept silent about loyalty risks in critical government positions—in the teeth of his deep personal conviction that they were being protected—because he should have felt himself bound by arbitrary decisions as to what issues are best left to the executive process. But McCarthy is of course *not* bound by such decisions. He makes his own. If McCarthy were to learn the figures on our production of atom bombs and felt that our supply was dangerously low, he would probably keep silent, reasoning that a short supply is less dangerous than Soviet knowledge of it. (McCarthy's record for acting responsibly in this area is, on the whole, excellent. He does not automatically reach for a megaphone every time he is displeased, his negotiations with the Greek ship owners being a case in point. Not until his Committee had concluded an agreement with them to ban commercial traffic to Red China did McCarthy make an announcement on the subject.)

To revert to the first question we raised: is McCarthy above all a publicity seeker, and is his traffic with the people nothing more than his way of gratifying a lust for national attention? This question neither McCarthy's friends nor his foes can answer. Motives of this sort can of course be advanced and defended to explain the activities of most public figures. But this is strictly a parlor game.

Only one thing is certain: McCarthy *receives* publicity—more publicity than any American save the President. There are several reasons for this. McCarthy deals with sensational issues, and sensation is newsworthy. And McCarthy, day in and day out, deals body blows to the soft underbelly of American Liberals, whose screams of anguish are so infrequent (by virtue of their entrenched power) that when they *are* made to scream, the occasion is, again, newsworthy. And, of course, having occupied the front pages for so long now, McCarthy has become a national figure, and the public is curious about national figures, particularly those who are controversial.

But to say that because McCarthy *gets* publicity, he does what he is doing simply because he *wants* publicity, is a specious piece of tendentious reasoning.* Such inferences about the motivations of public figures can of course never be conclusively refuted, but since the need for a public ventilation of the government's security derelictions is now firmly established, the presumption, in a world still prepared to concede that a concern for the commonweal *can* be genuine, ought to be that the Senator who met that need was motivated by a desire to serve the people. Obviously, McCarthy cannot carry issues to the people without getting their attention; and there is no way of focussing the people's attention on an issue without at the same time drawing attention to oneself. In short, McCarthy must be judged on whether his program is commendable—not on whether one of the program's concomitants is to keep McCarthy on the front pages.

It is curious that what is widely thought of as a contemptible aspect of Senator McCarthy's method actually amounts to nothing more than his intimacy with the people. McCarthy's continuous appeal to the people sorely aggravates the same Liberals whose certified faith in the people's judgment never extends to those situations in which the people disagree with the Liberals. Thus, if McCarthy had been repudiated at the polls on any of the several occasions when he invited a public verdict on his activities, the Liberals would have rushed forward to praise the overarching wisdom of the people. He was not repudiated; so the Liberals talk out of the other side of their mouths. The people, they tell us, were swept away by primitive passions—of the sort that never unsettle the Liberals, except when they contemplate McCarthy.

* Estes Kefauver's television crusade against crime is, of course, susceptible to the same interpretation. But Liberals were disposed to infer noble intent in this situation. Kefauver exposed to public view persons against whom charges of malfeasance in office, bribery, racketeering, theft, gambling and murder, had been made or *insinuated*. McCarthy exposed to public view persons charged with serving the interests of the Soviet Union. The Liberals, for reasons best understood by themselves, have sympathized with McCarthy's victims while worrying very little about Kefauver's. Yet it is McCarthy's victims whom the ordinary processes of the law clearly cannot reach, and for whom, therefore, Congressional hearings are especially in order.

The Use of Congressional Immunity

Not only does McCarthy accuse people on insufficient evidence, not only does he then proceed to publicize his charges against them, he also protects himself from any legal recourse they might have by hiding under Congressional immunity. So runs another Liberal indictment of McCarthy's method.

We have, throughout, stressed the substantive differences between processes of law and loyalty actions, and have warned against the danger of assimilating the two. At the same time, we have occasionally referred to the similarity between McCarthy's role and that of a public prosecutor. Should we be charged with inconsistency, our answer would be, simply, that both the similarities and the differences are *there*. Indeed, McCarthy has assumed the role of public prosecutor—but in a type of action that does not reach the courts and to which, therefore, the rules that govern court actions are inapplicable.

One of the similarities between McCarthy, the anti-Communist tribune, and the conventional public prosecutor lies in the fact that both enjoy a considerable immunity against legal action for libel and slander—*and would not be able to perform their functions without such immunity.* If a prosecutor, whose job it is to urge the jury to return a verdict of "guilty," could be held legally responsible for all the statements he makes in the course of a trial, he would be at the mercy of all vindicated defendants—and would be careful not to make statements that he *needs* to make to plead his case. It is not unusual for the prosecutor to sum up his case by informing the jury that that accused is a deceitful and practiced liar, a foul and callous adulterer, a degenerate thief, or a cold-blooded, cynical and ruthless murderer. Not infrequently the person so described walks out of the courtroom a free man. Free, that is, except that he cannot file suit against the prosecuting attorney for slander.

The privileges Senator McCarthy exercises in his present role are essentially those of the district attorney. They are also the privileges the framers of our Constitution *deliberately extended to our national legislators*—lest they fail, for fear of subsequent court action, to speak out against persons they deem to be public malefactors.

To furnish the sort of "proof" that would satisfy a court that

John Jones is pro-Communist remains in most cases impossible—
by definition of Communist conduct. Often McCarthy has had
nothing to go on but a set of facts amassed by State Department
or FBI investigators, which seemed to constitute strong *prima
facie* evidence that John Jones, currently with the State Department, is a loyalty risk. After exhausting other means of getting
Jones out of the Department, McCarthy makes a speech about
Jones on the floor of the Senate. Jones promptly says he will sue
McCarthy if he will waive his immunity. McCarthy refuses to do
so. *And he must refuse:* for to authenticate his charges, McCarthy
would have to furnish a jury with the original investigating reports; and neither the State Department nor the FBI can make
them available. But for his immunity, McCarthy would have to
preserve a discreet silence about Jones. In short, the monopoliza-
tion by the Executive of much of the evidence relevant to loyalty-
security cases is the major difficulty a Congressman faces in uproot-
ing security risks.

Another difficulty is of course the reluctance of Communists to
furnish evidence against each other. A case in point developed
from Elizabeth Bentley's public reiteration, early in 1949, of her
immunized charge before the House Committee on Un-American
Activities that William Remington had been known to her as a
Communist. When she repeated the statement over the radio,
Remington filed suit against the General Foods Corporation (the
program's sponsor), the National Broadcasting Company, and
Miss Bentley, asking $100,000 in damages. Miss Bentley named
persons who had known Remington as a Communist; but none of
them stepped forward, at that time, to testify in her behalf. The
result: the broadcasting company and the sponsor had to pay
$10,000 to Remington. Yet a few months later, the Justice Depart-
ment furnished evidence—and witnesses—firmly establishing Remington's membership in the Party. He was convicted for perjury.
McCarthy, too, has always to consider the Communists' conspiracy
of silence; and, but for his immunity, he could not get on with
his job.

A third difficulty for McCarthy (and everybody else who attempts to expose loyalty risks) is that even when he is fortunate
enough to obtain investigative reports from the executive agencies
he is not able to penetrate the secrecy which protects confidential
informants. Yet much information is given to the FBI and other
investigators by informants who will not permit their identity to

be revealed. It is the FBI's responsibility to appraise the reliability of X-9, who states that John Jones is a member of the Communist Party. But this does not help McCarthy, since X-9 is not prepared to come forward and reiterate his accusation against Jones in a court of law. Should McCarthy reveal X-9's testimony against Jones, who is still working in the State Department? Or should he take no action at all in order to avoid criticism for "abusing" Congressional immunity? The questions, it seems to us, answer themselves.

Again, there is the fact that the Communists and the pro-Communists are litigious beyond belief, determined, as always, to make the most of the legal and constitutional devices free society puts at their disposal. Louis Budenz testified to the Tydings Committee about a major policy decision of the Communist Party, made while he was still managing editor of the *Daily Worker:*

... The Communist Party—and this is something that everyone should know—agreed that after that period of 1945, that with the cold war beginning, all concealed Communists should sue anyone who accused them of being Communists, sue them for libel. As Alexander Trachtenberg [a high officer of the Communist conspiracy] who made the report, said, "This is not necessarily for the purpose of winning the libel suit. It is to bleed white anyone who dares to accuse anyone of being a Communist, so that they will be shut up." As a matter of fact, that became the policy.[2]

Budenz told of a lawsuit, undecided at the time he spoke, in which the defendant (who had charged the plaintiff with being pro-Communist) stood to lose $55,000 in *lawyer's fees alone*—win or lose.

Most relevant in this context are the obstacles the government had to surmount in proving what was altogether self-evident—that eleven top U.S. Communists were bent upon overturning our government by force and violence. It took an estimated two million dollars, an eight months' trial, a militia of lawyers, round-the-clock cooperation of the FBI, and the sacrifice of several valuable undercover agents, to persuade a jury that our top Communists were out to do something that every informed American has known for over twenty years they were bent on doing. But are we to believe that, lacking the resources of the federal government, individual Congressmen should have refrained over the years from stating that Eugene Dennis, Gus Hall, Benjamin Davis, *et al.* were revolutionary conspirators so as not to "abuse" Congressional immunity?

Finally, there is the sheer loss of time in litigation—a loss of time no busy man can afford. For example, McCarthy himself filed suit in 1952 against the *Syracuse Post-Standard,* charging libel. After nine months of pre-trial hearings, depositions, briefs, conferences, and correspondence, the newspaper, acknowledging guilt, gave McCarthy $16,500 as a settlement. McCarthy's lawyer's fees (he told us) were reasonable, just over $6,000. He therefore cleared about $10,000 which, as damages, was tax free. We commented to McCarthy that since the Syracuse paper had not said anything that many other papers had not also said, he might make a rather handsome living by filing suits against one rich paper after another. He might, indeed, McCarthy replied, and added: "But I would have to stop being a Senator. I cleared $10,000 from the Syracuse case, but I also spent what amounts to a total of two months of my time in connection with the suit. I haven't got time to file suits *and* to keep up with my work."

Paragraph 1, Section 6, Article I, of the Constitution was designed to encourage Congressmen to speak their minds. It promises them that ". . . for any speech or debate in either house they shall not be questioned in any other place." The guarantee is highly utilitarian, and McCarthy is by no means the only Congressman whom it has recently stood in good stead. Senators Kefauver, O'Conor and Tobey would have been hard put to defend some of the accusations and innuendoes they advanced in the course of their encyclopaedic investigation into American rascality.* Yet most of McCarthy's detractors would be among the first to insist that the Kefauver investigation was in the national interest.

It should, however, be recalled that Congressional immunity was written into the Constitution not to serve the Congressmen, but to serve the people. The decision of an early (1808) court specifically directed attention to this: "These privileges are thus secured, not with the intention of protecting the members against prosecution for their own benefit, but to support the rights of the people, by enabling their representatives to execute the functions of their office without fear of prosecutions, civil or criminal."[3]

All this is not to say, of course, that Congressional immunity *always* serves the public interest. Like all good things, it is subject

* For example: Why, Senator Tobey asked William O'Dwyer, had James Moran accompanied him on a wartime visit to Frank Costello's apartment— "To carry the little black bag?"

to immoderate use; and, even when exercised within normal limits, it can be exploited by evil men for antisocial purposes. But on the record, no McCarthy critic, in charging him with abuse of Congressional immunity, appears to be speaking with reference to any developed or even intelligible doctrine as to *what constitutes abuse of Congressional immunity.* Some appear to mean merely that Congressional immunity protects his activities more extensively than its creators could have intended—i.e., that McCarthy takes refuge in it "constantly." It is, however, easy to show that this is a gross exaggeration. In the Appendix, we list, side by side, the most damaging charges McCarthy has made, on the floor and off the floor; and the reader will see that it is on the rare, not the every-day, occasion that McCarthy avoids litigation by wrapping himself in Congressional immunity.

Some of his critics point out that even when McCarthy goes through the motions of waiving immunity for utterances made off the Senate floor, he has not actually done so, because he is quoting, or paraphrasing, previously immunized allegations. If this is what is meant by "abuse," the point is silly. If McCarthy quotes, outside the Senate, Budenz' immunized statement that Haldore Hanson was a member of the Communist Party, he is indeed just as immune as if he had quoted it inside the Senate—not because McCarthy is a Senator but because Budenz testified before a Senate Committee. But what do McCarthy's critics wish him to do?

Say, himself, in so many words, "Hanson is a Communist because *I* say so?" Since what McCarthy knows about Hanson he knows via Budenz, it would be foolish—and mendacious as well—for him to say anything except, *"according to Budenz,* Hanson was a Communist." By decrying McCarthy's not calling Hanson a Communist on his *own* authority, his critics in effect talk as if they wanted McCarthy to commit a previously uncommitted smear just to give Hanson a chance to file suit!

The denials by McCarthy's victims, it is further said, never catch up with his accusations, in part because Congressional immunity tilts the scales to the disadvantage of the "accused." Senator McCarthy strikes out at Jones and makes page 1; Jones retorts and makes page 15. And Jones can't get back at McCarthy because McCarthy is privileged.

Normally, the public figure has, indeed, readier access to the news pages. Most newspapers, however, appear to be aware of the inherent unfairness of such mismatched bouts and try to balance the scales. And when McCarthy is the accuser, this appears to be especially true. Not only, on the record, is the reply of the accused given equally prominent treatment in the papers, it is often much more extensive, and is often given editorial help on the side. The publicity given to Owen Lattimore's rebuttal when he appeared before the Tydings Committee in 1950 (to say nothing of the extravagant editorial reception of his book, *Ordeal by Slander*) is an instance in point. But Lattimore, some would answer, was a special case. The authors have, therefore, examined the treatment given to McCarthy's nine public Tydings cases by five newspapers —the *New York Times*, the *San Francisco Chronicle*, the *Washington Post*, the *St. Louis Post-Dispatch*, and the *Des Moines Register*. The results of this inquiry are detailed in the appendix. The upshot is that all these newspapers gave equally prominent space to the rebuttals and, in some cases, further editorial space in which to pass on their unfriendly opinions of McCarthy.

McCarthy's *own* position on the use of Congressional immunity is far from clear. He must often have regretted the impassioned promise he made on the evening of February 20, 1950, when he was pleading for the creation of what was to be the Tydings Committee. Senator Lucas had been trying to needle him into revealing there and then the names of the 57 supposed Communists on his list, and had said: "The Senator is privileged to name them all in the Senate, and if those people are not Communists, he will be protected. That is all I want the Senator to do. . . ."

I wish to thank the distinguished Senator from Illinois for his views [McCarthy answered], but I should like to assure him that I will not say anything on the Senate floor which I will not say off the floor. On the day when I take advantage of the security we have on the Senate floor, on that day I will resign from the Senate. Anything I say on the floor of the Senate at any time will be repeated off the floor.

Two months later, his critics, pointing out that he had made several charges in the Senate that he had not made off the floor, were demanding that he eat his words. The best McCarthy could manage by way of reply was this:

At that time I assumed [I] could get the files. Since then I have made statements about some six or seven individuals, furnished documentary proof. They have asked me to make statements off the floor. I have said that I will do that when they make their files available. . . . When they make those files available so they can be used, those statements will be made in public.

One of your questions is: "Will you make the statement in public?" The answer is: No. Number two: "Are you going to resign?" The answer is: No.[4]

McCarthy certainly had a point in insisting that he could not hope to defend himself in court without access to files not available to him in a lawsuit. Yet he would have done well to have taken specific note of this qualification two months earlier, when making his unqualified pledge.

McCarthy's present position, as expressed to the authors, is that he regards Congressional immunity as indispensable to the responsible discharge of Senatorial duty; and that no Senator has a right, much less a duty, to deprive himself of its protection. He is, however, prepared to waive immunity on all statements he has thus far made provided (1) he be given access to the security files of all persons who may sue him, and (2) that he be not held legally responsible for those of his statements made in *executive* session or those he *wished* to make in executive session but did not because the Tydings Committee would not let him. In our opinion, this proviso is entirely reasonable. We have seen (in the chapter on the Tydings Committee) how steadfastly McCarthy resisted pressure of various Democratic Senators to reveal in public session the names of the persons he was accusing, and how often he reiterated his request that the Tydings Hearings be held in executive session. Consequently, he does not and should not regard himself as responsible for the publicity given to the nine persons he named in open session *at the direction of Tydings* and his colleagues: Kenyon, Duran, Jessup, Brunauer, Hanson, Schuman, Shapley, Service and Lattimore.

But, in our opinion, McCarthy misses an essential point. In the first place, mere access to the files would not always give him the ammunition he needs to defend himself successfully against libel suits. In the case of Edward Posniak, for instance, the files would reveal that "an" undercover agent and "a" secret informant of the FBI knew him as a member of the Communist Party. Since neither the agent nor the informant could be counted on to come forward in McCarthy's defense, it seems highly improbable that McCarthy could defend himself should Posniak bring suit. So, too, in the Vincent and Hanson cases. Budenz might be willing to cooperate, but his word would hardly pass as courtroom proof of their membership in the Party—indeed it would probably be ruled inadmissible as hearsay evidence.

Yet, as we have argued above, Posniak, Vincent, Hanson, and Kenyon are clearly, under existing standards, security risks. The information against them should, therefore, have been brought to light. But McCarthy could bring it to light and relate it to the security problem only because of his immunity. For him to promise to say nothing under immunity that, given courtroom access to the files, he is not prepared to repeat off the floor, is to circumscribe his future usefulness in a manner the nation cannot afford.

The position we should like to see McCarthy adopt is this: "I am, in a manner of speaking, a professional hunter of security risks in government. I shall continue to search the security risks out until I am satisfied that the job is done, or until I am convinced that the Administration is doing the job to my satisfaction. I shall attempt to be scrupulously accurate—to the extent that one can be, given the executive blackout on security data—and reasonable in my judgments. But I intend to spend my time in the Senate, not in the courthouse. I shall therefore avail myself, unapologetically, of the immunity granted me by the Constitution." McCarthy himself *has* said: ". . . the freedom of Senators and Congressmen to speak unpleasant and embarrassing truths without fear of prosecution in lawsuits is at times abused. Rather than remove this freedom of speech, it would seem wiser for the voters to remove those who abuse that freedom of speech."[5]

Impugning the Loyalty of His Critics

FINALLY, some critics consider it characteristic of McCarthy that he imputes pro-Communism to everyone he disagrees with. Like most anti-McCarthy charges, this one is grossly exaggerated. Unlike many of them, however, it starts out from some incontrovertible facts.

For example, there is McCarthy's attack on Drew Pearson in December, 1950. McCarthy told the Senate:

> It appears that Pearson never actually signed up as a member of the Comunist Party and never paid dues. . . . [But] if the loyal American newspaper editors and publishers and radio station owners refuse to buy this disguised, sugar-coated voice of Russia, the mockingbirds who have followed the Pearson line will disappear from the scene like chaff before the wind. The American people can do much to accomplish this result. They can notify their newspapers that they do not want this Moscow-directed character assassin being brought into their homes to poison the well of information at which their children drink.
>
> [What is more, said McCarthy,] I have discussed this man Pearson with practically every former member of the Communist Party whom I have met during my recent and present investigation of Communists in Government. Almost to a man, they were agreed on a number of things: No. 1: That Pearson's all-important job . . . was to lead the character assassination of any man who was a threat to international communism. No. 2: That he did that job so well that he was the most valuable of all radio commentators and writers from the standpoint of the Communist Party. No. 3: In order to maintain his value, it was necessary that he occasionally throw pebbles at communism and Communists generally, so as to have a false reputation of being anti-Communist.[6]

Apart from recounting the aid Pearson had given to the Communists by his systematic attacks on hard anti-Communists, McCarthy based his charge against Pearson on one count: Pearson, he said, retained a leg-man and/or principal assistant, named David Karr, whom McCarthy identified as a member of the Communist Party. Pearson promptly denied that Karr was or had been a Communist. McCarthy impressively documented his allegation (1) by quoting from a report, drawn up by the office of the Executive Director and Chief Examiner of the Civil Service Commission in 1943, which unambiguously asserted that Karr was an active Communist, and (2) by citing testimony from Mr. Howard Rushmore, a former Communist, that as a staff member of the *Daily Worker* Rushmore had given Karr, also of the *Daily Worker,* assignments. "He had to show me his party card to get those assignments," Rushmore had added.[7]

With this and, as far as the public knew,* *only* this to go on (i.e., impressive testimony to the effect that Karr was, or had been, a Communist, and that he worked for Pearson), McCarthy ended up saying such things as the following:

"The relationship [between Pearson and Karr] is such that it is diffi- cult to know who is the master and who is the servant." "Pearson [is] . . . under the direction of David Karr. . . ." ". . . Pearson never actually signed up as a member of the Communist Party. . . . However, that has not in any way affected his value to the party; nor has it af- fected his willingness to *follow the orders of David Karr. . . .*" "One of Pearson's extremely important tasks, *assigned him by the Communist Party,* through David Karr, . . ." etc. "So again, Pearson was assigned the task—*assigned the job by the Communist Party,* through David Karr . . ." etc. "Again Pearson is *assigned the job by the Communist Party* through David Karr, . . ." etc. ". . . the man through whom Pearson receives orders *and directions from the Communist Party is one David Karr. . . .*" "*David Karr is the connecting link between Drew Pearson and the Communist Party.* He is the man who *assigns* to Pearson the impor- tant task of conducting a character assassination of any man who dares to stand in the way of international Communism."[8] [Italics added.]

McCarthy, in short, accomplished that rather improbable feat: he smeared Drew Pearson.

Much has been said about McCarthy's behavior in questioning James Wechsler of the New York *Post* in the course of an investi- gation of the State Department's overseas libraries. One of the charges against McCarthy that has arisen from this encounter— that McCarthy was seeking to intimidate the anti-McCarthy press —is pure nonsense;** but a further charge—that McCarthy was ad-

* It was not yet public knowledge that Drew Pearson had also employed another named Communist, Andrew Older, whom he had kept on even after he was exposed—because, in Pearson's words, he had hoped to "convert" him.

** Mr. James Burnham neatly dispensed with this allegation in an article in *The Freeman,* June 15, 1953, which concludes with the following para- graphs: "No sanctions of any kind were invoked or contemplated against either Wechsler or the newspaper which he edits. In the hearing, Wechsler was given total latitude, much beyond rules that might legally and properly have been invoked, to say anything he wanted at whatever length he chose. He was permitted to evade and avoid direct questions, to declaim and divert,

vancing a basically unsupportable standard for testing a man's loyalty—has some superficial plausibility to it, and merits brief consideration. McCarthy told Wechsler:

> I feel that you have not broken with Communist ideals. I feel that you are serving them very, very actively. Whether you are doing it knowingly or not, that is in your own mind. . . .
>
> I have no knowledge as to whether you have a card in the party. . . . Your purported reformation does not convince me at all. I know if I were head of the Communist Party and I had Jim Wechsler come to Moscow and I discovered this bright man, apparently a good writer, I would say, "Mr. Wechsler, when you go back to the United States, you will state that you are breaking with the Communist Party, you will make general attacks against Communism, and then you will be our ringleader in trying to attack and destroy any man who tries to hurt and dig out the specific traitors who are hunting our [sic] country." You have followed that pattern.

McCarthy, it is alleged, is actually saying that if you support Communist objectives you are, obviously, a Communist, and if you attack them, this is a deceptive maneuver, and you are still a Communist—unless, of course, you subscribe to McCarthy's formula for attacking them.

If McCarthy had intended to set up such a standard as a general yardstick for weighing a man's loyalty, he would indeed have embarked on a venture in sheer insanity. For such a standard, with one or another modification, would indict as disloyal absolutely everyone who disagrees with McCarthy's brand of anti-Communism. Now McCarthy may sometimes be imprecise; but heaven knows he is no lunatic. It is only the observer who is determined *not* to understand McCarthy who, on considering the context in

---

to introduce a written statement in a manner directly counter to the established ruling of the committee and the Senate, and to denounce the Chairman and other members of the nation's highest legislative body in a fashion that in most other countries would be deemed not merely abominable taste but actionable as contempt and libel. . . .

"Wechsler and McCarthy are political enemies. They condemn each other verbally in public. Where is the threat to free speech and free press in that? If McCarthy is trying to intimidate the press, then why is not the *Post,* with its unrestrained attack on what it describes as 'the reactionaries' of Congress, to be charged with intimidating the legislature and subverting the legislative process?

"Wechsler can hardly be confused in his mind about all this. For him and his political associates, 'free press,' and most of the other freedoms, are only clubs with which to beat their opponents—means, that is to say, to their ends."

which the above statement was made, will go on to wrench such a meaning out of it. McCarthy was not, be it noted, talking about just *any* American; he was talking about James Wechsler, an admitted former Communist. He was laying down a standard one may or may not endorse, but one we have no business confusing with a standard for testing the bona fides of persons who do *not* have Communist backgrounds.

With respect to the Wechslers, McCarthy is saying two things: (a) it is not unreasonable to suppose that Communist "renegades" who are now demonstrated *anti*-anti Communists, are pulling the wool over our eyes; for it is clearly conceivable that there are men around us who, for tactical reasons, have been instructed by the Party to feign conversion in order to attend more effectively to the Party's business; and (b) ex-Communists must therefore be looked at more skeptically than other persons when the question of their loyalty to the United States arises. They, McCarthy is saying, must prove their sincerity in a very particular sort of way—by doing their earnest best to expose the conspiracy of which they were a party; by disclosing, for example, the names of their former confederates. This is a special form of penance that McCarthy is in effect asking for. He may have gone too far, but he is reasonable in applying a standard *different* from that applicable to persons innocent of involvement in the Communist conspiracy.

Excepting his assault on Drew Pearson, McCarthy's unwarranted attacks have been directed, almost exclusively, at particular newspapers rather than individual newsmen. He is especially fond, for example, of referring to the *Washington Post* as the "Washington edition of the *Daily Worker*"; to the *New York Post* as the "uptown edition of the *Daily Worker*"; to the *Milwaukee Journal* as the "Milwaukee edition . . ." etc. Yet such statements are more uncouth than vicious; they can probably be dismissed, even, as jocular indulgences in what *Life* magazine has called "groin-and-eyeball" polemics. Not so, however, some of the more specific charges McCarthy has aimed at certain newspapers.

On one occasion, for example, McCarthy advised certain advertisers in Milwaukee to withdraw their support of the *Journal*. "Keep in mind when you send your checks over to the *Journal*," he said, "[that] you are contributing to bringing the Communist Party line into the homes of Wisconsin."

On another, he wrote about *Time:* "There is nothing personal about my exposing the depth to which this magazine will sink in using deliberate falsehoods to destroy *anyone who is hurting the Communist cause*. . . . I feel that I have the duty to let those advertisers [who buy space in it] know that *Time* magazine publishes falsehoods *for a purpose*. Those advertisers, who are extremely busy in their work, are entitled to have it called to their attention if unknowingly they are flooding American homes with Communist Party line material. . . ."[9] (Italics added.)

And, in describing the *Milwaukee Journal,* the *Madison Capital-Times,* the *New York Post,* the *Washington Post,* the *St. Louis Post-Dispatch,* and the *Portland Oregonian* as "consistently paralleling the editorial line of the *Daily Worker,*" McCarthy wrote:[10]

> They, of course, criticize Communism generally to obtain a false reputation of being anti-Communist. Then they go all-out to assassinate the character and destroy the reputation of anyone who tries to dig out the really dangerous under-cover Communists. . . . Some who read those papers may at first blush violently differ with me. However, you need not take my word. Make your own decision. First check the editorial policy which the *Daily Worker* consistently follows. Then determine for yourself the extent to which the above papers follow that editorial policy. Do not be deceived, however, by any general condemnation or tossing of pebbles at Communism generally. That is a perfectly safe sport which was indulged in even by Alger Hiss. The test is not whether they are willing to condemn Communism generally and the well-known, previously exposed Communists. The test is whether they follow a pattern of supporting or condemning the exposure of the sacred cows—the dangerous, under-cover Communists who have been promoted to positions of untouchability by the Communist and left-wing press.

And there we have it in McCarthy's own words—the reasoning which, he feels, justifies him in referring to the *Podunk Post* as the Podunk edition of the *Daily Worker*. And he has relied on it often enough to warrant its being treated as an integral part of his approach—if not, strictly speaking, a part of his method.

It would be preferable, from McCarthy's standpoint, if he had never attempted a logical explanation of his statements about these papers' and Pearson's Communist motives. Any way you look at it, of course, he is in these cases guilty of smearing. Had they occurred in the course of emotional responses to the uncounted smears and unmatched viciousness that all these persons and newspapers have heaped on McCarthy through the past few years, they might be understandable. But they did not, and therefore they cannot be classed with, say, letters from Mr. Truman to music critics.

This aspect of McCarthy's "method" is traceable to several untenable assumptions which, while they do not underlie his thinking at all times, certainly do so sometimes.*

ASSUMPTION A: *One cannot at one and the same time vigorously oppose Communism and McCarthy.*

Given a rigorously logical frame of reference, this assumption is, far from being palpably foolish, rather seductive. If McCarthy's activities are seriously damaging Communism, as at least McCarthy and the Communists are convinced, why indeed, should an anti-Communist object to them? But the matter is not this simple: McCarthy sometimes fails to see that, while there are certainly those who object to his activities *because* they are anti-Communist, there are also those who object to them because they don't *deem* them to be anti-Communist, or because they feel that, while they hurt Communism some, they hurt American institutions more.

ASSUMPTION B: *Distortion of the facts about McCarthy indicates not merely malice, unbalance, naivete, or unscrupulousness, but also pro-Communism.*

Why, McCarthy must often ask himself, should my critics distort and falsify the *facts* about what I do, unless it is because they are pro-Communists? But McCarthy should know that it is not only the Communists who distort and falsify information in order to discredit people whom they oppose. And many non-Communists do oppose McCarthy, heaven knows. Therefore, while it is undeniable that many—perhaps most—of McCarthy's enemies are guilty of imponderable crimes against justice, it does not follow that one of these crimes is pro-Communism.

ASSUMPTION C: *All anti-Communists are agreed as a matter of course that "reasonable doubt" of reliability is sufficient cause for removing employees from government service* (i.e., if you *don't* agree, you are not anti-Communist).

McCarthy would do well to realize that the merits of having a loyalty program *at all* remains a live issue with some clearly anti-

---

* We say "sometimes" because McCarthy has by no means impugned the loyalty of all his critics. McCarthy is on record as acknowledging the existence of "honest" criticism: "There are . . . the completely honest newspaper editors who are sincerely opposed to what I am doing. . . ." (*McCarthyism*, p. 89). McCarthy's failure to attack some of his most relentless and conspicuous critics bears out the fact that he resorts to his have-you-stopped-following-the-party-line technique on rather special occasions.

Communist Liberals. Most Liberals, of course, have long since conceded: their own front man, after all promulgated the Loyalty Order as far back as in 1947. But a *tough* loyalty program, one based on the "reasonable doubt" standard, is still bitterly opposed by a great many sincerely anti-Communist Liberals. And McCarthy's conviction—which we share—that one cannot be *effectively* anti-Communist and also oppose the "reasonable doubt" standard does not support the conclusion that one cannot be anti-Communist at all and oppose the standard.

ASSUMPTION D: *Since a vigorous security program is indispensable to legitimate anti-Communism, opposition to it is prima facie evidence of party-lining* (in a class with, say, declaring the Czechoslovak coup a "people's victory," or accusing the United States of having used bacteriological warfare in Korea).

The fact that a vigorous security program is geared to the national interest, while the kind the Liberals want is not, raises interesting questions about the wisdom and vision of the Liberals; but not about their loyalty. The issues involved in a hard-hitting loyalty program are issues that separate Americans from Americans, not Americans from Communists. It is, in any case, a pretty precarious business to impute pro-Communism to someone on the basis of that person's stand on a single issue. Sometimes it works. The informed American who asserts that there are no concentration camps in Russia is, in all likelihood, consciously following the Party line. The American who has been around a little and yet states that Soviet Russia has no aggressive or imperialistic ambitions, can almost be counted on to be pro-Communist. But opposition to the loyalty program is not such a definitive test. McCarthy ought to know this— "just like a grown man," as they say in Oklahoma. Consequently, he cannot accuse a newspaper of "following the Party line" merely because that newspaper advocates a toothless security program. The most he can do is to say that *in respect of security programs*, newspaper X and the Communists are saying one and the same thing— which, in this case, means exactly nothing.

And finally ASSUMPTION E: *Those people who have the interests of the United States at heart act in such a way as to advance those interests.*

This is the most fundamentally false of all McCarthy's assumptions; and the tragedy lies less in the fact that McCarthy sometimes falls back on it, than in the fact that the assumption should be false. Not only do different people have different ideas about what constitutes a good society; the world has always been crowded with pestiferous blunderers who are incapable of acting in such a way as to promote even their *own* ideal society, much less *the* ideal society. The proximate end McCarthy most ardently seeks—security of the Civil Service against Communist penetration—is also sought by a large number of his critics. And yet, most of these critics do get in McCarthy's way *every time* he attempts to advance the goal which they are supposed to have in common. This evidently baffles McCarthy, and he sometimes finds that there is no satisfactory explanation except that they are not, after all, anxious to achieve the goal they profess. It is at this point that he kicks over the traces and proceeds to impugn the loyalty of, say, the editors of the *Washington Post*. It was precisely this assumption that prompted McCarthy to impugn the loyalty of General George Marshall, to explain in terms of treason a series of Marshall's international blunders that undeniably redounded to the benefit of the Communists.* And this he must not do. Americans would rather be called dolts than traitors; and, all things considered—the law, the national ethic, our tradition—their preference should be respected insofar as the evidence permits.

McCarthy's sporadic reliance on these assumptions, this aspect of his "method" not only weakens his claim to responsible conduct, but seriously undermines his effectiveness. For one thing, in calling Drew Pearson and the *Milwaukee Journal* pro-Communist, he loses the opportunity to make the far more telling indictment of them that their performance invites; that, whatever their intentions, they do act in a way that advances the fortunes of Communism. For while Americans are by now fairly immune to the claims of doctrinaire Communism, they are still fearfully vulnerable to the blandishments of anti-anti-Communism. McCarthy has done well to concern himself with the threat of pro-Communists in the Civil Service. He would do even better to concern himself, equally, with the threat of circumspect anti-Communism. But to do this, he must force himself to recognize that the adherents of softness in combating Soviet Russia are, for the most part, persons genuinely concerned with the welfare of the United States.

* See Appendix, "The Marshall Episode."

McCarthy As Against His Contemporaries

FOR JOE MCCARTHY, Owen Lattimore is not a "conscious, articulate spokesman of Communism," but America's "top espionage agent"; Philip Jessup is not an inept statesman with an unexplained record of complicity with the Communist subversion of the Chinese Nationalists, but the *"pioneer* of the smear campaign against Chiang Kai-Shek," "the *originator* of the myth of the 'democratic' Chinese Communists"; the State Department is not lax, or even criminally negligent with respect to loyalty risks, it is "infested" with "57 Card-Carrying Communists" and four times this number of loyalty risks.

McCarthy can be depended on not to understate his case, which is what a great many people refer to when they talk about "Senator McCarthy's method." On the other hand, this aspect of McCarthy and his method must be judged with an eye to the fact that McCarthy is a publicist among publicists.

We would do well to remember that McCarthy was twenty-three, ambitious, and impressionable, when Franklin Roosevelt was elected President of the United States. The political techniques of the most important American political figure of our time must have dazzled and impressed him—much as they dazzled and impressed a people who set aside a tradition (which they were later, repentant perhaps, to legislate back into existence) in order to send him back to the White House again and again and again. Franklin Roosevelt campaigned for the Presidency four times. He did not see himself as running against a party which, in its own way, was trying to serve the country; he painted his opponents as "economic royalists," representatives of "greedy and selfish interests." For Roosevelt, all members of the Republican Party, all recalcitrants in the Democratic Party, and all Supreme Court Judges over the age of 65, were enemies of the Republic. He drew a sharp line that separated him and his followers from other Americans. Those on his side were wise patriots; those on the other side, self-centered rascals. The American people, depending on how they voted, were either fulfilling a glorious destiny, or committing suicide.

Two years after Joe McCarthy was elected to the Senate, and two years before he broke into fame as a result of a speech about the State Department, McCarthy witnessed the greatest political upset in the history of this country. In defiance of the predictions of almost all our political sages, with only token support from the influential members of his own party, faced with the active opposition of the vast majority of the nation's newspapers, Harry Truman outran the slick favorite from New York and went back to the White House for four years.

McCarthy, the politician, can be assumed to have studied the campaign of 1948 with care. Harry Truman lacked the suavity of his predecessor; but clearly, he had no intention of deserting Roosevelt's basic formula, i.e., that of persuading the people that their choice was not between two mildly different political parties, but between unscrupulous highwaymen and selfless public servants.

Said Mr. Truman of Republicans, in the week of September 26 to October 2, 1948: "They don't want unity. They want . . . the kind of unity that benefits the National Association of Manufacturers, the private power lobbies, the real estate lobbies and selfish interests."

Said Mr. Truman on October 19, to the International Ladies Garment Workers: "The Republicans plan a real hatchet job [on labor]. . . . The Taft-Hartley Law is only the beginning of the attacks they plan."

On October 30, in a final blast, Mr. Truman warned the country, *"Powerful forces, like those that created European Fascists, are working through the Republican Party [to] undermine . . . American democracy."*

Not only did Mr. Truman win the election hands down, he also won the enthusiastic support of America's Liberals. Their consciences were unruffled by Truman's indictment of twenty million voters as pawns of Fascism. And not because their consciences were dead; for they were quickly aroused eighteen months later when McCarthy insisted that there were 57 Communists in the State Department.

It is difficult, moreover, to argue that the political utterances of today are baser than those of yesterday. As a matter of fact, one commentator has publicly bemoaned the *deterioration* (mostly in terms of skill and color) of modern invective.[11] His article in *Life* was sub-titled, "The Hollow Chant Has, Alas, Replaced the Verbal Brickbat." He bemoans the passing of "an old and cherished rhetorical tradition: the *ad hominem* thrust or verbal brickbat. . . . Could such a gem of vilification as Senator John Randolph's great effort of 1826, 'He shines and stinks like a dead mackerel in the moonlight' emerge in the debates of the present generation of Congressmen?" We are reminded that Thomas Paine said of George Washington that he was "treacherous in private friendship and a hypocrite in public life." Thomas Jefferson was described as "an atheist, an adulterer and a robber," while Lincoln was classified, among other things, as "The baboon president, a low-bred, obscene clown." Theodore Roosevelt, William Jennings Bryan, Fiorello La Guardia, General Hugh Johnson, and Harold Ickes contributed handsomely to the glossary of American invective. Thus, though perhaps less so than a hundred years ago, public life remains hazardous. *

Let us look at short extracts from public utterances of three contemporary public figures, and begin with a classic—a campaign speech by candidate (now Senator) George Smathers, in which he informs an audience of backwoods Floridians about the character of his opponent:

Are you aware that Claude Pepper is known all over Washington as a shameless extrovert? Not only that, but this man is reliably reported to practice nepotism with his sister-in-law, and he has a sister who was once a Thespian in New York. Worst of all, it is an established fact that Mr. Pepper, before his marriage, practiced celibacy.

Or there is John L. Lewis paying his respects to management:

When we sought surcease from bloodletting, you proffered indifference; when we cried aloud for the safety of our members, you answered, "Be content, 'twas always thus." When we urged that you abate the stench, you averred that your nostrils were not offended. . . . When we spoke of little children in unkempt surroundings, you said,—"look to the State." . . . You profess annoyance at our temerity; we condemn your imbecility. You are smug in your complacency; we are abashed by your shamelessness. . . . To cavil further is futile. We trust that time, as it shrinks your purse, may modify your niggardly and anti-social propensities.

Joe McCarthy on the State Department, Dean Acheson, and other matters—from his celebrated Wheeling, West Virginia, speech of February 9, 1950.

* In fact, its toughness is sometimes envied by those engaged in more tranquil pursuits. In a "Plea for Literary Mayhem," (*Saturday Review*, April 11, 1953), Richard Hauser comments, "In political dispute we slash and hack and rip and bludgeon, and the arena is inevitably heaped high with mangled corpses and bloody survivors. But in our literary tussles a galloping leukemia sets in, and nobody ever gets hurt."

The reason why we find ourselves in a position of impotency [in international affairs] is not because our only powerful potential enemy has sent men to invade our shores, but rather because of the traitorous actions of those who have been treated so well by this Nation. . . .

This is glaringly true in the State Department. There the bright young men who are born with silver spoons in their mouths are the ones who have been worst. . . . In my opinion the State Department, which is one of the most important government departments, is thoroughly infested with Communists. . . .

As you know, very recently the Secretary of State proclaimed his loyalty to a man guilty of what has always been considered as the most abominable of all crimes—of being a traitor to the people who gave him a position of great trust. The Secretary of State, in attempting to justify his continued devotion to the man who sold out the Christian world to the atheistic world, referred to Christ's Sermon on the Mount as a justification and reason therefor, and the reaction of the American people to this would have made the heart of Abraham Lincoln happy.

When this pompous diplomat in striped pants, with a phony British accent, proclaimed to the American people that Christ on the Mount endorsed communism, high treason, and betrayal of a sacred trust, the blasphemy was so great that it awakened the dormant indignation of the American people.

George Smathers does his level best to make Claude Pepper a pervert by assonance, John L. Lewis persuades us that the managers of Pennsylvania's coal mines are indistinguishable from the managers of Siberia's salt mines, and Joe McCarthy represents Acheson as invoking divine sanction for Communism. Differences are not notable as regards the "method" of the three men in dealing with the opposition; differences—striking differences—however, emerge in our reaction to them. George Smathers comes out of it a bright and ingenious young man, John Lewis a lovable old sourpuss, Joe McCarthy a blackhearted son of a bitch.

It is here that we arrive at a central enigma in the uproar over McCarthy's "method"—the severity with which his verbal excesses are judged, as against the indulgence shown to other public figures whose language is, if anything, more distorted and more abrasive. This most perverse anomaly in Liberal behavior has occasioned surprisingly little comment. Outrage at McCarthy's generalizations about the Democrats, New Dealers, Dean Acheson, and the State Department, appears to have unbalanced the judgment of many of his critics, and blinded them to the extravagances on their side of the fence. Our Liberal statesmen, journalists, professors, and preachers ululate whenever the hyperbole is used against them;

but, in their mouths, it becomes a righteous weapon with which to smite down the Philistines.

When, for example, James Wechsler, editor of the *New York Post*, tangled with McCarthy over the question of his Communist background, Wechsler was widely hailed as a courageous newspaperman in the front line of those martyrs who, in behalf of freedom and decency, do battle with McCarthy. Now "Fighting" Jim Wechsler, clean of heart and heroic of posture, presides over a newspaper that divides its feature columns more or less evenly between attacks on McCarthy's "indiscriminate, reckless sensationalism," and serialized treatments of such subjects as "A Model's Autobiography," "Married Infidelity," and the alleged pro-Fascism or anti-Semitism of almost everybody James Wechsler disagrees with. The *Post* will feature an address by Alex Rose, union leader and officer of New York's Liberal Party, in which he advises the world at large that the Republican Administration is deliberately set on bringing about a national depression "in order to break the back of American labor unions." Yet two or three pages further on, in the same issue, a *Post* reporter or columnist or editorial writer will writhe in agony at the "lurid sensationalism of America's national disgrace"—Joe McCarthy, of course.

Most Liberals were silent as a tomb when Harry Truman accused Eisenhower, in 1952, of anti-Semitism, anti-Catholicism, "butchering the reputations of innocent men and women" and indulging in a "campaign of lies." As in the roughly similar circumstances of 1948, the Liberals (for the most part) simply refused to be unnerved or disconcerted by reckless and exaggerated charges—so long as they were being made by persons of whom they approved against persons of whom they disapproved.*

The Liberal attitudes towards investigating committees follow much the same pattern. The inquisitorial method is "understandable," or "indispensable," or even "desirable," if it is used to uncover or embarrass Wall Street racketeers (the Nye Committee), the anti-union practices of management (the LaFollette Committee), or the financial angels of right wing organizations (the Buchanan Committee). But the same method—even if more restrained and equitable in its application—is outrageous and fascistic when used to lay bare the activities of American fellow travellers (the Com-

* "It was a very dry campaign until Truman added some life to it," commented Professor Robert E. Lane of Yale University's political science department. (Yale *Daily News*, November 10, 1952.)

mittee on Un-American Activities), to expose the ideological impact of the Institute of Pacific Relations (the McCarran Committee) or to look into pro-Communism in the Voice of America (the McCarthy Committee).

An understanding that this schizophrenia of the Liberals exists (even if we do not pretend to know *why* it exists), is indispensable to an understanding of the issues treated in this book. For although the cliché runs, "I agree with Senator McCarthy's aims but I disapprove of his methods," it would reflect far more accurately the thinking of the Liberal if it said instead: "I agree with Senator McCarthy's methods, but I disapprove of his aims." For it is McCarthy's aims that demonstrably disconcert and frighten so many of his critics. They disapprove of McCarthy's *method* when it is used to further McCarthy's aims; but like it fine when it is used to further their own.

Since it is not, we maintain, McCarthy's method that underlies their opposition to McCarthy, it must, indeed, be something else; for we do, after all, know that they do not like McCarthy, even if we are not in a position to understand just why. But if it is at all possible to analyze their stated objections to McCarthyism, to understand just what it is they have in mind when they rail against McCarthy, it comes out more or less as follows: McCarthyism spells evil days ahead for our society; for McCarthyism has its roots in the desire of man to control the thinking of his fellow man. McCarthyism, with all its talk about the alleged dangers of Communism, is pushing us into an Age of Conformity.

And this fear, so serious and so moving, we shall have to consider carefully.

CHAPTER XIV

The New Conformity

Our "Reign of Terror"

FREEDOM of the mind, so high in our hierarchy of values, is said to be in an advanced state of atrophy in America—a result of McCarthy and McCarthyism. All conversations or discursive roads, from no matter where, lead to this subject. Perhaps most often, the theme is played under the solemn and sublime auspices of the baccalaureate ceremony. The President of college A, having been invited by the President of B to strike a blow for freedom of the mind at B's commencement exercises, can be counted on to deliver a good solid talk about Socrates and how the Athenian witch-hunters did him in for merely disagreeing with them. The modern parallel springs quickly to mind—all the more easily due to a certain negligence in pointing out the differences between Socrates and Lattimore. And the warning, subsequently echoed in lectures, editorials and sermons all over the land, is always there: we are moving into a new Age of Conformity. Behind every tree there is a McCarthyite—and, for that matter, behind every sapling: for even the misdirected exuberance of 1952's crop of college students is written down as a manifestation of the New Inquisition. Yes, it has been seriously suggested that McCarthy was the final cause that drove college men to forage in women's dormitories for panties and brassieres.*

* "Rabbi Blames 'McCarthyism' In College Raids/ He Says 'Danger' of Voicing Dissent on Big Issues Makes Campus Restless/ Rabbi Louis I. Newman, preaching yesterday at Temple Rodoph Sholem, 7 West 83 Street, attributed the current dormitory 'raids' by college students to 'McCarthyism' which, he said, makes serious discussion and dissent on major issues dangerous. 'A vast silence has descended upon young men and women today in the colleges of our country, and they find an expression for their bottled-up energies in foolish and unseemly "raids" upon dormitories,' Rabbi Newman said," etc., etc. *New York Herald Tribune*, May 25, 1952.

Only the most adventurous spirits among us, we are solemnly assured, would today dare to apply for a position in the civil service. For to do so is to invite first suspicion, then irresponsible persecution by some committee. Either you don't get the job—because sometime in your past you may have indulged an indepedent thought—or you do get it, whereupon you embark on a career of explaining your past to security personnel who, very likely, will frustrate any chance of advancement, and perhaps set you loose, to struggle through life with a blighted reputation.

Worse still, soon we shall not even have enough gumption left to object to this state of affairs; for we are being taught at college to take it and like it. We learn from a celebrated series of articles by Mr. Siegel in the *New York Times* that a deadening uniformity has become a characteristic of the campus. How, Mr. Siegel asks, can the student be blamed? In an age that does its intellectual business under McCarthy's auspices, the retaliation against freshness and originality—against thinking—is swift and sure. College students, knowing they must one day earn a living for themselves, prefer to succumb rather than to fight. Nor is it merely the undergraduate who feels the truths of Communism stirring within him that has to think twice about the future; the real, and furthermore the intended, victims of the oppression are those with *Liberal* ideas. Thus we find E. B. White, a humorist with a conscience, writing a deadly serious satire for the *New Yorker*, the sense of which is that were McCarthy so much as aware of the existence of Thoreau, he would damn him as a loyalty risk.*

Those of us who have not felt the Reign of Terror are warned not to take the threat lightly. The professional mourners at the wake of American freedom are unimpressed, in fact angered, by consolations, especially of the empirical sort. They appear to resent any distractions from their gloomy introspections.

Mr. Eugene Lyons tells,[1] for example, of a meeting at Swarthmore College, in 1951, of "six bold men"—a solemn conclave of what they themselves termed "the unterrified," calculated to prove that "Americanism is not yet extinct," but also calculated to suggest that it is on its last legs. A spate of books, all favorably re-

---

* Which, incidentally, Thoreau *was:* not because he is the author of *Walden,* to which Mr. White refers exclusively in his satire, but because he also wrote the stirring and magnificent essay on "Civil Disobedience." It would hardly have been in the national interest for Thoreau to have occupied a high position in the War Department, say, during the Mexican War.

viewed, have been sponsored by Cornell University and financed by the Rockefeller Foundation, and all of them conclude that freedom today is moribund. Professor Henry Steele Commager has announced that "we are now embarked upon a campaign of suppression and oppression more violent, more reckless, more dangerous than any in our history." Harold Ickes wrote shortly before his death that "if a man is addicted to Vodka he is, *ipso facto*, a Russian, therefore a Communist." Lester Markel, editor of the Sunday edition of the *New York Times*, heralds the advent of a "black fear in the country brought about by the witch hunters."

Naturally enough, Mr. Markel welcomes to the *Times'* Sunday Magazine Section Earl Bertrand Russell, who writes of America, "If by some misfortune you were to quote with approval some remark by Jefferson you would probably lose your job and find yourself behind bars." "The hardheaded boys," Mr. Bernard De Voto writes in *Harpers Magazine,* "are going to hang the Communist label on everybody who holds ideas offensive to the U.S. Chamber of Commerce, the National Association of Manufacturers, or the steering committee of the Republican Party." Lawrence Clark Powell, librarian of the University of California, writes for a British publication:[2] "In this time of inquisitional nationalism, I know that I run a risk in confessing that I possess a French doctor's degree and own an English car. And what dire fate do I court when I say that I prefer English books?" And when Dr. Ralph Turner, a professor of history at Yale, exposed the reign of terror to a convocation of Eastern College students, the latter, after due deliberation, voted McCarthyism a greater threat to America than Communism.

The notion that the United States is in the grip of a reign of terror as the result of the activities of Senator McCarthy, Senator Jenner, Congressman Velde, the House Committee on Un-American Activities *et al.*, is, of course, palpable nonsense. This is not to overlook the fact, however, that America has stiffened on certain political matters in the past five years. Joining a Communist front is no longer a profitable way to demonstrate concern for the downtrodden. Glossing over the barbarities of the Soviet Union in order to arrive at the Inner Truths of the Soviet "experiment" is no longer accepted as presumptive evidence either of objectivity or of wisdom. Nor can the party-liners now play their old game of putting aside one disguise and appearing overnight in another. Four months after their humiliation at the polls, the Progressives, acting through the National Council of Arts, Sciences and Professions, attempted a comeback by promoting a "Cultural and Scientific Conference for World Peace" at the Waldorf-Astoria in New York. The conference was practically hooted out of town, and the participants—hard Communists and Communist dupes—went back to their classrooms, offices, and newspapers to proclaim what has always been an invulnerable deduction to the Communists: that because the public refused to respond to the exhortations of the Communist Party, the day of Fascism has arrived in America.

Yes, America's back has stiffened. There is little doubt that the conference would have been a rip-roaring success in, say, 1938 or even in 1947. And the stiffening is in evidence elsewhere: Frederick Vanderbilt Field would not today be invited to direct a national research association. Howard Fast is no longer being lionized by respected American publishers. And Paul Robeson has ended his long career as the prima donna of American culture. What is more, none of these men could pass a security investigation for government employment; not even, *mirabile dictu,* for employment in the State Department.

America, in other words, is rallying around an orthodoxy whose characteristic is that *it excludes Communism;* and adherents of Communism are, therefore, excluded from positions of public trust and popular esteem.

The assertion that the growing firmness of the American people is also felt by any deviate from the line laid down at the last assembly of the National Association of Manufacturers is the red herring of our time. It was invented by hard-headed Communists, echoed by those Liberals who for the most part know not what they do, and popularized by those of our melodramatic clubwomen who hungrily devour whatever crumbs the Liberals throw their way.

As everyone knows, Liberal and Socialist activities, both organizational and propagandistic, have not only not been interfered with in any way, they are at peak intensity all over the land. The partisans of the Brannan Plan, of socialized medicine, of continued and increased federal preemption of state functions, of the closed shop, of doctrinaire international philanthropy, of Clement Attlee, of Pandit Nehru, are as numerous as ever, and are more vocal with each passing day. Their converts among college students, very far from concealing their advanced views with an eye to their career, assure themselves success by *proclaiming* these views. The Democrats, the ADA'ers, and the World Federalists, continue to organize and propagandize, on the campus and off; and continue, on the campus and off, to think of themselves as the wave of the future. Thus, the annual "Vermont Conference" at the University of Vermont, when it assembled in the spring of 1952, heard national issues discussed by a panel made up of Leon Keyserling, Sumner Slichter and James B. Carey; and international issues by a panel made up of Sidney C. Suffrin, Michael Straight and Saul K. Padover! In the course of a typical year's program, the Yale University Political Union plays host to an endless succession of well-known Liberals—and for good measure also invites Howard Fast and Corliss Lamont. Yet the Grand Sachem of McCarthyism, McCarthy himself, is meanwhile unable to inflict his reign of terror in his own bailiwick: in a period of 18 months, the University of Wisconsin invited Eleanor Roosevelt, Norman Cousins, Owen Lattimore and James Carey to complain about McCarthy's reign of terror to the student body.

How the New Inquisition visits its wrath on the Liberals is probably best indicated by the treatment accorded to the three major "victims" of McCarthy's campaign speech (October, 1952). Within six months of the speech, Archibald MacLeish received both the National Book Award and the Pulitzer Prize for poetry. Bernard De Voto received the National Book Award for History. It being one of the unusual years during which Arthur Schlesinger Jr. did *not* write a book, he collected his tithe from the politicians (rather than from the critics), who elected him co-chairman of the Americans for Democratic Action. In short, to say that Liberalism is on the run in America is akin to saying that Communism is on the run in Russia.

It is true, of course, that irresponsible statements are made now and then about men and women of pronounced Liberal views. But such statements are nothing new on the American scene, and they are probably received with greater impatience than ever before. For example:

—Early in 1952, Senator McCarthy learned that copies of Edmund Wilson's *Memoirs of Hecate County* were being forwarded

to Europe at government expense. Impulsively, and absurdly, Mc-
Carthy denounced government sponsorship of books which "follow the Communist Party line"—although it is notorious that Wilson turned his back on the Communists in the 30's and is the author
of some first-rate anti-Communist books and articles. *Memoirs of
Hecate County* is a vulnerable book on a lot of counts; and the
reason is obscure why it was selected for official distribution in the
first place; but it is no more pro-Communist than its author. And
McCarthy was told so in no uncertain terms by persons who, in
general, view his activities with much approval.[3] Here, McCarthy
himself was reckless; but "the forces of McCarthyism" did not support him on the point he was making. And Wilson's reputation as
the dean of America's literati is as secure as ever—a fact which is all
the more relevant to our thesis since he is an unrepentant socialist.

—A year after the "Hecate" incident, Norman Cousins, editor of
the *Saturday Review,* was one of several persons invited to Hagerstown, Maryland, to address a meeting sponsored by the Junior
Chamber of Commerce. Cousins was to speak under the auspices
of the United World Federalists.

A Hagerstown American Legionnaire rushed forward to protest—on the grounds that Mr. Cousins' name appeared in the files
of the House Committee on Un-American Activities. The Committee, when queried, revealed that Cousins' name did indeed appear
in its files, and in connection with the pro-Communist Waldorf
Conference. But, the Committee added, the files revealed that
Cousins had been the only anti-Communist speaker at the Conference, that he had been booed for criticising the USSR, and that
when the moment came for him to leave the Conference, he had
to be given police protection. Upon the release and digestion of
this information, Cousins received an apology from the American
Legion, and still another from the Junior Chamber of Commerce.
Mr. Cousins has certainly not suffered from the incident, as the
prosperity of his magazine and the success of his books and lectures
will affirm. And this in spite of the fact that the cause he most
persistently champions—World Federalism—is at sword's point
with the ideals of most American conservatives.

—One more incident. In May, 1953, a Baltimore policeman was
found listing the license numbers of automobiles parked in the
vicinity of a World Federalist rally. When queried, the policeman
reported that he was carrying out instructions he had received

from his immediate superior. What happened then? Almost immediately, the Governor of Maryland, no less, was publicly apologizing to all World Federalists everywhere, and, in fact, *affirming his
sympathy with their goals.*

In short, we have with us, as we have always had, men of scant
information and abundant ill-will. But the evidence simply does
not exist that their agitations constitute a national scandal, much
less a national threat. We will always have with us ignorant and
oblique attacks against the Left; just as we will always have with
us ignorant and malicious calumny upon the Right. The notion
that the former are more numerous or vicious or effective than the
latter cannot be supported by evidence. A dispassionate survey of
extremes of opinion and prejudice would surely conclude that, if
"hysteria" reigns in the United States today, it is a hysteria whose
blows are directed at the Right. Unwarranted charges of "reaction," "fascism," "anti-Semitism," "chauvinism," and "warmonger-
ing," are leveled every bit as frequently as unwarranted charges of
"Communism" and "socialism."*

If we are in the throes of a reactionary revolution which threatens independent thought, then at least we may, with Eugene
Lyons, derive some comfort from the world about us. "One conso-
lation," he writes, "as we face the propaganda portrait of a dis-
traught, hysterical America is that it implies a nation of heroes.
For the unterrified seem roughly equal to our entire population."
Of course the answer is that the jeremiads about the threat to free
and independent thought and speech are self-refuting; they come
from the tongues and pens of men who, in the very act of protesting
against tyranny, i.e. in exercising their right to express opinions
freely, expose their own hoax. "One evening recently," Mr. Lyons
writes, "I saw and heard Arthur Garfield Hays [counsel for the
American Civil Liberties Union], his mouth opened wide, in a
television screen close-up, shouting that in America no one any
longer dares open his mouth."

Recently, a refreshingly honest and objective admission came
from an unexpected quarter. The *New Yorker's* Mr. Richard Rovere, whom we hope we are permitted to call a card-carrying Liberal, wrote in the *New Leader* in the spring of 1952 that, while he

---

* A factual laboratory report on this phenomenon, with particular emphasis upon the handicaps suffered by anti-Communists, appeared in the American Legion *Monthly* in September 1951, in an article, "America's New Privileged Class," by Eugene Lyons.

yields to no man in hatred and contempt for Senator McCarthy, he is forced to admit that he has found that attacking McCarthy "is just about as dangerous as drinking my morning cup of coffee."*

* One of the authors quoted this statement of Mr. Rovere in a column on Senator McCarthy written for the *Spadea Syndicate* in the spring of 1953. Mr. Rovere objected as follows: ". . . What you reported me as saying was correct enough, but in both text and context you will find specified a place, time and condition of life. I said then, and I would say today, that it would be ridiculous for me or anyone in a similar position to lay claim to moral courage for attacking McCarthyism. But my case is, if not unique, special. I do not work for the State Department; I have no plans to run for Senator; I am not an editor of *Colliers*. I am in short unlikely to suffer any personal loss or damage as a consequence of my view, and therefore, while it would be pleasant to be able to regard myself as brave, I fear I've no grounds for doing so. But I think it is very different with many other people. . . ." Our point in this chapter, and in others in this book, is that it is *not* "different with many other people"; that it is only different with those people who are pro-Communist or whose record supports a reasonable doubt as to their reliability. And, of course, with those who are congenitally so meek, and worthless, that they would not dare endorse Camels for fear they might displease Lucky Strikes. But these timid men have no business to enter into public debate in the first place; and surely Mr. Rovere would not want to call their disappearance a loss to intellectual life.

The Question of Conformity

McCarthyism, we are saying, has narrowed the limits within which political proselytizing can safely go forward in the American community. The assertion that there is a "reign of terror" directed at all who disagree with Senator McCarthy, we are saying further, is irresponsible nonsense. But something is abroad in the land, and we have no objection to its being called a "reign of terror" provided it is clear that a metaphor is being used, and that the victims are the Communists and their sympathizers. We may concede that America has come to insist on "conformity," if you will, *on the Communist issue.*

One of the problems that arises is that of stating precisely what the conformity, encouraged by McCarthyism, actually involves: *what sanctions* are being imposed upon *what people* to discourage *what sort* of activity. Defining the conformity is difficult, if for no other reason than that its shape and coloring vary sharply from one part of the country to another, and from one field of activity to another. Another question entirely is whether we approve of the sanctions and of their being visited on the particular people they are being visited on. But there is a third question: What about the argument underlying the Liberals' determined assault on McCarthyism—the argument that "conformity," *in any area whatever,* is undesirable? A number of serious writers on the subject* profess to be disturbed not so much with the peculiar orientation of a "conformist" society, as with the fact that a conformity—*any* orthodoxy whatever—should exist at all. McCarthyism is bad, we are told, and must be bad, just to the extent that it obstructs the free flow of commerce in the "marketplace of ideas."

The objection requires thorough consideration—not because it is profound, but because it elicits reflexive and emotion-charged support from so many people who, for excellent reasons, are concerned with protecting "freedom of the mind."

Opposition to conformity of *any* sort arises from a failure to understand the ways of society, a failure to recognize that *some* conformity, in varying degrees and in diverse fields, has characterized every society known to man; and for the reason that some conformity is just as indispensable as some heresy.

The word "conformity" is too often used to connote collective adherence by an insensate and irrational society to an unimagina-

* e.g. Alan Barth, Alexander Meiklejohn, Zechariah Chafee, Jr.

tive and erroneous doctrine. Thus the frequent references to the "threat of conformity," to "arid conformity," to "stultifying conformity," and so on. The word "conformity" is not necessarily misused when it is given that meaning. But it is also a useful word to describe the prevailing value preferences of *highly civilized societies;* and in that sense conformity may be a blessing rather than something to be avoided. In short, we rightly deplore the "conformity" that obtained in Germany during the thirties—the orthodoxy which evokes so vividly the image of an authoritarian, secular, ethnocentric society, savage in its elimination of dissidents. But we may also speak of the "conformity" of English sentiment on, say, the subject of parliamentary government—and with some enthusiasm. In the one case, a nation was wedded to an evil social doctrine which it defended by imposing brutal punitive sanctions upon dissidents. England, however, is wedded to what we deem a highly commendable political process—and wedded to it by the voluntary acquiescence of all, or nearly all, of its citizens.

Our indictment of Nazi conformity is therefore based on two counts: (a) we don't like the values the Nazis encouraged, and (b) we don't like the fact that they violated persons who disagreed with them. Our approval of England's conformity with parliamentary rule is based on our approval of the institution of popular government, and also on our approval of the fact that Englishmen are not embarked on an active campaign against dissidents.

The conformity we are concerned with in this book—the one McCarthyism is promoting—resembles the English conformity on the first count: the vast majority of Americans are certainly in sympathy with those values Communism threatens. It is equally clear—as regards the second count—that McCarthyism (understood as including all the legal, economic and social measures that are being used to discourage adherence to Communism) has little in common with pogroms and concentration camps. But on this score the conformity encouraged by McCarthyism is not like contemporary English conformity either: for it *is* a calculated, purposeful national campaign levelled against Communist dissidents. Do we conclude, then—from this difference—that conformity, English-style, is desirable, while conformity, McCarthy style, is reprehensible?

It is easier to understand the conformity McCarthyism is urging, and the sanctions being used to promote that conformity, if we recognize that some coercive measures—i.e., restrictive sanctions of some sort—against dissidents are indispensable to the achievement of *any* conformity. *Coercion takes different forms.* It may be exercised through education, through social pressure, or through laws. But it must be exercised in one form or another if naturally diverse minds are to form a common tendency.

What Liberals fail to understand is that even the orthodoxies they approve of have not come about through spontaneous consent. To act as though the Paraclete had, one bright morning, breathed into the hearts of Englishmen their allegiance to parliamentary rule, is, among other things, to do a severe injustice to the thousands of men who devoted their lives to dislodging British absolutism. England had to fight for her form of government; and it was several hundred tumultuous years before popular rule emerged as the imperious and unchallenged orthodoxy that reigns today.

In short, we are apt to forget that conformity, in order to "be," must first "become." We cannot have our cake without first baking it. England's conformity with parliamentarianism does not, today, depend on coercive measures to preserve its supremacy, because it is *mature,* because it is institutionalized to the point that it goes virtually unchallenged. McCarthyism, however, involves an orthodoxy still-in-the-making; and therefore, as with all imperfect conformities, some coercive sanctions are being exercised in its behalf.

The sanctions imposed on behalf of favored values have often been violent, as when the guillotine was used as an instrument for winning converts to French republicanism, or when civil war and the Thirteenth Amendment were adopted as deterrents to slavery in this country, or when the Income Tax was written into our laws to encourage financial support of the government. Or, the sanctions may be relatively gentle: for example, the ubiquitous pressures which, for two decades now, have emanated from the classroom and from the bureaucrat's desk, from political podiums and from a preponderance of our literature, in behalf of the leviathan State.*

---

* As unabashed an acknowledgment of the Liberal orthodoxy being pressed in American schools today as the authors have ever seen appeared in an article in the July 1953 *Atlantic Monthly* written by Mr. Joseph S. Clark, Jr., Mayor of Philadelphia: "Fortunately, free compulsory education works for the liberals. . . . big business has not yet taken over American education. Adlai Stevenson has more supporters among schoolteachers and college professors than Tom Dewey. It is significant that what used to be called 'history' is now called 'social studies.' *Spiritually and economically, youth is conditioned to respond to a liberal program of orderly policing of our society by government,* subject to the popular will, in the interests of social justice." (Italics added.)

The sanctions imposed by McCarthyism are of both kinds. The legal sanctions, the anti-Communist *laws*, are, in a sense, "harsh" measures. The Smith Act, for example, punishes with imprisonment anyone who conspires to advocate the overthrow of the government by force. The McCarran Act harasses members of fellow-travelling organizations. The Feinberg Law denies employment to teachers who are members of subversive organizations. Miscellaneous laws and executive orders deny government employment to persons regarded as loyalty or security risks.

The social sanctions of McCarthyism are of the other, relatively mild variety—as when individual schools refuse to hire Communist professors, or radio stations close their doors to Communist artists, or labor unions deny membership to Communist workers. They are ordinarily milder because, in the absence of a law on the subject, there may be other schools, radio stations, and unions that will give the Communists shelter.*

To sum up, then, a drive for some conformity, and the turbulence often attendant on such a drive, are not unusual phenomena in our society or any other. And judging by past experience, if Americans, by the year 1999, learn to despise fellow-travelling with the same intensity and unanimity with which today they regard, say, slave-owning, it is predictable that the Liberals of that day will not bewail America's anti-Communist orthodoxy.

But we must probe deeper into the alleged threat to freedom of the mind posed by McCarthyism. Although the measures by which McCarthyism encourages conformity are clearly the same measures by which societies *have* traditionally protected favored values, Liberals are not obliged to *approve* of what societies have done in the past. They can repudiate *all* sanctions designed to influence opinion, past, present and future; and they seem to be doing this

---

* Although legal sanctions are almost invariably harsher than social ones, there is, theoretically at least, no *necessary* difference between them as far as the hurt to the victim is concerned. If, for example, *all* schools refuse employment to Communist teachers, the latter are as hard hit as they would be by a law forbidding them employment as teachers. And, looking at it the other way 'round, it is always possible to conceptualize a law that will accomplish precisely the measure of restriction that results from a given social sanction. The fact that laws are, just the same, usually more restrictive than social sanctions is highly important and, as we shall see later, relevant in deciding how free societies *ought* to go about achieving conformity on a given issue.

when they universalize about the evils of "thought control" each time the subject of McCarthyism is brought up.

It is perfectly true that the sanctions of McCarthyism (like those that have been used in the past on behalf of democracy, freedom for trade unions, and so on) *do* constitute "thought control" in the sense that they hack away, and are intended to hack away, at opposition to certain values. But to condemn these sanctions is to condemn the natural processes of society.

Freedom of the mind, we are told by the Liberals, is an absolute value; and thought control, "since it impairs this freedom," an absolute evil. Few Liberals are aware that the first of these statements does not necessarily justify the second. The only freedom that an individual may never sacrifice is, providentially, one that he will never be without: the freedom to act as a moral agent *at the choice level*—to select, as between whatever alternatives are left open to him, the one which most closely coincides with the "good." In religious terms, man's only absolute freedom is his freedom to earn salvation; and this freedom is irrevocable because man has a free will. The Russian serf, even within the area in which he is allowed by the State to act, can triumph over evil every bit as decisively as can the American freeman.*

* The religious-minded reader may feel we are stating the obvious, at this point; and the agnostic will surely tell us we are boring him. Nevertheless, the hazy notion is at large that the debate about "thought control" and "freedom of the mind" somehow involves religious absolutes. It is methodologically important, then, first to account for religious imperatives, and then to remove them from what is fundamentally a political discussion. Christianity justifies the assertion that freedom of the mind is an "absolute." But this freedom, as we say, is one that man will never be without. Freedom of the mind is never at stake if free will is postulated. (For the determinist, the concept is meaningless by definition.) What the "freedom of the mind" cultists are actually worried about is (a) *"guidance"* of the mind, and (b) derivatively, *freedom of action.* These are political considerations and actually do not affect man's moral standing. Though education and other pressures, social and legal, strongly dispose people to choose one course of action rather than another, it does not follow by any means that their moral freedom is impaired. The citizen of the Soviet Union, faced with conflicting accounts, *Pravda's* and the *Voice of America's,* of how the Korean war began, is strongly influenced to accept the *Pravda* account, and probably will; but this act of choosing between them takes place in an area that is beyond the reach of the MVD. And similarly, although many alternatives are never privileged to compete for a man's acceptance—as, for example, the idea of racial amalgamation may never so much as occur to the ethnocentric Southerner—man's freedom to choose among those alternatives he *does* consider is not affected. Likewise, the freedom to *perform* the chosen "good" does not affect a man's moral standing. If performance were the vital thing, then A, who chooses to

There remains, however, the alluring *political* argument that if democracy is to prosper, sanctions must not be used to delimit the number of ideas our minds consider, or to make one idea appear more attractive than another. Democracy, so the argument goes, thrives on the "free market in ideas," and to tamper with the market is, ultimately, to sabotage the machinery that makes possible enlightened self-government. In a democracy, therefore, every idea must be allowed to display its inherent attractiveness, so that it can be judged on its merits. All ideas must, so to speak, start out even in the race; and if an idea is to be rejected, this must be done by each individual for himself—free from coercion by his fellow men. McCarthyism embodies such coercion. Thus, *ipso facto* it is anti-democratic.*

Unquestionably, the claims of the free market in ideas are very strong. Hard experience through centuries has taught us to exercise self-restraint in insisting upon our own notions of what decisions society should make. Societies, we have learned, fare better when they have a wide selection of ideas from which to choose, if only because their citizens are then better able to articulate, and therefore to realize, their wants. But when the Liberals go on from here to formulate an inflexible doctrine which, in the name of freedom of the mind, would prohibit a society from exercising sanctions of *any* sort, and when they talk as if even the freest society could manage this feat, they are talking very dangerous nonsense.

Part of the Liberals' difficulty is that when they think of sanctions against ideas, they think in drastic terms. They think in terms of denying employment to, or imprisoning the carriers of, "objectionable ideas." They ignore altogether the areas in which the process of "controlling" thought takes a less dramatic form. They do not consider, and hence do not weigh, the more subtle, but infinitely

---

attend church on Sunday but cannot because all churches are shut down, would be less worthy in the eyes of God than B, who chooses to go to church and is so situated that he can go. In short, the *moral* requirements of freedom are met if we are able, *as we always are,* to dispose our minds to pursue the dictates of conscience, whatever they may be.

* A paradox is already evident in the premise of the Liberal theory: there is probably no idea in America more pervasive and more demanding of conformity than that of the "free market in ideas." How many schools fail to inculcate it? How many writers challenge it? How many politicians fail to do homage to it? And let the Liberal beware of the answer that, after all, it is a "good idea," etc. Though we agree that, in many respects, it is, the argument is fatal to his position.

more important sanctions through which societies defend favored ideas.

Our schools, for example, have thoroughly indoctrinated the average American with the virtues of democracy. A sanction of the subtle variety has been exercised; and one that will unquestionably affect his political judgment in a thousand ways favorable to one favored concept—the perpetuation of democracy. Where, again for example, social disfavor attends Jew-baiting, a sanction (not the less effective because it is subtle) is being imposed against racial intolerance. Once again, does anyone contend that polygamy is getting a fair break in the market of ideas?

In short, every idea presented to our minds, as we grow up, is accompanied by sanctions of approval or disapproval which add to, or subtract from, that idea's naked appeal. And these sanctions are "thought control"—whether they urge political conformity with democracy by jailing Communist conspirators, or aesthetic conformity with classicism by disparaging, in the classroom, musical romanticism.

The practice of thought control is so ubiquitous and so commonplace as to make us wonder at the success of the Liberals in frightening people with only one, the crudest, of its many manifestations. They turn the trick, it seems, by dramatizing the sanctions that are deliberately and purposefully imposed, while keeping silent about the haphazard process by which society subsidizes approved prejudices and preferences. And they disarm us by an impressive array of swear words which they apply only to the overt, dramatic type of sanction.

Not long ago, in the course of upholding (on the grounds of precedent) the constitutionality of Atlanta's banning of the movie *Lost Boundaries* (which dramatizes, among other things, the evils of Jim Crow), a U.S. District Court launched into a ringing Liberal lament, excoriating all such laws. The fate they deserve, the Court insisted, is "interment in the attic which contains the ghosts of those who, arrayed in the robe of Bigotry, armed with the spear of Intolerance, and mounted on the steed of Hatred, have through all the ages sought to patrol the highway of the mind."

The judge apparently disapproved the action taken by Atlantans to forbid the propagation of certain ideas on their screens. This, he suggested, was "thought control." Yet the question cannot be avoided: does the *withholding* of the ideas embodied in *Lost Boundaries* from audiences in Atlanta constitute "thought control" in some sense in which the *presentation* of those ideas to New York audiences does not? Was the Atlanta Board of Censors tampering with freedom of thought in some sense in which a dozen movie producers do not regularly do, month in month out, as they decide what pictures advocating what ideas shall be produced? Clearly, the *encouragement* of certain ideas on race relations can affect thought, just as the *discouragement* of these ideas can—as, for example, when they are suppressed. We may feel that it is a mistake to suppress such ideas; that Atlantans would profit from a sympathetic presentation of a Negro family's assimilation by white society. Yet this is merely a euphemistic way of saying that we would like to influence contrarily disposed minds in the direction of our own point of view—which is to plead guilty to the charge of thought control. We are certainly not less guilty than our fellow countrymen in Atlanta, who seek to incline minds the other way.*

In short, it is characteristic of society that it uses sanctions in support of its own folkways and mores, and that in doing so it urges conformity. What we call the "institutions" of a society are nothing but the values that society has settled on over the years and now defends by sanctions. Most of us take fierce pride in our society's institutions—quite reasonably, since it is our institutions that make us what we are. But it is well to remember that in exhibiting this pride, we are applauding just so many manifestations of conformity which were brought about by the practice of "thought control" through many generations.

Not only is it *characteristic* of society to create institutions and to defend them with sanctions. Societies *must* do so—or else they cease to exist. The members of a society must share certain values if that society is to cohere; and cohere it must if it is to survive. In order to assert and perpetuate these values, it must do constant battle against competing values. A democratic society, for example, dare not take for granted that the premises of democracy will, unaided (i.e., solely in virtue of their ideological superiority), drive Communism out of the market. If the contest were to be adjudicated by a divine tribunal, society could sit back with folded hands and watch the show. But it is not; and hence a concomitant of

---

* It should be noted that the Atlanta incident is cited merely to illustrate, *in terms of thought control*, the various sanctions and countersanctions commonly exercised. Other issues, highly important, but not relevant here, were raised when the Board of Censors, in counterattacking against Hollywood, invoked the power of the State.

man's selecting freedom as against Communism is his acting rationally in *behalf* of freedom and *against* Communism. If the contest were to be adjudicated by a divine tribunal, a society could afford to be capricious and patronizing towards the enemy's ideas. It could even afford to act on Liberal premises relating to "freedom of the mind"—by seeing to it, for example, that the New York *Daily Worker* circulated as many copies as the *New York Journal American*.

A hard and indelible fact of freedom is that a conformity of sorts is always dominant, as evidenced by such minutiae as that the *Journal American* and the *New York Post* are more heavily subscribed than the *Daily Worker*. And since a conformity of sorts will always be with us, the freeman's principal concern is that it shall be a conformity that honors the values he esteems rather than those he rejects.

This is not to say, of course, that society never makes mistakes in this area, and that the conformities selected by societies are, invariably, conformities with the eternal verities. Even free and enlightened men may use the power of sanctions in behalf of false and inferior values. But democracy is meaningless unless, having brought to bear on today's problems their intelligence, their insights, and their experience, freemen take vigorous action on behalf of the truth as they see it.

Thus Liberal spokesmen, who are forever warning us against attempting to get an inside run for our favored values, show a fundamental misunderstanding of the free society.

The Liberals are forever warning us about the dangers of coming down hard on those who oppose the basic values of our society. The Communist problem, for example, according to one of the Liberals' favorite lines of argument, is not inherently different from that which, prior to the Revolutionary War, our forefathers posed to the English; and we have no more business assuming our own infallibility *vis à vis* the Communists than the English had in assuming theirs *vis à vis* the American Revolutionaries. "In 1940," writes Alan Barth,[4] "the Alien Registration Act forbade all Americans to teach or advocate the duty or necessity of overthrowing by force or violence a government created by just such advocacy."

Two implications are clearly present in such a statement, namely, (a) that the revolution America is seeking to frustrate through the Smith Act and, one supposes, through McCarthyism in general, cannot be written off as morally reprehensible unless we are prepared to write off, in like manner, the Revolution to which we owe our existence as a nation; and (b) that the English ought not to have resisted our insurrectionary forefathers.

Both of these notions, we contend, are false, and the freeman must reject them as a matter of course: the one as contrary to his considered estimate of Communism, the other as politically egocentric to the point of sheer naivete.

We believe on the strength of the evidence, that the American Revolution against George III was a revolution in the interests of freedom and of civilization. But it does not follow that the English should have recognized it as such, and should, accordingly, have given it their blessing. Still less does it follow that the Communist revolution is in the interests of freedom and of civilization, and that we should give it *our* blessing. For each free society must decide these questions by its own lights as they arise, and there is no place to which it can turn for the kind of guidance that will exclude the possibility of error. Certainly not to such doctrines as "the divine right of revolution."

The individual freeman may, of course, find himself in disagreement with his society's decision. If so, it is his duty to resist the majority, even if it be very large, to just the extent called for by the intensity of his disagreement. But let him not deny society's right to consolidate around the institutions it favors. Or at least let him not deny this right in the name of a free society.

The preaching of the Liberals on the subject of conformity, as we have already suggested, does not conform with their practice. In the light of their own habits, their sense of outrage in the presence of McCarthyism becomes difficult to explain. For where movements are concerned that conform with Liberalism, the Liberals talk out of the other side of their mouths.

The drum-beating for a "bi-partisan" foreign policy, for example, insistent and deafening as it was during the post-war years (and is even today), is a call for "conformity" in one aspect of public affairs. And who has beat that drum more assiduously than the Liberals? Every time a diehard crosses the aisle and joins the bi-partisan ranks there is jubilation in the Liberal Camp. That no such acclamation greets the regeneration of a Louis Budenz, a Whittaker Chambers, or an Elizabeth Bentley, is something for which the Liberals have yet to offer a convincing explanation.

Where were the Liberals when the weapons they now forbid us

to use against the Communists were being used, fifteen years ago, against American fascists and against a number of Americans who were *not* fascists? And how do the Liberals account for their past and present ruthlessness in assaulting all persons, groups, or even ideas, that are out of harmony with the Liberal orthodoxy? That Liberal weapons have been effectively wielded, many a businessman, many a so-called isolationist, and many a hard anti-Communist can prove by pointing to his scars.

What is more, the Liberals have been signally successful in many of their drives for conformity. Not many years ago, for example, most Americans believed employers were entitled to recognize or not recognize labor unions as bargaining agents for workers as they themselves saw fit. But more and more Americans became convinced that the ends of social justice would be better served if workers enjoyed a stronger bargaining position. The Liberals, however, were not content with a slow evolution of public sentiment. They were in a hurry. And no sooner did they win a Congress and a President of their persuasion, than they passed a law making collective bargaining *mandatory*. The non-conforming employer could thenceforward (a) close up shop or (b) go to jail for contempt. It was, to be sure, the employer's actions rather than his thought that the Wagner Act was intended to control. But it has also proved an extremely effective instrument of creeping thought-control, since it has produced a gradual consolidation of public opinion around the ideas of its authors. If the collective bargaining clause of the Act were repealed tomorrow, a few employers might conceivably turn the unions out. But an overwhelming majority would not. Sixteen years of collective bargaining, sanctioned by law and by society, have so deeply implanted this practice in our public morality that it has become, quite simply, an American "institution."

The Liberals, in short, do want conformity—with Liberalism. The overriding sin, in their attitude toward McCarthyism as a drive toward conformity, is their duplicity. The fulminations of those Liberals who know what they are about are prompted not by a dread of conformity as such, but by the approaching conformity with values to which they do not subscribe.

To say that all societies encourage conformity leaves open the question of *how* they ought to encourage it. And there is a consensus that a society concerned with preserving individual freedom

will not take away from dissidents one iota of freedom that does not *have* to be taken away in order to protect its institutions.

The traditional view among libertarians has always been that freedom tends to be maximized for both majorities and minorities, and thus for society in general, if social sanctions are preferred to legal ones. This view has normally been supported by two arguments: (a) that the *genus State* (which goes into action when legal sanctions are imposed) has natural aggressive tendencies that tend to feed upon each successive new grant of power; and (b) that social sanctions more accurately reflect the real "lay" of community sentiment.

The first of these arguments is grounded in long centuries of experience which have taught us that the State has attributes one of which is a tendency to usurp functions that can be equally well and, in most cases, better performed by the citizens acting individually or through voluntary and spontaneous associations. The end result of such usurpations is, of course, fatal to freedom. Thus, wisdom instructs freemen not to whet the State's always enormous appetite for power by passing laws that add *unnecessarily* to the paraphernalia of the State.

The second argument rests upon what we have learned in the long pull of history about the plight of dissenting minorities, even in the freest societies. A legal sanction is, in theory, one hundred per cent effective: all the citizens are made to conform, even if only fifty-one per cent of them entertain the views that prompted the legislation. Thus, half the citizens of the State of New York, plus one, can, through control of the legislature, pass a law that will prevent Communists from teaching in any State school—even though half of the community, minus one, believes such a law to be bad or at least inadvisable. Social sanctions, by contrast, are effective roughly in proportion to the number of persons who wish to exercise them: if only fifty-one per cent of New Yorkers want Communist teachers kept out of the schools, and only social sanctions are used, then Communists will be kept out of, roughly fifty-one per cent of the schools; the minority is left free to resist the pressure exerted by the majority.

In other words, minorities remain freer when majorities content themselves with the degree of conformity they can achieve without calling in the police. Freemen, other things being equal, will ardently desire to maximize the minority's freedom; and to the extent that they do they will advocate social evolution rather than legal revolution. The freeman who objects to nudism may inflict social indignities on the sun cultist, but he will not advocate legislation outlawing nudist colonies. The freeman will join in making life uncomfortable for Gerald L. K. Smith, but will not back a law forbidding Smith to publish his scurrilous literature.

It is interesting that the Liberals have been far less concerned than libertarians about freedom for the minorities. They have a congenital fondness for passing laws, and a congenital distaste for waiting around while social sanctions engender conformity on this issue or that. The sure and swift machinery of the State fascinates them the way a *real* pistol fascinates youthful admirers of Hopalong Cassidy; their faith in it knows no bounds. Thus, for example, the proposed federal Fair Employment Practice Law is a sturdy rallying point for all Liberals; while the libertarian prefers to encourage racial conciliation through education and social pressures.

The balanced libertarian does not, to be sure, hold that the majority members of a free society must *never* be "in a hurry," and that in no circumstances may they take the short cut conveniently provided by the statute-book. He well knows there are times when legal sanctions must be used, and he knows we live in such times today. He will advise the majority not to adopt *unnecessary* legal measures of a restrictive character; but not to hesitate to adopt the *necessary* ones, i.e., those that the exigencies of the situation clearly call for.

Mr. Justice Holmes laid down a famous test by which free societies can distinguish between the unnecessary and the necessary in this area. The "clear and present danger" doctrine is useful, and, probably, the best we have. The doctrine is, of course, incapable of furnishing wholly objective and unvarying standards, as Supreme Court experience with it has proved.* But the central meaning of Holmes' test is clear and serviceable as applied to deeds as

---

* Holmes confined himself to ruling on the requirements that must be fulfilled before society restricts the freedom of *advocacy*. He did not, that is to say, propose that the same test be met by laws aimed at *actions*, while his standard seems to us equally as good for the one as for the other. The Supreme Court was wrestling with the Constitutional problem of how to reconcile the First Amendment with the right of a society to demand, on the level of utterance and publication, the conformity it needs for self-protection. The formula Holmes hit upon is dubious constitutional law. As Mikklejohn, Chafee and others have pointed out, the First Amendment states *unambiguously* that freedom of speech and of the press *shall not be abridged;* and it seems improbable that the founding fathers meant by it anything different from what they said. Holmes achieved a fairly happy balance between the right of the individual to advocate and the right of society to survive, but it was not an entirely honest way of amending the Constitution.

well as speech. It authorizes the use of legal sanctions against any activity that offers an imminent threat to the survival of existing institutions, or an imminent threat to the safety of persons or property. It forbids their use against all other deeds and utterances, and insists, indirectly, that a free society, when not in jeopardy, protect its values through the use of social pressure.

However we translate Holmes' test, most of us are agreed that activity on behalf of the enemy in time of war poses a clear and present danger.

We cannot avoid the fact that the United States is at war against international communism, and that McCarthyism is a program of action against those in our land who help the enemy. McCarthyism is (and, in our opinion, is likely to remain), nine parts social sanction to one part legal sanction. But that one part legal sanction is entirely legitimate. The resulting restrictions on a minority's freedom are certainly mild when compared with the drastic restrictions the majority imposes upon itself through such measures as military conscription. It is perhaps the crowning anomaly of present-day Liberalism that it should, on the one hand, sanction the total tyranny of compulsory military service, and yet balk at restricting the least freedom of our enemy's domestic allies.

Finally, the Liberals insist, our society cannot, even during wartime, afford to cut itself off from *innovation.* Whatever the emergencies of today, the argument runs, we must think about tomorrow. We must make sure that our conformity shall not be so rigid as to barricade our minds against new ideas. The most terrifying nightmare of our intellectuals is that America may some day pass the hemlock to a Socrates, hang a Thomas More, or force a Gal-

---

The Holmesian school—as well as the free speech absolutists—has always, it seems to us, begged the question *why* advocacy should be placed in a different category for this purpose from deeds. Quite evidently, the distinction cannot be justified on the grounds that speech is more valuable to the speaker than freedom of action is to the doer. If Jones wants to make a speech extolling the virtues of the Soviet Union, while Smith (who has no interest in politics) wishes to start a lottery—and if laws proscribing both activities are on the books,—to convince Smith that as a victim of thought control Jones is a good deal worse off than he will take some doing. Holmes was presumably concerned with the *utility* to society of freedom of speech, as against freedom of action. In fact, however, the two are, invariably, so intertwined that greater freedom in the one category tends to generate greater freedom in the other. Advocacy often influences actions, and action, through the roundabout process of "creeping thought control," often influences advocacy.

lileo to recant. It can happen here, we are warned, if we give Mc-Carthyism its rein.

This argument forgets that societies are, after all, educated as well as educable. It is one thing for society to give a hearing to new ideas, and quite another thing for it to feel impelled to put new ideas—simply because they are new or unorthodox—on a plane of equality with cherished ideas that have met the test of time. It is, for example, one thing to study Jean Paul Sartre and allow the free circulation of his books (which this country is doing) and quite another thing to give existentialist ideas the inside run in the curriculum of our university philosophy departments (which this country is not doing). It should after all be clear that a free market in ideas ceases to be free or a market if the latest huckster to arrive can claim his share of trade without regard to the quality or appeal of the commodity he is selling, and merely because he is a parvenu. The Liberals, bewitched as they are with the value of innovation, tend to forget that a free market is one where the customers can, if they so wish, keep on trading with the same old butcher.

Moreover, the argument tends to equate "innovation" with progress. The innovator can regale society with a cornucopia of wealth and happiness; but he can also open a Pandora's box. A measure of healthy skepticism about new ideas is not a sign of obscurantism —nor, necessarily, an indication of stagnancy. Most of what we correctly call progress is a matter of the natural development and growth of old ideas. The statement that the heterodoxy of today is the orthodoxy of tomorrow, which we hear so often in this connection, is a piece of absurd oversimplification. *One* of today's heterodoxies may become tomorrow's orthodoxy; but if so, then, by definition, the remainder will not. And today's heterodoxies are always numerous in a way that the cliché fails to recognize. Witness in our country the brief flowering and unlamented demise of Know-Nothingism and Ku-Kluxism—both of them heterodoxies that did not, on the morrow, become orthodoxies. Nor is it true, as the argument suggests, that there is net social gain, or progress, necessarily and as a matter of course, every time a heterodoxy displaces an orthodoxy. Societies often progress backwards.

Even so, progress *does* occur, and no intelligent society should adhere to a conformity so rigid as to make the airing of alternatives dangerous or impossible. Our major differences with the Liberals in this area have to do with whether McCarthyism tends in any such direction. And this brings us, at last, to the question: What is the actual extent of the conformity McCarthyism seeks to impose?

McCarthyism's Call to Conformity

McCARTHYISM, on the record, is not in any sense an attempt to prevent the airing of new ideas. It is directed not at *new* ideas but at *Communist* ideas, of which the last thing that can be said is that they are new or untried. The McCarthyites are doing their resourceful best to make our society inhospitable to Communists, fellow-travelers, and security risks in the government. To this end, they are conducting operations on two fronts: (1) they seek to vitalize existing legal sanctions, and (2) they seek to harden existing anti-Communist prejudices and channel them into effective social sanctions.

Valid laws and auxiliary Executive Orders prohibited Communists—or persons about whose loyalty or reliability there was a reasonable doubt—from holding government posts long before Senator McCarthy started talking; but they were frequently evaded, and sloppily administered. McCarthy and his allies have simply insisted that they be vigorously enforced. McCarthyism is primarily the maintenance of a steady flow of criticism (raillery, the Liberals call it) calculated to pressure the President, Cabinet members, high officials, and above all the political party in power, to get on with the elimination of security risks in government. In a sense, the major "victims" of McCarthy's drive for conformity have been those responsible for the so-called loyalty program, whom he has tried to inch into performing their clear legal duties.

On the second front, McCarthy has tied into fellow-travelers who have no tangible affiliation with the government. For example, he early aimed his fire at Harlow Shapley, Frederick Schuman, and Owen Lattimore.* McCarthy exposed their party-lining and did what he could to build up social pressure against them. He has not, or at least not yet, succeeded in eliminating them from positions of power and influence in national academic life: all three continue to teach at important universities. But there is no doubting the fact that they are less influential than they were before. Their pronouncements on foreign policy are no longer cited as

---

* To be sure, McCarthy first became interested in these men because of their alleged connection with the government. Insofar as their government affiliations were either past history or of a merely peripheral nature, it can be argued that he attacked them in the wrong context. But that is beside the point as far as the present question (what degree of conformity is McCarthyism attempting to bring about?) is concerned.

authoritative. Lattimore's future books about solutions in Asia are unlikely to become bestsellers.*

The conformity attendant upon McCarthyism, then, adds up to something like this: (1) *persons who conspire to overthrow the government by force* are subject to legal sanctions (the Smith Act, for example), primarily that of imprisonment; (2) *persons in public service about whose loyalty or security there is a "reasonable doubt"* are subject to legal sanctions (the various security regulations), primarily that of exclusion from government employment; (3) *persons other than government employees about whom there exist reasonable grounds for believing they are "pro-Communist,"* are to some extent subject to legal sanctions (possibly the McCarran Act or the Attorney General's list of subversive organizations), primarily that of having their activities officially labeled as "Communist" or "subversive" or (as with the Feinberg Law or the statutory loyalty oath requirements) that of being excluded from certain jobs; they are furthermore subject, increasingly, to social sanctions, primarily of the type that have been aimed at Lattimore and Schuman and Shapley.

These sanctions are not the same all over the country. In some localities, in sections of the Midwest for example, the sanctions hit people who might escape them elsewhere. In the rare instance, a single Communist-front affiliation may engender public hostility and bring down severe social sanctions on a man's head. In the academic arena of the East, by contrast, the level of enforced conformity is decidedly lower, and sometimes descends nearly to zero. Southern Baptist College X fires Jones when there are apparently no reasonable grounds for believing him to be a pro-Communist. But Harvard, Williams and Johns Hopkins retain Shapley, Schuman and Lattimore on their faculties when reasonable grounds abound for believing them to be pro-Communist.

The claim is often made that McCarthyism has as its ultimate objective the exclusion of Liberals from positions of power, prestige,

---

* We stress the discomfort that the three professors have suffered without attempting to balance it against the comfort they have presumably drawn from their apotheosis by the Liberals. It has for several years been a popular —and adroit—witticism among young academicians that "if *only* I were a Communist, then I could be sure I wouldn't be fired. They wouldn't dare!" The insecure professor who embraces Communism in order to frustrate the college president's attempt to get rid of him is the central figure in a recent novel about university life.

and influence in the American community; and that the present campaign against Communists and fellow-travelers is merely the thin edge of the wedge. It is therefore curious that the one instance which lent a modicum of factual support to this fear received little or no attention from Liberal publicists.

In October of 1952, Senator McCarthy delivered his widely heralded attack on Adlai Stevenson, which people generally expected would turn into an attempt to connect the Democratic candidate with Communism. With millions of listeners glued to radio and TV, McCarthy reached, not for a red paint brush, but for a list of some of Stevenson's top advisors: Archibald MacLeish, Bernard De Voto, Arthur Schlesinger, Jr. Was his point that these men were *Communists?* No, that was not McCarthy's point. His objection to these men was not that they were Communists, or even pro-Communists, but that they were Liberals—atheistic, soft-headed, anti-anti-Communist, ADA Liberals. And his major point turned out to be that this was sufficient reason for rejecting the candidate for whom they were serving as Edgar Bergens.

Whether the speech was a conscious effort to narrow the limits of tolerable opinion so as to exclude left-wing Liberals, only McCarthy can say. The fact that he has not reiterated the point suggests that, if this *was* his intent, he was not very serious about it. It is far more likely that he intended to deliver a traditional political campaign speech highlighting the disqualifications of his Party's opponents. But it may well be we have not heard the last of this idea. Some day, the patience of America may at last be exhausted, and we will strike out against Liberals. Not because they are treacherous like Communists, but because, with James Burnham, we will conclude "that they are mistaken in their predictions, false in their analyses, wrong in their advice, and through the results of their actions injurious to the interests of the nation. That is reason enough to strive to free the conduct of the country's affairs from the influence of them and their works."* But the real point, for our purposes, is that the mainstream of McCarthyism flows past the Liberals as gently as the Afton; and that the MacLeishs, De Votos and Schlesingers have no grounds for arguing that any sustained effort is being made to read *them* out of the community.

---

* Burnham was referring to "Wechsler and his political associates" (*The Freeman*, June 15, 1953). He was most clearly advocating *social* sanctions against them.

It is still only *Communist* ideas that are beyond the pale. And the evidence is convincing that the function of Senator McCarthy and his colleagues is not that of defining or creating a new orthodoxy with which individuals are being called upon to conform. The American community affirmed anti-Communism long before McCarthy started in. McCarthy's function has been to harden the *existing* conformity.

We are left with the final question: whether the conformity urged by McCarthyism is doing a service to America and, therefore, whether we should view it with approval. Certainly the vast majority of the American people have already given *their* answer to the question; for, after all, the approaching conformity is of their own making, and they must be presumed to approve what they are doing. Most Americans, the available evidence seems to say, favor anti-Communism, and tight security in the civil service. But we are asking, of course, whether the majority is *right;* and therefore we must take account of the misgivings of the intelligentsia. What should be said of their resolute and impassioned opposition to McCarthyism?

Simply this. They are confused, they have misread history, and they fail to understand social processes. What is more, they do not feel the faith they so often and so ardently express in democracy. There is only one alternative to this explanation: that they are opposed to the decline of Communist influence at home. The determination of the American people to curb Communism cannot be dismissed as a capricious, ignorant, or impetuous decision. There is, we contend, a great deal of difference between a society's harassing the exponents of an idea that has been thoroughly examined and found objectionable, and its harassing the exponents of an idea simply because it hurls a novel challenge at traditional notions. Our Schumans, Shapleys, and Lattimores have become unacceptable not because they are known to hold ideas and values at variance with those of the majority of Americans, but because they expound a *particular* set of ideas and values which Americans have explored and emphatically rejected, and because the propagation of these ideas fortifies an implacable foreign power bent on the destruction of American independence.

The ideas of the Schumans, Shapleys and Lattimores are not, as we say, new ideas; they are exploded ideas. America has had access to the literature of Communism for more than a generation. Everything from *Das Kapital* and *The Problems of Leninism* to month-lies, weeklies and dailies reflecting the least adjustment in the Party Line, has for years circulated freely in American classrooms, librar-ies, and living rooms. Communist missionaries have roamed the land to urge their ideas through the spoken word. In short, Amer-ica could hardly have given Communism a fairer or more exhaus-tive hearing without inviting over a dozen commissars to conduct an American Five Year Plan.

Having heard the case, America has rejected it. And because the case is championed by a mobilized, aggressive, titanic enemy state, America has gone further: she has turned to the offensive against Communism. We are at war, and there are many strategies, many tactics, many weapons, many courses of action open to us. Our lines could be advanced by innumerable enterprises, some foolish, some proper—by assassinating Malenkov, by atom-bombing Soviet industrial plants, by subsidizing a Russian underground, by pro-viding leadership and funds for prominent European and Asiatic anti-Communists, by imprisoning violators of the Smith Act, by purging the Civil Service, and by exposing and persecuting Com-munist apologists in whatever occupation they are engaged. One thing is certain: Communism will not be defeated—any more than freedom was won—by postulating the virtues of democracy and of Christianity as evident truths and letting it go at that.

McCarthyism, then, is a weapon in the American arsenal. To the extent that McCarthyism, out of ignorance or impetuosity or malice, urges the imposition of sanctions upon persons who are *not* pro-Communist or security risks, we should certainly oppose it. When persons about whose loyalty or security reliability there is *no* reasonable doubt are flushed from government service for secur-ity reasons, those responsible should be criticized and held to an accounting both at the polls and before investigating committees. Whenever the anti-Communist conformity excludes well-meaning Liberals, we should, in other words, go to their rescue. But as long as McCarthyism fixes its goal with its present precision, it is a movement around which men of good will and stern morality can close ranks.

CHAPTER XV

Afterword

CURRENT reports indicate that American intellectuals traveling abroad divide their time, more or less equally, between sight-seeing and apologizing for McCarthy. For Europeans, it seems, have lost faith in America, where McCarthyism is rife; they are for this reason, we are told, inclining more and more towards neutralism, toward a "balanced" view of the "two great powers that threaten the peace of the world."

The following is a letter to the *New York Times* (July 1, 1953) from a distinguished American scholar in the field of philosophy, visiting in Scotland for the purpose of delivering the famed Gifford Lectures at Saint Andrews University:

"I should like to report a strong impression," writes Professor Brand Blanshard, "which is the result of seventeen months abroad. It is this, that if there is one American who more than any other is injuring his country by un-American activities it is Senator McCarthy. We who are abroad have come to expect that his acts and ideas will be thrown in our faces wherever we go. We are tired of explaining him, listening to derisive laughter about him and apologizing for him.

"European liberals are for the most part disillusioned with Communism and would be ready to follow American leadership if they were persuaded that it was really liberal. But if they ever feel an impulse in this direction they open their newspapers next day to read that Mr. McCarthy is again scouring government offices and universities in search of men who have dared to utter liberal opinions, even in the remote past, and branding them as Communists and public enemies. Is it any wonder that Europeans put down their papers with a sigh and say: 'If that is what America is offering, we want none of it. We have rejected Communism precisely because we could not bear that sort of thing. You do not make it bearable to us by renaming it Americanism. If you ask us to choose between Communism and McCarthyism, we can only say: A plague on both your houses.'

"Many thoughtful Europeans would consider that in the work of undermining the American position in the world Mr. McCarthy has been of more use to the Russians than half a dozen of their crack divisions. I should agree."

Is this indeed what McCarthy has done to us in Europe? And is the best traveling American philosophers can do, in the circumstances, to endure, with Mr. Blanshard, the humiliation of acknowledging McCarthy as a fellow countryman, to apologize humbly for him, and to leave town with Europe's derisive laughter ringing in their ears?

Let us turn, for a short but first-hand account of the European position, to a few passages of what purports to be a fairly representative statement of prevailing European sentiment on the crisis of the day. We quote from a statement that appeared in *Time* magazine, October 12, 1953, putting forward the views of Mr. Tom Driberg, MP, introduced by *Time* as "an influential Christian socialist."

"Many Europeans and Asians," Mr. Driberg says, "mistrust the tendency to dragoon the whole world into two big-power blocs, each professing the noblest intentions and emitting, alternately, high-falutin slogans about democracy and Tarzanlike boasts of invincible might. We have seen this tendency in American and Soviet policy alike. We believe that it is wrong in itself, and likelier to lead to war than to peace.

"Many of us also feel impatient when, like kids after a street fight, each side accuses the other of having started it. Did the Russians start it in Czechoslovakia in 1948? Or the French in Indo-China in 1945? Or the British in Greece in 1944? Any competent attorney could make a case either way.

". . . After all, we agree on some issues with either side: with the Russians, we reject what seems to us the jungle philosophy of big-business capitalism; we stress political liberties as strongly as the Americans do—or did before the era of McCarthy. . . .

"Certainly Britain, and other Commonwealth countries, want to trade with China. Why not? . . . the Americans are destroying British and Commonwealth prosperity. As a socialist, I am an anti-imperialist; but the new imperialism of the dollar seems to me at least as harmful as the old imperialism. . . .

"To equate Soviet Russia with Nazi Germany is a dangerous oversimplification. They seem to me essentially different, in several ways: (1) ideologically, Communism is a Christian heresy, but Naziism was anti-Christian paganism; (2) hence, in practice, though there has been much cruelty in Russia, there is nothing comparable with the calculated horror of the gas chambers and the extermination of the Jews; (3) geographically and economically, the Soviet Union is far more self-sufficient and therefore not intrinsically expansionist. . . ."

Now let us first catch our breath and then, in the light of this exposition of the "neutralist" view, suggest a new approach for the traveling American philosopher shouldered with McCarthy's cross. Let us suggest that the next time an American professor is accosted by Europe's Christian Socialists, he say something like this:

"First, let's get *one* thing straight: A reign of terror does *not* exist in the United States. What about Mr. Blanshard—Phi Beta Kappa, senior professor of philosophy in Yale University, sometime co-president of the American Philosophical Association, member of the American Academy of Arts and Sciences? Why, Mr. Blanshard is, in respect of what he has told you about McCarthyism, a charlatan. He has, in fact, according to all academic rules, given his university grounds for dismissing him. Not, heaven knows, because he disagrees with McCarthy—in American colleges people are *hired,* not *fired* because they disagree with McCarthy—but because to make such a statement as that McCarthy is engaged in searching out 'men who have dared to utter liberal opinions, even in the remote past, and branding them as Communists,' is to say a demonstrable untruth, and the person who utters it, in the teeth of the evidence, is, demonstrably, ignorant or mendacious. Mr. Blanshard might just as well make claims to professional competence after informing his students that Socrates refused to escape with Crito because he was afraid of getting seasick.

"But Blanshard's fatuousness is in point only to the extent that such reign-of-terror talk beclouds the issue and commits European intellectuals to rather futile careers of swatting away at a straw man. For there are, indeed, aspects of McCarthyism that do horrify you, the Europeans, and will probably continue to horrify you. And this is because the United States and Europe are substantially *different* societies; and it is eternally true that one community will think well of another community in proportion as the second community resembles the first. And, in several essential respects, America does not resemble Europe.

"We are not accustomed, in most parts of America, to what you over here accept as a matter of course. The average American, unlike the average Frenchman, does not talk politics with his Communist barber in a friendly atmosphere of give-and-take, drink wine with his Communist neighbor, or have to inure himself to the antics of his Communist alderman. The American does not burn the midnight oil on election night because, like the Italian, he wonders whether the dawn will usher in a Communist government. The American does not, like the Englishman, have the slightest doubt in his mind as to who was responsible for the enslavement of Czechoslovakia, for the 'revolution' in Greece, or for the war in Indo-China; nor is he inclined to view Stalin as a 20th-Century Luther, or Russia as a land where, unlike Hitler Germany, 'horror' is not 'calculated.' And America, unlike England, does not barter with men who are shooting down her sons.

"Americans would not have tolerated, as France did until 1950, an avowed Communist as head of her atomic energy development program; and Americans, increasingly, will not tolerate, as England does, Communist domination of certain highly strategic trade unions.

"America, like England, has had her Fuchs, Pontecorvos, Mays, Burgesses and McLeans; but America, unlike England, has been deeply shocked by the successes of her traitors, and has resolved to frustrate them; for it is quite true that America is not prepared to accept the notion than an occasional traitor in this, and one in that government agency, is one of those consequences of 'political liberties' that we must put up with.

"The American, in short, is different from the European. Adlai Stevenson left his countrymen bewildered, if not humiliated, when he told them in the fall of 1952 that the wonder is not how *many* Communists there are in the United States but, considering the Great Depression, how *few* there are. For unlike the European, we do not live in the dread that the slightest—or even the greatest—convulsion in our economy, or in our politics, or in our culture, is going to deliver the man in the streets into the arms of a proletarian dictatorship.

"We believe, in short, that the average American is too balanced, too mature, too responsible to undulate in rhythm with the average European. America is simple. America understands pro-Communism, and she understands anti-Communism; but she is bewildered by 'non-Communism.' You may call this stolidity on her part, a sign of dogmatism, of ignorance, of absolutism. Call it what you will. It is there. And McCarthyism reflects it.

"Yet we in America are by no means united. McCarthyism is the source of violent controversy in this country, as you well know.

This is partly the result of ignorance, partly the result of success-ful Communist propaganda. But it is also because a number of peo-ple in America look at the order of things in Europe and then, rue-fully, at the state of affairs in America. These people are, by and large, our intellectuals. Whether it is coincidence or causality, our intellectuals are fired by the things that fire Europeans, and they are not perturbed by the things that do not perturb Europeans—Com-munism, for example.

"These Americans are engaged in a battle against McCarthyism, and in the balance hangs the future of America, the question whether the American mind will be set in the European mold or whether it will hang on to its characteristics, and indulge its pres-ent 'stolid' instincts.

"A considerable number of Americans support McCarthy not only in his fight to prevent America from becoming Communized, but also in his fight to prevent America from becoming like Europe. For us Communism is the *worst* fate on the horizon; but there are *other* fates that we would avoid, one of them being the fate of Europe, whom we see today as a weary and cynical community of pettifogging nations whose deterioration is not only measured by the strength of her Communist minority but the weakness of her non-Communist majority.

"Senator McCarthy is certainly no more critical of you than you have been and are likely to continue to be of him; in point of fact, he has on no occasion, not even in his Comrade-Attlee speech, spoken so intemperately or so distortedly about Europeans as Euro-peans regularly speak about him. So be it, for this is beside the point. We do not anticipate or even propose a reconciliation, and we do not anticipate, and *certainly* do not propose a compromise. Whatever help Europe chooses to extend in the fight against Com-munism is help that she extends in the defense of herself, and that help will reflect the extent to which she wishes to resist Commu-nism, not the extent to which she consents to go along with a country in which McCarthy is a national figure. We do not, there-fore, intend to get rid of McCarthy. We believe that on McCarthy-ism hang the hopes of America for effective resistance to Commu-nist infiltration. And if and when McCarthy broadens out, and there have been indications that he will, his spirit may infuse American foreign policy with the sinews and purpose to crush the Communist conspiracy. Only then can we afford to do without McCarthy."

Appendix

Appendix A

Communist Front Connections of McCarthy's "Public Cases"

THE FOLLOWING are the fronts with which, McCarthy charged, the nine "Public Cases" had been connected—together with descriptions of the evidence McCarthy adduced to back up his allegations. We list only those fronts mentioned by McCarthy that are backed up by an executive or a legislative citation. In by no means every case, it should be noted, did McCarthy list *all* the fronts his public cases had been connected with. We refer, specifically, to Miss Kenyon and Drs. Schuman and Shapley. The following symbols will be used: For the Attorney General—"AG"; for the House Committee on Un-American Activities—"HUAC"; for the California Committee on Un-American Activities—"CUAC"; for Tydings Committee Hearings—"TCH."

DOROTHY KENYON

1. *American Committee for Anti-Nazi Literature.* Sponsor, March 1939, as indicated by organization's letterhead. Miss Kenyon had no recollection of sponsorship. TCH, p. 182.
    Cited as a Communist front: CUAC report, 1948, p. 334.
2. *American Committee for Democracy and Intellectual Freedom.* Member, in 1940. Miss Kenyon admitted membership. TCH, p. 181.
    Cited HUAC report, June 25, 1942, p. 13, and March 29, 1944, p. 87; CUAC report 1948, p. 12.
3. *American-Russian Institute, N. Y.* Sponsor of dinner honoring FDR, May 1946. Miss Kenyon admitted sponsorship. TCH, p. 202.
    Cited: AG, April 27, 1949.
4. *Associated Blind, Inc.* Sponsor, as indicated by organization's letterhead. (No date.) Miss Kenyon had no recollection of sponsorship. TCH, p. 202.
    Never officially cited, but identified as a Communist front by HUAC report, Appendix IX, 1944.
5. *Citizens Committee to Aid Striking Seamen.* Member Advisory

Committee, January 1937, as indicated by organization's letterhead. Miss Kenyon had no recollection of membership. TCH, p. 182.

> Never officially cited, but identified as a Communist front by HUAC report, Appendix IX, 1944.

6. *Conference on Pan-American Democracy.* Sponsor, November 1938, March 1939. Miss Kenyon admitted sponsorship. TCH, p. 180.

> Cited: AG, June 1, 1948; HUAC report, March 29, 1944, pp. 161, 164; CUAC report, 1947, p. 210.

7. *Consumer's National Federation.* Member, 1937. Miss Kenyon admitted membership, but stated she got out soon afterwards because "I did not like the . . . company that I was keeping." TCH, p. 189.

> Cited: HUAC report, March 29, 1944, p. 155; CUAC report, 1943, p. 102.

8. *Consumer's Union.* Miss Kenyon denied Consumer's Union membership, stating she had been a member of Consumer's Research, parent of Consumer's Union. TCH, p. 180.

> Cited: HUAC report, March 29, 1944, p. 153; CUAC report, 1943, p. 102.

9. *Coordinating Committee To Lift The (Spanish) Embargo.* Sponsor, 1939. Miss Kenyon admitted sponsorship. TCH, p. 196.

> Cited: HUAC report, March 29, 1944, pp. 137, 138; CUAC report, 140, 1947, p. 210.

10. *Descendants of the American Revolution.* Member of the Advisory Board. Miss Kenyon admitted membership "in the middle 30's," but stated, "I got out . . . as fast as I could." TCH, p. 203.

> Cited: HUAC report, June 25, 1942, pp. 18, 19; CUAC report, 1948, p. 336.

11. *Film Audiences for Democracy.* Member Advisory Board, October, 1939, as indicated by organization's letterhead. Miss Kenyon had no recollection of membership. TCH, p. 182.

> Cited: HUAC report, March 29, 1944, p. 150; CUAC report, 1948, pp. 193, 238.

12. *Films for Democracy.* Member Advisory Board, April 1939, as indicated by organization's letterhead. Miss Kenyon had no recollection of membership. TCH, p. 182.

> Cited: HUAC report, March 29, 1944, pp. 149, 150; CUAC report, 1948, p. 238.

13. *Gerson Supporters.* Signed organization's letter, supporting the appointment of Simon W. Gerson, February 1938. Miss Kenyon had no recollection of doing so. TCH, p. 182.

> Cited: CUAC report, 1948, p. 34.

14. *Greater New York Emergency Conference on Inalienable Rights.* Sponsor, February 1940, as indicated by organization's convention program. Miss Kenyon had no recollection of sponsorship. TCH, p. 182.

> Cited: HUAC report, March 29, 1944, pp. 96, 129; CUAC report, 1948, p. 61.

15. *Lawyers Committee on American Relations with Spain.* Member, 1938, 1939. Miss Kenyon admitted membership. TCH, p. 181.

Cited: HUAC report, March 29, 1944, pp. 168, 169; CUAC report, 1948, p. 335.

16. *League of Women Shoppers.* Sponsor, 1935, 1936. Miss Kenyon admitted sponsorship, and stated she withdrew "a year or so" after its founding in 1935. TCH, p. 179.

Cited: HUAC report, March 29, 1944, pp. 121, 181; CUAC report, 1943, p. 100.

17. *Milk Consumer's Protective Committee.* Member Advisory Board, April 1940, as indicated by organization's letterhead. Miss Kenyon had no recollection of membership. TCH, p. 182.

Cited: New York City Council Committee investigating the Municipal Civil Service Commission.

18. *National Citizen's Political Action Committee.* Member. (No date available.) Miss Kenyon admitted membership: "I was very happy to be a member of the PAC." TCH, p. 193.

Cited: CUAC report, 1948, p. 38.

19. *National Council of American-Soviet Friendship.* Sponsor, November 1948, as indicated by organization's letter of invitation to rally honoring "Red Dean" Canterbury. Miss Kenyon admitted sponsorship in 1943, but stated that she withdrew "some three years later," and in 1949 addressed letter of protest to the organization because her name was still carried as a sponsor. TCH, p. 180.

Cited: AG, December 4, 1947; HUAC report, March 29, 1944, p. 156; CUAC report, 1948, pp. 321, 322, 327.

20. *Political Prisoners Bail Fund Committee.* Sponsor, January 1935, as indicated by organization's letterhead. Miss Kenyon admitted sponsorship. TCH, p. 180.

Never officially cited but identified as a Communist Party front by HUAC report, Appendix IX, 1944. (HUAC reports in Appendix IX that the Political Prisoners Bail Fund Committee worked closely, in the middle thirties, with the International Labor Defense. This latter organization was called the "legal arm of the Communist Party" by Attorney General Biddle /*Congressional Record*, Sept. 24, 1942/; legislative committees identified it as such several years before. /HUAC, Jan. 3, 1939, pp. 75-78; Massachusetts House Committee on Un-American Activities, *Report*, 1938, pp. 198, 342./)

21. *Schappes Defense Committee.* Signed letter asking for Schappes' release, October, 1944. Miss Kenyon had no recollection of signing the letter and denied she had been a member of the committee. TCH, pp. 182, 196.

Cited: AG, April 27, 1949; HUAC report, March 29, 1944, p. 71; CUAC report, 1948, p. 55.

22. *Testimonial Dinner for Ferdinand C. Smith.* Sponsor, September, 1944. Miss Kenyon had no recollection of sponsorship. TCH, p. 191.

Never officially cited, but identified as a Communist front by HUAC report, Appendix IX, 1944.

23. *Veterans of Abraham Lincoln Brigade.* Signed open letter to

F.D.R., protesting attacks on the organization and decrying war hysteria, as indicated by *Daily Worker* paid advertisement, Feb. 21, 1940. Signed press release entitled "For America's sake: break with Franco Spain," March, 1945. Miss Kenyon denied membership or affiliation. TCH, p. 181.

> Cited: AG, December 4, 1947; HUAC report, March 29, 1944, p. 82. CUAC report, 1948, pp. 94, 382.

24. *Washington Committee to Lift Spanish Embargo.* Name used in organization's open letter January 1939. Miss Kenyon had no recollection of affiliation. TCH, p. 181.

> Cited: CUAC report, 1948, pp. 335, 336.

PHILIP JESSUP

1. *American Law Students Association.* Member, Faculty Advisory Board (1940) as indicated by organization's letterhead. Jessup acknowledged serving on an Advisory Board which "may have been this one." TCH, p. 263.

> Never officially cited, but identified as a Communist front by HUAC report 448, Appendix IX, 1944.

2. *American Russian Institute of New York.* Sponsor of two dinners given by that organization (1944 and 1946). Jessup acknowledged sponsorship of both dinners. TCH, p. 226.

> Cited: AG, April 27, 1949.

3. *National Emergency Conference.* Sponsor (May, 1939) as indicated by organization's list of sponsors. Jessup stated, "I am willing to assume that I consented to have [my name] put on the list." TCH, p. 269.

> Cited: HUAC report, March 29, 1944, p. 49; CUAC report, 1948, p. 115.

4. *National Emergency Conference for Democratic Rights.* Sponsor February 1940 as indicated by organization's letterhead. Jessup had no recollection of sponsorship, thought it likely that organization automatically listed sponsors of its predecessor, the National Emergency Conference. TCH, p. 270.

> Cited: HUAC report, March 29, 1944, pp. 48, 102; CUAC report, 1948, pp. 112, 327.

NOTE: Senator McCarthy has also asserted that Jessup was affiliated with the Coordinating Committee to Lift the Spanish Embargo (Congressional Record, June 2, 1950, p. 8109) and the China Aid Council (Pamphlet "Let Them Fall," September 1951.) For reasons that appear in the text, the allegation with reference to the CCLSE appears to be unfounded. Similarly, the evidence later published in "Let Them Fall" is insufficient to establish Jessup's connection with the CAC.

Esther Brunauer

1. *American Youth Congress.* Signer of call to annual meeting (1938). Mrs. Brunauer acknowledged affiliation. TCH, p. 296.
> Cited: AG, December 4, 1947; HUAC report, June 25, 1942, p. 16; CUAC report, 1948, p. 179.

2. *Friends of the Soviet Union.* Presided at meeting (June, 1936). Speaker at another meeting (June, 1934). Mrs. Brunauer acknowledged her part in both meetings. TCH, p. 296.
> Cited: AG, December 4, 1947. HUAC report, January 3, 1939, p. 78; CUAC, report, 1948, pp. 65, 244, and 321.

NOTE: Senator McCarthy also asserted Mrs. Brunauer supported the Consumer's Union, and that she was a member of the Committee for Concerted Peace Efforts. Evidence failed to support the alleged connection with Consumer's Union. The Committee for Concerted Peace Efforts has never been cited as a Communist front.

Harlow Shapley

1. *American Committee for Democracy and Intellectual Freedom.* Member, as indicated by organization's letterhead (September 1939).
> Cited: HUAC report, June 25, 1942, p. 13; CUAC report, 1948, p. 112.

2. *American Russian Institute,* New York. Member, Board of Trustees, as indicated by *New York Times* (December 12, 1947).
> Cited: AG, April 27, 1949.

3. *Civil Rights Congress.* Sponsor of organization's Bill of Rights conference (June, 1949).
> Cited: AG, December 4, 1947; HUAC report No. 1115, September 2, 1947, pp. 2, 19; CUAC report, 1947, p. 187.

4. *Committee for the First Amendment.* Signer of organization's statement protesting the HUAC investigation of the motion picture industry (October, 1947).
> Cited: CUAC, report, 1948, p. 210.

5. *Committee of One Thousand.* Sponsor, as indicated by organization's press release (March 5, 1948).
> Cited: CUAC report 1948, pp. 34, 35.

6. *Congress of American Women.* Speaker at organization meeting, as indicated by *Daily Worker,* (September 23, 1947).
> Cited: AG, June 1, 1948; HUAC report No. 1953, April 26, 1950; CUAC report, 1948, pp. 228-31.

7. *Conference on Pan-American Democracy.* Signer of organization's open letter defending Luis Carlos Prestes, Brazilian Communist Party official, as indicated by the *New Masses* (December 3, 1940).
> Cited: AG, June 1, 1948; HUAC report, March 29, 1944, pp. 161, 164; CUAC report, 1947, p. 210.

8. *Eisler Defense Committee.* Signer of organization's statement on Gerhart Eisler, as indicated by *Daily Worker,* (June 28, 1947).

> Cited: HUAC report No. 1115, September 2, 1947, p. 13.

9. *Independent Citizen's Committee of the Arts, Sciences and Professions.* Vice-chairman, as indicated by organization's letterhead (May 1946).

> Cited: HUAC report No. 1954, April 26, 1950; CUAC report, 1948, p. 262.

10. *International Worker's Order.* Gave interview to organization's publication, *Fraternal Outlook,* (March, 1949).

> Cited: AG, September 24, 1942, and December 4, 1947; HUAC, report, January 3, 1939, p. 78; CUAC report, 1948, pp. 267, 268, 271.

11. *Joint Anti-Fascist Refugee League.* Sponsor, as indicated by organization's letterheads (September 8, 1944; April 28, 1949); also chairman of organization's reception committee for Irene Joliot-Curie, (March 31, 1948).

> Cited: AG, December 4, 1947; HUAC report, March 29, 1944, p. 174; CUAC report, 1948, pp. 270, 271.

12. *League of American Writers.* Signer of organization's open letter, as indicated by *Daily Worker* (July 31, 1940).

> Cited: AG, June 1, 1948; HUAC report January 3, 1940, p. 9; CUAC report, 1945, pp. 121, 122, 126.

13. *National Council of the Arts, Sciences and Professions.* Chairman, when organization sponsored the Waldorf Peace Conference (Cultural and Scientific Conference for World Peace, 1949).

> Cited: HUAC report No. 1954, April 26, 1950.

14. *National Emergency Conference for Democratic Rights.* Signer of organization's letter, as indicated by *Daily Worker,* (May 13, 1940).

> Cited: HUAC report, March 29, 1944, pp. 48, 102; CUAC report, 1948, pp. 112, 327.

15. *National Federation for Constitutional Liberties.* Signer of organization's statement urging military commissions to Communists, as indicated by *Daily Worker* (March 18, 1945).

> Cited: AG, December 4, 1947; HUAC report, March 29, 1944, p. 50; CUAC, 1948, pp. 201, 327.

16. *New Masses.* Signer of open letter appearing in publication's (April 2, 1940) issue attacking Grand Jury for questioning its editors and employees.

> Cited: AG, September 24, 1942, p. 7688; HUAC report, March 29, 1949, pp. 48, 75; CUAC report, 1947, p. 160.

17. *New York Conference for Inalienable Rights.* Signer of organization's open telegram, as indicated by *Daily Worker* (September 17, 1940).

> Cited: HUAC report, March 29, 1944, p. 149.

18. *Progressive Citizens of America.* Vice chairman (1946-1948).

> Cited: CUAC report, 1947, p. 369.

19. *Spanish Refugee Appeal.* Sponsor, as indicated by organization's letterhead (February 26, 1946).

Cited: CUAC report, 1949, p. 359.

20. *Teacher's Union.* Speaker at organization meeting, as indicated by *New York Times* (April 18, 1949).

Identified: CUAC report, 1948, p. 379.

21. *United Public Workers of America, CIO.* Speaker at Union meeting, as indicated by *Daily Worker* (April 16, 1948).

Cited: CUAC report, 1948, p. 379.

NOTE: Senator McCarthy asserted that Dr. Shapley was also affiliated with the Conference Against Anti-Communist Legislation, Citizens to Abolish the Wood-Rankin Committee, and the National Committee to Defeat the Mundt Bill. There is no evidence that these organizations have been either officially identified or cited as Communist fronts.

FREDERICK SCHUMAN

1. *American Committee for the Protection of Foreign Born.* Sponsor, as indicated by organization's letterheads (March, 1940, June 23, 1948).

Cited: AG, June 1, 1948; HUAC report, March 29, 1944, p. 195; CUAC report, 1947, p. 44.

2. *American Council on Soviet Relations.* Signer of one of organization's open letters.

Cited: AG, June 1, 1948; AG, *Congressional Record,* September 24, 1952, p. 7688; HUAC report, March 29, 1944, p. 174; CUAC report, 1948, p. 65.

3. *American League for Peace and Democracy.* Sponsor of organization subsidiary, The China Aid Council, as indicated by organization's letterhead (August 31, 1948).

Cited: AG, June 1, 1948; HUAC report, January 3, 1939, pp. 69-71; CUAC report, 1943, p. 91.

4. *American-Russian Institute, New York.* Sponsor.

Cited: AG, April 27, 1949.

5. *American Slav Congress.* Sponsor.

Cited: AG, June 1, 1948; CUAC report, 1948, p. 35; HUAC report No. 1951, April 26, 1950.

6. *Civil Rights Congress.* Sponsor, as indicated by program of organization's initial meeting (April 27, 28, 1946).

Cited: AG, December 4, 1947; CUAC report, 1947, p. 87; HUAC report, No. 1115, September 2, 1947, pp. 2, 19.

7. *Committee for a Boycott Against Japanese Aggression.* Signer of organization's appeal for Japanese boycott. (undated.)

Cited: CUAC report, 1948, pp. 147, 319, 365.

8. *Friends of the Soviet Union.* Speaker for organization as indicated by organization's hand bills (February 25, 1934; January 16, 1936).

Cited: AG, December 4, 1947; HUAC report, January 3, 1939, p. 78; CUAC report, 1948, pp. 65, 244, 321.

9. *League of Professional Groups for Foster and Ford.* Signer of organization's open letter urging the election of the Communist Party ticket (1932).

Cited: CUAC report, 1948, pp. 196, 246.

10. *National Citizens' Political Action Committee.* Member, as indicated by official organization membership list (August, 1944).

Cited: CUAC report, 1948, p. 38.

11. *National Conference on American Policy in China and the Far East.* Sponsor, as indicated by organization program, January 23, 1948.

Cited: AG, July 25, 1949.

12. *National Council of the Arts, Sciences and Professions.* Member (1948, 1949).

Cited: HUAC report, No. 1954, April 26, 1950.

NOTE: Senator McCarthy asserted that Professor Schuman was also affiliated with the African Aid Committee. There is no evidence that this organization has been officially cited or identified as a Communist front.

Appendix B

The Controversy Over the Loyalty Files

THE TYDINGS COMMITTEE dismissed Senator McCarthy's non-public cases as "old" cases, declaring that they had been reviewed and cleared by previous congressional committees. It also endorsed their previous "clearance." For it announced that a review of the State Department's relevant loyalty files (Senator McCarthy had repeatedly claimed they would substantiate his charges) had completely satisfied it that McCarthy was accusing persons whose reliability was beyond a "reasonable doubt."

But even before the Committee had announced its conclusions about the material that lay in the files, McCarthy challenged the validity of *any* finding the Committee might arrive at, on the ground that the files had been "raped," and that the Tydings Committee was being shown records from which all damaging data had been removed. And the two Republican members of the Committee further complicated the matter by insisting that the Committee's examination of the files, such as they were, was superficial; and hence its findings inconclusive. Thus a sharp issue was drawn; and much that has been said and written about this issue is tendentious and uninformed. In an attempt to dispel that confusion, we present here a chronological résumé of the relevant events through the spring and summer of 1950.

February 20: Senator McCarthy claims that the State Department's secret loyalty files will prove his case.

February 22: The Senate directs the Tydings Committee to "procure by subpoena and examine the complete loyalty and employment files of the Department of State" concerning persons charged with disloyalty.

March 14: Senator Hickenlooper complains of the Committee's failure to obtain the files (President Truman refused to furnish them), maintaining that it is impossible to conduct an adequate cross-examination of McCarthy's targets without access to these files. Senator Tydings states he is trying to persuade Truman to hand over the files and adds that he has not subpoenaed them because he believes that the Secretary of State, as long as the President backs him up, is legally entitled to ignore a committee subpoena of this kind. "I have in the circumstances asked for the files as a gentleman, not as a sheriff. . . ."*

March 22: Tydings appeals to President Truman to release the files.

March 28: Truman refuses to release them, arguing that their release would cause "serious prejudice to the effectiveness of the Federal Bureau of Investigation as an investigative agency," "embarrassment and danger to confidential informants," and "injustice and unfairness to innocent individuals."**

March 29: Tydings subpoenas the files of the State Department, the Justice Department, and the Civil Service Commission.

The relevant subpoenas are duly ignored, and the Committee does not attempt to exact compliance through legal process.

May 4: Truman changes his mind and announces that the loyalty files on McCarthy's cases will, after all, be made available to the Committee.

May 5: McCarthy charges that the files have been "raped," "skeletonized," "tampered with."

June 16: The Tydings Committee receives the files of 70 of the persons mentioned by Senator McCarthy in his February 20th speech. In his letter of transmission, Peyton Ford, Deputy Attorney General, informs Tydings: "The Federal Bureau of Investigation furnished me a record of *all* loyalty material furnished the State Department in these cases. The State Department files have been checked, and I can assure you that *all* of the reports and memoranda furnished the State Department are contained in the files."† (Italics added.)

June 16–25: The Tydings Committee examines the files.

June 21: Tydings announces to the press he has received a letter from Deputy Attorney General Ford assuring him that a special FBI inquiry has established the falsity of Senator McCarthy's charge that the files have been stripped. The FBI investigation, Tydings asserts, has proved: "That the files are intact, that they have not been 'raped,' 'skeletonized,' or 'tampered with' in any way, and that the material turned over to the State Department by the FBI is still in the files."‡

* *Tydings Hearings,* p. 225.
** Letter from President Truman to Senator Tydings, Mar. 28, 1950.
† Letter from Peyton Ford to Senator Tydings, June 16, 1950.
‡ *New York Times,* June 22, 1950.

June 26: Fulton Lewis, Jr., reports that Tydings' claim is not true, that the FBI has *not* made an examination of the files.

June 27: McCarthy writes J. Edgar Hoover, "I would ... greatly appreciate knowing whether or not the FBI actually has conducted any examination of the files in question and if so, whether your department has actually found the files to be complete with nothing having been removed therefrom."

July 10: Hoover replies to McCarthy, "The Federal Bureau of Investigation has made *no* such examination and therefore is *not* in the position to make *any* statement concerning the completeness or incompleteness of the State Department files." (Italics added.)

July 12: McCarthy releases the documents on which he bases his charge that the files were stripped. These documents are affidavits from four persons who had been employed by the Department on a temporary basis in the Fall of 1946 and assigned to a "file project," the purpose of which, they said, was to remove from the personnel files of Department employees all derogatory information. According to two of the affiants, some or all of the derogatory information was destroyed. A third stated he assumed that some or all of it was destroyed. The fourth individual disclaimed any first-hand knowledge as to whether the data had been destroyed or not.

July 12: The State Department answers McCarthy. His charge is "absolutely false" and "a characteristic distortion of facts." "No derogatory information concerning personnel of the Department has been destroyed. ... The so-called stripping process which Senator McCarthy attributes to evil and treacherous motives was actually a thorough-going reorganization of the Department's personnel files—not its loyalty and security files, which were and are separately maintained in a security division wholly removed from the personnel operation. ..." "To the Department's knowledge the data culled from the personnel files was not destroyed except in the case of material such as duplicate documents, routine inter-office transmittal sheets, superseded forms, etc. ..." "... A new filing system ... entailed the removal, for transfer to a more appropriate repository, of various other data not necessary to those operations, such as duplicate copies of investigation reports already in the security files [of the security division]."*

July 13–17: The FBI examines the files that had been turned over to the Tydings Committee.

July 17: Attorney General McGrath reports that "the FBI in-

* State Department press release (*Tydings Report*, pp. 171-72.)

vestigation reveals that [as of July 13] the files contain all FBI reports and memoranda furnished to the Department in these cases prior to the time they were turned over to your committee. . . ."*

June 20: The Tydings Committee, in its final report, states (a) ". . . *we have carefully and conscientiously reviewed each and every one of the loyalty files relative to the individuals charged by Senator McCarthy. . . . In no instance have we found in our considered judgments that the decision to grant loyalty and security clearance has been erroneously or improperly made in the light of existing loyalty standards;"* (b) *Senator McCarthy's charge that the files have been stripped is "distorted and false."** (Italics added.)

July 20: Senator Henry Cabot Lodge formally registers his "individual views" on the Committee's investigation, with special attention to the examination of the loyalty files. He says:

. . . After having read a representative cross section of the 81 loyalty files, the conviction was reached that *the files alone did not furnish a basis for reaching firm conclusions of any kind and that to attempt to conclude with respect to an individual case on the basis of the files alone would be a most half-baked and superficial procedure unfair alike to the government and to the employee in question. The files which I read were in such an unfinished state as to indicate that an examination of each file would be a waste of time. . . .*

There were, for example, many instances in those files which I read where hostile and serious allegations were made about the employee concerned but which, insofar as the files were concerned, were left unexplained. Where one could expect to find some rebuttal or explanation, there was nothing. For some reason the files which were prepared were inadequate from the standpoint of a senator who was trying to come to a conclusion on the basis of the files alone. *In some of the most important cases the report of the FBI full field investigation was not included.* It should be noted that the sub-committee was allowed to see the files only under such stringent limitations as to preclude our getting much essential information and as to make our work extremely cumbrous. We were not only bound and specifically forbidden from discussing any individual case by name outside of the room in the White House where we saw the files, but we were also forbidden from taking any notes from the White House. *We were categorically denied the help of technical career personnel, such as FBI men, to help in the files.* No assistance from the sub-committee's professional staff was permitted.† [Italics added.]

* Letter from J. Howard McGrath to Senator Tydings, July 17, 1950.

** *Tydings Report*, pp. 10, 170.

† *State Department Employee Loyalty Investigation*, Senator Lodge's *"Individual Views,"* pp. 19, 20.

Sept. 8: J. Edgar Hoover confirms Attorney General McGrath's July 17 report that the files given to the Tydings Committee had been checked and found intact.*

The foregoing clearly leaves a number of questions unanswered. It does not answer the question whether the loyalty files were intact at the time the Committee saw them. For, contrary to Senator Tydings' claim, the FBI had not certified that the files were complete *at the time the Committee examined them*. It could not have done so, since it did not check the files until over three weeks *after* the Committee completed its examination.

Are there grounds then, for supposing that the Tydings Committee did not in fact have access to the complete files? Certainly, in view of the affidavits on the "stripping" incident, McCarthy was justified in expressing skepticism as to the integrity of the files. On the other hand, the incident was more or less satisfactorily explained by the Department (e.g., by Mr. Carlisle Humelsine's testimony in 1953):

In answer to McCarthy's questioning about the 1946 "file project," Humelsine acknowledged that the Tydings Committee and the Department had been wrong in stating that the material the four affiants had been instructed to extract from the personnel files was not derogatory. But the purpose of the project, he stated, had been to segregate security material and place it in separate files. The waste baskets and cardboard boxes into which the material had been put were, he added, temporary receptacles in which it was to remain only until proper filing cabinets were available. If any material was destroyed, said Humelsine, it was merely to get rid of a second copy where there was duplication.**

This all seems plausible enough. But the fact remains that McCarthy's witnesses were never asked to appear before the Committee to back up and expand their affidavits. For example, it would be relevant to ask, in the light of the Department's claim that only duplicates were destroyed, whether the affiants had come across duplicates while screening out derogatory data from the personnel files. Until their affidavits are repudiated, or discredited by evidence on the other side, an element of mystery will continue to surround the 1946 "stripping" project.

But even if the files *were* raped in 1946, it is not likely that the

---

* Letter from J. Edgar Hoover to Senator Tydings, September 8, 1950.
** *Hearings, Subcommittee of Senate Committee on Appropriations, 1953,* pp. 526-28.

Tydings Committee's review was affected by such interference. For in 1947 the FBI was directed by the President's Executive Order to assist in the administration of the loyalty program. Assuming that the names of the persons whose files had been stripped were submitted to the FBI, the derogatory evidence destroyed in 1946 was presumably developed anew in 1947.

But bearing in mind that the FBI did not itself vouch for the integrity of the files until *after* the Tydings Committee had looked at them, the possibility exists that the files were incomplete when the Committee saw them. For it may be that they had been tampered with by other Department employees at other times.

That the State Department had at least been negligent in looking after its files is proved by testimony before the McCarthy Committee in 1952. For example, the testimony of Mrs. Helen B. Balog, supervisor of the Foreign Service File Room, revealed among other things:

(1) That "10 or 11" different files are kept on Department personnel, and that "three or four hundred" persons have access even to those that are highly confidential.

(2) That one such person, who had access to the confidential personnel files of the Foreign Service, spent "practically the entire year of 1949" going back and forth to the file room, and on "quite a number" of occasions worked alone in the file room at night. The person in question was John Stewart Service;

(3) That derogatory material is frequently removed from an employee's dossier before the dossier is sent up to a promotion panel "because they [personnel officials] did not want the panel's mind to be unnecessarily prejudiced against a man;"

(4) That on one occasion "in 1951 or 1952" an order had come down to burn a letter of a derogatory nature that had been a part of an employee's dossier;

(5) That documents in the file are neither numbered nor otherwise recorded; and hence it is never possible to ascertain whether material borrowed from the files has been returned, or whether documents have been filched. Mrs. Balog gave an example of what can happen. She herself, she said, had noticed a letter of recommendation filed in the dossier of a Foreign Service Officer who was later dismissed. Some time later, an FBI agent came around and asked to look at the file. Mrs. Balog went through it and noted that the letter of recommendation was missing. "And by whom was

that missing letter signed?" counsel asked. "Owen Lattimore," said Mrs. Balog.*

It is, then, not at all surprising that Senator Lodge should have said the files were in an "unfinished state," and "in some of the most important cases the report of the FBI full field investigation was not included."

Let us assume, however, that *all* the derogatory information available on the persons McCarthy had named was laid before the Tydings Committee; so that the Committee was correct in insisting it had consulted the complete files. Even then we must still recognize that the Committee had no business claiming that it had found in them a refutation of McCarthy's charges.

When he presented his report to the Senate, Senator Tydings vastly amused himself by teasing Senators Hickenlooper and Lodge for having taken, respectively, the time to read only nine and twelve of the files.** But Senator Lodge's account of the "examination" makes it clear that any study of the file was little short of futile. To expect a United States Senator to arrive at a meaningful evaluation of an employee's security credentials in the circumstances that surrounded the Committee's work is absurd. Not only were the Senators denied the aid of FBI or State Department security officials in evaluating the significance of particular data (e.g., the significance of an affiliation with a given Communist front at a given time); they were forbidden to bring along their own assistants. Not even Robert Morris, Assistant Committee Counsel and an expert in this business, was allowed to help. Any one who has seen a raw security file is aware of the difficulties faced by a layman who tries to make any sense out of it.

This is not to say, of course, that the Committee members gained from the files no *insight* into the Department's security program. Senator Hickenlooper, after reading some of the files, spoke as follows to the Department's top security official, John Peurifoy:

I am of the opinion . . . [that] the State Department as well as other departments . . . have leaned over backward . . . to protect individuals, and we have done it to the prejudice of the interests of the public. In other words our loyalty boards have held too rigidly to the "proof be-

* *Hearing, Senate Investigating Committee,* February 4, 1953, pp. 3, 5, 10, 13, 14.
** *Congressional Record,* July 20, 1950 (bound), p. 10711.

yond all reasonable doubt" theory which is the [rule] in criminal cases.
They have demanded a greater degree of proof than is often possible to
produce, and frankly in some of the departments [that] . . . are very
sensitive . . . they have kept people on where the evidence seems strong
that they are a bad security risk. Even in your own Department you
have kept them on because of the failure to be able to produce unquestioned proof of membership in the Communist Party. . . . I have read
some of these files. I haven't been able to read all of them, and *I don't
hesitate to say on this record that the ones I read I would say almost
without exception I would not keep in the State Department. I would
not have them around.** [Italics added.]

In this connection, Senator McCarthy had warned the Committee months before it looked over the files that it would be futile to
examine them without the aid of expert advice. When urging the
Committee to obtain Esther Brunauer's file, McCarthy had said,
"I might say also, I am not trying to advise the Committee but in
all sincerity, I don't think the members of the Committee will be
any more competent than I would be to go over and examine those
records personally. I think you will have to have on your staff individuals who have been in this type of work for some years, who
have taken some part in those records, so that you will be able to
get everything out of it."**

The Committee cannot itself be blamed for the regulations that
governed its examination of the files. This was the responsibility
of the Executive, acting through the Justice Department. But the
Committee's majority members *must* be blamed for having accepted the relevant regulations without protest and, most particularly, for having pretended that the examination of the files had
yielded *"proof"* that the State Department's security division was
efficient and McCarthy wrong. For example, the Committee was
not straightforward enough to point out that, for reasons that have
yet to be explained, it was given files on only 70 of McCarthy's 110
cases (all 70 of them, incidentally, Lee-list cases). The Committee
thus blandly cleared a third of McCarthy's cases without having
had even a cursory look at their files.

Among the State Department files the Tydings Committee did
obtain, and presumably study, were those of an employee *who had
been engaged in recruiting spies for the Communist underground;
of another who had been identified by FBI informants as a member of the Communist Party; of another who had been associated*

---

* Tydings Hearings, p. 1254.
** *Ibid.*, p. 86.

with members of a spy ring; and of a number of employees who were clearly unqualified, on security grounds, to work in a sensitive agency. This information was spelled out in the files (or so, at any rate, both the Committee and the State Department, in vouching for the integrity of the files, have assured us). And yet, the Tydings Committee included all these employees in its blanket finding that no one worked in the State Department whose loyalty could be questioned.

Appendix C

Statistical Breakdown of Lee List and McCarthy List

BACKGROUND AND DISPOSITION OF CASES GIVEN BY McCARTHY TO THE TYDINGS COMMITTEE

The lists of names given by Senator McCarthy to the Tydings Committee break down into three classifications: (1) Public Cases, (2) Numbered cases, (3) Non-Public and Non-Numbered cases. McCarthy's public cases are treated in detail in the text. Complete information on McCarthy's two non-public, non-numbered cases (Theodore Geiger and Oliver Edmund Clubb) is not available. There follows, therefore, a breakdown of McCarthy's numbered list alone, and also the breakdown of a comparison between the McCarthy and the Lee lists.

It will be noted that the figure 110, used in the text as representing the total number of names given by McCarthy to the Tydings Committee, is arrived at by subtracting from the public cases (9), the numbered cases (107), and the non-public and non-numbered cases (2), those cases, indicated below, which were either not identified or else duplicated (6). A final warning: two of the public cases are also numbered cases, thus bringing McCarthy's names to a total of 110.

LIST OF McCARTHY CASES THAT WERE NOT INCLUDED IN THE LEE LIST:

1. Gustavo Duran
*2. Haldore Hanson
3. Dorothy Kenyon
4. Owen Lattimore

5. Frederick Schuman
6. Harlow Shapley
*7. John Stewart Service

Total Public Non-Numbered Cases: 7†

8. Theodore Geiger

*9. Oliver Edmund Clubb

Total Non-Public Non-Numbered Cases: 2

*10. Case No. 15
11. Case No. 19

*12. Case No. 21
*13. Case No. 22

*14. Case No. 23
*15. Case No. 24
*16. Case No. 25
*17. Case No. 26
 18. Case No. 27
*19. Case No. 77
*20. Case No. 82
*21. Case No. 84
*22. Case No. 86
*23. Case No. 87
*24. Case No. 88
*25. Case No. 90

*26. Case No. 91
*27. Case No. 92
*28. Case No. 93
 29. Case No. 94
*30. Case No. 95
*31. Case No. 96
*32. Case No. 97
*33. Case No. 98
*34. Case No. 102
 35. Case No. 103
 36. Case No. 106
*37. Case No. 107

Total Numbered Cases: 28

Total non-Lee Cases: 37

* Working for the State Department at the time the Tydings Committee met.
† (Philip Jessup is a numbered non-Lee case; Esther Brunauer is a numbered case and also a Lee case.)

McCarthy's Numbered Cases

59 Individuals on McCarthy's List were employed by the State Department as of February 20, 1950

6 had been cleared under Executive Order 9835 before February 20, 1950, and were not being reprocessed in June, 1951: (Cases 38, 89, 93, 95,* 98, 107.)

19 were cleared under Executive Order 9835 between February, 1950, and June, 1951: (Cases 21, 22, 25, 26, 31, 36,* 43, 51,* 58, 60,* 63, 64, 68,* 79, 82,* 86, 91, 100.)

26 were being investigated under Executive Order 9835 as of June, 1951: (Cases 1, 2,* 6, 7,* 15,* 23, 24,* 32, 34,* 37,* 40,* 41, 46,* 47,* 48, 49, 50, 52, 54, 55, 56, 59,* 70, 84, 85, 102.)

7 had never been investigated under Executive Order 9835 as of June, 1951: (Cases 83, 87, 88, 90, 92, 96,* 97.)

1 resigned in December, 1950, while investigation under Executive Order 9835 was pending (Case 77.*)

———
Total 59

* Not in the State Department as of the 1st of January, 1953.

Employment dates of those who were no longer with the State Department in January, 1953

Case		Case	
2	4/24	47	3/44
7	9/45	51	8/43
15	4/47	59	9/45
24	3/49	60	9/45
34	8/45	68	6/46
36	8/45	77	10/45
37	12/48	82	45(?)
40	11/45	95	45(?)
46	11/45	96	45(?)

48 Individuals on McCarthy's List were not working for State Department as of February 20, 1950

35 had previously been employed by the State Department.

> 11 resigned or were terminated before December, 1947. (Cases 9, 12, 16, 17, 44, 47, 66, 67, 75, 99, 103.)

> 24 resigned or were terminated after December, 1947. (Cases 3, 4, 5, 8, 10, 11, 13, 14, 18, 27, 30, 35, 39, 45, 53, 57, 61, 62, 69, 71, 73, 74, 81, 94.)

> Of the 24

>> 14 had never been investigated under Executive Order 9835. (Cases 3, 4, 5, 10, 11, 14, 18, 30, 35, 57, 71, 73, 74, 94.)

>> 5 had been cleared under Executive Order 9835. (Cases 8, 13, 27, 45, 61.)

>> 4 resigned while security investigations were pending. (Cases 39, 53, 62, 69.)

> (Data on Case 81 unavailable.)

6 had applied for work with the State Department. (Cases 20, 28, 29, 72,* 78, 101.)

> 5 secured other government posts. (Cases 78, 101 [Treasury], 29 [Public Health], 28 [Commerce], 72 [Army].)

---

* No. 72 was singled out in McCarthy's speech as an *anti-Communist* who was unfairly discriminated against by the Department when he applied for work.

   1 worked for the Department of Commerce. (Case 19.)

Data on Case 106 unavailable.

   2 never fully identified. (Cases 76, 104.)**

   3 were duplications. (Cases 22 and 105; 80 and 85; 65 and 89.)

Total 48

** Civil Service Commission has no record of the two persons involved having had federal employment.

Appendix D

List of Persons Accused by McCarthy

(The following—as complete a list as the authors have been able to compile—are persons whose loyalty McCarthy has, in however remote a way, challenged. The period covered is from February 9, 1950, to January 1, 1953. On the left we quote those of McCarthy's statements that have been made on the floor of the Senate, which immunizes him. On the right we list the statements made off the floor, which are, of course, immunized only when he repeats testimony originally heard under the cloak of immunity. We have selected those of McCarthy's characterizations that are the most derogatory, thus those that make out the strongest case for the charge that he is a "reckless smearer."

ROBERT WARREN BARNETT

"The letter of charges against the Barnetts—both Robert Warren Barnett and his wife, Mrs. Robert Warren Barnett—charges them with close association and constant contact with known Soviet espionage activity." (*Congressional Record*, p. 9707, Aug. 9, 1951.)

ESTHER BRUNAUER

"At that time I pointed out that one Esther Caukin Brunauer, who was holding a top job in the State Department, I pointed out that the evidence showed that her husband had been a member of the Communist Party and was active therein, that she belonged to a number of Communist-front organizations, and that she was one of Alger Hiss' assistants at San Francisco.

"Incidentally, her assistance to Hiss has since been denied by

"Another case was Esther Brunauer, a $10,000 a year State Department official. She also belonged to a sizeable number of organizations named as fronts for the Communist Party. For example, she was chairman of a meeting of the American Friends of the Soviet Union, [at] which the principal speaker was a well known Communist and a frequent writer for the official Communist Daily Worker. Brunauer was a signer of the call to the annual

her, but on page 419 of this State Department publication we find that Brunauer was one of the assistants of Hiss.

"Incidentally, as a member of Unesco she has been able to travel rather freely to other capitals of the world. The evidence shows contacts in those capitals with members of Communist delegations." (*Congressional Record*, May 8, 1951 p. 5058.)

meeting of the American Youth Congress which was publicly known to be completely dominated by the Communist Party. She admitted that her husband had Communist connections and had been a member of the Young Communist League." (Wisc. Retail Ford Dealers Assoc., Milwaukee, Aug. 6, 1950.)

STEPHEN BRUNAUER

"For example, his very good friend, Noel Field, a known Communist and espionage agent, spent night after night with Stephen Brunauer, who had access to all the top secrets in the explosive section of our Navy. Field then left the country, and has since disappeared behind the iron curtain, taking with him all information which his friend Brunauer had given him. . . . What forced the Navy to take action was that it appeared during the atom-spy investigations that Stephen Brunauer was involved." (*Congressional Record*, May 8, 1951, p. 5058.)

"Brunauer, an admitted former member of the Young Communist League, was suspended from his job as head of the Navy's high explosives section where he was engaged in top secret work. He resigned before the Navy's Loyalty Board could complete questioning him and dispose of his case." (*McCarthyism*, p. 13.)

GERTRUDE CAMERON

(Miss Cameron was named by McCarthy on the Senate floor, August 9, 1951, as having been one of the persons whose name he had given to the Tydings Committee a year earlier. McCarthy pointed out that Miss Cameron was currently in loyalty-security channels in the Department, but he gave no particulars against her.)

NELSON CHIPCHIN

(Mr. Chipchin was named by McCarthy on the Senate floor, August 9, 1951, as having been one of the persons whose name he had given to the Tydings Committee a year earlier. McCarthy pointed out that Mr. Chipchin was currently in loyalty-security channels in the Department, but he gave no particulars against him.)

LAUCHLIN CURRIE

"The Stilwell-Davies group took over in China in 1942. Soon thereafter, Lauchlin, at the White House, and John Carter Vincent, and subsequently Alger Hiss at the State Department were exercising their influence at the Washington end of the transmission belt conveying poisonous misinformation from Chungking. The full outlines of Currie's betrayal have yet to be traced.

. . . In this connection it should be recalled that Currie issued an order on White House stationery depriving the Republic of China of 20,000 German rifles." (*Congressional Record,* June 14, 1951, p. 6574.)

"Just turn back a page of history to 1945. This Lauchlin Currie was administrative assistant to the President. This is the same Lauchlin Currie who has been named under oath by Elizabeth Bentley as the man who tipped off her Russian espionage agents that we were about to break the Japanese Code. . . . This is the same Lauchlin Currie whose picture I hold in my hand, with a picture of Harry Dexter White, John Abt, and Alger Hiss—all named under oath repeatedly as Communists. . . ."

"At that time Lauchlin Currie was Administrative Assistant to the President. The Joint Chiefs of Staff approved sending vast amounts of German captured arms to those fighting Communism in China. After the Joint Chiefs of Staff and Eisenhower had approved the shipment—after vast quantities had left German ports destined for our allies in China—Lauchlin Currie, Truman's administrative Assistant, the man named by Bentley and Chambers, signed an order on White House stationery ordering that all this

military equipment be destroyed."
(Columbia County Republican
Club, Portage, Wisc., Sept. 9,
1950.)

JOHN PATON DAVIES

"Incidentally, since I wrote the State Department, Davies has been cleared, despite the vast amount of information on his communistic activities." (*Congressional Record*, p. 9708, Aug. 9, 1951.)

"Davies has been suitably rewarded by Dean Acheson for his sell-out of an ally. Davies serves in Washington as a member of the State Department's Policy Planning Committee, where he is strategically placed to help further the betrayal he began in Chungking." (*Congressional Record*, June 14, 1951, p. 6574.)

"John P. Davies, who was accused by General Hurley of operating behind his back to support the Communists and who, in his official reports to the State Department, adopted the thinking of Agnes Smedley, a known Communist agent, whom he described as one of the 'pure in heart' in China."

"In their recommendations to Washington both [Davies and Service] followed the Communist Party line." (*McCarthyism*, pp. 33, 35.)

GUSTAVO DURAN

"Now let us see what happens when individuals with Communist connections are forced out of the Department. Gustavo Duran who was labeled (I quote) 'a notorious international Communist' was made assistant to the Assistant Secretary of State in charge of Latin American affairs. He was taken into the State Department from his job as a lieutenant colonel in the Communist International Brigade. Finally, after intense congressional pressure and criticism, he resigned in 1946 from the State Department—and ladies and gentlemen, where do you think he is now? He took over a high-salaried job as Chief of Cultural Activities Section in the office of the Assistant Secretary

"I presented to the Committee the complete Army Intelligence report showing that he was active in secret Communist operations in Europe and that he was regional head of S. I. M. a counterpart of the Russian Secret police." (Isaac Walton League, Fond du Lac, Wisc., July 30, 1950.)

General of the U. N." (*Congressional Record,* Feb. 20, 1950, p. 1956.)

ARPAD ERDOS

(Mr. Erdos was named by McCarthy on the Senate floor, August 9, 1951, as having been one of the persons whose name he had given to the Tydings Committee a year earlier. McCarthy pointed out that Mr. Erdos was currently in loyalty-security channels in the Department but he gave no particulars against him.)

HERBERT FIERST

"A memorandum of August 2, 1946 by Mr. Bannerman, one of the security officers in the Department of State, is to the effect that physical surveillance showed that this man Fierst was in constant contact with members of an espionage group and that he recommended Communists for State Department employment, and was engaged in a number of other Communist activities." (*Congressional Record,* p. 9707, Aug. 9, 1951.)

JOHN TIPTON FISHBURN

(Mr. Fishburn was named by McCarthy on the Senate floor, August 9, 1951, as having been one of the persons whose name he had given to the Tydings Committee a year earlier. McCarthy pointed out that Mr. Fishburn was currently in loyalty-security channels in the Department but he gave no particulars against him.)

THEODORE GEIGER

"I may say for the Senator's benefit, in connection with Mr. Geiger, that the day the President made the statement that there were no Communists in the Government, we received a telephone call from one of the men who served in the same Communist cell as Mr. Geiger. . . . He [Mr. Robert Morris] developed, I think, either 3 or 4 witnesses who were in Mr. Geiger's Communist cell. They said 'We will come down and testify before the Committee as to Geiger's Communist activities.'" (*Congressional Record*, p. 1091, July 25, 1950.)

" 'There is a case of a man named Theodore Geiger. He has been an employee of the State Department. He is now one of Paul Hoffman's top assistants. He is doing work that is quasi-State Department in character. I [Mr. Robert Morris] have gone and gotten some witnesses together who will testify that he was a member of the same Communist Party unit as they were, and I think we would be delinquent if in the face of this evidence that is now on record . . .'" (Quoted from *Tydings Committee Hearings* in *McCarthyism*, p. 74.)

HAROLD GLASSER

"Another of the men whom Acheson refused to turn his back upon was Harold Glasser. Glasser also was named under oath by a government witness as a Communist." (*McCarthyism*, p. 31; citation: *Congressional Record* [unbound], Dec. 6, 1950, p. 16336.)

STELLA GORDON

(Miss Gordon was named by McCarthy on the Senate floor, August 9, 1951, as having been one of the persons whose name he had given to the Tydings Committee a year earlier. McCarthy pointed out that Miss Gordon was currently in loyalty-security channels in the Department but he gave no particulars against her.)

Haldore Hanson

"Is the Senator also aware of the fact that Haldore Hanson, who as I say was running a Communist paper in Peiping, China, some 15 years ago, and today is the head of the technical staff on planning for Point 4, and that Budenz testified that Hanson is one of the men who is considered to be among the top Communists in the country— so much so that Budenz said he carried Hanson's name around with him. Is the Senator aware of that fact?" (*Congressional Record*, May 24, 1950, p. 7599.)

"Here is a man who worked on the Communist edition of a magazine; who praised Communists; who was co-editor of a Communist paper in China; who was named by a Government witness under oath as a member of the Communist Party." (Izaak Walton League, Fond du Lac, Wisc., July 30, 1950.)

Ruth Marcia Harrison

"I will not read all the charges. One is that she belonged to a vast number of Communist fronts, plus a Communist organization; that she belonged to the Young Communist League, was a paid-up member of it." (*Congressional Record*, Aug. 9, 1951, p. 9707.)

Myron Victor Hunt

(Mr. Hunt was named by McCarthy on the Senate floor, August 9, 1951, as having been one of the persons whose name he had given to the Tydings Committee a year earlier. McCarthy pointed out that Mr. Hunt was currently in loyalty-security channels in the Department but he gave no particulars against him.)

Philip C. Jessup

"Prof. Jessup must therefore be credited by the American people

"I would like to discuss with you the case of one of the individuals

with having pioneered the smear campaign against China and Chiang Kai-Shek, and with being the originator of the myth of the (democratic) Chinese Communists.

"From that time onward we witnessed the spectacle of this three-horse team of smears and untruths thundering down the stretch—Jessup's publications, *Far Eastern Survey*, the *Daily Worker*, and *Isvestia*. What an effective job they did can best be demonstrated by the fact that this was the line which the State Department followed in formulating its far-eastern policy, right down to the last comma. . . .

"In this connection it should be noted that Dr. Jessup was also quite a joiner. Perhaps he was also a dupe in this respect, but it is rather significant that the only organizations that he so prolifically joined were Communist-front organizations. . . .

"I personally have stated that I thought that Jessup was a well-meaning dupe of the Lattimore crowd. However, I do not think the decision on that point is up to me; but rather, it is up to the Congress and the American people. . . .

"One can understand a person standing by his friend on a private basis; but Dr. Jessup, as Ambassador-at-large, represents the American people. He is supposed to be aware of the dangerous tactic of infiltration as practiced by Stalin's police state. To put it mildly, Jessup's reaction to gross disloyalty seems obtuse. He can say without qualification and as a most important public official, that he can see no reason whatever to change his opinion about Hiss'

whom I consider most dangerous to this country. As I said before, when I gave this on the Senate floor, they shouted, McCarthy you gave this under Senatorial immunity. I am talking about Philip C. Jessup, the Ambassador-at-large. . . . He has not only a great affinity for Communist causes, he has a great affinity for Communist employees, Communist friends, Communist-money supported publications, and a great affinity for Communist public supported organizations." (New York City, Veterans of Foreign Wars, Aug. 30, 1951.)

"Whether or not Mr. Jessup was a dupe, don't think for a moment that the Communists did not know what they were buying when they paid thousands of dollars to enable his publication to act as the lead horse in that 3-horse team which so effectively convinced a sizeable number of individuals in the State Department and a great mass of honest, sincere, loyal Americans that the Communists in China were not Communists at all and that Chiang Kai-shek represented everything that was evil." (Washington, D. C., American Newspaper Editors Society, April 20, 1950.)

veracity, loyalty, and integrity, even though an American jury has convicted him of perjury and what amounts to far-reaching espionage on damaging evidence which satisfied the jury and a Federal judge that Hiss beyond reasonable doubt, has proved to be an underground Communist agent.

"This is in the very best Acheson tradition of 'not turning one's back' on treason." (*Congressional Record*, March 30, 1950, pp. 4402-4.)

Mary Jane Keeney

"Then there was a Mrs. Mary Jane Keeney from the Board of Economic Warfare in the State Department, who was named in a F.B.I. report and a House Committee report as a courier for the Communist Party while working for the Government. And where do you think Mrs. Keeney is—she is now an editor in the U.N. Documents Bureau." (Speech to Ohio County Women's Republican Club, Wheeling, West Virginia; read into the *Congressional Record*, February 20, 1950, p. 1956.)

Dorothy Kenyon

"I took a typical case in order to show just what it meant to be cleared by the Loyalty Board. It was a case in which the Board had documentation with respect to 28 organizations which had been declared to be Communist-front organizations. They had not been declared Communist-front organizations by McCarthy, but they had been declared Communist-front organizations by the Attorney General, the House Un-American

"As you know, the first case presented to the Committee was of one Judge Dorothy Kenyon. The case consisted of photostatic documents showing membership in and sponsorship of 28 Communist-front organizations, named as such not by me, but by the Attorney General, or Congressional Committees. I erred. Judge Kenyon's files show membership in exactly 52 organizations of this type—not 28—but at the time I had obtained

Activities Committee, the California Committee, the Coudert Committee. I presented her case to the Committee to show that 28, according to our exhibits, showed her name, and showed that she was a sponsor of the organizations. The Committee did not even go through the motions of calling her and asking her 'Judge, why did you join? Were you a dupe, or did you join purposely?' That was the importance of the Kenyon case. (*Congressional Record,* p. 4380-81, Mar. 30, 1950.)

"Here again we have this prominent State Department official, Judge Kenyon, crying aloud in anguish for a fellow red." (*Tydings Hearings,* p. 68.)

photostatic proof of only 28 instances. . . .

"The State Department's Loyalty Board, however, never once questioned Judge Kenyon personally or by mail, regarding her penchant for fronts. Nor have her views regarding the conviction of Alger Hiss been entertained [investigated?] by the State Department as an obvious indication of how she thinks." (American Newspaper Editors Society, Washington, D. C., April 20, 1950.)

Leon Keyserling

"The evidence before the McCarran committee is to the effect—that evidence has not yet been made public, and I hesitate to make it public except that I think the Senate should have the information at this time—the sworn evidence before the McCarran Committee is to the effect that Leon Keyserling had been approached and asked to join the Communist Party. At the time he said he agreed with all the principles of the party except that he would not agree on the necessity for a so-called "black belt" or Negro republic in the South. He would not agree with the Communist Party on that point. I am referring now to the sworn testimony before the Board. He also disagreed with the Communist Party's theory that the United States could be communized only through a bloody revolution." (*Congressional Record,* April 21, 1952, p. 4153.)

Mrs. Leon Keyserling

"The evidence presented to the Board [Commerce Department's Loyalty Board] shows that Mrs. Mary Dublin Keyserling had been a member of the Communist Party and that she belonged to an unlimited number of Communist fronts." (*Congressional Record,* April 21, 1952, p. 4153.)

Owen Lattimore

"Subsequently, in executive session, I told the subcommittee, that I thought this man was one of the top Communist agents in this country. Today, I intend to give the Senate some documentation to show that he is a Soviet agent and also that he either is, or at least has been a member of the Communist Party. . . .

"He is undoubtedly the most brilliant and scholarly of all the Communist propagandists, and also the most subtle of the evangelists who have deceived the American people about the Chinese Communists. . . .

"Thus we have the picture of Lattimore using his high office in the O.W.I. to spread the Communist line for China thru a Chinese Communist whose son now awaits being seated as a representative of the Chinese Communists in the U.N.; and it is important to point out that Lattimore's maneuver was based upon fraud and misrepresentation in his intended decep-

"Budenz testified he attended Communist Politburo meetings of the Communist Party and that at one of those meetings a Party line change was transmitted from Moscow to the Politburo from Owen Lattimore via Frederick Vanderbilt Field.

"Budenz testified unequivocally that his official information was that Lattimore was a member of the Party and that one of the tasks assigned to Lattimore was to recruit Communist and fellow-traveler writers to sell to the American people and to the State Department the Communist Party line on China.

"Budenz further testified that Lattimore was a member of a Red cell in the Institute of Pacific Relations—the job of which was to sell the Communist line on China.

"Budenz testified that top secret instructions which went out to Communist leaders throughout the country were seen by him and that they bore Lattimore's Party identi-

tion of his superior." (*Congressional Record*, March 30, 1950, pp. 4374-75, 4385-86.)

fication symbol 'XL'" (Republican Rally, Wauwatosa, Wisc., Sept. 14, 1950.)

PAUL LEFANTIEFF-LEE

"His file in the Navy Department, which was transmitted to the State Department, shows that he took secret State Department documents, which were found in his room and picked up by naval intelligence. That is shown by the naval intelligence report." (*Congressional Record*, Aug. 9, 1951, p. 9708.)

ESTHER LESS
(also known as Esther Less Kopelewich)

(Miss Less was named by McCarthy on the Senate floor, August 9, 1951, as having been one of the persons whose name he had given to the Tydings Committee a year earlier. McCarthy pointed out that Miss Less was currently in loyalty-security channels in the Department but he gave no particulars against her.)

DAVID DEMAREST LLOYD

". . . another individual whom I discussed last year because of his communistic activities—a man who was then on the payroll of the Defense Establishment, but loaned to the President and working in the White House. Since then this individual has been promoted to a $17,500-a-year job. I believe that his correct title is Administrative Assistant to the President. In view of his promotion to a job of considerable power in the White House, I felt in duty-bound called upon to give the Senate some further picture of this man, David Demarest Lloyd." (*Congressional Record,* Jan. 15, 1952, p. 193.)

VAL LORWIN

"I understand that two of the individuals [from a list McCarthy had read to the Senate] were suspended [pending adjudication of loyalty and security charges].They are ... and Val Lorwin. (*Congressional Record,* August 9, 1951, p. 9708.)

"Lorwin was suspended under the State Department's Loyalty Program (according to a letter received from the Chairman of the Civil Service Loyalty Review Board in June, 1951)." (*McCarthyism,* p. 13.)

DANIEL F. MARGOLIES

"Originally the appointment of this man was disapproved on the ground that he was a bad loyalty and security risk. He was hired anyway." (*Congressional Record,* August 9, 1951, p. 9707.)

PEVERIL MEIGS

"The next case is that of Peveril Meigs. Meigs was No. 3 on my list. He was not No. 3 in order of importance but merely accidentally No. 3 on the list. He was allowed to resign from his job with the State Department with a clear record. The State Department made no notation on his record to the effect that he was under investigation. He got a job in the Military Establishment. The Army loyalty board called hearings on Meigs and he was ordered discharged from the Army." (*Congressional Record,* May 26, 1952, p. 5963.)

"On February 20, I believe, I laid before the Senate the case of Peveril Meigs. The State Department held a hearing. They knew

"Meigs was allowed to resign from the State Department with a clear record. He then obtained a job with the Military Establishment. He was discharged from that job under the Loyalty Program." (*McCarthyism,* p. 13.)

that they could not conceivably clear Peveril Meigs, even with the type of Board which they have. What did they do? They notified him that he would not be cleared, so he then resigned, went over to the Army and got a job in the Army, with no notification to the Army that this man was an extremely bad security risk because of close association with espionage agents. It was only after we called the Army's attention to the case that the Army Loyalty Board took the case up, and of course, they promptly ordered him discharged." (*Congressional Record,* January 15, 1952, p. 192.)

Ella M. Montague

"She worked for the Amtorg Trading Corp. The testimony before three different committees is that only top members of the Communist Party could work for Amtorg." (*Congressional Record,* August 9, 1951, p. 9707.)

Philleo Nash

"As to the matter developed by the FBI there are nine principal points:

"1. That Philleo Nash, the President's adviser, had been in close contact with the Communist underground in Washington.

"2. That he had been a close friend and a close associate of one of the convicted Canadian Communists.

"3. We shall skip that one; some of these Mr. President, I think should not go into the *Record.*

"4. Also omitted.

"5. That he has financially contributed to the support of the Canadian *Tribune,* the official organ of the Communist Party in Canada.

"6. That during the early forties parts of the Communist spy ring in Canada were using his home in Toronto as a point of rendezvous, and some of them were living there.

"7 & 8. I believe we had better skip.

"9. That Philleo Nash in the early forties was attending Communist meetings and had officially joined the Communist Party." (*Congressional Record,* Jan. 29, 1952, p. 581.)

Franz Leopold Neumann

(Mr. Neumann was named by McCarthy on the Senate floor, August 9, 1951, as having been one of the persons whose name he had given to the Tydings Committee a year earlier. McCarthy pointed out that Mr. Neumann was currently in loyalty-security channels in the Department but he gave no particulars against him.)

Olga V. Osnatch

"She worked for the Russian Embassy in Turkey for 3 years. Then with the Russian Welfare Society and so forth. One of the significant things here, of course, is that the Russians do not hire people in their embassies unless they are Communists." (*Congressional Record,* Aug. 9, 1951, p. 9707.)

Edward G. Posniak

"An FBI agent who joined the Communist Party at the request of the Bureau in 1937 and was ex-

"In 1948 Letters of Charges were filed against Posniak after the reports of 9 FBI investigators were

pelled from the Communist Party in 1948 and whose record as an informant was one of complete reliability, stated that [Posniak] . . . was a member of the Communist Party and personally known to him as such. . . . " (*Congressional Record*, July 25, 1950, p. 10928.)

(McCarthy did not reveal Posniak's name when he synthesized the FBI report; Senator Wayne Morse, however, who had knowledge of the matter, immediately identified the man McCarthy was speaking of as Edward Posniak.)

presented to the State Department. . . .

"At the time of the hearing he was cleared by a 2 to 1 vote of the State Department loyalty panel. After I gave the Senate a résumé of the 9 FBI reports on Posniak, his loyalty-security case reopened and he was allowed to resign while his case was pending. He has since been before a federal grand jury, but as far as is known at the time this is written, no action has been taken on his case." (*McCarthyism*, p. 29.)

PHILIP RAINE

"He is tied up, in the letter of charges, very closely with Robert T. Miller, who has been identified under oath several times as a Russian espionage agent." (*Congressional Record*, August 9, 1951, p. 9708.)

WILLIAM REMINGTON

"I stated to them [the Tydings Committee] that they would find in his file the statements of men who were in the Communist movement with him, showing that he also was a member of the Communist Party." (*Congressional Record*, July 25, 1950, p. 10913.)

"Remington was convicted in connection with his membership in the Communist Party and sentenced to 5 yrs. Evidence presented at his trial showed that he had supplied secret government documents to a Soviet courier." (*McCarthyism*, p. 13.)

ROBERT ROSS

(Mr. Ross was named by McCarthy on the Senate floor, August 9, 1951, as having been one of the persons whose name he had given to the Tydings Committee a year earlier. McCarthy pointed out that Mr. Ross was currently in loyalty-security channels in the Department but he gave no particulars against him.)

SYLVIA SCHIMMEL

(Miss Schimmel was named by McCarthy on the Senate floor, August 9, 1951, as having been one of the persons whose name he had given to the Tydings Committee a year earlier. McCarthy pointed out that Miss Schimmel was currently in loyalty-security channels in the Department but he gave no particulars against her.)

FREDERICK SCHUMAN

"Was the Senator aware at the time he cleared Frederick Schuman that Frederick Schuman had belonged to 35 organizations which had been officially labeled either by the Attorney General or by a Congressional Committee as front-supported organizations doing the work of the Communist Party?" (*Congressional Record,* Dec. 19, 1950, p. 16747.)

"Another is Dr. Frederick Schuman whose job was to lecture and train State Department employees who were to be placed in Communist trouble spots.

"He was associated with a vast number of organizations officially listed as fronts for and doing the foul work for the Communist Party. For example he was a member of the American Council on Soviet Relations, the American Russian Institute, Civil Rights Congress, the Friends of the Soviet Union, and on and on. He also headed up a campaign for Wallace for President." (Izaak Walton League, Fond du Lac, Wisc., July 30, 1950.)

JOHN STEWART SERVICE

" . . . the same John Service who in 1944, according to General Patrick Hurley's papers, advocated that we torpedo Chiang Kai-shek, and who officially as a representative of the State Department said that the only hope of Asia was Communism. The same John Serv-

"Service was named by our Ambassador to China as one of the men who was serving the cause of Communism in China. He asked the President to remove Service. He said that this man's actions are not good for the United States, they are good for Russia. While in

ice was later picked up by the FBI on charges of espionage." (*Congressional Record,* Jan. 5, 1950, p. 1973.)

China, Service, in secret recommendations to the State Department, urged that the Communists were the only hope of China. Later Service, and five others were picked up by the FBI. . . . Among other things, the FBI produced microphone recordings from a hotel room which showed that Service had turned over to a known Communist, not only State Department documents, but also secret military information." (Speech in Baltimore, Md., Sept. 15, 1950.)

HARLOW SHAPLEY

"I pointed out to the Senate that Shapley had headed up this outfit that the State Department called a tool of Russia and a sounding board for Communist propaganda." (*Congressional Record,* Feb. 20, 1950, p. 1973.)

"Shapley was Chairman of a conference held in New York in March, 1949, which President Truman denounced as a tool of Russia and a sounding board for Communist propaganda. But what does Acheson do? He rewards Shapley, the Chairman of the Conference which Truman called a tool of Russia, by giving him an appointment to represent the State Department on a U.N. Commission—paid for, of course, largely out of your pockets. The list of Communist-front organizations to which he belonged is legion." (Isaac Walton League, Fond du Lac, Wisc., July 30, 1950.)

WILLIAM T. STONE

"Stone's Communist activities are legion, and I will not attempt to describe all of them. It is of some interest to note that he was one of the co-editors of *Amerasia. Amerasia* has been described by the FBI as a 'tool of Soviet espionage.'" (*Congressional Record,* Aug. 9, 1951, p. 9706.)

"Another typical case of State Department 'clearance' is that of William T. Stone. On March 22, 1946, the State Department Security Office made the following recommendation on Stone:
" 'In behalf of the above-mentioned, it is recommended that action be instituted to terminate his services with the State Department immediately. It is suggested,

to achieve this purpose, that an appropriate officer of the Department should inform Mr. Stone that his continued employment in the Department is embarrassing to the Department and he should be given an opportunity to resign. If he should not resign voluntarily, action should be immediately instituted under Civil Service Rule No. 3 to terminate his service with the Department.'" (*McCarthyism,* p. 30, quoting Third Supplemental Appropriation Bill 1951, Senate Appropriations Committee, April 17, 1951, p. 408.)

FRANCES M. TUCHSER

(Miss Tuchser was named by McCarthy on the Senate floor, August 9, 1951, as having been one of the persons whose name he had given to the Tydings Committee a year earlier. McCarthy pointed out that Miss Tuchser was currently in loyalty-security channels in the Department but he gave no particulars against her.)

JOHN CARTER VINCENT

"Vincent is charged with being a member of the Communist Party, and to the best of my knowledge he is also charged with espionage activities while in Switzerland." (*Congressional Record,* Aug. 9, 1951, p. 9706.)

"John Carter Vincent, State Department official repeatedly accused in Congress of pro-Communist operations. . . .

"John Carter Vincent, who has been named under oath as a member of the Communist Party."

"In 1944 Lattimore and John Carter Vincent (named by a government witness under oath as a Communist), upon the recommendation of Lauchlin Currie (named under oath as a member of a Communist spy ring), accompanied Vice President Henry Wallace on a tour of China." (*McCarthyism,* pp. 30, 33, 62.)

Appendix E

Press Coverage Given to McCarthy's Nine Public Cases

DOROTHY KENYON

St. Louis Post-Dispatch

Mar. 8, p. 1. "McCarthy Names Woman in State Dept. Red Inquiry"

Mar. 14, p. 1. "McCarthy's Red Charges Denied by Judge Kenyon" 2 columns (hereafter referred to as cols.) This story includes McCarthy's accusations against Shapley, Duran, and Service on p. 6A.

Mar. 9, p. 4A. quotes from Kenyon telegram to Tydings Committee calling McCarthy's charges "outrageous and maliciously false."

New York Times

Mar. 9, p. 1. "McCarthy Says Miss Kenyon Helped 28 Red Front Groups," over 2 cols.

Mar. 15, p. 1. "Miss Kenyon Cites Patriotic Record to Refute Charges" (Reply about equally prominent), approx. 3 cols.

San Francisco Chronicle

Mar. 9, pp. 1, 7. "McCarthy's Spy Hunt—Senator Accuses Dorothy Kenyon Ex-UN Delegate," 1 col. Jessup named in same story but less conspicuously; much space devoted to Kenyon denial.

Mar. 15, p. 7. "Outrageous Charges," ½ col.

Des Moines Register

Mar. 9, pp. 1, 6. Kenyon mentioned very inconspicuously under headline "Wrangling by Senate Group Delays Probe—Tydings Tries to Put McCarthy on Spot," 2½ cols.

Mar. 15, p. 8. "Dorothy Kenyon is 'Not Disloyal' says Hickenlooper after Hearing," over 1 col. of Kenyon reply.

Washington Post

Mar. 9, pp. 1, 5. "Ex-Judge Hurls Lie at McCarthy's Red Charge," 3-col. story.

Mar. 15, pp. 1, 2. "Miss Kenyon Denies Red Link Before Senate Unit," 2 cols.; picture of Kenyon on front page.

HALDORE HANSON

St. Louis Post-Dispatch

Mar. 13, pp. 1, 6. Accusation and Hanson press statement.

Mar. 28, pp. 1, 6A. Hanson denial—not headlined.

New York Times

Mar. 14, pp. 1, 4. "McCarthy Accuses Point Four Official," over 2 cols.

Mar. 29, p. 3. "McCarthy Is Dared To Drop Immunity—Hanson Testifies He Will Sue for Libel if Accuser Makes Charge Outside Congress," 2-col. story and picture.

San Francisco Chronicle

Mar. 14, pp. 1, 8. "Disloyalty Hearing—Senator McCarthy Names 3 More Communists," over 1 col.

Mar. 29, p. 5. "McCarthy Challenged—Hanson Calls on Senator to Repeat His Charges Without Immunity," over 1 col. large headlines.

Des Moines Register

Mar. 14. Hanson not mentioned at all; only Brunauer and Lattimore. No coverage of his reply either.

Washington Post

Mar. 14, pp. 1, 3. Hanson mentioned under headline "McCarthy Adds Four, Including Lattimore to Pro-Red Roster," 3-col. story.

Mar. 29, p. 2. "McCarthy Juggled Facts, Hanson Says," 1 col.; large headline; picture of Hanson.

ESTHER BRUNAUER

St. Louis Post-Dispatch

Mar. 13, p. 1. Same story as Kenyon reply.

Mar. 28, p. 6A. "angrily denied McCarthy's accusations," same story as Hanson denial.

New York Times

Mar. 14, p. 4. Same story as Hanson; less prominent.

Mar. 28, p. 3. "Red Leaning Denied by Mrs. Brunauer," over 2 cols.

San Francisco Chronicle

Mar. 14, p. 8. not named until tag-end of Lattimore-Hanson story. Separate headline, p. 8., short story "Woman Denies Charge by McCarthy." No coverage of Brunauer's reply of the 27th.

Des Moines Register

Mar. 14, p. 7. no story; only picture and caption.

Mar. 28, p. 9. Brief reporting of Brunauer's testimony.

Washington Post

Mar. 14, pp. 1, 3. "McCarthy Adds Four, Including Lattimore to Pro-Red Roster," 3-col. story.

Mar. 28, pp. 1, 2. "Mrs. Brunauer Hits Charges; Reveals Threats to Family"; bottom of page; over 1 col.

PHILIP JESSUP

St. Louis Post-Dispatch

Mar. 8, p. 9A. Jessup named inconspicuously in continuation of Kenyon story.

Mar. 20, pp. 1, 6. Large headline: "Jessup Accuses McCarthy of Shocking Disregard for Interests of Our Country." Very prominent 3-col. story with lengthy quotes from Jessup's statement.

New York Times

Mar. 9, p. 1. Less prominently named in same story as Kenyon: over 2 cols.

Mar. 16, p. 20. Short item: "Jessup Calls Charges Baseless."

Mar. 21, p. 1. "Jessup Denounces McCarthy Charges as Danger to U.S." 3½ col. story but mostly in continuation on p. 25. Supporting letters from Marshall and Eisenhower quoted in full.

San Francisco Chronicle

Mar. 9, pp. 1, 7. named less conspicuously in same story as Kenyon accusation.

Mar. 21, p. 1. "Criticism of State Dept.—Marshall 'Shocked' by Attack on Envoy Jessup; Truman Backs up Acheson," 1 col.

Mar. 21, p. 7. "Charges 'In Effect' Aid Communism—Jessup Counterattacks, Accuses McCarthy," over 1 col.

Des Moines Register

Jessup accusation not mentioned.

Mar. 21, pp. 1, 6. Large page-width headline "Marshall, Ike Back Jessup," 2-col. story.

Washington Post

Mar. 9, p. 5. inconspicuously reported accusation in Kenyon story.

Mar. 21, pp. 1, 5. "Jessup Lashes Sharply at McCarthy," 2 cols.; picture; texts of letters backing Jessup quoted separately on front page.

OWEN LATTIMORE

St. Louis Post-Dispatch

Mar. 13, p. 1. about 1 col. including Brunauer and Hanson accusations.

Mar. 27, pp. 1, 2A. "Moonshine, Is Lattimore Reply to McCarthy Charge He Is Red Spy in State Dept.," over 2 cols.

April 6, pp. 1, 4. "Lattimore Calls McCarthy Chinese Nationalist Dupe," over 2 cols.; prominent.

May 3, pp. 1, 5. Lattimore denial of all charges against him and wife.

New York Times

Mar. 14, p. 4. less prominently mentioned in same story as Hanson.

Mar. 28, p. 1. dismissed McCarthy charges as "Pure Moonshine," small sub-headline.

April 7, p. 1. "Lattimore Denies He was Ever a Red; Tydings Clears Him," 3 cols.

April 21, p. 1. "Lattimore Accused by Budenz as a Red," Over 4-cols. mostly on p. 2.

May 3, pp. 1, 2. "Lattimore Calls Budenz 'Informer,' Lying for a Profit," 2½ cols.

San Francisco Chronicle

Mar. 14, pp. 1, 8. not very conspicuously mentioned in same story as Hanson.

Mar. 28, p. 1. "McCarthy's Charges Called 'Moonshine,'" 1 col.

Mar. 29, p. 1. Short item: "Lattimore Calls Charges 'Hallucination.'"

April 7, p. 1. "Spy Investigation—FBI Files Cleared Lattimore, Tydings Says; but McCarthy Doesn't Believe It"; prominent story.

April 21, pp. 1, 7. "McCarthy Charges—Lattimore Called a Spy by Budenz, but General Asserts He's Loyal Citizen" (refers to ex-MacArthur aide), over 2 cols.; very prominent continuation of story with large pictures of hearings.

May 3, pp. 1, 6 "McCarthy Disgraceful, Budenz Lies for Profit, Says Owen Lattimore," over 2 cols.

Des Moines Register

Mar. 14, No story; only picture and caption, p. 7.

April 7, p. 5. "Lattimore's FBI Record Called Clear"; over 2 cols.; pictures.

April 20, pp. 1, 8. page-width headline: "Retired General Backs Lattimore." Budenz accusation not headlined but reported at length, 3-cols.

May 3, p. 6. "Senate Urged by Lattimore: End 'Nonsense,'" 2 cols.

Washington Post

Mar. 14, p. 1. "McCarthy Adds Four, Including Lattimore to Pro-Red Roster," 3 cols.; picture on front page.

April 7, pp. 1, 21. "Files Clear Lattimore, Tydings Says." Subtitle: "Far Eastern Expert Declares McCarthy Charges Are 'Lies'; Calls Senator Dupe," nearly 4 cols.

April 21, pp. 1, 2. "Reds Called Lattimore Communist, Budenz Says," over 4 cols.; picture of both on front page.

GUSTAVO DURAN

St. Louis Post-Dispatch

Mar. 14, p. 6A. Duran mentioned under headline of Kenyon denial. His reply to charges mentioned in same story.

New York Times

Mar. 15, p. 1. Mentioned in same story as Kenyon reply.

San Francisco Chronicle

Mar. 15, p. 1. Name not headlined in reporting of accusations.

Mar. 15, p. 7. "'Full of Errors'—ExSpaniard and Former State Dept. Official Says McCarthy is Wrong." Short story.

Des Moines Register

no mention.

Washington Post

Mar. 15, p. 2. Accusation and denial in same story as Service, Schuman, Shapley. Over 2 cols.

HARLOW SHAPLEY

St. Louis Post-Dispatch

Mar. 14, p. 6A. Accusation and reply to press. Same story as Schuman, etc.

New York Times

Mar. 15, p. 1. same story as Kenyon reply.

San Francisco Chronicle

Mar. 15, p. 1. "Disloyalty Charges—McCarthy Names Four More, Including Shapley; State Dept. Issues Denials," less than 1 col.—partly devoted to Kenyon Denial.

Mar. 15, p. 7. "Shapley Calls Story Untrue—and Boring." Pictures of Kenyon, Shapley and Schuman on this page and 3 separate short stories on replies of Shapley, Schuman and Duran.

Washington Post

Mar. 15, p. 2. Accusation and reply reported along with Duran and Schuman. Over 2 cols.

FREDERICK SCHUMAN

St. Louis Post-Dispatch

Mar. 14, p. 6A. Accusation reported in same story as Service, Shapley.

New York Times

Mar. 15, p. 1. Accusation in same story as Kenyon reply.

Des Moines Register

No mention.

San Francisco Chronicle

Mar. 15, p. 7. Short story on Schuman denial of charge.

Mar. 15, p. 1. Accusation—name not headlined.

Washington Post

Mar. 15, p. 2. Accusation and reply reported with those of Duran and Shapley.

JOHN S. SERVICE

St. Louis Post-Dispatch

Mar. 14, p. 6A. Service mentioned under headline of Kenyon reply.

June 22, p. 7A. Long story on Service answer with voluminous quotes from his statement; picture.

New York Times

Mar. 15, p. 1. Same story as Kenyon reply.

June 23, pp. 1, 4. "Service Concedes He Briefed Jaffe" sub-heading: "But State Dept. Officer Denies He Turned Over Data on Secret Military Plans." 4 cols.

San Francisco Chronicle

Mar. 15, p. 1. Accusation not headlined.

June 22, pp. 1, 5. "Amerasia Inquiry—Service Denies Passing Any Secret Data," over 1 col.

Des Moines Register

Accusation not reported.

June 23, pp. 1, 7. "Briefed Jaffe on China War, Service Says"; Sub-head: "But Denied Revealing Vital Secrets," over 3 cols.

Washington Post

Mar. 15, p. 2. Same story as Kenyon denial; accusation of Service not headlined.

June 23, pp. 1, 14. "Service Says China Charges Are Unfounded," approx. 3 cols.

Appendix F

The George Marshall Episode

SENATOR McCARTHY delivered a 60,000 word speech on the floor of the Senate, on June 14, 1951, examining the career of General George Marshall and concluding, on the basis of the evidence he presented, that Marshall is "steeped in falsehood," and that he has "recourse to the lie whenever it suits his convenience." McCarthy concluded his survey of Marshall's career by asking,

How can we account for our present situation unless we believe that men high in this Government are concerting to deliver us to disaster? This must be the product of a great conspiracy, a conspiracy on a scale so immense as to dwarf any previous such venture in the history of man. A conspiracy of infamy so black that, when it is finally exposed, its principals shall be forever deserving of the maledictions of all honest men. . . . What can be made of this unbroken series of decisions and acts contributing to the strategy of defeat? They cannot be attributed to incompetence. If Marshall were merely stupid, the laws of probability would dictate that part of his decisions would serve his country's interest.

McCarthy has said that he did not call Marshall a traitor. Strictly speaking, he is correct. And, in fact, a year after making his speech, McCarthy wrote "If [Marshall] . . . made mistakes, that is no disgrace. Only those who do nothing make no mistakes. To prove that Marshall made mistakes does not indict Marshall of being either incompetent or of following the Communist cause"; and to the direct question, "Did you accuse Marshall of being a traitor," McCarthy answered, "No."*

It is, however, unreasonable to conclude, on the basis of the paragraphs quoted above, that McCarthy was charging Marshall with anything less than pro-Communism. In doing so, McCarthy aroused more resentment than with any other single act in his stormy career—save, possibly, his attack on Philip Jessup.

Marshall was not a typical "McCarthy case." McCarthy did not

* *McCarthyism, op.cit.*, pp. 68-69.

impugn Marshall's loyalty on the ground that he had belonged to a number of Communist fronts; or that he had been seen at clandestine meetings of the Party; or that he had filched secret documents and turned them over to members of a Soviet spy ring. Rather, McCarthy impugned Marshall's loyalty on the grounds that, over a period of years, his policy decisions advanced the Communist cause and retarded our own. He reconstructed Marshall's public record after delving laboriously into the memoirs of Leahy, Churchill, Mark Clark, Sherwood, Stimson, Byrnes, Stettinius, Welles, Hull, Arnold, Deane, Chennault, and Daniels—almost all of them highly vocal *admirers* of General Marshall. McCarthy moved from *their* reconstruction of wartime strategy and wartime and postwar diplomacy to an analysis of Marshall's role in shaping allied policy. He concluded that, on those issues in which the interests of the western powers and those of Russia conflicted, Marshall consistently sided with the policy urged by Russia. McCarthy therefore inferred that Marshall was pro-Communist.

On McCarthy's showing, the crucial matters in Marshall's record were:

(1) his inordinate anxiety to launch a second front at a time when we were manifestly unprepared to do so;

(2) his insistence that the Russians be allowed to reach eastern Europe ahead of the Allies;

(3) his insistence that we appease Russia at Teheran and Yalta in order to woo her help in the Far East;

(4) his siding with Stalin at Teheran on the strategy of the war;

(5) his directives to his subordinates that the Russians be indulged in their refusal to make available to us statistics on their "forces, their weapons, and their plans";

(6) his allowing the Communists first access to Berlin and Prague, and his failure to provide for a western corridor to Berlin;

(7) his insistence at Yalta that we make territorial and other concessions to Stalin;

(8) his role in formulating our anti-Chiang Far Eastern policy;

(9) his personal impact on that policy while in China;

(10) his pressure on Truman to extend further lend-lease aid to Russia;

(11) his suppression of the Wedemeyer report which warned against our China policy;

(12) his proposal that we withhold military aid from Nationalist China;

(13) his "sabotage" of the military-aid program with which we finally went to China's assistance;

(14) his fixing of the thirty-eighth parallel as a dividing line between free and Communist Korea;

(15) his refusal to prosecute vigorously the war against the North Koreans;

(16) his advocacy of a European security pact which excludes Western Germany, Spain, Greece or Turkey;

(17) his backing of American demobilization.

The evidence that Marshall made common cause with the Russians on these vital issues is, as McCarthy claimed, indeed overwhelming; but it does not, as McCarthy claimed it did, add up to party-lining of the sort that raises reasonable doubts as to loyalty. Almost all Marshall's decisions were backed by other military men and other diplomats whose attitude toward the Soviet Union (however appalling it may seem, especially in retrospect) cannot be described as treasonable. Every one of Marshall's actions is explainable in terms of the deeply imbedded premises that were being acted upon by many non-Communists of the day: (a) the Germans must at all costs be diverted from their attacks on Soviet Russia, whose capitulation would prolong the war indefinitely; (b) Soviet Russia must at all costs be placated lest she make a separate peace; (c) the best means of assuring peaceful postwar international relations is to indulge Soviet Russia in all or, at any rate, most of her territorial ambitions; (d) Soviet Russia's entry into the Pacific War is indispensable to a quick victory over Japan; (e) peace in China can result only from American pressure on Chiang to "broaden the base" of his government to include the Chinese Communists.

Marshall, then, is obviously not in the same class with a John Service, or a John Vincent, whose duties and qualifications called for expert reporting and shrewd interpretation of facts on which policy-makers like Marshall were to rely.

The most—and perhaps the least—that can be said of Marshall is that the premises he acted upon, the decisions he made and clung to so stubbornly, and, finally, his short-sightedness, probably merit him the title of America's most disastrous general. And if McCarthy had excised two paragraphs from it, his 200-page speech would have added up to some such statement as that—and a very impressive statement to boot.

McCarthy's conclusions about Marshall differed from the conclusions which he normally draws concerning his targets in that they were based on a dangerous and unusual brand of reasoning which, followed to its logical conclusions, would also brand Roosevelt and Truman as disloyal. In assessing a man's primary loyalties, we cannot base our deductions on the *effects* of that man's behavior. Thus, while the *impact* of Marshall's career did, beyond any doubt, decisively aid the Communist cause, one has no grounds, given all the evidence, for concluding that Marshall wished it to do so. As we have pointed out, every one of Marshall's decisions between 1942 and 1946 is explainable in terms not necessarily pro-Communist. It is true that put together they become progressively more disturbing as a pro-Soviet pattern emerges. But only the observer who postulates rationality as the generator of every human decision, who overlooks the element of irrationality in human action, sees purpose lurking behind every pattern. In studying the record of George Marshall, McCarthy failed to take into account man's irrationality; he forgot that more often than not men stumble into patterns.* He also missed the main point: a balanced and rational observer would not fix attention on the question whether Marshall *intended* to aid the Soviet Union; his concern would be whether he had helped Communism consistently, and if so, whether, given his demonstrated ignorance or incompetence, it makes sense for an anti-Communist society to retain such a man as its master global strategist.

McCarthy's critics have insisted that his method is not only bad in itself, but entails disastrous consequences for those on whom it is visited, e.g., in terms of wrecked reputations, social and economic ostracism, etc. It is therefore in point to ask whether Marshall has been damaged by McCarthy's assault.

Marshall's loyalty is not doubted in any reasonable quarter. On the other hand, Marshall no longer rides as high as he once did in the esteem of his countrymen. This is in part because of McCar-

---

* It is interesting that two famous societies, one imaginary, one real, adopted this approach in this area. In exercising their prerogative of *ostracism*, the question that interested the ancient Greeks was not so much whether a leader had *intended* to damage Athens, but whether, in their opinion, he *had* damaged it or threatened to do so; in which case he was exiled for ten years. In his *Thoughts on the Government of Poland*, Rousseau proposed that the Polish parliament meet upon the death of the king to determine whether or not, while ruling, he had satisfactorily served the nation. If the king lost out in this post-mortem, his memory was to be publicly disgraced and his family's goods confiscated.

thy's exposure, but mostly because of America's growing disillusionment with the shape of the new world its wartime leaders, among them Marshall, forged for it. To the extent that McCarthy, through his careful analysis of Marshall's record, has contributed to cutting Marshall down to size, he has performed a valuable service. For McCarthy is quite right in saying that "if the history of [the past ten years] . . . is to be understood, Marshall's record must be understood."

As regards his imputation of treasonable motives to Marshall, McCarthy deserves to be criticized, even if Marshall's general reputation for loyalty did not suffer. McCarthy's judgment here was bad. It is in a class with Winston Churchill's estimate of Stalin ("Personally I cannot feel anything but the most lively admiration for this truly great man, the father of his country. . . .").* Neither estimate is typical of the judgment of either man.

* The argument that Churchill should be forgiven because, obviously, he did not really *believe* what he said about Stalin, whereas McCarthy must be condemned because he probably *did* believe what he implied about Marshall, rests on an interesting code of morality.

Notes

CHAPTER II

1. *Congressional Record,* July 18, 1946, pp. 9389-90.

CHAPTER III

1. *Hearings on Communist Espionage in the United States,* House Committee on Un-American Activities, August 30, 1948, pp. 1291-1300.
2. *Report,* p. 14.

CHAPTER IV

1. Jack Anderson and Ronald May, *McCarthy: The Man, The Senator, The "Ism"* (Boston; Beacon, 1952).
2. *Senate Appropriations for 1953,* p. 427.
3. "Loyalty and Security Principles and Procedures Relating to Employees of the State Department," VC1, June 8, 1948.
4. *Congressional Record—Senate,* July 24, 1950, p. 10968.
5. *The McCarthy Record,* The Independent Citizens' Committee on McCarthy's Record (Milwaukee, 1952), p. 81.
6. *Senate Appropriations for 1953,* pp. 376-77.
7. "Memorandum to All Employees," June 8, 1948; and subsequent "Regulations and Procedures, Section 390, Loyalty and Security of Employees."
8. *Senate Appropriations for 1953,* p. 382.
9. *Appropriations Committee, U.S. Senate, for [fiscal] 1951,* p. 601.
10. *Ibid.,* pp. 610, 611.
11. *House of Representatives, Committee on the Judiciary, Special Subcommittee to Investigate the Department of Justice* (transcript), Mar. 23, 1953, Vol. 27, pp. 4295-97.
12. *Ibid.,* p. 4322.
13. *Ibid.,* p. 4336.
14. *Ibid.,* Vol. 28, p. 4362.
15. *Report,* p. 12.

CHAPTER V

1. "Report of Preliminary Investigation of Senator William Benton's Charges against Senator Joseph R. McCarthy Relating to Senate Resolution 187, United States Senate, Committee on Rules and Administration, Subcommittee on Privileges and Elections, January, 1952."
2. *Tydings Committee Report,* p. 149. Hereinafter referred to as *Tydings Report.*

Chapter VI

1. State Department Employee Loyalty Investigation. *Hearings Before a Subcommittee of the Committee on Foreign Relations* (Hereinafter referred to as *Tydings Hearings*), p. 1.
2. Senator Joseph McCarthy, *McCarthyism, The Fight for America* (New York; Devin-Adair, 1952), p. 75.
3. *Tydings Report*, p. 72.
4. *Ibid.*
5. *Tydings Hearings*, p. 10.
6. *Ibid.*, p. 6.
7. *Congressional Record*, Feb. 20, 1950 (bound), pp. 1953, 1959, 1973.
8. *Ibid.*, p.1955.
9. *Ibid.*, p. 1959.
10. *Ibid.*, pp. 1972-73.
11. *Ibid.*, p. 1967.
12. *Ibid.*, p. 1963.
13. *Ibid.*, p. 1973.
14. *Ibid.*, Mar 30, 1950 (unbound), pp. 4434, 4435.
15. *Ibid.*, Apr. 5, 1950 (unbound), pp. 4957, 4958.
16. *Tydings Hearings*, p. 15.
17. *Ibid.*, p. 17.
18. *Ibid.*, p. 17.
19. *Ibid.*, p. 18.

Chapter VII

1. *Tydings Hearings*, p. 18.
2. *Ibid.*, p. 18.
3. *Ibid.*, pp. 23, 24.
4. *Ibid.*, p. 50.
5. *Ibid.*, p. 176.
6. *Tydings Committee Hearings: Appendix* (Hereinafter referred to as *Tydings Appendix*), pp. 1557, 1558.
7. *Ibid.*, p. 1557.
8. *Ibid.*, pp. 1558-59.
9. *Tydings Hearings*, p. 185.
10. *Tydings Appendix*, p. 1560.
11. *Tydings Hearings*, p. 187.
12. *Ibid.*, p. 208.
13. *Ibid.*, p. 29.
14. *Ibid.*, p. 32.
15. *Ibid.*, p. 68.
16. *Subcommittee of the Senate Committee on Appropriations*, Feb. 28, 1950, pp. 596, 601.
17. *Tydings Hearings*, pp. 20 ff.
18. *California Committee on Un-American Activities, Report*, 1948, p. 91.
19. *Tydings Hearings*, pp. 25, 26.
20. *Ibid.*, p. 71.
21. *Tydings Report*, p. 47.

22. *Ibid.*, pp. 46-48.
23. *Daily Worker*, Feb. 21, 1940, p. 4.
24. *Tydings Report*, p. 48.
25. *Tydings Hearings*, pp. 50, 52.
26. *Ibid.*, p. 76.
27. *Ibid.*, p. 74.
28. *Ibid.*, p. 74.
29. *Ibid.*, p. 82.
30. *Ibid.*, p. 76.
31. *Ibid.*, p. 76.
32. *Ibid.*, p. 80.
33. *Ibid.*, p. 81.
34. *Ibid.*, p. 76.
35. *Ibid.*, p. 81.
36. *Ibid.*, p. 81.
37. *Ibid.*, p. 77.
38. *Ibid.*, p. 78.
39. *Ibid.*, p. 78.
40. *Ibid.*, p. 342.
41. *Ibid.*, pp. 348, 350.
42. *Chicago Tribune*, Dec. 13, 1939; *Tydings Hearings*, p. 352.
43. Haldore Hanson, *Humane Endeavor*, p. 303.
44. *Ibid.*, pp. 349, 350.
45. *Tydings Report*, p. 34.
46. *Tydings Hearings*, p. 359, (*Pacific Affairs*, Sept., 1938, p. 290).
47. *Ibid.*, p. 358.
48. *Ibid.*, p. 591.
49. *Tydings Report*, p. 37.
50. *Humane Endeavor*, pp. 241 ff.
51. *Ibid.*, p. 294.
52. *Ibid.*, pp. 31, 32.
53. *Ibid.*, pp. 30, 31.
54. *Ibid.*, pp. 311-12.
55. *Ibid.*, pp. 217 ff. for this and similar references.
56. *Ibid.*, p. 310.
57. *Ibid.*, p. 279.
58. *Ibid.*, p. 273.
59. *Ibid.*, pp. 29, 324.
60. *Ibid.*, p. 324.
61. *Manual of Departmental Regulations*, State Department, June 8, 1948.
62. *Tydings Hearings*, p. 28.
63. *Ibid.*, p. 100.
64. *Ibid.*, p. 247.
65. *Ibid.*, p. 229.
66. *Ibid.*, pp. 256, 257.
67. *Ibid.*, p. 273.
68. *Tydings Report*, p. 43.
69. *Congressional Record*, Mar. 30, 1950 (bound), pp. 4403, 4404; June 2, 1950 (bound), pp. 8001, 8003.
70. *Ibid.*, Mar. 30, 1950 (bound), p. 4402.
71. *Ibid.*, June 2, 1950 (bound), p. 8001.
72. *Ibid.*, June 2, 1950 (bound), p. 8000.

73. *Ibid.*, Mar. 30, 1950 (bound), p. 4403.

74. *Ibid.*, p. 4404; June 2, 1950 (bound), p. 8003.

75. *Ibid.*, Mar. 30, 1950 (bound), p. 4405.

76. *Tydings Report*, p. 42.

77. Letter from Senator Paul Douglas to Prof. Franz Boas, Hon. Chairman, National Emergency Conference for Democratic Rights, Sept. 20, 1940.

78. *New York Times,* Jan. 31, 1939, p. 2.

79. *Ibid.*, Sept. 21, 1939, p. 17.

80. *Tydings Report*, p. 41.

81. *McCarran Committee Report* (hereinafter referrerd to as *McCarran Report*), p. 225.

82. *Tydings Report*, p. 42.

83. *McCarran Report*, p. 100.

84. *Ibid.*, pp. 101, 102.

85. *Ibid.*, p. 103.

86. *Far Eastern Survey*, Nov. 15, 1944.

87. *McCarran Report*, pp. 147-48.

88. *McCarran Hearings*, pp. 494-95; *McCarran Report*, pp. 147-48.

89. *McCarran Hearings*, pp. 122, 123.

90. *Tydings Hearings*, pp. 497-98.

91. *McCarran Hearings*, p. 5225.

92. *New York Herald Tribune*, Sept. 1, 1940.

93. *New York Times*, Aug. 31, 1940.

94. *McCarran Hearings*, p. 22.

95. *Tydings Report*, p. 41.

96. State Department Press Release, No. 310, Apr. 3, 1950; *Tydings Report,* p. 272.

97. *McCarran Hearings,* p. 81.

98. *Ibid.*, p. 9.

99. *Tydings Report*, p. 42.

100. *McCarran Hearings*, p. 4938.

101. *Ibid.*, pp. 5359-60.

102. *Tydings Report*, p. 41.

103. *Ibid.*, p. 39.

104. *Tydings Hearings*, p. 267.

105. See *Hearings before Senate Foreign Relations Committee on Appointment of Philip Jessup*, pp. 686-872.

106. *McCarran Report*, p. 148.

107. *McCarran Hearings,* p. 1049; *Hearings on Jessup's Nomination*, pp. 714-21.

108. *McCarran Hearings*, pp. 927, 2500.

109. *Ibid.*, p. 1551.

110. *McCarran Report*, p. 212.

111. *Hearings on Jessup's Nomination*, p. 722.

112. *McCarran Hearings*, pp. 844-46.

113. *Tydings Appendix*, p. 1789.

114. *Tydings Hearings*, p. 84.

115. *Ibid.*, p. 86.

116. *Ibid.*, p. 84.

117. *Ibid.*, p. 84.

118. *Tydings Appendix*, pp. 1789, 1790.

119. *Tydings Report*, pp. 29, 30.

120. *Tydings Hearings*, p. 84.

121. *New York Times*, Apr. 26, 1943.
122. *Tydings Hearings*, p. 310.
123. *Ibid.*, p. 85.
124. *Ibid.*, pp. 296, 305.
125. *Tydings Report*, p. 29.
126. *Tydings Hearings*, p. 86.
127. *Ibid.*, pp. 296, 297.
128. *Tydings Report*, p. 29.
129. *Tydings Appendix*, p. 1523.
130. *Tydings Hearings*, p. 91.
131. *Ibid.*, p. 297.
132. *Tydings Report*, p. 29.
133. *Special Committee on Un-American Activities, Report*, Mar. 29, 1944, p. 154.
134. *Tydings Hearings*, p. 84.
135. *Ibid.*, p. 307.
136. *Ibid.*, p. 307-309.
137. *Ibid.*, p. 307.
138. *Tydings Report*, p. 28.
139. *Tydings Hearings*, p. 87.
140. *Ibid.*, p. 307.
141. *Ibid.*, pp. 300, 303.
142. *Ibid.*, p. 294.
143. *Tydings Appendix*, pp. 1563-64; *Tydings Report*, p. 30.
144. *Tydings Report*, p. 30.
145. *Washington Times-Herald*, June 6, 1946 (*Tydings Appendix*, pp. 1532-33).
146. *Tydings Hearings*, pp. 142-71.
147. *Ibid.*, p. 162.
148. *Ibid.*, p. 167.
149. *The Red Decade* (Bobbs Merrill, 1941), p. 314.
150. *Soviet Politics at Home and Abroad* (Knopf, 1946), p. 582.
151. *Tydings Hearings*, p. 110.
152. *Ibid.*, p. 112.
153. Letter from Senator Wherry to Secretary Byrnes, Aug. 2, 1946 (*Tydings* Appendix, p. 1544).
154. *Ibid.*
155. Letter from Assistant Secretary Russell to Senator Wherry, Sept. 14, 1946 (*Tydings Appendix*, p. 1544-45).
156. *Tydings Appendix*, p. 1545.
157. *Ibid.*, p. 1546.
158. *Ibid.*, p. 1544.
159. *Ibid.*, p. 1866.
160. *Ibid.*, p. 1547.
161. *Ibid.*, p. 1547.
162. *Ibid.*, p. 1865.
163. *Ibid.*, pp. 1866-70.
164. *Ibid.*, p. 1866.
165. *Ibid.*, p. 1868.
166. *Ibid.*, p. 1869.
167. *Tydings Hearings*, p. 113.
168. *Ibid.*, p. 121.
169. *Ibid.*, p. 111.

170. *Ibid.*, p. 121.
171. *Ibid.*, p. 119.
172. *Tydings Report*, p. 30.
173. *Tydings Hearings*, pp. 131, 133; *Congressional Record*, Jan. 5, 1950 (unbound), p. 90.
174. *Tydings Report*, p. 78.
175. *Ibid.*, p. 93.
176. *Tydings Hearings*, p. 1408.
177. *Tydings Report*, p. 82.
178. *Ibid.*, p. 94.
179. *McCarran Report*, p. 224.
180. *Tydings Report*, pp. 73, 74.
181. *Tydings Hearings*, pp. 277-86.
182. *Congressional Record*, Mar. 30, 1950 (unbound), p. 4436.
183. *Tydings Hearings*, p. 92.
184. *Ibid.*, p. 440.
185. *Ordeal by Slander* (Little, Brown and Company), p. 5.
186. *Tydings Report*, p. 72.
187. *Ibid.*, pp. 3200-3201.
188. *Ibid.*, pp. 3494-96.
189. *Tydings Hearings*, p. 746.
190. *Tydings Report*, p. 63.
191. *Tydings Hearings*, pp. 887-89.
192. *Ibid.*, pp. 491-93.
193. *Ibid.*, p. 805.
194. *Tydings Report*, p. 56.

Chapter VIII

1. *Tydings Report*, pp. 6, 7.
2. *House of Representatives, Appropriations Committee for 1949*, p. 176.
3. *House Appropriations Subcommittee for 1947*, p. 192.
4. *Congressional Record*, Vol. 94, p. 2063.
5. *Ibid.*, pp. A1912-A1924.

Chapter IX

1. *Tydings Hearings*, p. 2513.
2. *Congressional Record*, July 24, 1950 (unbound), p. 10971.
3. *Ibid.*, July 24, 1950 (unbound), p. 10977.
4. *Ibid.*, July 20, 1950 (bound), p.10699.
5. *Ibid.*, July 24, 1950 (unbound), p. 10977.
6. *Ibid.*, July 17, 1950 (bound), pp. 10396-97.
7. *Ibid.*, July 24, 1950 (unbound), p. 10977.
8. *Tydings Hearings*, p. 2519.
9. *Ibid.*, p. 2522.
10. Proceedings, U.S. District Court for District of Columbia, Sept. 29, 1945, *United States v. Philip Jaffe et al.*
11. *Parts Manufacturing Co. v. Lynch* (129 F 2d 841).
12. *Harris v. United States* (331 U.S. 145), 1946.
13. *Congressional Record*, June 6, 1950 (bound), p. 8114.

14. *Tydings Report*, p. 95.
15. *Ibid.*, p. 95.
16. *Tydings Hearings*, pp. 11, 12.
17. See Letters from Senator McCarthy to Senator Tydings, Mar. 20 and 24, 1950, Apr. 5, 1950.
18. *Tydings Hearings*, p. 257.
19. *Ibid.*, p. 491.
20. *Ibid.*, p. 767.
21. *Ibid.*, p. 697.
22. *Ibid.*, pp. 701-702.
23. *Ibid.*, p. 706.
24. *Ibid.*, p. 733.
25. *Tydings Report*, p. 148.
26. Ibid., p. 93.
27. *Ibid.*, pp. 93, 146.
28. *Congressional Record*, July 20, 1950 (bound), p. 10712.
29. *Ibid.*, (bound), pp. 10708, 10716.

Chapter X

1. *Hearings, Committee on Appropriations*, U.S. Senate, 82nd Congress, 1st Session, 1951, p. 408.
2. *IPR Hearings*, p. 30.
3. *Ibid.*, p. 107.
4. *Hearings, Committee on Un-American Activities*, 80th Congress, 2nd Session, p. 508.
5. *IPR Hearings*, Aug. 22, 1951, p. 625.
6. *Senate Appropriations for 1953*, p. 1722.
7. *IPR Report*, p. 244.
8. Whittaker Chambers, *Witness*, p. 31.
9. *IPR Hearings*, Part 2, Aug. 4, 1941, p. 439.
10. *Hearings held before Subcommittee on Privileges and Elections of the Committee on Rules and Administration*, U.S. Senate, July 3, 1952, pp. 223, 225.

Chapter XI

1. *Senate Appropriations for 1953*, p. 981.
2. *Tydings Report*, p. 15.
3. *Senate Appropriations for 1953*, 461 ff.
4. *Hearings before the Senate Permanent Subcommittee on Investigations of the Committee on Government Operations*, Aug. 19, 1953.
5. *New Republic*, Feb. 4, 1952.
6. *U.S. News and World Report*, Nov. 23, 1951, p. 23.
7. *New York Journal American*, Nov. 6, 1951.
8. *Congressional Record, Senate*, July 24, 1950, p. 10968.

Chapter XIII

1. *IPR Report*, p. 224.
2. *Tydings Hearings*, p. 506.

3. *Coffin v. Coffin* (1808) 4 Mass. 1, 3 Am. Dec. 189—quoted in *Mc-Carthyism, op. cit.*

4. Speech to the American Society of Newspaper Editors, Apr. 20, 1950.

5. *McCarthyism, op. cit.*, p. 17.

6. *Congressional Record,* Dec. 15, 1950.

7. Hearings before a subcommittee of the Senate Committee on Immigration and Naturalization quoted in *Congressional Record,* Dec. 19, 1950.

8. McCarthy's speech against Pearson was delivered in three sections, Dec. 15, 19, 1950 and Jan. 5, 1951. See *Congressional Record* for these dates.

9. *McCarthyism,* pp. 91, 92.

10. *Ibid.,* pp. 89, 90.

11. *Life,* Oct. 23, 1950, "The Art of Vituperation," by Winthrop Sargent.

Chapter XIV

1. "Is Freedom of Expression Really Threatened?" *American Mercury,* Jan., 1953.

2. *Books of the Month,* 1952.

3. E.G., *The Freeman,* editorial, June 30, 1952.

4. Alan Barth, *The Loyalty of Free Men* (New York; Viking, 1950), p. 103.

Index

Index